East-West European Economic Interaction

The Vienna Institute for Comparative Economic Studies organises a series of international workshops concerned with problems of East-West European economic interaction, guided by an International Steering Committee consisting of:

Carlo Boffito, Milan
Jósef Bognár, Budapest
Oleg Bogomolov, Moscow
Bernard Cazes, Paris
Gerhard Fink, Vienna
John P. Hardt, Washington
Norbert Kloten, Stuttgart

Rikard Lang, Zagreb
Friedrich Levcik, Vienna
Aleksander Lukaszewicz, Warsaw
Philipp Rieger (Chairman), Vienna
Christopher T. Saunders, Brighton, UK
Peter Sydow, Berlin, GDR
Dragomir Vojnić, Zagreb

The present volume is based on Workshop Session XII held in Athens, Georgia, USA, 1989.

Workshop Papers so far published:

Vols 1–4 A list of these titles can be obtained and copies can be ordered from The Vienna Institute for Comparative Economic Studies, P.O. Box 87, A-1103 Vienna, Austria. The remaining volumes are available from Macmillan. Series Editor: Philipp Rieger, Chairman of the Workshop
Vol. 5   East and West in the Energy Squeeze (1980)
Vol. 6   East-South-West: Economic Interactions between Three Worlds (1981)
Vol. 7   Regional Integration in East and West (1983)
Vol. 8   East-West Trade and Finance in the World Economy (1985)
Vol. 9   Industrial Policies and Structural Change (1986)
Vol. 10   Macroeconomic Management and the Enterprise in East and West (1988)
Vol. 11   East-West Economic Relations in the 1990s (1989)
Vol. 12   The Impact of Governments on East-West Economic Relations (1990)

The Impact of Governments on East-West Economic Relations

Edited by

Gary Bertsch
Professor, Department of Political Science
University of Georgia

and

Steven Elliott-Gower
Assistant Director, Center for East-West Trade Policy
University of Georgia

NEW YORK UNIVERSITY PRESS
Washington Square, New York

Director: Prof. Dr Dr F. Levcik

Manufactured in Great Britain

First published in the U.S.A. in 1991 by
NEW YORK UNIVERSITY PRESS
Washington Square
New York, NY 10003

Library of Congress in Cataloging-in-Publication Data
The Impact of governments on East-West economic relations / edited by
Gary Bertsch and Steven Elliott-Gower.
   p. cm. — (East-West European economic interaction : vol. 12)
Papers from the 12th Workshop on East-West European Economic
Interaction held Apr. 1–5, 1989 at the University of Georgia in
Athens : organized by the Vienna Institute for Comparative Economic
Studies.
Includes bibliographical references and index.
ISBN 0–8147–1159–6 (cloth)
1. International economic relations—Congresses. 2. East-West
trade (1945–)—Congresses. 3. Soviet Union—Commercial policy—
Congresses. 4. Europe, Eastern—Commercial policy—Congresses.
5. Europe—Commercial policy—Congresses. I. Bertsch, Gary K.
II. Elliott-Gower, Steven. III. Wiener Institut für Internationale
Wirtschaftsvergleiche. IV. Workshop on East-West European Economic
Interaction (12th : 1989 : Athens, Ga.) V. Series : East-West
European economic interaction : 12.
HF1359.I47 1991
337—dc20   90-22560
                                          CIP

PREFACE

Reforming a planned economy is inevitably a difficult process of compromise among different interest groups. Some of the reform measures have unfavourable economic and social side-effects for various societal groups, and, of course, some of the compromises, being ill-advised, produce undesired outcomes for all interest groups. However, for the outsider the alternation between decentralizing and recentralizing measures makes it unclear whether reform is proceeding or stopping again. The East European governments could certainly achieve a much more positive Western response to reform actions by clarifying the underlying ideology of reform and by moving even faster towards Western-style democracy and market regulation.

In turn, Western governments could exert a strong and positive influence on the reform process by reacting more quickly and decisively to reforms in the East; by facilitating the entry of reformist CMEA countries into international economic organizations, for example, or by lifting outdated trade restrictions in response to positive changes in the East. Most West Europeans feel strongly that economic cooperation with the East should be promoted in order to get the CMEA countries moving more decidedly towards reform.

Many questions have to be decided over the next few years including: where Western assistance could be most decisive for perestroika; whether a "wait and see" policy would harm East-West relations; what the role of a future "Common European House" (of EC, EFTA, and CMEA countries) is in the world economy; what the role of international organizations, such as the UN, UNCTAD, GATT, and IMF is in establishing global economic security; and what organization (like the GATT) could develop and implement a code of conduct for trade between countries with different economic systems. The chapters in this volume address these and other crucial questions.

Gerhard Fink

The Vienna Institute for
Comparative Economic Studies

FOREWORD

The University of Georgia in Athens, Georgia, U.S.A. was host to the twelfth in the series of *Workshops on East-West European Economic Interaction*, organized over the last fifteen years by The Vienna Institute for Comparative Economic Studies (WIIW), under the guidance of an International Steering Committee. In this period the Workshops had in fact developed into a series of truly international gatherings of economic and policy experts concerned with manifold vital economic aspects of world-wide policy interplay. The Workshops have from their inception proved themselves a veritable school of reform and of well founded criticism of dogmatic trains of thought. They contributed substantially to mutual understanding between participants from East and West.

The discussions at the Twelfth Workshop focused on the growing role of governments in developing - or containing - East-West economic relations. Both East- and West Europeans maintained the desirability of active support by Western governments of the East European countries' endeavours in changing their economic and political institutional settings. They held that this would be in the mutual interest of all concerned. American participants, on the other hand, because of security and foreign policy reasons wanted to see tangible results of ongoing reforms in East Europe and the USSR before lifting some of the governmental impediments to East-West relations.

* * *

ACKNOWLEDGEMENTS

The papers presented at the Workshop were prepared for publication in this volume by *Gary K. Bertsch* and *Steven Elliot-Gower* of the *University of Georgia*. To me remains the pleasant duty of expressing to them my appreciation for having undertaken an arduous task.

Particular thanks are due to *The University of Georgia* for hosting the Workshop and for material assistance.

Grateful acknowledgement of generous financial support is made to *The Ford Foundation* and to *The German Marshall Fund of the United States*.

We thank *Austria's Federal Ministry for Foreign Affairs* for giving financial assistance for transportation of the Austrian participants.

Gerhard Fink organized the workshop, guided by the Steering Committee, and with the support in administrative matters of *Gerlinde Schöfbeck*. *Victoria Goode* assisted in the running of the workshop, and *Kevin Lasher* assisted the editors in proofreading the pages of this book, which were typed by *Teresa Williams*. *Renate Garbacz* re-formatted and prepared the camera-ready copy of the typescript.

We can rely, as always, on the valued cooperation of Mr. *T.M. Farmiloe* of the *Macmillan Press Ltd.* in producing a volume to be proud of.

Philipp Rieger
Chairman of the Workshop

TABLE OF CONTENTS

PART III - EASTERN EUROPE

PART IV - WESTERN EUROPE AND JAPAN

PART V - PROSPECTS

INTRODUCTION

Gary K. Bertsch
Steven Elliott-Gower[1]

The chapters and commentaries in this volume are a part of history. That may sound like a particularly grandiloquent statement but it is true in a number of respects. In the most narrow sense, this volume represents the proceedings, an historical record, of the 12th international Workshop on East-West European Economic Interaction held at The University of Georgia, April 1-5, 1989.

In another, pejorative, sense critics might say that the chapters are a part of history in that the events of late 1989 and early 1990 date the chapters, and that they are therefore passé. It is undeniably true that many of the chapters contain dated information or talk in the future tense about events that have now transpired. Some of them do not anticipate the sheer pace of reform throughout Eastern Europe. Certainly they do not foresee the tumbling of communist governments throughout the region; (but then who did?). Some, both by American and East European authors, may be criticized as representative of the "old thinking". However "historical" some of these chapters may be, it should be remembered that history is never irrelevant to the present and the future. The perceptive reader (perhaps the "historical" reader) will find many clues in this volume to the future of the Soviet Union, Eastern Europe, East-West economic relations and, of course, the role and impact of governments in this area. Contemporary value and relevance may be found even in what may seem the most anachronistic piece; the "new thinking", for example, can be most appreciated when contrasted to the old.

Having said this, most of the chapters and commentaries here reflect the new thinking. The authors are aware of the mistakes of the past, the limitations of centralized planning, the dangers of ideology, and the futility of mutual suspicion and confrontation. They are sensitive to the need for and global significance of political and economic reform in the East, the challenges faced, and the new roles that governments must play in the transitional period. Indeed, while we should be wary of "social engineering", some of the chapters may be considered blueprints for reform. And what makes these especially

---

[1] Co-Director and Assistant Director, respectively, Center for East-West Trade Policy, University of Georgia, Athens, Georgia, U.S.A.

significant to the present and future is that the fact that, in a number of cases, they were written by scholars who are now policymakers. At about the time of the workshop in Georgia, for example, Soviet academics Bogomolov and Shmelev were elected to the People's Congress of Deputies. Valtr Komarek, whose reformist proposals were long-ignored by the communist government in Czechoslovakia, was appointed First Deputy Prime Minister after the revolution in his country. Other reform-minded East European scholars, whose ideas are included here, have also become more politically influential in their respective countries since the first part of 1989 when they wrote their chapters. Moreover, given their expertise and the rapidly growing interest in East-West economic relations, many of the Western contributors to this volume have been invited to take part in the governmental policy debates in their respective countries. Indeed, the editors were asked to report to the U.S. Senate Foreign Relations Committee on East-West economic relations shortly after the end of the workshop.

All of this is, of course, particularly significant in terms of the central theme of this volume, the impact of governments on East-West economic relations in the 1990s. Governments have undoubtedly had the determining influence on East-West economic relations. More important than their influence, however, has been their motivation. In the past they were primarily motivated by political, security, and ideological considerations. Commercial considerations were of little significance. In the present period, the cold war motivations, and the roles and impact of governments in East-West economic relations are undergoing profound changes. The changes are healthy and long overdue, and they open new opportunities for more constructive, meaningful, and economically beneficial relations between East and West. Economic and political obstacles remain but, at the time of writing, they are beginning to disappear. In the United States, for example, after a lengthy period of indecision, cold war restrictions on East-West trade are being slowly dismantled. However, we are still in a transitional period, and we must continue to identify and address the critical issues surrounding East-West economic relations in an effort to inform the debate, promote mutually beneficial economic relations and, ultimately, to help stabilize East-West relations. This volume is a small part of that process.

Two editorial notes should be made here. First, given the fact that English is not the native language of most of the authors, we were obliged to make some grammatical and stylistic changes to many of the chapters. However, we erred on the side of caution and where there was a danger of interfering with the substance of a chapter, we left well enough alone. Second, with twenty-five chapters and twelve commentaries, we were also obliged to edit some of the longer pieces to keep the total manuscript within a managable length.

It should also be noted that, in keeping with the tradition of the workshop series and resulting proceedings, the opinions expressed by the contributors here are their own individual views and do not necessarily reflect those of their institutions or governments.

Finally, on behalf of The University of Georgia, we should like to thank the workshop series' International Steering Committee for selecting Athens, Georgia as the site of the 12th Workshop. It was a remarkably rewarding experience for us and, to use the current parlance of American politics, we are pleased to be "in the loop".

PART I - THE SOVIET UNION

Chapter 1

PERESTROIKA AND EAST-WEST ECONOMIC INTERACTION

Nikolai Shmelev[1]

There is nothing in the nature of a planned economy that should require autarchy or self-imposed isolation from the world economy. The Soviet Union's long-term quest for maximum self-sufficiency was primarily dictated by political circumstances. These circumstances have changed.

A deep perestroika of the Soviet economic system is impossible without active participation in the international economic system and without using the advantages and benefits of the international division of labour. By opening up its economy, the Soviet Union is beginning to try to integrate itself in the world economy. This means that in the long run the possibility of foreign markets should become an important consideration in the selection of an optimal structure of production, investments and scientific research. This also means that the export and import of capital to and from the Soviet Union should become not an exotic or occasional phenomenon but the norm. In the progress towards an "open economy" it is necessary to distinguish between current problems and long-term purposes.

The most acute problems facing the Soviet economy are: the failure to meet domestic consumer demand, the threat of inflation, and an intolerably high budget deficit. These are interrelated problems and their solution is possible only when they are dealt with as a set. Of course, internal solutions to

---

[1] Institute of U.S.A. and Canada Studies, Academy of Sciences of the USSR, Moscow, USSR.

these problems are most important but external factors also have a considerable role to play.

As of 1989, "hot" money (i.e., that awaiting the appearance on the market of the required goods) now amounts to 75-100 billion roubles (according to different estimates). At the current level of a budget efficiency of the consumer import of 800-1000 per cent this means that a one-off import of industrial consumer goods of $7.5-15 billion could fully alleviate the acuity of this problem. Furthermore, in order to meet consumer demand and balance the budget with increased revenues the Soviet Union needs a stable, regular import of $3-5 billion of consumer goods a year. It is especially urgent during the first part of the 1990s, until the new Soviet government's structural policy and the new economic mechanism encouraging quality and a high scientific and technological level of manufactured products start to bring tangible results.

Given an unfavourable world situation for Soviet exports and the difficulties of restructuring to produce more fully manufactured goods, it is difficult to finance the necessary increase in imports, but not impossible. First, imports of grain and a number of other kinds of foodstuffs can be reduced owing to various modes of stimulation of domestic production and reducing loss and spoilage of agricultural produce. Secondly, it is possible to, at least temporarily, reduce Soviet imports of equipment for large-scale heavy industry projects with long repayment periods, and to increase imports of machinery and equipment for the light and food industries. Thirdly, gold and foreign-exchange reserves may be used, and a certain manoeuvring in our activities and obligations in various parts of the world. Fourthly, there are opportunities for increased international borrowing not only for the import of equipment for the consumer industry but also for the direct import of consumer goods.

Under existing conditions short-term international credit is not the most effective way of solving the problem. Medium- and long-term international credit is needed and, of course, not only government credits, but also private international credit on generally accepted commercial terms. The money for servicing such credits can be partly obtained by cutting grain imports and some other kinds of traditional imports such as industrial pipes. There are also prospects for an expansion of Soviet exports as a result of the measures undertaken now to promote the export activities of Soviet industrial enterprises.

A full opening of the Soviet economy is a long-term objective and it can hardly be reached before the end of the 1990s. To achieve this objective, it is necessary to create a number of preconditions which are either unavailable or only beginning to be developed now.

Despite the problems, it is necessary for the Soviet Union to reduce its dependence on energy and raw materials exports for hard currency earnings and to increase its export of manufactured industrial goods. The problem is not simply one of increasing investment in export-oriented, especially high technology, industries. Soviet manufactured exports must achieve much higher levels of competitiveness with new marketing techniques and maintenance programs. An important step towards accomplishing this qualitatively different level of competitiveness is granting Soviet state and cooperative enterprises free access to foreign markets and, as Wladimir Andreff notes in this volume, free use of hard currency profits. It is also time to create powerful and competing trade associations; intermediaries of "trade house" type. Industrial cooperation with foreign firms, joint ventures, formation of regional or industrial "free economic zones" also provide promising methods of improving the competitiveness of Soviet exports of goods and services.

The reform of domestic wholesale prices will make it possible to establish a true and single exchange rate of the rouble. This will create conditions for a direct objective relationship between domestic and foreign trade prices.

A gradual shift during the coming years towards a wholesale trade with the means of production will mean the formation of preconditions for the domestic convertibility of the Soviet rouble. The Soviet and foreign holders of the rouble will obtain, at last, a physical opportunity to spend their money in the domestic Soviet market for what they need.

The establishment of a true exchange rate of the rouble and a shift towards free wholesale trade will make the rouble partly convertible, (i.e., convertible for our enterprises and their foreign partners). Another hotly debated way in which the rouble might become fully convertible over time is the creation (as in the 1920s) of a parallel "chervonny" (high-carat) rouble which would be freely convertible into foreign currencies and which would gradually displace the present non-convertible rouble from circulation. Both these ways lead to the same goal but it is difficult to say which of them is more effective.

A partial convertibility of the rouble will provide the necessary economic conditions for the development of industrial cooperation, joint ventures and "free economic zones;" that is, for a stable and regular import of foreign capital into the Soviet economy on generally accepted commercial principles. Today such conditions are lacking, and the Soviet Union's long-term cooperation with foreign partners rests mainly on mutual enthusiasm rather than mutual economic interest.

The shift towards a convertible currency, especially at its early stages, brings up the issue of additional sources for the regulation of temporary fluctuations of the trade and payment balances. All these sources are known and international borrowing is not the least important. The prospects of closer cooperation between the Soviet Union and international monetary and financial institutions should not be excluded in this connection.

Of course, the prospects of "opening" the Soviet economy depend mainly, but not only, on the Soviet Union itself. Full participation of the Soviet Union in international economic affairs, and the opening of its vast domestic market is also in the interests of other countries. Thus, in view of positive changes in the international political climate, the time has come to eliminate remnants of the Cold War that impede economic cooperation. There are many such impediments. The most significant among them being: first, the discrimination of the Soviet Union on the domestic markets of certain Western countries, including the United States; secondly, unreasonable controls on exports of Western high technology goods for the civil sectors (controls on military-oriented products being more or less natural); thirdly, political assessments of a normalization of economic relations with the West in terms of a new "Marshall Plan", even though socialist countries do not need such a plan but rather generally accepted commercial forms of international economic interaction; fourthly, political attempts to hinder Soviet membership of or, at least, more active cooperation in such international organizations as the GATT, IMF, and the World Bank.

Does perestroika of the Soviet economy need the assistance of the West? Yes, it does. But it needs assistance not charity. Assistance differs from charity in that it is mutually beneficial. The issue is not only one of the Soviet Union's economic problems but of new opportunities opened up by perestroika in global economic, technological, and scientific cooperation from which everybody will benefit.

Chapter 2

THE SOVIET ATTITUDE TOWARD INTEGRATION IN THE WORLD ECONOMY

Jerry F. Hough[1]

On the surface, it seems foolish for an American to write about the changing attitude of the Soviet government toward integration into the world economy when other chapters here are written by leading advisers to the Soviet government on the question. It would be clearly ridioulous for an American to explore current Soviet attitudes on current questions such as membership in the GATT or promotion of a United Nations conference on world economic interests.

Yet, there is perhaps a reason for a Westerner to try to put the question in broader perspective. For a series of reasons the question of integration into the world economy is extremely sensitive in the Soviet Union, and a Westerner is less constrained in trying to put the changes in a broader perspective. Although the issue cannot be expressed openly, the fundamental question in the United States on Soviet-American relations is the possibiity of conducting a successful policy of "liberation" that John Foster Dulles and others enunciated in the 1940s. If Soviet economic reforms are doomed to failure either because of lack of popular support or conceptual failures, then the United States is clearly likely to continue the policy of the Reagan administration of putting maximum economic and political pressure on the Soviet Union and Eastern Europe in order to destroy "the Evil Empire" once and for all.

2.1 Soviet public statements on foreign economic policy

It is perfectly obvious that the question of integration into the world economy has been a sensitive one in the Soviet Union. When Mikhail Gorbachev travelled to Leningrad in May 1985, he stated that it was not accidental that his first trip outside Moscow was to Leningrad. He could not, however, remind his audience that Peter had originally built the city as a "window to the West" and that his trip there symbolized an intention to return to such a policy.

---

[1] Professor of Political Science, Duke University, Durham, North Carolina, U.S.A.

Indeed, Gorbachev's speech in Leningrad was barely covered in the central press, and his assertion that his choice of Leningrad had symbolic meaning was not printed. Indeed, the most potentially explosive sentence of all was not even included in the version of the speech published in his collected works. This was a cryptic statement that East Germany had interesting experiences in the foreign economic sphere. It has long been clear that the quality of East German goods has been the highest in the socialist world because East German manufacturers have free access to the West German market and must raise the quality of their goods to meet the foreign competition on that market. Either Gorbachev did not find it useful to make the point publicly, or perhaps he had it cut out when someone explained the explosive implications of the seemingly innocuous sentence that had been included by some speechwriter.

The same caution was displayed in the introduction of joint ventures. Despite the growing glasnost in economic debates during 1986, the advocacy of joint ventures, especially with capitalist countries, was virtually absent from the Soviet press of that year. The decree on joint ventures was ready for publication by late November 1986 and was scheduled to appear in mid-December at the time of the Central Committee plenary session that had been called to discuss democratization. The plenum was postponed for a month because of the riots in Kazakhstan, and the publication of the decree was also postponed. It appeared in *Isvestiia* on the very day that the Central Committee convened, and hence public attention was focused on the proposals for democratization of elections, not on joint ventures.

Since this time the attention given to foreign economic questions in the Soviet media has increased. Joint ventures have become particularly "fashionable". Yet, every knowledgeable specialist is aware that joint ventures never have been that serious a part of any country's foreign economic policy and that they tend to run into difficulties. Successful integration into the world economy has entailed acceptance of 100 per cent ownership, and (notably as in the Pacific countries) an active export strategy at a stage of economic development when the quality of exported goods is still low by contemporary standards. (The goods are priced at low enough levels to compensate for their quality.) Indeed, part of a successful policy of integration into the world economy is the initiation of a policy of investment abroad by the developing country as it becomes industrially more advanced.

Just as the Soviet press has not included frank disussion of the implications of the experience of the GDR, so it has carried little sophisticated analysis of the experience of the Pacific countries and the Third World. *Voprosy ekonomiki* - the major economics journal of the institute headed by the Leonid Abalkin - carried almost no articles in 1988 that even dealt with foreign economic policy in part. The journal, *Mirovaia ekonomiia i mezhdunarodnye otnosheniia* (The World Economy and International Relations), did have several articles on foreign economic matters, but surprisingly few given the presumed focus of the journal. Even these articles were extremely cautious in comparison with the articles dealing with the problems in the domestic sphere in other journals. N. Shmelev co-authored an article asserting that "international competition is an obligatory condition of dynamic scientific-technical progress", and then presenting a number of steps for the Soviet Union to take.[2] However, the article did little to document, let alone dramatize the reasons for the assertion about international competition. The few other articles in the journal that dealt with the foreign economic sphere, even in part, were less explicit.

The question is why has there been so little discussion of the foreign economic imperatives of economic reform?

One possible answer - and it is the dominant one given in the United States - is that Soviet economists are basically incompetent, especially on foreign economic questions. They are seen as men who were trained in the Leninist view of foreign economic relations and who are so obsessed with the United States that they do not seriously study the experience of the Pacific countries, let alone the experience of the Third World countries that is really relevant to a semi-developed country such as the Soviet Union. Even in their domestic arguments they make statements about the impossibility of improving quality and quantity simultaneously that suggests a lack of awareness that quality and quantity improved most rapidly at the same time in the Pacific countries. And, of course, the logical conclusion of this conventional view is that with such incompetent economists, it is not surprising that the leadership does not know what it is doing. Some Americans holding the conventional view regret the situation they see, but basically this view is the main justification for an American policy of destabilization rather than economic cooperation.

In my view, however, we should take much more seriously the possibility that Gorbachev was right in January 1989 when he insisted that he does have

---

[2] V. Spendarian and N. Shmelev, "Problemy povysheniia effektivnosti vneshneekonomicheskikh sviszei", *Mirovaia ekonomiia i mezhdunarodnye otnosheniia*, no. 8 (1988), p. 11.

a strategy of economic reform and that it makes much more sense than that articulated in public. We should not forget that many of the most competent economists in the Soviet Union work not in the academy which - in the Soviet Union as abroad - tends to be academic, but in the much-maligned bureaucracy. The people one occasionally meets in these circles are extremely sophisticated, and they, rather than scholars outside the government, have the major impact on policy. And, above all, we should not forget the extreme political sensitivity of the issue of ingretation into the world economy. Indeed, we must understand that the question runs far deeper than repudiation of the Stalinist economic model and hence must be handled with extreme caution for that reason alone.

Clearly the extreme caution with which the Soviet leaders have approached the necessary raising of retail food prices indicates a fear of the sort of riots that accompanied the increase of meat prices in 1962 in the Soviet Union and the attempt to increase meat prices in Poland in 1970, 1976, and 1980. While an increase in food prices is particularly explosive, subjecting Soviet workers to foreign competition also raises great fears. If the workers think that unemployment will result from their inability to meet the foreign competition, they will be especially alarmed. In addition, however, they have been told for decades that Western capitalists inherently exploit their workers. The thought of working under such capitalists is already a frightening idea, but the thought of being forced to compete with exploited workers abroad - especially with those in the Third World who produce the low-quality, low-wage goods with which the Soviet Union must compete - is just as unsettling. The worker will naturally think that to compete with a foreign factory, all the more so one with better technology, a Soviet factory manager must exploit and overwork labour as much as or more than the foreign capitalist. The reality of such perceptions is not the politically important fact. Their existence is what is important, and they rest on seven decades of unchallenged propaganda.

Integration into the world economy is also ideologically problematical in the extreme. Soviet reformers can claim - rightly or wrongly - that Lenin would not have undertaken collectivization in 1929 nor abolished the private and cooperative sector in the city. They can claim to be returning to the essence of Marxism-Leninism in the reforms that they are now advocating and introducing. In the foreign economic sphere, they can refer vaguely to Lenin's policy of promoting foreign concessions (Averell Harriman had one in the republic of Georgia), but if they begin writing honestly about the last year in which Lenin was leading a fierce battle against Bukharin and other leaders

- including even Stalin to some extent - on the question of integration into the world economy, they would find themselves in deep trouble.

In fact, the central issue of 1922 was the extension of the New Economic Policy (NEP) to the foreign economic sphere. Lenin had repudiated the huge Russian foreign debt at the time of the revolution and had nationalized foreign property without compensation. As two leading American economists wrote in the early 1920s, the Soviet leaders "by rejecting the very foundations upon which international credit and commerical intercourse among civilized nations is built, isolated Russia from the rest of the world."[3] It was as if Brazil had decided in the late 1980s to repudiate its foreign debt altogether and nationalized all foreign property without compensation. The British prime minister, Lloyd George, was interested in ending the Russian isolation, and at the 1922 International Economic Conference in Genoa, he offered a compromise on the question.

A large number of top Soviet officials wanted to negotiate with the West and also to end the monopoly of the foreign trade ministry in the conduct of foreign trade. Lenin was absolutely adamant - almost hysterical on both questions[4] - and, supported by Trotsky, he carried the day. By doing so, he made inevitable the kind of domestic mobilization of resources - what Gorbachev called the Trotsky-Preobrazhensky policy of the peasantry - that occurred in 1929. Clearly reformers who want to interpret Lenin's views in order to delegitimate the agricultral decisions of 1929 cannot ignore Lenin's attitudes and policies on foreign economic questions that made the agricultural decisions virtually inevitable.

But if the fear of arousing workers' fears and the impossibility of using Lenin to legitimate an opening to the West seriously limits the ability of Soviet scholars and spokesmen to lay out a clear foreign economic strategy, we are left with a problem in assessing that strategy. Perhaps the inability of Soviet economists to freely discuss the issue means that the vast majority of them have not really thought seriously about the issue and do not understand it. However, in my opinion, those who are guiding Soviet policy are far more sophisticated than they can demonstrate in public.

---

[3] Leo Pavlovsky and Harold G. Moutton, *Russian Debts and Russian Reconstruction* (New York: McGraw-Hill, 1924), pp. 4-5, 55, 152 and 167.

[4] See A.O. Chubarian, *V.I. Lenin i formirovanie sovetskoi vneshnei politiki* (Moscow: Nauka, 1972), pp. 261-281.

13

2.2 The political, economic and international interests of the Soviet government

If it is the case that Soviet public statements about foreign economic policy do not and cannot represent real Soviet thinking on the subject, how then do we understand what is going on? In my opinion we must examine the political, economic, and international interests of the Soviet leadership and then hypothesize a strategy that best serves those interests. We must then look at the actual steps that the Soviet Union has been taking to see whether they correspond to the steps that have been hypothesized.

In my opinion, Mikhail Gorbachev has three major interests that are relevant in understanding his foreign economic stategy.

First, Gorbachev must maintain control over a very different population than existed in the Soviet Union in the 1960s, let alone in earlier decades. In 1964 when Khrushchev was overthrown, the Soviet Union had 30 million people with a complete secondary education or better, while the political-administrative elite between the ages of 50 and 60 was the Brezhnev-Grishin generation that was born between 1905 and 1915. In 1989 the Soviet Union had 125 million people with a complete secondary education or better, 61 per cent of the population over the age of 17, and the political-administrative elite between the ages of 50 and 60 was born between 1930 and 1940.

The passage of the Brezhnev-Grishin generation from the scene is of great significance. The theory of totalitariarism was correct in insisting that totalitarian movements rested for their social support upon populations that were especially insecure because of being subjected to special stress. The shocks to which the German population was subjected between 1915 and 1923 are well-known, but W.W. Rostow's analysis of virulent communism as "the disease of the transition" was based on the assumption that the Russians at the turn of the century were living through particularly stressful times because of the speed of industrialization, the heavy emphasis upon foreign investment, the disintegration of the tsarist political system, and the defeats of Russia in the Crimean War, the Russo-Japanese War, and World War I.

The Russians born in the 1920s and the 1930s, however, had a very different set of experiences. Stalinism paradoxically nurtured the seeds of its own destruction. Censorship and political repression meant that the youth were raised in a much more stable time; the xenophobic policy of the post-war era that cut off the youth from foreign culture gave it a correspondingly intense exposure to Russian literature of the 19th century and the Western values it

14

expressed; and, finally, the necessities of winning World War II led Stalin to speak of the United States and Great Britain as peace-loving countries, and this inevitably undercut the effort to maintain a rigid ideological analysis of capitalist countries after the war. Whatever the reasons, we met today's political-administrative elite when they were teenagers in the 1950s. They were not afraid of contact with the West as were members of the Brezhnev-Grishin generation, but instead they were extremely attracted to Western music, Western clothes, Western souvenirs, Western films, and so forth.

The great British specialist on the Soviet Union of the 1950s, Edward Crankshaw, was utterly contemptuous of the Brezhnev-Grishin generation in a book published in 1959: "Nothing in this world is more depressing to contemplate than the average Soviet official of high or low degree at present between the ages of forty and sixty... Those who started their rise in their thirties during the great purges of twenty years ago...are incomparably the worst". He had a very different view of the generation born in the 1920s: "The Soviet Union's great hope lies in the young - those under thirty-five [i.e., born after 1924]... In a dozen professions in which Party control is particularly rigid - in the Foreign Service, in the Law, in journalism, in economics, in the higher civil service with its many branches, in the armed forces, in the university faculties, you will meet well-turned-out young men in their thirties, usually Party members, relaxed and easy in manner, often with a pleasantly ironical approach to life, and very much in touch with realities of every kind... I have been talking of the cream of the younger men beginning to rise in what are called the liberal professions and the State and Party service. Until the last decade young men of comparable ability would not have dreamt of this sort of career". [5]

The person who was 35 years old in 1959 was 65 years old in 1989. Those who were young in that year are correspondingly older today. Despite of all the talk about a privileged bureaucracy in the Soviet Union, the Soviet managerial-bureaucratic class has been extremely underprivileged: it has not been able to read free newspapers, to shop in Paris, or to vacation on the Greek Isles; it must live in two-bedroom and three-bedroom apartments; it must endure an extraordinarily egalitarian wage and social policy, without having the ability to discipline the work force; it does not have the security provided by

---

[5] Edward Crankshaw, *Khrushchev's Russia* (Baltimore: Penguin Books, 1959), pp. 91, 127 and 130.

the ownership of property. From Western Europe a century ago to Brazil and South Korea today, the growth of a managerial middle class has been associated with sharply increased pressure for a more liberal political system. The vote for Boris Yeltsin in Moscow makes clear what should have been obvious earlier. Gorbachev had to worry about accommodating the desires of the new middle class in the bureaucracy and the labour force.

Yet, no one in any country likes the reversal of a social policy that guaranteed total job security, highly subsidized prices, and an absence of inflation. The same people who want a wide selection of goods on the shelves are not going to be happy with the increase in prices that is necessary to achieve it. A number of governments around the world tried to ween publics away from excessively protective social welfare policies but the process has never been painless, and it must be handled with care if stability is to be maintained.

The second interest that Gorbachev must pursue is the rebuilding of the power of the Soviet state. Obviously Brezhnev did not consider this interest compelling, but he had only a short time to live by the late 1970s and clearly he was indifferent about his place in history. In longer term perspective, however, the decline of the Soviet Union as a great power has been quite severe in the last decade, and the continuation of the trend will create increasingly severe problems as China and India, each with a billion people, become modern industrial powers in the 21st century. The interests of national defense demand a modernization of the economy to meet that threat.

To some extent, Gorbachev gives the appearance of a man who is truly interested in his place in history who really wants to transform Russia, and it is likely that that motivation alone will drive him. The issues of Soviet power and of political stability are closely related. Those socialist countries that have been successful in achieving national goals have been quite stable politically, but those in Eastern Europe that have been associated with a reduction in national power and independence have been unstable. If the Soviet people become convinced that the Soviet system dooms the Soviet Union to second-class status as a country and will leave the country ill-prepared to defend itself against China and some American technological breakthrough in the 21st century, the Soviet system will become as unstable as any in Eastern Europe.

The third interest that Gorbachev must pursue - and in a sense it is the most important - is to find an economic reform that will actually work. Many Western economists speak about the introduction of market prices, a convertible rouble, an excessive money supply, and so forth, and imply that only conservatism stands in the way of quick solutions. Much of this analysis is extremely misguided. The Third World experience with movement away from subsidized prices suggests that it must be done very carefully, while the movement to a fully convertible currency is a very slow process. India is a long way from one now, while even France is only now introducing full convertibility. The talk about excessive money supply is unsophisticated in the extreme. Oleg Bogomolov puts the amount of cash and savings accounts in the Soviet Union at 360-370 billion roubles.[6] That is 1,300 roubles per person, and is grossly too small a stake for an economy that is going to ask its citizens to invest in housing, cooperatives, shares of factories, and the like. Even if none of the Soviet money were used for consumption, there would still not be enough money in circulation to pay for down payments on apartments, let alone productive investment.

Clearly the Soviet leadership cannot simply accept the advice of some Western and radical Soviet economists in favour of straightforward radical reform, for the result would be economic disaster. The problem is to find a path of transitional reform that moves the Soviet Union forward toward a better-functioning economy without creating economic chaos in the interim.

It is no simple task. How does one increase the money supply needed for investment while ensuring that people do not simply try to spend the money on consumer goods and drive up prices? How does one introduce market prices before introducing competition between plants, for otherwise plants and ministries in monopoly or semi-monopoly positions will simply take advantage of the situation to raise prices in an unjustified manner? But how does one introduce competition without giving plant managers the right to adjust prices, for variation in price is one of the main - if not the main - instruments of competition?

Similarly reform is not easy for purely technical reasons. For example, a law on enterprises introduced on January 1, 1988 simply could not have any meaning in 1988, for the supply plans for 1988 had already been established during 1987, and this is only one example of the way that decisions must be interrelated with a planning process that is always producing key decisions at least a year before they are enacted. Indeed, one leading economist is pro-

---

[6] *Argumenty i fakty*, no. 3 (1989).

bably right in saying that the most worrying development of 1988-1989 is that the five-year plan to begin in 1991 is "quietly, quietly" being formulated.

There are other technical problems even more serious. The Soviet Union simply has had no experience with a great variety of questions that are crucial to a market economy. It has no experience with the taxation of business, with the development of depreciation rules, with the definition of legitimate business expenses, and the like. Its banking system has not even had checking accounts, let alone experience with determining creditworthiness, with securing mortgages, and so forth. The long-time monopoly of foreign trade means that few in the country have experience with the rules of foreign trade, let alone the peculiarities of fluctuating exchange rates or the sharp practices of international traders. The list could go on and on.

Some Westerners, uncertain about how they would handle the transition, simply think that the task is impossible and that reform must fail. Such a view is clearly too pessimistic, for many countries have shown growth during difficult periods of transition. Gorbachev's problem is to find a sequence of steps that will achieve positive results without paralyzing himself with the search for perfection. He must try to mobilize support for reform without prematurely building excessive expectations, while he obscures the costs of reform from the population.

2.3 Economic reforms and the pace of economic intergration

Given Gorbachev's set of interests and the dilemmas they create, there is good reason for Gorbachev to have followed a path of reform that is not unlike that which he has actually followed. So long as the Central Committee elected in 1981 remained in power, Gorbachev needed to act with special caution, but by the time the party congress had met in March 1986 to elect a new Central Committee, the planning process for 1987 had already begun. As a consequence, little could be done in 1986 except a series of radical statements at the congress to open up the debates on economic reform and then the preparation of a series of essentially experimental laws on individual labour, cooperatives, and joint ventures that were to be tested out in 1987. In addition, at the end of 1986 major reorganization occurred in the administration of foreign trade, with the Ministry of Foreign Trade being merged with the State Committee on Foreign Economic Ties and with the new ministry closing the old ministry's monopoly control of foreign trade.

In 1987 everyone commented on the limited character of the legislation that was passed. The law on individual work legalized only part-time work, and the law on unearned income restricted the right of individuals to engage in the distribution of goods. The laws on cooperatives and joint ventures were very restrictive and, in practice, the number of enterprises that were established was quite small. Yet, if looked upon in light of the desirability of small-scale experimentation and learning, the 1987 experiment made considerable sense. And, whatever the impact of the new laws, they embodied a most enormous change in ideology which had crucial long-term significance.

The decision to begin with the creation of cooperatives was very well calculated. Since Lenin had endorsed cooperatives, the support of small-scale cooperatives was a logical first ideological step on the road to selling shares in state enterprises. It also was a logical first step in opening up the supply system by multiplying suppliers. And it also made political sense, As the experience of the Palestinian revolution - and of all revolutions - shows, revolution is a young man's activity. The Palestinian revolt began when the drop in oil prices closed lots of young Palestinian employment opportunities in the Gulf States and blocked their chance for upward mobility. The Soviet leaders too have to worry about teenagers and people in their early twenties as potential leaders of demonstrations and a free trade union movement, but the legalization of cooperatives gives ambitious young people the possibility of achieving their advancement within the system. A young worker who has the chance to move into the middle class has little incentive to stay on the assembly line and organize a trade union, and if its potential leaders are siphoned off into the middle class, the Soviet working class may be more quiescent than it otherwise might be.

The mystery of 1987 was the failure to conduct significant agricultural experimentation. Indeed, although agricultural reform had come very early in East European and Chinese reform, it was hardly even discussed in the burgeoning debate on economic reform in the Soviet press, which concentrated overwhelmingly on industrial reform. Conceivably it was felt that agricultural reform in a developed economy such as the Soviet Union could not succeed until laws were passed that began to reform the food industry and the agricultural supply industries; perhaps the fear of urban unrest in the face of inflation of food price increases was a worry.

The concentration on industry in the debates of 1987 reflected the fact that the major new legislation being prepared was the law on the enterprise. It deeply disappointed the radical reformers in its inconsistency, but, as already indicated, no law could have had an impact in 1987 because the supply plan was already in place. The real question is whether the new law on enterprise had an impact on the planning process of 1987. Formally it did, for the proportion of supplies distributed by state orders declined to below the 40 per cent level in 1988, but it remains unclear what this meant in practice.

The major developments in 1988 were, first the broadening of the law on cooperatives and the rapid growth of the number of people working in cooperatives; and, second, the introduction of serious experimentation in the agricultural sphere. The number of people working in the cooperatives reached 500,000 by mid-1988 and 1,500,000 by early 1989, and, although problems of regulation had to be faced, the types of cooperative activity expanded. In agriculture, Gorbachev became increasingly insistent on the introduction of the lease system in agriculture. In practice, the necessary reductions in the size of state deliveries did not take place, and the lease movement remained quite restricted. However, if this is seen in light of the earlier practice of introducing a one-year experiment under the guise of passing a new law, normal progress was finally beginning in agriculture.

Indeed, the first major development in 1989 was a plenary session of the Central Committee on agriculture that was extremely radical in the version of history it presented, in its endorsement of independence for the peasant (even the possibility of withdrawal from the collective farm), and in its promise of an eventual end of all state deliveries. The leadership also announced a decision that was absolutely indispensable; namely that the reform would be phased in during a transitional period. What remains unclear is the speed with which change will occur during the transition. Much of that will be determined during the compilation of the plan for 1990.

Clearly the early 1990s will also see a significant acceleration of reform in the foreign trade area. The right to trade abroad is being extended to all state and cooperative enterprises; the joint venture law has been considerably liberalized; a first experimental domestic auction of foreign currency is being introduced; laws legalizing foreign economic zones are imminent. One should also note the foreign policy steps that have been taken so facilitate the development of foreign economic relations. Emigration of Jews has been increased in an attempt to relax the Jackson-Vanik amendment while substantial concessions have been made to China to promote an improvement of economic relations with it. Most important of all, Gorbachev has made very major changes in the military realm - both a virtually unilateral withdrawal of the

SS-22 missiles and a unilateral reduction in troops - in order to reduce the sense of threat in Europe.

The question is how rapidly will the expansion of foreign economic relations be? Obviously many of the changes introduced in 1989 were in the same experimental category as steps taken earlier. As such, their major impact will be felt in the early 1990s. Obviously a really large-scale increase in foreign economic activity depends not only on an increase in the freedom of Soviet economic enterprises to undertake it, but also on their having an incentive to do so. So long as the Soviet enterprises have a captive domestic audience, they have relatively little reason to test the much more rigorous foreign market. Real changes in the supply and incentive system promised in existing legislation must be introduced into practice.

There will be a significant expansion in Soviet foreign economic relations early in the 1990s. The most serious indicator will be relations with Japan. The Soviet Union has a major geostrategic interest in the Japanese-American security relationship, for an independent Japan would almost surely increase its military budget above the 1 per cent of GNP level and might eventually even acquire nuclear weapons. Yet, Japan is the major economic power with excess capital that it seeks to export, and the Soviet Union has an absolute imperative in developing a strong economic relationship with it, partly to lessen its dependence on West Germany. The signs of a movement to rapidly improving Soviet-Japanese relations are likely to lead to the solution of the Northern Territories issue.

The truly interesting question is the extent to which integration of the Soviet Union into the world economy is part of its reintegration into world civilization. All of the signs suggest that the Soviets, consciously or unconsciously, have decided that facing a billion Chinese and a billion Indians, they want to join the 600 million person West European home that has been created in the post-war period from the Elbe to San Francisco and be part of a billion Europeans facing the world of the mid-21st century. For this reason alone there are no analogies between the present and Brezhnev's policy in the 1970s, and the opening of the Soviet Union to the world economy is likely to go much faster than we expect.

Chapter 3

SOVIET FOREIGN TRADE REFORMS AND THE CHALLENGE TO EAST EUROPEAN ECONOMIC RELATIONS WITH THE WEST

Wladimir Andreff[1]

3.1 Introduction

Since Mikhail Gorbachev took office there has been a great amount of un-certainty surrounding perestroika, particularly its possible effects on East-West economic relations. In 1985, the introduction of major economic reforms seemed to represent the main hope of seeing these relations improve in the long term.[2] At the present time, despite the relative decline in East-West trade throughout the 1980s, a certain number of studies have attempted to deter-mine whether this hope can be based on the reform of Soviet foreign trade.

If the Soviet reform is effectively implemented it will have a substantial impact not only on relations between the Soviet Union and the West, but also on relations among the other European CMEA countries and Western Europe. This side effect of the Soviet reform may influence trade between the Six[3] and the West as well as foreign investment flows; in particular Western investment capital which might prefer the vast Soviet market rather than the smaller markets in the rest of Eastern Europe. Forecasting such side effects is even more difficult than forecasting more general trends concerning East-West eco-nomic relations.

However, according to John Pinder, the Soviet reform of its domestic eco-nomy and foreign trade is likely to have one of the following consequences:[4] 1) not much change, 2) a tendency for the CMEA to become more inward-oriented, or 3) an economy which is more open to market mechanisms, both

---

1) Professor of Economics, University of Social Sciences at Grenoble, France.

2) P. Marer, "Economic Policies and Systems in Eastern Europe: Commonalities and Differen-ces", in U.S. Congress, Joint Economic Committee, *East European Economies: Slow Growth in the 1980's* (Washington, D.C.: U.S. Government Printing Office, 1985).

3) Bulgaria, Czechoslovakia, the GDR, Hungary, Poland and Romania.

4) J. Pinder, "The EC and Eastern Europe under Gorbachev: How Normal Could Relations Become?" in *The Economies of Eastern Europe under Gorbachev* (Brussels: NATO, 1988).

at home and abroad, with a more marked orientation towards the world market and trade with the West. The first hypothesis is possible. It would mean that the side effects of the Soviet reform will be overruled by other factors influencing trade between the Six and the West; such as the situation on international markets, the trends in oil prices, and policies adopted by the Six to modernize their industry, balance their hard currency trade and manage their external debt. Such factors should not be neglected, but if they are stressed in the analysis, little can be learned about the impact of the Soviet reform on the relations between the Six and the West. If only to give some food for thought during this discussion it is preferable to adopt another hypothesis.

The hypothesis of the CMEA becoming more inward-oriented is the least likely of the three. First of all, it would be in contradiction with the main orientations adopted by the CMEA summit meeting in June 1984 which argued in favour of expanding trade relations with the West.[5] Even East German economists clearly stated that there could be no other policy at present than the overall orientation of the economy towards exporting to hard currency markets.[6] The resolution adopted by the Soviet Council of Ministers in December 1988 makes it all the more unlikely that the Soviet Union will voluntarily fall back on the CMEA. The Joint Declaration on the establishment of official relations between the European Economic Community and the CMEA, signed in June 1988, may be considered by some of the Six (particularly Hungary) as a sort of guarantee against such an inward-oriented solution.[7]

Thus we intend to adopt the hypothesis that the Soviet reforms, if implemented,[8] will modify the external economic relations of the Soviet Union and the Six but will not lead to greater inward-orientation. The questions to be

---

[5] L. Csaba, "Politique économique et planification dans les pays du C.A.E.M.", *Revue d'Etudes comparatives Est-Ouest*, XVIII, no. 2 (Juin 1987).

[6] G. Nötzold, "Perspektiven der sozialistischen ökonomischen Integration und die intersystemaren Wirtschaftsbeziehungen", *Wissenschaftliche Zeitschrift der Karl Marx Universität Leipzig* (Gesellschafts- und Sprachwissenschaftliche Reihe, 32, no. 4, 1983).

[7] W. Andreff, "Les relations économique entre le Conseil d'Assistance Economique Mutuelle et la Communauté Economique Européenne", in W. Andreff, éd., *Réforme et commerce extérieur dans les pays de l'Est* (Paris: Editions L'Harmattan, à paraître, 1989).

[8] It would be particularly interesting to analyse the chances of the Soviet reform actually being carried through; such an analysis would involve studying the internal administrative and economic mechanisms in the Soviet Union and would lead us off our present subject. We presume that the reform will bring about at least some changes in comparison with the 1970s and 1980s.

examined, then, are: whether these changes will affect relations between the Six and the West; whether or not they are likely to improve these relations; whether the Six, in their relations with the West, will have to cope with competition caused by the new trade links between the Soviet Union and the West; and, in this case, in what way the Six will change their economic policy to deal with this new competition. These questions cannot be examined without making some assumptions about the environment of the Soviet foreign trade reform and of the relations between the Six and the West. From this point of view, we believe that three variables are of crucial importance: the price of oil, the reactions of Western firms to the new legislation in Eastern Europe concerning direct foreign investment, and the likely results of the industrial modernization programmes implemented by the Six since 1983[9] and of the CMEA's 20-year long "Comprehensive Programme of Scientific and Technological Progress" launched in 1985.[10] Of the Six we will pay particular attention to Hungary and Poland, inasmuch as they have already carried out a significant reform of foreign trade and have made real efforts to attract joint ventures with foreign firms on their own territory.

3.2 The reform of foreign trade in the Soviet Union and in Eastern Europe

From 1979 to 1982 the Six went through a period of severe economic difficulties which included a substantial "external constraint" in the form of trade deficits and hard currency debts.[11] This situation was analysed in terms of economic crisis by Western economists.[12] An international conference organized by the Academies of Science of the six countries of the CMEA (Romania did not take part) preferred to describe this period as a phase of economic disequilibrium illustrated in particular by shortages, and looked forward to the likelihood of a return to a more balanced situation (or

---

[9] W. Andreff and E. Brunat, "La notion de modernisation industrielle dans les économies socialistes et son analyse", *Economies et Sociétés - Cahiers de l'I.S.M.E.A.*, série G, no. 43, tome XXII (Fevrier 1988).

[10] R. Evstigneev, "State Scientific and Technological Policy and Incentives for Enterprises", in C.T. Saunders, ed., *Industrial Policies and Structural Change* (London: Macmillan Press, 1987).

[11] W. Andreff and M. Lavigne, "La constrainte exterieure dans les économies du C.A.E.M.", *Economies et Sociétés - Cahiers de l'I.S.M.E.A.*, série HS, no. 29, tome XIX (Avril 1985).

[12] W. Andreff and M. Lavigne, "A Way Out of the Crisis for the CMEA Economies?" *Soviet and Eastern European Foreign Trade*, XXIII, no. 3 (Fall 1987).

"sbalansirovannost").[13] Here we are at the very roots of the revival of economic and foreign trade reforms in several CMEA countries in the 1980s.

The implementation of reforms demands time. The initial reaction of the Six in the early 1980s was to adopt strict adaptation policies. Large-scale adaptation processes were thus introduced in various East European countries to change their economic situation, improve their trade balances, and deal with their external debt. Although it would have been better to improve the balance of payments with the West by means of hard currency exports, this was practically impossible. The only acceptable way was to reduce imports.[14] The outcome of this adaptation was twofold : from 1982 on, the foreign trade balance between the Six and the West was transformed from a deficit into a surplus (with the exceptions of Bulgaria and Hungary); however, at the same time trade between the Six and the West began to grow more slowly and later to decline.

This sort of adaptation is a short-term measure. In 1983 a Czechoslovakian economist published a paper in the Russian journal, *Voprosy Ekonomiki*, proposing a much more complete set of adaptation policies, which can no doubt be seen as the harbinger of present-day reforms.[15] Among Seregiova's medium-term measures were: the proposed adaptation of the physical structures of production and input consumption to changes on the world markets; a more efficient use of raw material and equipment; and an increase in the value added of export products. Long-term measures included: the consolidation of the production bases for energy and raw materials; the intensification of agriculture in order to reduce import dependence; and the development of new industrial sectors, such as electronics, computer engineering, robotics and biotechnologies. This was in fact the first draft of what was to become the policy of industrial modernization needed in order to carry through the foreign trade reform in the Six countries.

The same analysis could not a priori be applied to the Soviet Union, at least as long as oil prices were high on the international market, and therefore

---

[13] K.I. Mikulski, ed., *Problems of Proportionality in a Socialist Economy* (Moscow: Ekonomika Publishers, 1984).

[14] S. Ladyka, "The Evolution of East-West Economic Relations: Past Tendencies and Future Prospects", in P. Bozyk, ed., *Global Challenges and East European Responses* (Warsaw: Polish Scientific Publishers, 1988).

[15] J. Seregiova, "Change in International Trade and European Countries of Comecon", *Voprosy Ekonomiki*, no. 9, (1983).

the Soviet Union did not labour under a substantial external constraint. This helps us to understand a certain form of Soviet "benign neglect" until 1984.[16]

This cannot be seen after 1985 when Gorbachev came to power and petrol prices fell. The fall in Soviet export earnings has reduced its purchasing power in the field of high-technology equipment from developed market economies. This type of external constraint (previously unknown to the Soviet Union), coincided with Gorbachev's desire for reform and his economic advisers' opinion that the country was (and is) in a state of "pre-crisis"[17] which could only be resolved by restructuring the economic system. This is the context within which Soviet foreign trade reform is taking place. It involves not only changes in foreign trade strategy but also in the organization of foreign trade.

Gorbachev has repeatedly stated that the Soviet Union is in favour of the strongest possible development of its international economic relations. As Aganbeguian has emphasized, the Soviet Union accounts for roughly a fifth of world industrial production but only a twentieth of world trade. Between 1975 and 1985, Soviet trade with the West increased by only one-third and stopped increasing since 1981. It has even decreased since 1985. Western countries' share of Soviet foreign trade fell from 33.6 per cent in 1980 to 23.0 per cent in 1986.[18] The main objective is thus to decentralize foreign trade, to eliminate existing barriers between domestic and external markets, and to link performance in external markets more closely with wages and profits of those enterprises involved. The medium-term objective is to create a strong export-oriented complex within the Soviet economy; one which would considerably alter the country's export structure in favour of manufactures and other sophisticated products.[19]

Soviet strategy concerning its economic relations with the West is aimed, not only at increasing exports of finished goods, machinery and equipment, but also at increasing the degree of processing of exported raw materials,

---

[16] W. Andreff, "The External Constraint in the Economic Crisis of East European Countries", in P. Zarembka and T. Ferguson, eds., *Research in Political Economy*, vol. 8 (Greenwich, Connecticut: Jai Press Inc., 1985).

[17] A.G. Aganbeguian, *Perestroika: le double défi soviétique* (Paris: Editions Economica, 1987).

[18] O.T. Bogomolov, "The Importance of External Relations in the Development of Eastern Europe: Case Study of the Soviet Union", in Bozyk, ed., *Global Challenges and East European Responses*.

[19] I.D. Ivanov, "Restructuring the Mechanisms of Foreign Economic Relations in the U.S.S.R.", *Soviet Economy*, 3 (July-September 1987).

fuels and foodstuffs. The principal Soviet goal is to become a major world exporter of machinery, equipment, and technology. According to Ivanov, the country has a long record in exporting machinery, particularly machine tools, aviation technology, optics, cars, and mining, agricultural, transportation and other equipment.[20] However, machinery is still a long way from dominating Soviet exports; in 1984 it accounted for only 12 per cent of their total value compared to 22 per cent in 1970.

The Soviet Union's foreign trade strategy is also aimed at imports. Bulk imports of grain, metals, and some basic chemicals have to be substituted domestically, the saved currency being reallocated. In machinery-related sectors, more imports will be used for modernization and less for new construction. The machine building sector will be the leading importer, followed by agriculture, the energy sector, infrastructure and consumer goods industries. It is expected that purchases of consumer goods will be partly redirected from Western Europe and Japan to developing countries.

Programmed development of export sectors implies the construction (up until the mid-1990s) of a strong domestic potential for the steady development of Soviet industrial exports, especially machinery. Priority industries in the years to come will be machine tools, electronics, electrical engineering, computers, robotics, and data processing; as well as chemistry as a source of new materials. In the energy sector, the country will continue to be self-sufficient in fuels and to export them, while accelerating the development of nuclear energy and natural gas. Overall machinery production for 1986-1990 is expected to increase by 40-45 per cent while the share of new products in total machinery shipments should be increased by anything up to 13 per cent annually. But a massive restructuring of Soviet exports cannot be achieved overnight. Accordingly, traditional export items ought not to be neglected so long as they are still competitive. Additional production of pulp, paper, cement, plastics, and other processed goods are envisaged within the plans.

Foreign trade organization has been reformed in order to support this new strategy. In August 1986, the CPSU Central Committee and the USSR Council of Ministers enacted two basic resolutions: one entitled "On measures to improve the management of foreign economic relations," and a second entitled "On measures to improve the management of economic, scientific and techno-

---

[20] I.D. Ivanov, "The Soviet Union in a changing global economic setting: the prospects for trade-oriented growth", UNCTAD/ST/TSC/4 (April 25, 1986).

logical cooperation with Socialist countries". With the application of these two resolutions on January 1, 1987, the monopoly exercized by the Ministry of Foreign Trade was abolished and the right of direct access to the international market was accorded to 21 ministries and administrations as well as 68 Soviet enterprises and economic associations (obedinenija). A State Commission for Foreign Economic Relations (GUK) was set up under the USSR Council of Ministers to direct foreign economic activities.

The Soviet Enterprise Law, enacted in June 1987, stipulates that the foreign commercial transactions of each enterprise should be treated as an integral part of its overall business performance, thus directly influencing the volume of its profits and the formation of reinvestment and social development funds. In order to get enterprises really interested in exporting, the new mechanism allows them to retain part of the proceeds of foreign currency transactions. These funds may be freely spent on imports of products and technologies needed for purposes of modernization, internal sales and exports. The idea is to eventually make all Soviet industries and enterprises self-financing in foreign currency for the period 1991-1995. As for the legislation covering cooperatives in the Soviet Union (passed on May 26, 1988), it stipulates that those cooperatives which are involved in industrial activities can be given the right to directly carry out import-export operations if their activities are competitive in the foreign market.

In November 1988, the overall organization of Soviet foreign trade could be described as follows.[21] The list of Soviet agencies allowed to sign commercial contracts with foreign firms included: the 22 foreign trade organizations which depend on the Ministry of Foreign Economic Relations; the foreign trade organizations belonging to the 65 sector Ministries at federal and republic levels, the 150 or so enterprises and economic organizations authorised to deal directly abroad, an indeterminable number of competitive cooperatives, the Soviet exporting associations created in 1988, one independent joint-stock company (Sovfintrade created in October 1988), a certain number of towns such as Moscow, Leningrad and Vyborg possessing a foreign currency account, and, finally, joint venture companies established in the Soviet Union with foreign capital participation.

---

[21] A. Tiraspolsky, "Cooperation U.R.S.S.-Ouest: les nouveaux partenaires des firmes occidentales", *Le Courrier des Pays de l'Est*, no. 334 (Novembre 1988).

A statutory order passed on December 2, 1988 gives all State enterprises and cooperatives the right to trade directly abroad,[22] on the condition that they are able to justify doing so on grounds of their competitiveness and export capacity! The rest continue to go through foreign trade organizations. This order took effect on April 1, 1989 (the first day of our deliberations at The University of Georgia!) and a new customs tariff was expected early in 1990. The rouble's exchange rate should also be lowered early in 1991. Soviet enterprises will then be able to exchange part of the foreign currency which they have earned on an internal currency market in the Soviet Union.

The Soviet Union's new foreign trade strategy and its reorganization offer a challenge to most of its trade partners, in both West and East. It is quite possible that the rapid introduction of reforms in certain East European countries is a spin-off from Soviet reforms; though with important differences among countries. However, we cannot conclude, as Derix does, that "the rules governing foreign trade have remained practically unchanged over the last 25 years, up until the moment when reforms started to be talked about".[23] Admittedly Romania (which had not modified its strategy of reducing foreign debt at any price) is the least reform-oriented country among the Six (at least until December 1989). Even Honnecker's GDR, despite its hostility to Soviet-style perestroika, made changes in its foreign trade: the State monopoly on foreign trade was emasculated and combines are now able to sign contracts abroad and hold on to foreign currency made through exports. In addition, the GDR gives less importance than other Eastern countries to the purchase of turnkey factories,[24] preferring to buy high-tech inputs from the West in order to incorporate them in its own capital goods.

Generally speaking, Bulgarian and Czechoslovakian reforms appear to follow, with a certain delay, a line close to that of Soviet perestroika. In Bulgaria, enterprises operate on the basis of accountability, independence and self-financing, foreign exchange transactions included. Interest rates on loans

---

[22] V. Mytarev, "Relations économiques extérieures: orientations 1989", *Actualités Soviétiques*, no. 830 (Décembre 30, 1988).

[23] H.H. Derix, "Außenwirtschaftsreformen in 'sozialistischen' Ländern - ein intrasystemarer Vergleich", *Deutschland Archiv* (August 1987).

[24] W. Andreff and I. Samson, "Das internationale Umfeld der bilateralen Beziehungen Frankreich-D.D.R. innerhalb des Welthandelsaustausches", in C. Luft, ed., *Außenhandelsbeziehungen und Wirtschaftskooperation zwischen der D.D.R. und der Republik Frankreich* (Berlin: Hochschule für Ökonomie Bruno Leuschner, 1988).

in foreign currencies are set according to international financial market conditions. In the long run, Czechoslovakia aims for convertability of the crown to
be ensured by realistic exchange rate policies and a gradual transition to a
unified, single exchange rate for all commercial and non-commercial transactions, applicable with regard to all currencies. In the GDR, Bulgaria and
Czechoslovakia, however, trade with the West occupies a relatively modest
place out of total foreign trade (Table 3.1), and in Romania, the policy of
austerity and the unpredictable measures inspired by the personal power of Mr
Ceaucescu were crucial factors until December 1989. These observations
would indicate, above all, the possibility of Soviet competition in respect of
Hungary and Poland in Western markets.

Table 3.1

**Percentage shares of foreign trade between the CMEA countries
and the West in total trade of CMEA countries
(1980-1987)**

	Exports			Imports		
	1980	1984	1987	1980	1984	1987
Bulgaria	15.8	9.1	6.7	17.2	13.8	15.1
Czechoslovakia	21.8	16.2	14.9	24.3	15.1	17.5
GDR	29.3	31.6	28.6	34.6	30.4	32.3
Hungary	34.0	34.2	35.9	39.5	34.8	41.0
Poland	34.4	34.6	41.5	35.1	29.5	39.6
Romania	34.8	37.2	34.0	31.2	19.9	12.5
Soviet Union	32.0	28.7	20.8	35.4	30.0	22.8

Source: United Nations, Economic Commission for Europe, *Economic Survey of Europe
in 1987-1988* (New York: United Nations, 1988).

The reform of Hungary's foreign trade entered a new stage in the 1980s,
especially since 1985 when perestroika was launched in the Soviet Union. The
number of enterprises having direct access to foreign markets rose from 136
in 1980, to 254 in 1985, and to over 1,000 in 1988.[25] In 1985 Hungary

---

[25] I. Salgo, "Décentralisation ou réforme? L'organisation du commerce extérieur hongrois dans
les années 1980", in Andreff, ed., *Reforme et commerce extérieur.*

repealed the restrictions covering Western imports which had been introduced in 1982 to deal with its balance of payments problem;[26] new legislation simplifying the acquisition procedure for foreign trade licences was introduced in December 1985. Late in 1987 the official authorization, which had until then been necessary before engaging in any direct trade with organizations outside the CMEA, was done away with, and since January 1, 1988 any enterprise has been able to register for foreign trade transactions. Since the beginning of 1988, small private entrepreneurs in Hungary have also been able to ask for a direct export licence for their products; over 200 products from private enterprises have obtained a licence in only a year.

In October 1987, the 1982 Polish economic reform entered a second stage, reckoned to be more radical. In line with the February 1982 law, the Minister of Foreign Trade can now issue authorizations called "concessions" to legally constituted organizations, allowing them to export and import certain products. The exporting enterprise can use part of what it makes in foreign currency through a special foreign currency retention account. Since 1983 foreign currency coming from such accounts is sold; and since May 1987 sales on this internal foreign currency market have been organized twice a month with the resulting price of the dollar being close to the black market rate.[27] Since 1982 the official value of the zloty has been fixed on the basis of a group of foreign currencies obtained from exports (in the same way as the Hungarian forint has been fixed since the same year). Since January 1988, "concessions" have also been given to trade intermediaries; the concessionaries finance all their foreign currency expenditure themselves using their export income on the internal market or through bank loans. Another 1988 innovation has been the possibility of engaging in trade in certain products without any previous authorization; the list kept by the new Ministry of External Economic Cooperation contains 78 export products and 20 import products.

It would appear that accelerating foreign trade reforms in Hungary and in Poland (taking place at the same time as those in the Soviet Union) are a first "side effect" of the Soviet reforms. Being the countries most open to the West,

---

[26] J. Hamori and A. Inotai, "Hungary and the European Communities: Facts, Trends, Prospects", *Trends in World Economy*, no. 57 (1987).

[27] For example, the exchange rate for the dollar reached 1429 zlotys on April 13, 1988. The official dollar rate at this time was 398 zlotys. K. Szymkiewicz, "Le commerce exterieur: 'locomotive' de la réforme économique en Pologne", *Le Courrier des Pays de l'Est*, no. 334 (Novembre 1988).

32

Hungary and Poland are also the best observation posts when trying to predict the possible effects of competition created by the reform of foreign trade in the Soviet Union.

3.3 The impact of Soviet reforms on East-West trade

Between 1980 and 1984, the growth rate (in dollars) of Western imports coming from the Soviet Union was 0.7 per cent per year on average, and 1.2 per cent for Western exports to the Soviet Union. The corresponding percentages for the Six were respectively 2.5 per cent and 10.7 per cent according to UNEEC figures (1988). Soviet trade with the West fell slightly in value between 1984 and 1987, being far below forecasts (*Table 3.2*), while the Six's trade with the West began to grow again at a rate which was equal to or greater than forecasts. Under such conditions, one would expect the Soviet Union to try to catch up with the export and import levels forecast for 1990 through strong growth in exchanges with the West. The growth rates necessary for such a recovery are high (10.3 per cent for exports, 9.4 per cent for imports) but probably not out of reach if foreign trade reform succeeds. The appearance of a Soviet trade deficit in 1990 is likely,[28] but this will only become serious in 1995 if the tendency to catch up, shown between 1987-90, is maintained (*Table 3.2*).

In such a situation the Soviet Union would find itself in strong competition with the Six in Western markets. The Six's trade with the West has grown rapidly between 1984 and 1987, especially in terms of the Six's imports. If this trend continues, the Six's trade surplus in foreign currency would become a worrying deficit in 1990 and unbearable in 1995, especially in Hungary. It is thus likely that the Six will undertake a massive effort to export to Western markets in conjunction with the Soviet Union to limit the growth of their foreign debt. Foreign trade reforms will doubtless contribute to this effort. One could thus forecast, in global terms, an increase in competition between the Soviet Union and the Six in Western markets.

---

[28] Soviet trade with the West has already shown a deficit of $ 1.6 billion for the first quarter of 1988.

Table 3.2

Foreign trade between the West and CMEA countries: achievement and forecast (1984-1995)

(average annual rates of growth calculated
from value in millions of current dollars)

	Forecast 1984-90[a]	Forecast 1984-87[a]	Forecast 1987-90[a]	Achievement 1984-87[b]	Foreign "Recovery" 1987-90[c]	Trade Balance		
						1987[b]	1990[c]	1995[c]
Western imports from the USSR	2.4	-2.5	7.6	-4.1	9.4	-350	296	2,497
Western exports to the USSR	4.3	1.6	7.1	-1.4	10.3			
Western imports from the Six	7.0	4.5	9.5	7.1	6.9	-1,007	3,907	20,407
Western exports to the Six	13.2	14.8	11.6	14.8	13.0			
Western imports from Hungary	6.4	1.6	11.4	12.1	0.9	337	1,215	3,212
Western exports to Hungary	10.8	12.8	9.0	14.5	7.3			
Western imports from Poland	8.2	6.0	10.5	8.3	8.2	-780	-942	-1,682
Western exports to Poland	9.4	7.8	11.1	10.3	8.5			

[a] Calculated from data published in United Nations, Economic Commission of Europe, *Symposium on East-West Business Opportunities and Trade Prospects, Thessaloniki, Greece, September 8-11, 1986,* (New York: United Nations, 1986).

[b] Calculated from United Nations, *Economic Survey of Europe in 1987-1988.*

[c] The "recovery" rate of growth is calculated as the rate necessary to achieve the forecast for 1984-90 once the rate achieved in 1984-87 is taken into account. The Western foreign trade balance is then estimated taking the "recovery" rate as the trend to 1990 and 1995 (a negative value of balance being a deficit for the West).

This initial conclusion should be regarded as being all the more likely if two trends are confirmed: international political detente and weak economic growth in the West. It has been shown that the intensity of Soviet commerce with the West has been fundamentally determined by two factors, political detente and the price of oil.[29] Mr. Gorbachev's policy is clearly to rebuild a climate favourable to expanded East-West trade. In addition, Western economic growth, especially in Western Europe, could make Soviet and East European exports more dynamic.[30] If the recovery becomes stronger in the West, future competition between the Soviet Union and the Six in Western markets would be less tough than if Western growth continued to slow down.

A more detailed analysis allows us to identify the principal areas in which the Soviet Union and the Six are in competition within Western markets (*Table 3.3*). Looking at the fifteen main export markets open to socialist countries in the West between 1980 and 1987, four situations can be distinguished. Soviet market share of total CMEA exports is very high in Finland and Japan, leaving little room for products exported by the Six. In Spain, Soviet products continue to increase their market share; foreign trade reform should maintain this trend. On the other hand, when compared with the Six, the Soviet Union has continued to lose its market share in France, the United States, Austria, and Switzerland. These countries could constitute an area of strong growth if the Soviet Union tried to get back into a position of strength in these four markets. For the other six countries under consideration, there is already open competition between the Soviet Union and the Six, as shown by the fluctuations in their respective market shares. Soviet market share generally increased between 1980 and 1984, sustained by the high price of oil, decreasing between 1984 and 1987 when prices fell. If the price of oil remains around $17-18 dollars per barrel, in the future, the Soviet Union will not be able to maintain or increase its share of these six markets unless it increases exports of manufactured products. Such a trend can already be seen in the British market between 1984 and 1987. On the other hand, it seems less likely that the Soviet Union would be able to compete with the Six in Canada and Australia.

---

[29] A. Nagy, "Changes in the Structure and Intensity of East-West Trade", *Acta Oeconomica*, 35, nos. 3-4 (1985).

[30] G. Wild, "Perspectives de croissance en Europe de l'Est et commerce avec l'Ouest", *Le Courrier des Pays de l'Est*, nos. 309-310-311 (Août-Septembre-Octobre 1986).

Competition between the Soviet Union and the Six could also affect imports of Western products necessary for rapid and successful industrial modernization, assuming the availability of sufficient foreign currency. In this respect, West first Germany should remain the main supplier both for the Soviet Union and for the Six, given the size of its lead over other Western countries. It should, however, be noted that in 1987, West Germany reoriented its activities somewhat towards the Six rather than the Soviet Union, as compared with

Table 3.3

**Market shares of the Soviet Union and of the Six
on leading Western markets[a]**

Leading Western markets for East European exports (ranked as in 1987)

	1980		1984		1987	
	USSR	Six	USSR	Six	USSR	Six
FRG[b]	47.0	53.0	60.2	39.8	45.7	54.3
Italy	57.7	42.3	66.5	33.5	55.7	44.3
France	67.9	32.1	66.9	33.1	57.7	42.3
Finland	86.1	13.9	88.5	11.5	84.8	15.2
Japan	87.8	12.2	77.0	23.0	83.3	16.7
United Kingdom	61.5	38.5	48.6	51.4	51.5	48.5
Netherlands	55.7	44.3	76.2	23.8	60.3	39.7
Austria	43.3	56.7	43.1	56.9	30.5	69.5
USA	31.9	68.1	25.7	74.3	22.1	77.9
Belgium-Luxembourg	68.3	31.7	81.9	18.1	46.3	53.7
Sweden	46.1	53.9	51.9	48.1	46.8	53.2
Spain	58.5	41.5	60.0	40.0	70.0	30.0
Switzerland	67.6	32.4	57.2	42.8	38.4	61.6
Canada	21.9	78.1	10.7	89.3	10.9	89.1
Australia	17.8	82.2	11.7	88.3	12.1	87.9

[a] Share of the Soviet Union and of the Six in each major Western market, as a percentage of total East European exports to each Western country.

[b] Trade between the FRG and the GDR is not included. For instance, in 1987 the Soviet Union's share in total Eastern European exports to the FRG was only 25.4 per cent, once GDR exports to the FRG are taken into account.

Source: OECD Monthly Statistics of Foreign Trade.

Table 3.3 (continued)

Market shares of the Soviet Union and of the Six
on leading Western markets[a]

Leading Western suppliers of East European imports (ranked as in 1987)

	1980		1984		1987	
	USSR	Six	USSR	Six	USSR	Six
FRG[b]	46.3	53.7	53.5	46.5	44.2	55.8
Italy	46.6	53.4	64.0	36.0	61.4	38.6
France	53.1	46.9	66.2	33.8	56.8	43.2
Finland	88.6	11.4	91.9	8.1	90.4	9.6
Japan	77.5	22.5	83.7	16.3	78.2	21.8
United Kingdom	40.3	59.7	56.4	43.6	44.1	55.9
Netherlands	35.8	64.2	36.2	63.8	31.6	68.4
Austria	22.6	77.4	36.9	63.1	27.6	72.4
USA	39.3	60.7	78.6	21.4	67.4	32.6
Belgium-Luxembourg	47.3	52.7	57.9	42.1	46.3	53.7
Sweden	35.1	64.9	37.8	62.2	31.5	68.5
Spain	48.1	51.9	61.1	38.9	54.4	45.6
Switzerland	28.0	72.0	26.0	74.0	32.1	67.9
Canada	74.2	25.8	88.2	11.8	80.7	19.3
Australia	85.0	15.0	70.7	29.3	79.9	20.1

a Share of the Soviet Union and of the Six in each major Western market, as a percentage of total Eastern European imports from each Western country.

b Trade between the FRG and the GDR is not included.

Source: OECD Monthly Statistics of Foreign Trade.

1980. The Soviet Union's four main suppliers after West Germany are Finland, Japan, Australia, and Canada. The two of these should remain favoured suppliers for they also buy a not insignificant share of their imports from the Soviet Union rather than from the Six in foreign currency. On the other hand, the relative share of supplies to the Soviet Union (mostly made up of cereals and food products) from Australia and Canada could decrease if Soviet agricultural reform[31] manages to reduce these imports. In every other Western

---

[31] This reform is based on the state leasing of land to peasants who work it for a period which can now extend to 50 years.

market, purchases by the Six and the Soviet Union are in competition for manufactured products, machines and capital equipment produced in the West. The limits of this competition are defined by the ability to finance imports; the Soviet Union's financing capacity diminished between 1984 and 1987. Finally, the United States, which was a more important supplier for the Six than for the USSR in 1980, has reversed this situation in 1987 as a result of better U.S.-Soviet political relations.

The structure of the Soviet Union's and the Six's commerce with the OECD countries, in terms of products (Table 3.4), indicates which products are the most likely to be the object of competition between the Soviet Union and the Six. Fuels represented over 80 per cent of Soviet exports to the West in 1983 and remained above 70 per cent in 1986. This should continue to decline, not only as a result of the Soviet Union's new foreign trade strategy but also because of the growing difficulty in increasing the country's level of oil production and because of current oil and gas prices. These same reasons should encourage the Soviet Union to restrict oil supplies to the Six, part of which is subsequently re-exported to the West in exchange for foreign currency. The reduction in the importance of fuels as part of East European exports should, on the other hand, reinforce competition in terms of other products. If the Soviet Union manages to increase the share of engineering products in its exports to the West (3.5 per cent in 1986), it will come up against competition from the Six who are following a similar strategy with a more favourable export structure (12.9 per cent in 1986). Everything depends on the successful outcome of industrial modernization programmes.[32] It would appear that the Soviet Union cannot compete with the Six in food industry exports where Hungary, Poland and Bulgaria are competitive, any more than it can in chemicals, textiles and metals where the Six have a greater export capacity to the West.

The importing of engineering products could also constitute an area of competition between the Soviet Union and the Six. East European purchases will be centred around the engineering products necessary for industrial modernization throughout the CMEA. The Soviet Union slightly reduced the proportion of engineering products within its imports from the West before

---

[32] The share of engineering products in the Soviet Union's exports to the EC has already increased from 10 per cent to 21 per cent between 1983 and 1986, though this is due above all to the fall in oil prices. Andreff, "Les relations économique entre le Conseil d'Assistance Economique Mutuelle et la Communauté Economique Européenne".

Table 3.4

Structure of East-West trade,
by commodity in 1986
(per cent)

	OECD exports	USSR imports	OECD exports	Six imports
Food industry	17.2	7.7	11.8	16.3
Fuels	1.1	71.9	2.9	21.8
Ores and minerals	0.8	2.1	1.2	2.2
Chemicals	13.6	4.6	23.0	11.6
Engineering products	35.2	3.5	39.2	12.9
Wood, furniture, paper	5.5	4.1	4.4	8.2
Textile, apparel	5.3	0.3	7.5	14.2
Metallurgy	18.3	4.7	6.2	10.0
Construction materials and miscellaneous	3.0	1.1	3.8	2.8
Total	100.0	100.0	100.0	100.0

Source: CHELEM Data Bank of the Centre d'Etudes Prospectives et d'Informations Internationales, Paris, and A. Tiraspolsky, "Cooperation U.S.S.R.-Quest: les nouveaux partenaires des firmes occidentales", Le Courrier des Pays de l'Est, no. 334 (November 1988).

1986, but this should increase again.[33] On the other hand, engineering products have increased within total imports from the West for the Six between 1983 and 1986, especially in Hungary, where they rose from 29.9 per cent to 33.8 per cent, and in Poland, where they rose from 25.9% to 33.9%. In contrast with this, competition should be reduced between the USSR, the GDR, Romania and Czechoslovakia for purchases of food products from the West if perestroika helps to increase Soviet agricultural productivity. On the other hand, if the Soviet Union imports more consumer goods from the West, as it did in 1988 in order to stimulate the Soviet population to work harder, there will be hardly any competition with the Six, most of whom are net exporters of such products to the West (e.g. textiles, clothing, furniture).

---

[33] According to Soviet figures, the proportion should increase from 40.7 per cent in 1986 to 41.4 per cent in 1987 at current prices.

In 1987, the Ministries and enterprises which were affected by foreign trade reform accounted for some 46 per cent of Soviet exports of machinery and equipment. This confirms that engineering products are at the centre of possible competition between the Soviet Union and the Six. However, the potential of such competition should not be overrated. Between 1975 and 1983, the only engineering products whose exports underwent rapid growth in the Soviet Union were those produced by the watch & clock making industry, as well as aeronautics and mining equipment.[34] Given the time necessary for industrial modernization, competition is unlikely to be more intense before the mid-1990s. Moreover, the capacity of the Six to export engineering products to the West is also limited, except to some extent in the GDR. For the two countries now engaged in radical reforms, the following observations should be taken into account: in Hungary only 24 per cent of industrial exports towards hard currency markets come from new industries, whereas 40 per cent come from traditional industries and 36 per cent from raw material-based industries.[35] Moreover, Marer found that during 1978-84, Hungary's imports of manufactures generally and of machinery and equipment specifically declined by 2-3 per cent per annum.[36] In Poland the proportion of manufactures in exports to the West fell by 18 per cent between 1982 and 1984.[37]

As far as imports of engineering products are concerned, competition between the Soviet Union and the Six is likely to be concentrated on a few countries. The main Western suppliers of machinery and equipment to the Soviet Union are Finland, Italy, the FRG, Japan, France and, in some years, Austria. Finland and Japan have few trading links with the Six. Competition for the purchase of engineering products is therefore likely to affect the four other countries, and perhaps above all Austria, whose sales are far more oriented towards the Six than towards the Soviet Union. In any case, whether discussing imports from or exports to the West, the amount of competition

---

[34] H. Wienert and J. Slater, *Transfert de technologie entre l'Est et l'Ouest. Les aspects commerciaux et économiques* (Paris: O.C.D.E., 1986).

[35] B. Botos, "The Structure of Our Industrial Foreign Trade and the Process of Internationalization", *Soviet and East European Foreign Trade*, XXIV, no. 2 (Summer 1988).

[36] P. Marer, "Hungary's Foreign Economic Relations in the mid-1980s: A Retrospective and Predictive Assessment", in *The Economies of Eastern Europe*.

[37] B. Kaminski, "Poland's Foreign Trade in the 1980's: Complex Challenges and Simple Responses", in *The Economies of Eastern Europe*.

between the Soviet Union and the Six will depend greatly on the the intensity and rate of industrial modernization.

It is of course too soon to judge the outcome of the modernization of East European industries. The task is an enormous one in the Soviet Union where part of the industrial infrastructure is obsolete; for example, 55 per cent of machining equipment is more than ten years old. The introduction of quality control in 1986 showed that few Soviet products were up to Western standards; only 14 per cent according to the state-controlled body in charge of standards (Gosprimka). Nevertheless, compared with other industries, it has been the output of the engineering complex in the Soviet Union which has grown most rapidly: by 7.3 per cent in 1986, 4.6 per cent in 1987, and 7.0 per cent during the first half of 1988. This has also been the case for labour productivity in the engineering complex, which rose by 6.9 per cent in 1986, and by 4.1 per cent and 7.9 per cent in the following two years.[38] Within this complex the best performances have been achieved respectively by: electrical engineering, machine tools and instrument building, followed by energy engineering, the tractor industry, and vehicle building. Agricultural production, which should contribute to Soviet import substitution, has experienced slower growth than the engineering complex, with 5.0 per cent in 1986, 3.5 per cent in 1987 and 2.8 per cent during the first half of 1988. The corresponding figures for the production of fuel and energy (the Soviet Union's main export to the West) are 5.7 per cent, 3.2 per cent and 3.2 per cent.

Thus we can observe some initial signs of industrial modernization in the Soviet Union, but these are as yet insufficient for Soviet competitiveness on Western markets to be of any real significance. All the more so since modernization is also under way in the other East European countries. In the GDR, growth in engineering products has been rapid since 1983, and more particularly in the fields of electronics, computers, and robotics.[39] In Czechoslovakia, the share of the engineering complex in industrial production rose from 30.8 per cent in 1980 to 33.8 per cent in 1985,[40] and in 1987 growth was even more rapid for electrical engineering and electronics. This last observa-

---

[38] U. Weissenburger and H. Machowski, "Perestroika has yet to make an impact: the Soviet economy in 1987/88", DIW Economic Bulletin (November 1988).

[39] I. Samson, "La modernisation des activités productives en R.D.A.", Economies et Sociétés - Cahiers de l'I.S.M.E.A.

[40] J. Blaha, "La modernisation en Tchécoslovaquie", Economies et Sociétés - Cahiers de l'I.S.M.E.A.

tion can also be applied to Poland, where the sector which has grown most rapidly since 1984 has been engineering products, and to Bulgaria[41], which has given special priority to microelectronics, optical electronics, and laser technology. In Hungary, emphasis has been laid on pharmaceuticals, motor vehicles, vacuum technology, and communications and medical equipment. However, in 1987 the output of engineering products was not much above the average for the rest of industry. Indeed, Gueullette has pointed out that in the Hungarian mechanical engineering industry 474 new products were introduced in 1980 and 389 in 1985, as well as 357 products having been modernized in 1980 and 384 in 1985.[42] Thus industrial modernization is really taking place in the CMEA, and does play a part in improving competitiveness. However, the rate of change is not necessarily in line with the radical nature of the economic reforms.

The reforms are supposed to make the socialist economies more sensitive to international prices. It may reasonably be believed that the Soviet Union, like the Six, would react once again to any sharp variation in fuel prices and, if the reform carries on being implemented, to any variation in the relative fuel price compared with that of engineering products. The Soviet Union, which had cut the amount of crude oil and petroleum products it sold to the West between 1984 and 1985 from 80 to 65 million tons, did react to the fall in prices[43] by increasing its sales to the West: 78 million tons in 1986 and 84 million tons in 1987. A similar trend can be observed in the export of Soviet natural gas with the fall in international prices between 1985 and 1987. The Six do not have the capacity to react to international fuel prices since they are not producers (with the exception of coal in Poland and oil in Romania). Consequently, the share of fuel in the Six's export revenue from the West has fallen since 1985. These foregoing considerations bring some new light on our analysis concerning the competition between the Soviet Union and the Six on Western markets: this only holds for a situation in which there are no sharp and substantial variations in fuel prices. A substantial rise in these prices would

---

[41] M. Kaser, "Trends in trade and economic co-operation among countries having different economic and social systems", UNCTAD/ST/TSC/9, (November 5, 1987).

[42] A. Gueullette, "La modernisation de l'appareil productif en Hongrie", *Economies et Sociétés - Cahiers de l'I.S.M.E.A.*

[43] The price at which Soviet crude oil and petroleum products were sold on Western markets is estimated at an average of $ 28.7 a barrel in 1984, $ 27.2 a barrel in 1985, $ 15.4 dollars a barrel in 1986 and $ 17.9 a barrel in 1987.

42

indeed allow the Soviet Union to maintain its previous export structure, to continue to have easy access to hard currency, to avoid sharply accelerating its industrial modernization drive and entering into competition with the industrial products of the Six on Western markets. However, in the present state of the world oil market such a hypothesis is unlikely to be realized.

3.4 Joint ventures with Western capital in East Europe

Three CMEA countries had already adopted legislative measures which enabled joint ventures to be undertaken on their territory in the 1970s: Romania (1971), Hungary (1972), and Poland (1976). In Hungary and Poland the legislation has been liberalized several times, particularly in 1985 in Hungary and 1986 in Poland. The present movement of economic reform recently led the Soviet Union to implement similar legislation from January 1987 on, and this has also been the case in Czechoslovakia since January 1989.[44] Meanwhile, in 1980 Bulgaria took statutory measures to allow the establishment of joint ventures with Western capital. The last East European country to accept such joint ventures was the GDR, although its close relations with the FRG lessened the need for joint ventures. The first effect of this aspect of the economic reforms has been an increase in the number of joint ventures with western capital (*Table 3.5*), from 23 in 1983 to 319 in 1988 and from 514 to 1019 if we take into account the "Polonia" (i.e., investment in Poland by Poles living abroad).

After some hesitation in 1987, Western joint ventures in the Soviet Union increased after August 1988. And significant reforms in December 1988, allowing the foreign partner to have more than a 49 per cent shareholding and foreign citizens to become managing directors, were designed to encourage more joint ventures in the Soviet Union.

The main aims of the Soviet joint venture legislation are as follows: the acquisition of high technology in order to develop the export potential of the Soviet Union, and the development of import substitution as well as training in management and foreign trade.[45] The same type of explanation can be given for the other socialist countries welcoming East-West joint ventures: the need to modernize existing enterprises, the introduction of new technology (thus

---

[44] In fact 10 joint ventures were set up in Czechoslovakia before this law was passed.

[45] M. Lavigne, "Les sociétés mixtes en U.R.S.S.: aspects juridiques et financiers", *Le Courier des Pays de l'Est*, no. 315 (Fevrier 1987).

Table 3.5

Number of joint ventures with Western capital located in CMEA countries
(1983-1988)

	Year end 1983	Year end 1985	1988	Month
Bulgaria	3	9	10	October 1987
Czechoslovakia	0	0	10	October 1988
GDR	0	0	0	
Hungary	11	46	160	April 1988
Poland	0	0	19	July 1988
Romania	9	7	5	October 1987
USSR	0	0	105	September 1988
	23	62	309	
"Polonia"	491	712	700	December 1987
Total	514	774	1,009	

Source: UNCTC, *Transnational Corporations in World Developments: Trends and Prospects* (New York: United Nations Centre on Transnational Corporations, 1988); and data from *Business Eastern Europe*.

improving productivity and product quality), the increase in hard currency earnings from exports, the development of R&D capacity and the acquisition of modern management methods.[46] Consequently, the Soviet Union on the one hand, and Bulgaria, Czechoslovakia, Hungary, and Poland, on the other, are in competition to attract Western investment. The competition is especially keen between the Soviet Union and Hungary and Poland. How this competition will develop largely depends on the strategy adopted by Western companies. It is often recognized Western companies are attracted to East European countries because of the still unconquered socialist markets and the

---

[46] J. Monkiewicz and M. Lebkowski, "Les enterprises à participation étrangère installées dans les pays socialistes. Etude comparative", *Revues d'Etudes comparatives Est-Ouest*, XVIII, no. 1 (Mars 1987).

skilled and well-disciplined manpower available at relatively low cost.[47] We could even add, at the present time, the attraction of a labour force which industrial modernization is making more flexible, in particular in Hungary and Poland, and increasingly so in the Soviet Union. However, it would seem that it is the sheer size of the Soviet market which is of the greatest interest to Western firms. If this is so, Soviet competition in this field will have a sort of crowding out effect on Western capital, turning it away from Hungary or Poland as firms opt for the Soviet Union. There are two signs that this may well be the case: the Soviet Union's success in attracting joint ventures since late 1988, and the case of China which, because of the size of its market, attracted some $9 billion of direct foreign investment between 1979 and 1987 and more than 4,000 joint ventures. The entry of Western capital into the Soviet Union ought not to change the terms of competition between the Six and the Soviet Union on the industrial markets of the West, at least in the short term. More than half of the joint ventures which have been set up in the Soviet Union are service companies or, in any case, are not involved in industrial production. Similarly only 5 of the 19 new joint ventures set up in Poland manufacture engineering products.

3.5 Conclusion: towards more liberal economic reforms?

Two factors, which in the interests of space we have not taken into account, may yet alter the competition between the Soviet Union and the Six. The relaxing of COCOM export controls would be likely to step up competition for imports of Western equipment. On the other hand, if the Soviet Union demanded that its East European partners (which are in its debt) increase their exports of industrial products to the Soviet Union, then several East European countries (with the exception of Romania and Hungary) would be less able to stand up to future competition from Soviet products on Western markets while still settling their debts in transferable roubles. Nothing that has happened recently within the CMEA suggests that the Soviet Union will have any more success than before in obtaining repayment of the debts of its socialist partners in this way.

In order to resist the possible crowding out effect on Western capital, East European countries will undoubtedly have to take even more liberal measures.

---

[47] S. Ladyka, "The Evolution of East-West Economic Relations. Past Tendancies and Future Prospects", in Bozyk, ed., *Global Challenges and East European Responses*.

New legislation is, in principle, to be implemented in 1989 in Poland, Czecho-slovakia, and Hungary; (and, with the events of late 1989, in the GDR, Bulgaria, and Romania as well). Certainly in the case of Poland, Czecho-slovakia, and Hungary, the Western partner in joint ventures is to be allowed to obtain a majority shareholding. Hungarian law stipulates that if the Western firm's stake is less than 50 per cent, then no permit will be required from either the Ministry of Trade or Finance. Competition within a framework of greater liberalization will continue with the opening of the special economic zones in the Soviet Union, Hungary, and on the Baltic (Poland). Foreign trade should also continue to become more easily accessible in the Soviet Union and the rest of Eastern Europe. From West to East, as Ladyka points out, we can forecast huge reserves of mutual trade.

This, of course, will only be the case if the external debt of the socialist countries does not prevent that mutual trade from developing.

PART II - THE UNITED STATES

Chapter 4

U.S.-SOVIET TRADE POLICY IN THE 1980s

Richard F. Kaufman[1]

The U.S.-Soviet trade relationship shifted in the 1980s from one where barriers were being thrown up to one where bridges are being rebuilt. The process seems likely to continue so long as overall relations between the superpowers improve. To what extent it will make a substantial difference in future trade flows is impossible to tell. Trade over the past 10 years has been both erratic and stagnant. As *Table 4.1* shows, U.S. agricultural exports were volatile; other exports and imports failed to grow. If inflation is taken into account, the trends in all categories would be downward. There was a considerable increase in exports to the Soviet Union in 1988, but mostly in agricultural products. Not surprisingly, trade policies and relations underwent important changes in this decade. How and why they changed are the subjects of this chapter.

4.1 Trade relations deteriorate, 1980-1982

The 1980s began with both sides engaged in different kinds of trade restriction. The Soviet Union was still following policies that assured its own relative isolation from the West: insulation of enterprises from foreign competition, strict control of imports, exports, and foreign exchange, and barriers against

[1] General Counsel, Joint Economic Committee, U.S. Congress, Washington, D.C., U.S.A.

Table 4.1

U.S.-Soviet trade, 1979-1986

(millions of dollars)

	1979	1980	1981	1982	1983	1984	1985	1986	1987	1988
U.S. Exports (FAS):										
Total	3,604	1,510	2,339	2,589	2,002	3,284	2,423	1,248	1,480	2,768
Agriculture	2,855	1,047	1,665	1,855	1,457	2,817	1,864	647	923	2,162
Non-agricultural	749	463	674	734	545	467	558	600	557	606
U.S. Imports for Consumption (CIF):										
Total	873	463	387	248	367	600	443	605	470	649
Agriculture	15	10	12	11	11	11	9	16	22	20
Non-agricultural	858	452	375	237	356	589	434	589	448	629

Source: U.S. Department of Commerce.

foreign investment.[2] The United States obliged by following policies to keep the West away from the Soviet Union.

In the Soviet Union, prospects were poor for continued growth of trade with the West. Much of the increase during the previous decade was because energy price rises in the early 1970s added greatly to Soviet hard currency earnings from oil exports. The fall of world energy prices was a blow to Moscow's hopes of earning enough hard currency to expand imports of Western goods and technology. The lack of competitiveness of Soviet manufactured goods in world markets and increased requirements for agricultural imports added to the problem of inadequate hard currency.

For what were likely political and economic reasons, trade policy was tightened. The 11th 5-Year Plan (1981-1985) gave a smaller role to foreign trade than did the previous plan. In November 1981, the chairman of Gosplan stated that the communist countries' share of foreign trade would be increased

---

[2] For discussions of Soviet protectionist policies see Jerry F. Hough, *Opening Up The Soviet Economy* (Washington, D.C.: The Brookings Institution, 1988), pp. 9-12; and Harry Harding and Ed. A. Hewett, "Socialist Reforms and the World Economy", in John D. Steinbruner, ed., *Restructuring American Foreign Policy* (Washington, D.C., 1989), pp. 162-65.

during the period of the plan.[3] By implication, the West would receive a smaller share. That year, imports from the West of non-agricultural products were reduced, as were purchases of machinery and equipment; it was the start of a downward trend. Over the next five years, equipment orders from the West declined by about 30 per cent from the previous five-year period, and orders from the United States declined by more than 65 per cent.[4] *Table 4.2* shows Soviet total exports and imports by region for the years 1981-1987, and the sharp decline in the shares of the developed countries.

The United States chose first to deny and then severely limit its trade with the Soviet Union, not because of the nature of its political and economic system, but because of perceptions of the Soviet threat to national security interests and American values. During the period of detente, when Soviet trade rose to modest proportions, the perceptions and the signals were mixed. The policy of encouraging peaceful trade was combined with controls over strategic exports, and laws were enacted withholding most favoured nation (MFN) status and official credits. Nevertheless, U.S.-Soviet trade turnover reached a record $4.5 billion in 1979.[5]

When President Ronald Reagan took office, there were new sanctions in place denying the Soviet Union some grain and certain energy equipment and technology. These measures had been initiated in the last year of the Carter administration in response to the Soviet invasion of Afghanistan. Efforts were also underway to strengthen the national security controls administered by the Western allies.

Despite strenuous objections to U.S.-Soviet trade prior to his election, Reagan opposed the limited grain embargo during his campaign, siding with those who argued it was hurting American farmers more than the Soviets, and he lifted it in April 1981, three months after taking office. A broad review of

---

[3] Joan P. Zoeter, "U.S.S.R.: Hard Currency Trade and Payments", in: U.S. Congress, Joint Economic Committee, *Soviet Economy in the 1980's: Problems and Prospects*, Part 2 (Washington, D.C.: Government Printing Office, 1983), p. 495.

[4] Hertha W. Heiss, "U.S.-Soviet Trade Trends", in U.S. Congress, Joint Economic Committee, *Gorbachev's Economic Plans*, vol. 2 (Washington, D.C.: Government Printing Office, 1987), p. 464; Joan F. McIntyre, "The U.S.S.R.'s Hard Currency Trade and Payments Position", in *ibid.*, p. 478 (Table 2).

[5] For an examination of the dynamics of America's Soviet trade policy, see Gary K. Bertsch, "U.S. Policy Governing Economic and Technological Relations With The USSR", in *Gorbachev's Economic Plans*; for a detailed history of the subject, Phillip J. Funigiello, *American-Soviet Trade In The Cold War* (Chapel Hill, 1988).

Table 4.2

Soviet Union: total trade, 1981-1987
(billions of current U.S. dollars)

	1981	1982	1983	1984	1985	1986	1987
Soviet exports by region:							
Total	79.4	87.2	91.7	91.5	86.9	97.0	104.5
Communist	43.4	47.1	51.0	51.9	53.2	65.0	68.6
Developed countries	24.4	26.2	26.7	26.4	22.5	18.8	22.2
Less developed countries	11.6	13.8	13.9	13.2	11.2	13.2	13.7
Soviet imports by region:							
Total	73.2	77.8	80.5	80.3	82.9	88.9	95.2
Communist	37.2	42.5	45.5	47.0	50.6	59.4	65.5
Developed countries	25.4	26.2	25.4	24.2	23.3	22.7	22.2
Less developed countries	10.6	9.1	9.6	9.1	9.0	6.8	7.5

Source: U.S. Congress, Joint Economic Committee, *Allocation of Resources in the Soviet Union and China - 1987*, Part 13 (Washington, D.C.: Government Printing Office, 1989), p. 68.

East-West policy conducted in the first year of the Administration concluded there would be continued linkage of trade with security and political concerns, and that multilateral export controls should be strengthened. The recommendations that came out of the review were considered to be restrained.

Hard-liners in the Defense Department were opposed to any easing of trade restrictions, and urged a tightening of export controls over technology which could contribute significantly, directly or indirectly, to Soviet defence industries. Top officials in the Departments of State, Commerce, and Agriculture, and in the Office of U.S. Trade Representative, took positions that were somewhat more moderate. They favoured trade with the Soviet Union in "non-strategic" areas but recognized that trade policy could not be separated from national security and foreign policy. There was a greater sensitivity among non-defence officials to the need for allied support for controls, and of the risks of U.S. unilateral actions. These officials were also more willing to take into account the needs of commercial interests.[6] Agricultural products were viewed by all to be an exception. The State Department, responding in 1981 to a question from a congressional committee about the Administration's Soviet trade policy said: "Although we cannot divorce our policies from overall Soviet behaviour, even in the area of nonstrategic trade, it is expected that the Soviet need for imported agricultural commodities will continue to offer exceptional export potential for U.S. farmers".[7]

Early in President Reagan's first term, events brought about a sudden stiffening of the U.S. position. The imposition of martial law in Poland in December 1981 seemed to confirm the worst fears of the hard-liners who assigned responsibility for it to the Soviet Union. Reagan reacted by imposing a number of economic sanctions against the Soviet Union and he warned of more to come. In the statement announcing his actions, the President said: "The Soviet Union bears a heavy and direct responsibility for the repression in Poland. For many months the Soviets publicly and privately demanded such a crackdown. They brought major pressures to bear through now-public letters to the Polish leadership, military maneuvers, and other forms of intimidation. They now openly endorse the suppression which has ensued".[8] Among the sanctions was suspension of licenses for the export of oil and gas equipment, including pipelayers. Some of the allies announced sanctions of their own but none as far-reaching or serious as the United States'.[9]

Seven months later, in June 1982, Reagan stated that the oil and gas sanctions would apply to foreign subsidiaries and licensees of U.S. firms, and that the purpose was to delay construction of the Soviet gas pipeline to Western Europe. This attempt to extend unilateral export controls extra-territorially was met with defiance from the European allies and strong opposition at home from the business community and Congress. In November 1982, Reagan terminated the extraterritorial restrictions and, in addition, reduced

---

[6] U.S. Congress, Joint Economic Committee, *East-West Commercial Policy: A Congressional Dialogue With The Reagan Administration* (Washington, D.C.: Government Printing Office, 1982).

[7] *Ibid.*, pp. 3-8.

[8] The Presidential Statement issued December 29, 1981, can be found in U.S. Congress, Joint Economic Committee, *East-West Commercial Policy*, p. 66.

[9] Jack Brougher, "The United States Uses Trade To Penalize Soviet Aggression and Seeks to Reorder Western Policy", in U.S. Congress, Joint Economic Committee, *Soviet Economy in the 1980's*, p. 439.

controls over U.S. oil and gas equipment to the level prior to the imposition of martial law in Poland. The reason given for ending the pipeline sanctions was an agreement with the allies to review trade policies with the Soviet Union, strengthen controls on strategic items, and establish procedures to monitor financial terms and harmonize export credit policies.[10]

4.2 Trade relations improve, 1983-1988

The period of the short-lived pipeline sanctions represents the lowest point in U.S.-Soviet trade relations during the Reagan administration. While there were other incidents that caused friction, such as the Soviet downing of a Korean airliner in September 1983, and various accusations and acts of espionage, none provoked major new sanctions. From 1982, there was slow and steady improvement in trade relations.

Progress toward better relations was brought about in two ways: bilaterally, in actions involving both governments, and unilaterally, in actions taken by one of them.

Agriculture provides the best example of bilateral actions that assured a degree of continuity for a major part of the trade relationship. The 1975-1981 long-term grain sales agreement was extended for one year in August 1981 and again in 1982. In April 1983, Reagan indicated U.S. willingness to negotiate a new long-term agreement, and one was concluded a few months later. That agreement has been extended to the last quarter of 1990.

Under the current agreement, U.S. grain sales to the Soviet Union have recovered to the pre-embargo levels, although the U.S. share of total Soviet imports has declined owing to the Soviet decision to diversify its sources. A dramatic fall in U.S. wheat exports occurred in 1986 for two reasons: reduced demand in the Soviet Union, and a shift to suppliers in the European Community where lower, subsidized prices were available. American wheat exports bounded up in 1987 after the United States decided to offer its own subsidies.[11] *Table 4.3* shows annual Soviet grain imports from the United States since 1976. It will be noted that even during the period of the partial grain embargo there were substantial imports from the United States.

---

[10] *1982 Congressional Quarterly Almanac* (Washington, D.C., 1983), pp. 165-166.

[11] For U.S. grain exports to the Soviet Union under the long-term grain agreement, see Economic Research Service, *CPE Agriculture Report* (January/February 1989), p. 14.

Table 4.3

Soviet grain imports from the United States
(marketing years 1976/77 - 1988/89
in millions of tons)

	1976/77	1977/78	1978/79	1979/80	1980/81	1981/82
Total wheat and corn	6.2	14.6	15.5	8.0	9.5	13.9
Wheat	3.1	3.5	4.0	2.2	3.8	6.1
Corn	3.1	11.1	11.5	5.8	5.7	7.8

	1982/83	1983/84	1984/85	1985/86	1986/87	1987/88[a]
Total wheat and corn	14.1	18.6	7.0	8.2	14.6	14.6
Wheat	7.6	2.9	0.2	4.1	9.0	4.0
Corn	6.5	15.7	6.8	4.1	5.6	10.2

[a] Data as of March 20, 1989.

Source: U.S. Department of Agriculture.

Other bilateral activities concerned the reopening of formal communications disrupted by the Carter and Reagan sanctions. These activities had the effect of improving the atmosphere for discussing commercial relations and facilitating business dealings. The Agreement on Economic, Industrial, and Technical Cooperation, signed in 1974, was kept from lapsing in 1984. It calls for each government to facilitate the leasing of office space, hiring of staff, issuance of visas, and other requirements of business people operating in a foreign country. The Working Group of Experts established under the agreement was reactivated and met in Moscow in 1985, the first such meeting since 1978.

A direct result of the Moscow meeting was the May 1985 reconvening of the Joint US-U.S.S.R. Commercial Commission (JCC), which had also been dormant since the Soviet invasion of Afghanistan. Its function is to provide a forum to discuss bilateral problems, such as the lack of access to markets. It was agreed in the 1985 meeting that the Soviet government would resume contacts with U.S. firms and the U.S. administration would seek legislation to end the embargo on certain Soviet fur skins.

There have been numerous other meetings and exchanges. In 1986, the U.S. Commerce Department took part in a Soviet trade show in which 60

American firms participated.[12] At the conclusion of the April 1988 meeting of the JCC, a joint statement was issued saying the governments recognized that "prospects for a substantial expansion of trade relations are related to progress on other issues of mutual interest, including humanitarian affairs", an acknowledgment of the link between trade and human rights issues.[13]

The most significant unilateral steps taken by Moscow to directly improve trade relations concern the reform of the trade structure and joint ventures. These actions pertain to Soviet trade with the West generally, but they also create opportunities for American firms and can have an important influence on attitudes in Washington. The question is whether they will succeed in the sense that trade and investment are significantly decentralized and decontrolled. The steps taken so far to make it possible for Western business firms to deal directly with Soviet enterprises and end users, and to open markets to foreign investments have prompted a favourable response in U.S. policy-making circles.

4.3 American policies and debates

The decision by President Reagan in April 1982 to seek a new long-term grain agreement assured significant continuity in U.S.-Soviet trade relations. In addition to agriculture trade, official American-Soviet science and technology exchanges were allowed to go forward, and there were more than 160 such meetings in 1982.[14] The President said, in a press interview on May 1983: "There seems to be a misperception that we're interested in some kind of trade war with the Soviet Union, and we're not at all", citing as evidence the willingness to negotiate a new grain agreement. He went on to say that he was concerned about Soviet expansionism, and that he objected to transfers of "high technology" that can contribute to the Soviet military buildup, and to subsidized trade and credits.[15]

---

[12] Heiss, "U.S.-Soviet Trade", pp. 451-54.

[13] John P. Hardt and Jean F. Boone, "U.S.-Soviet Commercial Relations in a Period of Negotiation", *Congressional Research Service Issue Brief*, IB88065, (May 31, 1988), p. 4.

[14] A list of the exchanges can be found in U.S. Congress, *East-West Technology Transfer*, pp. 42-57.

[15] Reagan interview with foreign television journalists, (May 26, 1983).

Reagan's comments were a fair statement of U.S. policy. In 1984, the Administration gave Congress a more formal explanation of its policies.[16] The Administration's views can be summarized as follows: First, there was no policy of economic warfare against the Soviet Union, but there was a policy of linkage. "We recognize the benefits of mutually advantageous trade as long as it is in harmony with our overall political and security objectives". Second, the government would continue to use trade sanctions for foreign policy objectives and to register disapproval of Soviet conduct in such matters as human rights violations, and invasion and repression of other countries. Third, the government would seek to restrict the flow of critical Western technology to the Soviet Union that could contribute substantially to the improvement of Soviet military capabilities either directly or indirectly. And, finally, the United States would follow a policy of restricting preferential credits to finance exports, in cooperation with other Western countries.

During the next four years, controversy and conflict over U.S.-Soviet trade, within the Administration and Congress, and between the two branches of government, were recurrent and sometimes bitter. There were officials in the Administration, especially in the Defence Department, who favoured the confrontational tactics used in the pipeline dispute and who urged more restrictive policies in the name of national security, and others who believed adequate consideration was not being given to national economic interests and the business sector. Many in Congress advocated more moderate policies, and there were some who sided with the hard-liners in the Administration. The debate boiled up periodically when egregious examples of technology transfers were brought to light, and when business leaders complained about lengthy delays in the reviews of export applications subject to export controls. All the same, the stated policies were unchanged through the end of Reagan's presidency.

However, beginning in 1985, there were modifications of the laws concerning export controls in East-West trade which may be indicators of more profound changes to come. As some of them represent tightening and some loosening of the restrictions on trade, and many concern U.S. relations with the Western allies, the ultimate direction of policy in this area is unclear. There has also been considerable debate in recent years over the Jackson-Vanik amendment and the subject of Western lending to the Soviet Union.

---

[16] U.S. Congress, *East-West Technology Transfer*, pp. 8-24.

Export Controls

In the 1985 renewal of the Export Administration Act, the law that authorizes export controls, Congress attempted to limit the president's authority to impose controls for foreign policy objectives. It also exempted from licensing requirements the export of products with relatively low-level technology--such as personal computers--to COCOM countries, and shortened the time for granting licenses for high-technology products. At the same time, the 1985 Act imposed sanctions against foreign firms that violate U.S. controls, required licenses for controlled goods sold to certain foreign embassies, and increased the penalties for violations of the Act.[17]

The Export Administration Act was not scheduled to be renewed again until 1989. But the ineffectiveness of the 1985 reforms, rising complaints from the business community about the enforcement of the export controls, and the release in 1987 of a study by the prestigious National Academy of Sciences, revived the controversy.[18] In its study, the Academy praised the Administration for revitalizing COCOM, but faulted it for not fulfilling the 1985 congressional mandate to decontrol items based on foreign availability, for trying to control too many items, for giving the Defence Department too great a role in the review process, and for conflict and confusion in the administration of the controls.

The study emphasized that the original intent of COCOM was to restrict the flow of goods and technology to the East solely for national security reasons. The goal of U.S. policy, it was stated, should be to improve the multilateral control system to the point where removing controls from West-West trade is possible. One of the features of U.S. policy that interferes with this goal is the use of foreign policy trade sanctions to penalize Soviet behaviour "without

---

[17] U.S. law authorizes export controls to preserve national security, promote U.S. foreign policy objectives, and prevent domestic shortages. The United States coordinates its controls with its Western allies through COCOM, but also imposes some controls unilaterally. For a brief discussion of the background, procedures, and controversies surrounding export controls, and recent legislation, see Glennon J. Harrison and George Holliday, "Export Controls" *Congressional Research Service* IB87122, (updated February 27, 1989).

[18] National Academy of Sciences, *Balancing the National Interest: U.S. National Security Export Controls and Global Economic Competition* (Washington, D.C.: National Academy Press, 1987).

56

clearly distinguishing them from strategic controls and without consultation with our allies".[19]

Many recommendations were made for improving the export control system. Among the most important were: first, limiting the coverage of U.S. and COCOM controls to items whose acquisition would significantly enhance Soviet military capabilities and that are feasible to control; second, maintaining unilateral controls only on a temporary basis or for limited, unique national security circumstances; and third, preserving a clear separation between the use of unilateral controls for foreign policy purposes, and the system of multi-lateral controls for national security purposes.

In 1988, Congress enacted additional amendments to the Export Administration Act as a part of the Omnibus Trade and Competitiveness Act. Again, some aspects of export controls were eased and others tightened. Several provisions carried forward recommendations of the National Academy of Sciences and reflected the Academy's emphasis on West-West trade. Among the amendments intended to relax controls were those requiring that items subject to unilateral U.S. national security controls be decontrolled, unless efforts are underway to negotiate multilateral control or an item is unique to the United States; that determinations of foreign availability take no longer than nine months; and that the Defense Department consider only national security, not foreign policy, in its reviews of export applications. On the other hand, retroactive sanctions were placed on the Toshiba Machine and Kongsberg Vaapenfabrikk firms, for their diversion of advanced technology and equipment to the Soviet Union, and higher penalties for violations of controls were enacted.

When the 1988 legislation was pending in Congress, the House and Senate conference report recommending it for final action stated: "The conferees explicitly endorse the goal of an export license-free zone among COCOM countries and expect the Administration to work diligently to achieve this objective as soon as possible". The Act directed the Secretary of Commerce to determine which countries could be relieved from licensing requirements for exports of U.S. controlled goods because of the existence of effective export control systems. In November 1988, the Secretary reported that, based on a review of the available information on foreign export control systems, he was unable to determine at that time that any of them are presently effective.

---

[19] *Ibid.*, p. 144.

However, the Secretary promised to continue efforts to eliminate controls for COCOM countries, and agreed with Congress that for U.S. export control policy to be effective it had to be implemented as part of a multilateral effort, "especially in light of the European Community movement towards barrier-free internal trade by 1992".[20]

The Commerce Department also stated that measures had been taken to improve the administration of export controls, that procedures introduced during 1988 "greatly reduce" the paperwork burden of U.S. exporters, and that on average only five days are required to process license applications to COCOM countries. In March 1989, Commerce announced that it had removed unilateral restriction "on a broad group of goods and technology", previously controlled for national security purposes. According to Commerce, the value of license applications filed in the financial year 1988 for the items decontrolled was $240 million.[21]

The 1988 trade legislation contains two provisions related to East-West issues other than export controls. The embargo on the Soviet fur skins was ended, fulfilling the commitment given at the 1985 meeting of the Joint Commercial Commission. This issue was debated in the Senate where an amendment was offered to tie the lifting of the embargo to the conditions concerning freedom of emigration contained in the Jackson-Vanik amendment. Adoption of the amendment would have kept the embargo in place. After it was pointed out that the Administration, the House of Representatives, and the National Conference on Soviet Jewry opposed the amendment, it was defeated by a wide margin.[22]

There was also a technical change in the anti-dumping laws concerning imports from non-market economies (NMEs). Under the new law, when dumping is alleged against a product imported from an NME the United States will use a factors approach to determine the fair value. In the factors approach, information is obtained about the quantity of the labour and capital factors that went into production of the product in questions in the NME country where it was produced. The prices of those inputs in a comparable market economy

---

[20] U.S. Department of Commerce, "Review of the Effectiveness of Export Control Systems Pursuant to Section 5(b) (2) of the Export Administration Act of 1979 as Amended by Section 2415 (a) of the Omnibus Trade and Competitiveness Act of 1988", (November 1988).

[21] "U.S. Removes Unilateral Export Controls on a Broad Group of Items", *U.S. Department of Commerce News*, BXA-89-8, (March 2, 1989).

[22] *Congressional Record*, (August 2, 1988), pp. S10590-91, S10593, and S10658-60.

are then used to calculate the price of the product in question. Previously, a surrogate producers approach was used, among other methods, in which the price of a comparable product was obtained from a third country. The Administration proposed changing this part of the anti-dumping law several years ago, urging yet a different method. East European countries have indicated they prefer the approach adopted in the 1988 Act because it allows them to demonstrate their actual factor inputs and provides greater certainty to the process.

Jackson-Vanik, MFN, and Official Credits

The Jackson-Vanik amendment to the Trade Act of 1974 provides that MFN treatment and government credits cannot be extended to any NME country that denies its citizens the right to emigrate. The debate over it and other statutory restrictions on U.S.-Soviet trade, such as the Stevenson amendment to the Export-Import Act, has been lively since U.S.-Soviet relations began to seriously improve.[23] Speaking in 1986, Senator Robert J. Dole, then majority leader of the U.S. Senate, expressed the widely held view in Congress that the Jackson-Vanik restrictions would not be removed until the situation with respect to Jewish emigration changed. Dole held open the hope that the issue might be resolved between President Reagan and General Secretary Gorbachev at one of their summit meetings. He added that there would have to be broad-based bipartisan support before there was any change in the amendment.[24]

Administration officials have made similar statements about the need for changes of Soviet emigration practices, and for a consensus in Congress and among private interest groups, before Jackson-Vanik can be reconsidered. The issue was not resolved in the summit process, but beginning in 1987, Jews

---

[23] The Stevenson amendment to the Export-Import Bank Act of 1974 places a ceiling of $ 300 million on new Export Import loans to the Soviet Union, unless the President makes a determination that it is in the national interest to increase the ceiling and Congress adopts a concurrent resolution of approval. It and other statutory restrictions adopted in the same period were intended to give Congress a role in decisions to finance Soviet trade. Another example is the Byrd amendment to the 1974 Trade Act, prohibiting all government agencies, except the Commodity Credit Corporation, from extending new credits in excess of $ 300 million unless Congress approves.

[24] Remarks by Robert J. Dole, April 24, 1986, in Margaret Chapman, ed., *Forum on U.S.-Soviet Trade Relations* (Washington, D.C.: American Committee on U.S.-Soviet Relations, 1987), pp. 61-62.

were allowed to leave the Soviet Union in large numbers, and by the fall of 1988 the annual rate of emigration was high enough to cause U.S. policy-makers and Jewish organizations to begin thinking about removing the legal barrier. In his December 1988 speech before the United Nations, Gorbachev indicated that new laws would be passed liberalizing emigration practices, and in early 1989 the requisite consensus in the United States appeared to be forming, as a number of members of Congress and private groups began suggesting that the amendment be waived.[25]

Commercial Borrowing

The increase in Soviet commercial borrowing from the West has provoked widespread interest and commentary in Washington from the news media, private persons, and government officials. Proposals for new legislation to control commercial lending to the Soviet Union have been made, a number of congressional committees have held hearings, and an interagency task force has issued a report on the subject. High-level interest in the subject was triggered by concerns about the apparent rapid rate of increase of Western credits to the Soviet Union and its allies, and assertions that untied and subsidized loans were being used by the Soviet Union to finance military spending and other activities harmful to the West.

Those concerned about the problem alleged that in 1986 alone total East bloc borrowing from the West was $24 billion, and that the total amount of East bloc debt increased to about $127 billion by the end of 1987. Announcements in the fall of 1988 that West European banks had offered $5-6 billion in lines of credit to the Soviet Union intensified the concerns. Some viewed these developments as part of an "economic offensive" against the West, linked to Soviet efforts to gain admission to GATT, the IMF, and the World Bank, and more aggressive actions to acquire militarily relevant Western technology.

Two aspects of the debate that ensued are noteworthy. First, most of those who warned against the dangers of growing Soviet involvement in Western credit markets were careful to say that they supported trade with the Soviet Union. Their objection was to untied loans: the use of which could not be monitored, the possibility that some loans were being subsidized by West European governments, the lack of adequate information about Soviet external

---

[25] Alyson Pytte, "Jackson-Vanik Limits on Trade Come Under New Scrutiny", *Congressional Quarterly*, (February 25, 1989), pp. 400-404.

debt, and the risks that default could potentially disrupt Western credit markets.

Senator Bill Bradley, one of the outspoken critics of Western lending practices, argued that it would be better for the West and Soviet reformers if the Soviets financed imports by increasing civilian exports than by borrowing because, among other reasons, the extensive contacts with the West that would accompany a civilian export strategy would encourage decentralization and a greater role for the market. Bradley's view that trade with the Soviet Union was desirable but that it should not be subsidized, was widely held. Then Congressman Jack Kemp, author of a bill that would have required U.S. banks to publish the details about any untied loans to the Soviet Union, asserted that he was not against trade with the Soviets.[26]

A second important aspect of the debate was the measured response of Congress and the Administration to the warnings of dire consequences if present trends continued. Six congressional subcommittees held hearings in 1987 and 1988 to examine Soviet economic reforms. All dealt with trade and finance issues, and two looked closely into the questions that had been raised about Soviet borrowing from the West. The hearings played a useful educational role, demonstrating that some of the assertions about Soviet borrowing and Western lending practices were exaggerated, and placing the subject in a proper perspective. Some concerns were substantiated, such as the need for more information about the Soviet economy and better monitoring of its international financial activities.[27]

Equally significant was the report of an interagency task force set up by the Administration to look into Western lending to the Soviet Union and its allies. This group, established under the auspices of the National Security Council

---

[26] Testimony of Senator Bill Bradley and Representative Jack Kemp, U.S. Congress, House Committee on Banking Finance and Urban Affairs, Subcommittee on International Finance, Trade and Monetary Policy, Hearing on *Bank Lending to Warsaw Pact Nations*, (September 22, 1988), pp. 63 and 14.

[27] See hearings on U.S. Congress, Bank Lending to Warsaw Pact Nations, especially the testimony of Don Green, Roger W. Robinson, Jr., and Richard C. Neu, pp. 40-48. Also, U.S. Congress, House, Committee on Foreign Affairs, Subcommittees on Europe and the Middle East, and International Economic Policy and Trade, Hearings on *United States-Soviet Trade Relations*, (1987); U.S. Congress, Joint Economic Committee, Hearings on *Economic Reforms in the U.S.S.R.*, (1987); U.S. Congress, House, Committee on Foreign Affairs, Subcommittee on Europe and the Middle East, Hearings on *United States-Soviet Relations: 1988*, vol. 1, (1988); and U.S. Congress, House, Committee on Small Business, Hearings on *Perestroika and its Implications for the United States*, (1988).

(NSC), was made up of representatives of the NSC, the Departments of State, Treasury, Commerce, and Defence, the Economic Policy Council, and the Central Intelligence Agency.

One of the major conclusions of the task force was that, while the hard currency debt of the Soviet Union and its East European allies had risen in nominal terms in recent years, most of the increase was due to the depreciation of the dollar against other major currencies. The Bank for International Settlements estimated that Soviet bloc gross debt to Western lenders at constant exchange rates increased by only 14 per cent or $13 billion from 1981 through 1986, and net debt (gross debt less deposits) adjusted for exchange rate changes had actually fallen. Gross borrowing by the Soviet Union, after adjusting for exchange rate changes, increased by only $8.4 billion in 1985-1987. The task force also concluded that Western commercial lenders appeared to be comfortable in assessing the Soviet Union's creditworthiness, in part because of Soviet gold reserves valued at more than $30 billion, and that there was no subsidization of commercial bank lending. Finally, it was found that Soviet borrowing from 1983 through 1987 was largely untied, but that in 1988 it was largely tied.[28]

Colin L. Powell, then National Security Advisor to the President, in a speech before the American Stock Exchange, commented favourably on the work of the task force, and added that the $5-6 billion in lines of credit recently announced appeared to be tied to Soviet purchases of Western light industrial equipment and consumer goods, would be drawn over a period of years, and were not likely to have any discernable effect on Soviet military preparedness. Non-strategic trade with the Soviet bloc, Powell said, would continue to grow. Rejecting proposals for the United States and its allies to control general-purpose (untied) lending by Western banks to the Soviet bloc, the National Security Advisor said: "Vigilance, not alarm, is the correct policy response".[29]

4.4 Conclusion

U.S.-Soviet trade policies can be seen as the products of dual protectionist systems. On the Soviet side, protectionism is systemic in an economic sense,

---

[28] U.S. Department of the Treasury, *Report of the Special Interagency Task Force on Western Lending to the Soviet Bloc, Vietnam, Libya, Cuba, and Nicaragua*, (November 1988).

[29] Remarks by Lt. Gen. Colin L. Powell, American Stock Exchange Conference on U.S. Perspectives, (November 8, 1988).

supplemented with political decisions about particular trade issues and trade partners. On the American side, selected protectionist policies are directed at perceived Soviet threats to national security and strongly held values such as human rights. Soviet policy is also influenced by a perceived American military threat.

The results are the same regardless of the origins of protectionist policies; trade relations are obstructed but what needs to be done to remove the obstacles differs. On a theoretical level all such trade problems may be soluble. As a practical matter, in the case of the Soviet Union and the United States, some of them may be intractable. For example, so long as each is seen as an adversary and a military threat to the other, full "normalization" of trade will not be possible.

This dualistic view of the subject underlines the necessity for analysts to look at the two sides. What is unusual about the 1980s is that there were initiatives in both countries to address some of the underlying causes of U.S.-Soviet protectionism. In addition to the bilateral improvement in overall relations, a precondition to progress in the trade area, each has taken important steps. The most fundamental changes may be in the area of military policy.

Continued progress in arms control and a reduction in military burdens would go far towards moderating the mutual hostile perceptions of the two countries. The fact that the Soviet leadership has announced its intention to reduce military spending, and that U.S. military spending has been constrained since 1985, is encouraging. However, it will take actual reductions in spending and capabilities to change perceptions.

It goes almost without saying that Gorbachev's reforms are beginning to open up the Soviet economy to international market forces. The August 1986 action, breaking up the foreign trade monopoly, has been supplemented by the December 1988 decree criticizing the implementation of the earlier action and increasing the impetus for decentralization. The recent decree also eases some of the constraints on joint ventures. Soviet officials (including some whose work appears in this volume) now attribute some of the root causes of the Soviet Union's economic difficulties to industry's segregation from foreign markets.[30] If, as one Western observer believes, the December 1988 decree is a step away from government regulation of foreign trade and toward market

---

[30] Ivan Ivanov, "Restructuring the Mechanism of Foreign Economic Relations in the U.S.S.R.," *Soviet Economy*, (July-September 1987), p. 195.

regulation, the possibility of meaningful improvement in U.S.-Soviet trade relations will be greatly enhanced.[31]

Among the challenges for the United States are the need to rationalize and contain export controls, and to respond appropriately to Soviet actions and signals. Again, there are signs of progress. The Reagan administration, prodded by Congress, began the process of streamlining the enforcement of export controls, achieving better cooperation with the Western allies, and de-emphasizing the use of controls for foreign policy objectives. U.S. policy seems to be moving toward a more targeted definition of the products and technologies that should be subject to controls. Concerning the statutory prohibitions on MFN and official credits, the government so far has responded correctly to signs of changes in Soviet emigration policy by indicating a willingness to consider waiving Jackson-Vanik. In some respects, the controversy over Soviet borrowing in Western commercial markets was the most encouraging development. The government's deliberative and analytical response was exactly right.

---

[31] Marie Lavigne, "Prospects for Soviet Trade Reform", (Institute for Defense Analysis: Alexandria, Virginia, 1989), processed, p. 16.

Chapter 5

U.S. EAST-WEST TRADE POLICY

Carol Rae Hansen[1]

5.1 Current and past policies

Since 1917, U.S.-Soviet commercial policy has followed a cyclical pattern of high peaks of interchange alternating with deep troughs of mutual economic isolation. The variations in policy on each side have turned on the perceived need to balance the benefits of trade against the political costs - that is, the potential loss of security and diplomatic leverage. Although the United States and the Soviet Union have never been major trading partners, trade has become important to key sectors, particularly agriculture. Following a substantial upturn in commercial relations during the period of detente (1971-1974), U.S.-Soviet economic relations over the next decade shifted steadily from cooperation to confrontation. In particular, the Soviet invasion of Afghanistan in 1979 and the imposition of martial law in Poland in 1981 triggered economic reprisals from the United States, including the 1980 grain embargo, restrictive foreign policy controls on exports, and reductions in credit and bilateral exchange programs.

However, beginning in 1985, the prospects for expanding U.S.-Soviet commercial exchange began to improve with increased contacts and discussions between the two superpowers. This was due, in part, to an easing in strained relations between the superpowers. It was also, apparently, partly the result of heightened concern for American competitiveness, and the recognition that America's economic stature was considered more critical in determining how it weighed its superpower status in the world.

In 1987, progress accelerated with American initiatives as well as with joint U.S.-European efforts to reform the COCOM process. Soviet interest in improved commercial relations also grew in 1987, culminating in a strong emphasis on trade at the Washington summit. More recently, some 450 U.S. businessmen met in Moscow for trade meetings in 1988 under the sponsorship of the U.S.-USSR Trade and Economic Council. In addition, on April 14, 1988 the two countries concluded a protocol to the June 1974 Long-

---

[1] Fellow, The Johns Hopkins Foreign Policy Institute, Washington, D.C., U.S.A.

Term Agreement to Facilitate Economic, Industrial, and Technical Cooperation. It specifically included joint ventures, under the monitoring of a Joint U.S.-USSR Commercial Commission.

Ironically, despite the intense interest often focused on the issue, and their combined GNP of over $ 6 trillion, the United States' and the Soviet Union's trading relationship has been quite limited. In fact, although it has the world's second largest economy, the Soviet Union is not a major trading nation, and its dependence on foreign trade is relatively small. As with the United States, Soviet imports are approximately equal to one-tenth of national income. Those imports, however, are primarily capital goods and do not serve the large and pent-up consumer demand of 270 million Soviet citizens, whose personal consumption in the early 1980s amounted to only 34 per cent of personal consumption in the United States despite hundred of billions of roubles in underutilized savings.[2]

Moreover, more than one half of the trade it does undertake occurs within the shelter of the guaranteed markets and comparatively stable prices of the CMEA. "It imports only about $ 30 billion annually from the West - an amount which makes its import market for Western products about the same size as Switzerland's."[3] The value of Soviet imports from the West has remained relatively constant over the past seven to eight years but has declined in percentage terms from 36 per cent in 1975 to 26 per cent in 1986; similarly, Soviet exports to the West have also declined as a percentage of their total exports, from 25 per cent in 1975 to 19 per cent in 1986. In addition, as a percentage of East-West trade, the U.S.-Soviet share is quite small. Although the United States and the Soviet Union are the world's two largest economies, the volume of their trade is a mere 1/2000th of total world trade.[4]

In fact, despite enhanced efforts on both sides to remove impediments to trade, trade remains minimal. In 1988 U.S. exports to the Soviet Union amounted to $ 2,768 million, of which agricultural exports were valued at $ 2,162 million. The United States accounted for 1.7 per cent of Soviet imports

---

[2] Aleksandr Zaichenko, "O khlebe nasushchnom", *Moskovski novosti*, no. 34 (1988).

[3] Malcolm Baldrige, "U.S.-Soviet Trade", in Margaret Chapman, ed. *Forum on U.S.-Soviet Trade Relations* (Washington, D.C.: American Committee on U.S.-Soviet Relations, 1987), p. 10.

[4] Yevgeniy G. Kutovoy, "The Soviet Perception of Trade and Economic Relations with the United States", in Chapman, ed. *Forum on U.S.-Soviet Trade*, p. 158.

in 1988 and 0.04 per cent of Soviet exports.[5] By comparison, in 1986, Soviet trade with the FRG was roughly $ 11 billion, $ 9 billion with Finland, $ 4.7 billion each with France and Italy (in 1985), and $ 4 billion with Japan.[6]

Many factors combine to ensure that the volume of U.S.-Soviet trade is small: the non-convertibility of the rouble, significant restrictions on investment in the Soviet Union, a growth in Soviet-CMEA trade, U.S. sanctions imposed for foreign policy purposes that led to a diversification of Soviet grain imports, Gorbachev's desire to reduce the Soviet Union's vulnerability to Western sanctions, COCOM's strategic export controls, credit limitations, the Soviet's conservative import policy, and Soviet hard currency shortages, among others.

Several underappreciated Soviet policies play a major role in reducing trade possibilities. As will be discussed further, for all his interest in using Western technology to speed his modernization drive, Gorbachev is also currently pressuring Eastern Europe to sell it much greater quantities of manufactured goods. Like his predecessors, Gorbachev hopes to both reduce the Soviet Union's dependence on Western sources of supply as well as conserve scarce foreign exchange. As a result, since 1981, the communist countries' share of Soviet trade has increased steadily while the industrialized West's share has fallen.

Many who criticize strictly enforced Western COCOM controls argue that they are major impediments, leaving few open sectors for trade, other than agriculture. However, the impact of COCOM controls may be greatly overestimated. For all the restrictions, if Gorbachev makes the policy choice to import, U.S. firms can sell a wide range of modern equipment and technology needed in the Soviet Union that is not subject to COCOM controls. Nor have the COCOM controls been the main obstacles to joint ventures. Soviet receptivity to such deals has stimulated considerable activity in this field. The International Chamber of Commerce and the Soviet Chamber of Commerce have already established a joint task force to evaluate the Soviet legal and administrative requirements for establishing joint ventures, and a variety of West European, Japanese and American firms have expressed interest, including Monsanto, Occidental Petroleum, Archer-Daniels-Midland, Combustion Engineering, McDonald's, Chevron, Ford, Honeywell, and Siemens. And in April 1988 seven American firms (RJR Nabisco, Archer-Daniels-Midland, the

---

5) U.S. Department of Commerce, "Data on Soviet Statistics", (February 21, 1989).

6) Kutovoy, "The Soviet Perception of Trade".

Mercator Corporation, Eastman Kodak, Johnson and Johnson, Chevron, and the Ford Motor Company) formed the American Trade Consortium to accomplish as a group what the individual firms could not negotiate.

5.2 U.S. policy goals

Preserve technology security

Since World War II, the primary concern looming over all discussions of U.S.-Soviet trade has been the issue of technology security. Today, maintaining technological superiority is a cornerstone of Western military planning. The United States and its NATO allies rely on superior technology to offset the greater number of systems fielded by the Soviets and their allies. Recognizing the West's technological advantage, immediately after World War II the Soviet Union began a systematic effort to acquire Western technology. This effort, coordinated at the highest levels of the Soviet government, continues to erode the West's technological advantage while saving Warsaw Pact countries many billions of dollars in research and development.[7]

To counteract this threat, the United States and its NATO allies (less Iceland, plus Japan) formed COCOM. This informal organization embargoes exports of strategic products and technologies to communist nations.

In the United States, the Export Administration Act (EAA) of 1979 defines the U.S. approach to export control in conjunction with COCOM. This Act requires the Department of Defense (DOD) to develop and maintain a Military Critical Technologies List (MCTL).[8] These critical military issues continue to serve as a brake on expanded U.S.-Soviet trade. However, the 1988 Omnibus Trade and Competitiveness Act, continues the liberalization of export controls initiated by the 1985 Export Administration Amendments Act, thus securing a greater consensus in and out of government, while maintaining key protections.

Preserving technology security through the use of export controls is problematic for two reasons. First, there are no well-defined criteria that can be used to determine whether a given technology will enhance significantly Soviet

---

[7] *AMC Guide to Technology Security*, prepared for the Army Material Command, Deputy Chief of Staff for Intelligence, by the Critical Technologies Group, the International Technology Division, Los Alamos National Laboratory and Orion Enterprises, Inc. (Los Alamos, NM and Fredericksburg, VA: November, 1987). p. 1.

[8] Ibid.

military capabilities. Second, technological security requires technological progress which can only be achieved through a free exchange of technical information among Western countries and the maintenance of a healthy economy. Thus, export controls must not interfere with economic and technological relations among Western nations. This is sometimes difficult to do.

Plan a secure export strategy for grain

The Long Term Grain Agreement (LTGA) ended in October 1988, and a new agreement was negotiated in November 1989; it was put into effect retroactively on the same terms, and expires December 31, 1990.

Despite this continuity, the issue of joint ventures in agricultural technology may join grain sales as a focus of key interest in U.S.-Soviet agricultural trade. As always, the United States must face the question of whether it should encourage expansion of this trade, given the Soviet's refusal in the past to abide by the terms of the LTGAs, and given the question of subsidized credits. As always, securing a sensible long-term strategy to promote American grain exports in the most cost-effective, least-disruptive fashion will be the primary policy goal. It remains a difficult goal to achieve, but an important one, for securing long-term grain markets for America's farmers with their bumper crops is an extremely high, but often unappreciated, priority for the United States.

Ironically, in spite of the problems with Soviet adherence to the LTGA and the advisability of credits, the U.S.-Soviet grain trade is sometimes highlighted as an example of the kind of stability needed to make the U.S.-Soviet relationship effective. Such stability, built upon legislative and executive cooperation, as well as upon a long-term, embargo-proof Executive Agreement and mutual interest is suggested as a model for future economic relations.

This problem is likely to be a central one for the relationship for some time. Both the United States and the Soviet Union share an interest in secure, stable long-term grain agreements but their preferred source of market no longer is mutual. The Soviet Union is probably still America's preferred market for high volume purchases but the United States is no longer the Soviets' preferred major grain source. Primary motivations also diverge. The United States wants a dependable outlet for grain surpluses, a more stable international grain market, and an improved balance of payments. By contrast, the Soviets want to intelligently manage their dependence on a U.S. market subject to foreign policy sanctions, to enhance their indigenous capacity in the near-term, and to diversify their sources in the meantime.

Since Mikhail Gorbachev's ascent in 1985, he has focused on agriculture as the leading sector in his economic reforms. Historically, the Soviets have been big producers of food grains such as wheat and rye, but their recent decision to expand their livestock herd has led to a growing demand for U.S. feed grains and oil concentrates such as corn and soybeans. Their poor ability to produce these has boosted import requirements, particularly from the United States, which has a distinct comparative advantage in production. Moreover, with the 1988 Soviet grain harvest some 40 million tons below the plan of 235 million tons, the smallest harvest since 1985, the Soviets were forced to buy even more grain on the world market than they had expected, further straining the state budget. As a result, U.S.-Soviet trade was up in 1988 over 1987 by 87 per cent almost exclusively due to heavy Soviet purchases ($ 2,162 million) of U.S. agricultural commodities. The sale of U.S. agricultural exports to the Soviet Union grew 143.2 per cent over 1987.[9]

Poor food availability is the driving impetus for the Soviets, and a report released by the State Committee for Statistics said that 1988's poor harvest has resulted in a "tense" food situation in the Soviet Union.[10] In 1988 *Izvestia* reported that if the food problem was not solved in two to three years, the people "will bury reform."[11]

Promote human rights

The Jackson-Vanik amendment to the 1974 Trade Act and the issues of emigration and the granting of MFN are perhaps the most symbolic expression of America's concern for human and religious rights in the Soviet bloc, but there are several other areas of significance that directly affect U.S.-Soviet trade. These are high on the list of economic discussions between Bush and Gorbachev, following the first specific inclusion of human rights in the agreed-upon agenda at the Washington summit in 1987. Policy issues of immediate or continuing relevance include: Soviet emigration, slave labour, religious persecution, enforced emigration, and a variety of other human rights issues.

---

[9] Department of Commerce, Office of Eastern Europe and Soviet Affairs (March 6, 1989).

[10] *Tass*, in English (January 21, 1989).

[11] David Remnick, "Soviet Await Benefits of Gorbachov Reforms", *The Washington Post* (August 18, 1988), p. 4 (original draft).

A new impetus has been added to the human rights debate by the Slepak Foundation, and its Principles for ethical American business investment in the Soviet Union. By May 1989 members in both houses of Congress had already introduced reporting legislation patterned on the successful introduction of the Sullivan Principles into U.S. law. A broad, bi-partisan range of human and religious rights activists, labour leaders and environmentalists joined forces to persuade U.S. business to use its considerable clout for reforms.

Promote and improve export controls

In the post-war period the United States has authorized the use of export controls for three purposes: to preserve national security, to prevent domestic shortages and inflation, and to promote U.S. foreign policy objectives. All three types of export controls have been controversial. The U.S. goal has always been to further the purposes of its export control policy without undermining the competitiveness of U.S. exports in global markets.

In the late 1980s the United States and its COCOM partners showed great commonality of interest. Ironically, Deputy Under Secretary of Defense for Technology Security Stephen Bryen, a noted advocate of tight technology controls, was indirectly partially responsible for this eventual easing in COCOM relations. His efforts to tighten surveillance (by hiring more customs agents, for instance), to streamline export licensing by cutting red tape and processing time, to publish the once-secret list of embargoed products to broaden public and business support, to computerize the application and licensing process, and to broaden the number of low technology goods that could be sold to the Soviet Union without an export license met justifiable criticisms of the COCOM process while boosting compliance and efficiency.

However, some controversy continues in COCOM, especially over controls on computers. The issue is a crucial one because of the direct and significant input that computers and microprocessors have into almost all contemporary military systems.[12] Apparently, less than 38 per cent of computers brought into the Soviet Union or built there are allocated to civilian use, and that per-

---

[12] See Judith Thornton, "Trade, Export Controls and Computer Technology", paper submitted to the Johns Hopkins Foreign Policy Institute's U.S.-Soviet Agenda Project, 1988, p. 4 (original draft).

centage fell sharply between 1983 and 1986.[13] American officials are justifiably concerned about computer sales to the Soviet Union.

Promote export competitiveness

For over forty years, the United States has been the prime motivating force behind the promotion of free trade. At base, it remains primarily concerned with the economic vitality of the free world, and desires a preeminent role. Promoting a vibrant and competitive U.S. export sector is a crucial component in this process.

Export markets have also become increasingly vital to the U.S. domestic economy. According to a National Academy of Sciences' study, they now represent a significant and growing share of total sales in a number of key industrial sectors and are especially critical to the success of the high-technology sector accounted for 42 per cent of manufactured exports in 1985. Moreover, in some industries, remaining competitive in world markets is essential to maintaining their share of the domestic market because foreign competitors that dominate the international market may in some cases enjoy economies of scale not available to U.S. producers limited to domestic sales.[14]

5.3 The special case of Soviet and East European reforms

A fundamental question is: is it in the interests of the United States for Soviet reforms to succeed? U.S.-Soviet trade today carries "the potential for making U.S.-Soviet economic relations an important political as well as economic phenomenon."[15] Conditions have changed, and with them new opportunities have emerged. For the Soviet Union, Gorbachev's dual policy of perestroika and interdependence are such that "if he succeeds in pushing his domestic reform program forward, he will have established a basis for expanding foreign economic relations to facilitate progress on the domestic

---

[13] Ibid., p. 2.

[14] National Academy of Sciences, *Balancing the National Interest: U.S. National Security Export Controls and Global Economic Competitiveness* (Washington, D.C.: National Academy Press, 1987), p. 152.

[15] Edited transcript of a Johns Hopkins Foreign Policy Institute meeting, "The Twin Threat of Congress and the Allies", in the U.S.-Soviet Roundtable Series; featured speakers: Drs. John Hardt and Paula Stern, p. 1.

front and provided the foundation for expanding U.S.-Soviet economic relations."[16]

However, the development of economic relations cannot be divorced from the political environment within which they exist. Thus, improved U.S.-Soviet economic relations across-the-board cannot be achieved without achieving first a "normalization of relations in the key areas of arms control, regional issues and human rights, among others. Simply signing an INF accord, however, is not enough; greater progress is required in terms of conventional arms balances and START..."[17] Thus, improved bilateral relations promote trade, not vice versa.

There is general agreement in the West that unless Gorbachev can show some successes, the whole process of reforms will be in danger. In fact, Gorbachev's preoccupation with the enormous challenge of radical reform is a potentially important incentive for reaching an accommodation with the West on a broad range of issues in order to obtain a "breathing space" permitting a focus on domestic issues. The easiest accommodations with the West could be in terms of economic issues, and the United States should be able to use that incentive to conclude agreements with the Soviets.

The key issues for the U.S. in the reform process are: a) Would success in modernization and efficiency changes require the Soviet Union to lower the priority of military programs? b) Would these successes cause the Soviet Union to move toward a market simulating economy, and shift bilateral competition from military to economic and political arenas? c) If so, might pressure on conformity in Eastern Europe be reduced, with a substantial pull-out of Soviet troops from Eastern Europe? d) "Alternately, might a more efficient economy allow the Soviet Union to improve and expand its military priority in the future?"[18]

"If Gorbachev does succeed in paving the path to reform, Gorbachev may require further interdependence to gain momentum. Joint ventures could be critical to the success of the program in political and economic terms. There are three kinds of joint-ventures deserving mention in this respect. These would involve the development of 'hard, good' food (that for which there is the

---

16) Ibid., p. 2.

17) Ibid., p. 2.

18) Ibid.

greatest demand), and its delivery to the stores, as well as the development of energy resources, specifically oil in the short-term."[19]

In each of these three key areas, joint ventures with the United States would be very helpful in boosting Soviet efficiency and productivity, as well as lower cost. Marketing and quality control are crucial areas wherein U.S. multinational corporations could play a key role. The first two areas, producing food and getting it on the table are of vital urgency and are clearly not the product of state-of-the-art technology; they will not be prohibited by COCOM controls. The need for greater efficiency and lower unit costs for food is vital, as a typical Soviet family of four with two income earners currently spends 59 per cent of its income on food, versus about 15 per cent in the U.S. If a Soviet family tried to match the typical American diet, they would spend a full 90 per cent of their income.[20]

U.S. technology, and Western products in general, may become especially important to the Soviets "if, as many expect, Soviet factories fail to meet ambitious production targets for new machinery."[21] The Soviets are now eager to buy Western imports that will boost efficiency, reduce raw material inputs, or save energy.

The structure of trade is likely to change, as the Soviets hope to get more mileage out of their import component. Greater emphasis will be made on manufactured imports, especially transport equipment, heavy construction machinery, and machinery in general, particularly in the area of oil and gas technology. In the industrial field, they are also particularly interested in computer-aided design and manufacturing techniques developed in the West. In addition, they are less interested in building new factories, and much more interested in modernizing them. They consider the licensing and sale of Western commodities in the Soviet Union and joint ventures as a means of obtaining key technology, but they are very anxious not to become dependent on foreign sources for that technology. Their preference is for quickly producing the technology themselves, after learning about it via joint ventures or limited sales. This desire may come in conflict with Western corporate strategies, which are to gain long-term access to the Soviet market.

---

[19] Ibid., p. 3.

[20] Ibid.

[21] Daniel Franklin, "Soviet Trade with the Industrialized West", *SAIS Review*, 8, no. 1 (Winter/Spring 1988), p. 82.

74

In attempting to promote democracy in Eastern Europe, the United States faces a classic dilemma: "Is the U.S. best served by a forthcoming economic relationship which might serve to increase East European well-being and autonomy, but might ease the economic burden of empire borne by the Soviet Union? Or, alternately, is the United States better served by a policy of denial which may heighten economic and social tensions in the region and maximize costs to Moscow?"[22]

The United States has consistently supported the former position, but not without considerable soul-searching. The current debate over Gorbachev's reforms, and whether or not the United States should support them through greater trade with the Soviet bloc, will bring this dilemma back to the fore. The United States can exert substantial leverage on East Europe countries, due to their relatively small economies, the severe economic difficulties that most have faced in recent years, and the Western orientation of their societies. Indeed, most East European states push for closer contact as a means of overcoming their economic malaise and promoting exports.

5.4 Future concerns

Despite its small volume and dollar value, U.S.-Soviet trade has repeatedly caused significant problems over the past fifteen years for the United States and its allies. Rather than diminishing, many of these concerns have been growing as the world trading system becomes more interconnected and significant as a percentage of U.S. GNP, and as the Soviets have become more outward-oriented.

Disputes with Western Europe

The prospect of continued intra-Western disputes is probably the most immediate danger posed by East-West trade. Since the damaging gas pipeline imbroglio of 1982 the West has struggled to avert new confrontations, and NATO, COCOM, and the Organization for Economic Cooperation and Development have all conducted studies in an attempt to harmonize Western positions and defuse tensions. Unfortunately, although the pipeline issue and

---

[22] Francis T. Miko, "U.S. Interests, Issues, and Policies in Eastern Europe", appendix 5. *East European Economies: Slow Growth in the 1980s, Volume 1. Economic Performance and Policy*, (Washington, D.C.: Selected Papers submitted to the Joint Economic Committee, Congress of the United States, October 28, 1985), p. 255.

its legacy were addressed, key differences still divide the allies. First, the European allies view trade with the East as economically beneficial, and as a means of human contacts, while the United States has traditionally looked at East-West trade as a weapon, rather than an end in itself. Second, West European countries almost universally support security controls to deny communist countries militarily significant goods and know-how, but they criticize U.S. foreign policy controls, which are intended to protest objectionable foreign and domestic activity. The West European position is somewhat hypocritical, as these countries have supported foreign policy controls against such states as Idi Amin's Uganda and South Africa. Third, the Europeans criticize America's "light-switch" policy of turning trade on and off, citing its economic costs; the United States has been willing to accept what the Presidential Commission estimates as a $ 7.6 billion loss in export sales to the U.S. economy annually.[23] Fourth, the Europeans criticize U.S. attempts to exercise licensing control over reexports of U.S.-origin products from one foreign country to another; they disagree with this "extra-territorial" application of U.S. law, and argue that the United States does not have jurisdiction over actions taken by foreign citizens that are undertaken outside the territory of the United States. The United States agues, by contrast, that it is merely seeking to ensure through the controls that products that were licensed for export from the United States to a particular foreign country do not find their way to proscribed destinations.

Finally, for its part, the United States criticizes virtually all its allies for spotty government enforcement and indifferent business controls. Indeed, some of America's closest allies have legislation that is intended to block U.S. extra-territorial jurisdiction. The United States is concerned that it loses business as a result. While U.S. firms tend to err on the side of caution by refusing questionable business or by carefully requesting export approval from DOD, many foreign firms accept such orders and ship the goods. Many foreign buyers also offer considerable premiums if control requirements, and their subsequent delays, are illegally dispensed with. American firms find it difficult to compete with such uneven enforcement of agreed-upon COCOM controls. The United States tends to compensate for such problems by "going it alone";

---

[23] Gary K. Bertsch, "U.S.-Soviet Trade and the National Interest: Assessing the Costs and Benefits", in Chapman, ed., *Forum on U.S.-Soviet Trade Relations*, p. 42.

or, by stepping up unilateral foreign policy controls in addition to COCOM's lists. This only exacerbates intra-Alliance frustrations.

Export competitiveness

Since 1949 America's leaders have experienced a constant tension between efforts to control militarily significant high technology exports while preserving Western business access abroad. The current law still leaves the United States with a dilemma in the Gorbachev era: to tighten or loosen export controls. Some critics of the 1979 Export Administration Act seek to tighten controls, arguing that the Soviet military indirectly benefits from uncontrolled sales of Western technology.

The Reagan administration supported this line of thought, with more restrictive licensing procedures, pressure on the allies to adopt more restrictive policies, a stronger DOD role in reviewing applications, and a greater investment in enforcement efforts. They argued that the Soviet's Military Industrial Commission (VPK), which coordinates the development of all Soviet weapons and the Soviet program to acquire Western technology, spent about half a billion roubles a year ($ 1.4 billion in 1980 purchasing power) in collecting Western technology.

Proponents of this tight control position stated that "According to the Soviets, about one-third of the VPK requirements are totally or partially fulfilled annually, strongly suggesting that Western industrial security, counter-intelligence, export controls, and other efforts do have an effect. But, each year the number of VPK requirements grows by about l5 per cent. This is a strong indication that the expanding Soviet military industrial program continues to rely on Western technical solutions and advances. It also indicates increased collection success and user expectation."[24]

The cost to the United States and to the West of Soviet success is substantial. The Department of Defence estimated in 1986 that Western technology acquired through *legal* channels alone in 1985 could have, had they been successful, saved the Soviet military $ 4.6 to $ 12.0 billion; cost the United States and its allies $ 5.0-$ 13.2 billion; degraded the NATO/Warsaw Pact military balance, particularly in critical aspects of ASW; and contributed to the

---

[24] Central Intelligence Agency, *Soviet Acquisition of Militarily Significant Western Technology: An Update* (Washington, D.C.: The Central Intelligence Agency, September, 1985), p. 6.

Soviet/Pact military technology base, particularly in automated production and control, sensors, and telecommunications.[25]

Advocates of the alternative position believe that the United States has over-reacted and controls many items of marginal military utility, at best. They claim that controlled items are available abroad, that U.S. licensing procedures are cumbersome, slow, and unpredictable, and that U.S. firms are made uncompetitive in the process. The Export Administration Amendments Act of 1985 was a compromise between the two positions, and passed after a bitterly-fought fight within the Administration and in the Congress that resulted in much soul-searching.

Both the U.S. House and Senate passed comprehensive trade bills in 1988 that included significant amendments to 1979 EAA; they were united in the 1988 Omnibus Trade and Competitiveness Act. Both bills had provisions that curbed the role of the Defence Department in the license review process; reduced licensing requirements for exports to COCOM countries; eliminated licensing requirements for low-technology items; reduced reexport license requirements; defined "foreign availability" and established a timetable for making determinations of foreign availability; sought to reduce the size of the Commodity Control List; and reduced unilateral controls while strengthening multilateral control mechanisms through COCOM and through bilateral agreements. The illegal sales of submarine-related technology to the Soviet Union by the Japanese company Toshiba Machine and the Norwegian firm Kongsberg Vaapenfabrikk have heightened congressional interest in these issues, and led to both an effort to rationalize and simplify the control process, as well as to toughen penalties for those who break U.S. law and flout COCOM regulations.

U.S.-Soviet grain trade

Ironically, in the United States, the U.S.-Soviet grain trade is seen as the single most divisive economic issue of the relationship; yet, at the same time, it has been the grain trade that has endured during some of the worst periods in U.S.-Soviet relations. Two intractable problems interact to pose often severe strains both on domestic U.S. politics as well as in terms of relations with our grain-producing allies. The first of these is America's growing agricultural

---

[25] *The Technology Security Program: A Report to the 99th Congress, Second Session, 1986* (Washington, D.C.: The Department of Defense, 1986), p. 11.

dependence on Soviet purchases at highly subsidized rates and the Soviet Union's casual refusal to abide by the terms of the Long Term Grain Agreement (LTGA). Each of these issues came to a head in 1988 with the expiration of the five-year LTGA.

The adverse policy consequences of the LTGA are apparent: America has lost its predominant share in its major purchaser's market, it has upset close allies, and continuing conflict within the Administration and between the Administration and Congress threatens domestic farm policy and U.S. agricultural export strategies. Perhaps most dangerous is the fact that it is *only* with heavy subsidies that the United States has regained any of the Soviet wheat market.

Although the United States remained a major supplier of grain to the Soviets, Argentina, the EC, Australia, and Canada became dominant during the last few years, until the United States again regained a major position through its very heavy subsidies. In fact, the Soviets concluded in 1986 major LTGAs with both Canada and Argentina, with Canadian sales surpassing U.S. sales by 4.2 MMT in 1986-87.[26] This diversification of the Soviet market has hit the United States hardest in wheat sales: U.S. wheat exports to the Soviet Union accounted for 27 per cent of its imports in 1984, but in 1985, the figure had dropped to 5 per cent.[27]

The danger of U.S. farm policy held hostage by U.S.-Soviet foreign relations in an election year was probably the most serious consequence in 1988. Recent history in this area is not encouraging. Many argue that the unprecedented subsidies applied by the Department of Agriculture from 1985-87 were tied to Administration desires to promote an arms treaty. Certainly, they came at a particularly awkward moment, in the midst of the farm crisis, and faced substantial high-level opposition. "The list of Cabinet-level opponents of this congressional initiative was impressive. It is reported to have included the Secretaries of State and Defence, the National Security Adviser, and the Director of the Central Intelligence Agency."[28] As the Reagan administration drew to a close, and worked to achieve further arms control agreements, many feared that America's farm policy would become hostage to foreign

---

[26] John P. Hardt and Jean F. Boone, "Soviet Agriculture: U.S.-USSR Grain Sales and Prospects for Expanding Agricultural Trade", (Washington, D.C.: The Congressional Research Service, November 4, 1987), p. 5.

[27] Ibid.

[28] Roger W. Robinson, Jr., "The Security Dimensions of U.S.-Soviet Trade", in Chapman, ed., *Forum on U.S.-Soviet Trade Relations*, p. 97.

policy. The current high subsidies have been sustained in 1989 and are described by many as linked to a possible START treaty as well as to a desire to expand market share.

Policy disagreements in Washington

Critics of the policy disagreements that often seem to pervade East-West trade argue that blame can be laid with "a fundamental overlap of jurisdiction among the principal line agencies: the Departments of Commerce, Defence, and State. The administrative structures established by the executive branch have not proven effective in resolving in a coherent and timely fashion the frequent policy differences that occur among these agencies ..."[29]

An equally divisive issue, credit, is currently building like a thunderhead on the horizon. Due to low world oil prices and its inability to generate much foreign exchange through the sale of manufactured goods, the Soviet Union has found credit to be a very important determinant of the level of U.S.-Soviet trade. At the same time, a small but vocal cadre of American business reminescent of those who campaigned to open the China market is lobbying hard to remove all restrictions against free trade and credits with the Soviet bloc.[30]

Many observers consider this the key agenda item today, and characterize it as "the future pipeline controversy".

The debate over extending credit to the Soviets is a hot one, but it must be resolved before the United States can move forward in bilateral trade relations. U.S. government credit is currently limited by provisions of the Trade Act (Jackson-Vanik and Byrd amendments) and the Export-Import Bank Act (Stevenson amendment). The Stevenson and Byrd amendments would restrict U.S. government credits to the Soviet Union to $ 300 million should other barriers (the Jackson-Vanik amendment linking MFN status to emigration policy) be removed or waived."[31]

---

[29] National Academy, *Balancing the National Interest*, p. 160.

[30] Such as the US-USSR Trade and Economic Council. Its President James H. Giffen, when asked whether the United States really has an interest in helping make the Soviet Union "an economic superpower", he replied "I think we do". See William E. Simon, "Should We Bail Out Gorbachev", *The Reader's Digest* (September, 1988), p. 66.

[31] Ibid., p. 10.

In the fall of 1988 several hearings were held in the House and the Senate specifically on the issue of extending private and government credits to the Soviet bloc.[32] Key issues concerned better coordination among the West on lending policies, the fear that the Soviets were subverting normal disclosure requirements to use the same oil and gold as collateral many times over to secure deals, and excessively favourable credit rates offered by Western banks.

Most troubling is the fear that the Soviets are borrowing with "untied" loans in the West (about 80 per cent of recent loans) to save scarce foreign exchange needed to enhance the Soviet military machine and sell arms to its allies at concessional rates. Members of Congress point to the 1987 recommendation of the Institute for International Finance against untied loans, and PlanEcon estimates that the Soviets' lending to developing world clients ballooned from $ 13 billion in 1980 to $ 49 billion in 1987, much of it to finance Soviet arms. In 1986, the Soviet Union is alleged to have spent over one-third of its hard currency earnings to support Nicaragua, Cuba, and Vietnam, as well as for intelligence activities. Figures cited by members and staff of Congress include the almost 3 per cent real growth in Soviet military spending in both 1986 and 1987, almost double the growth rate of 1981-86.

Trade enthusiasm

In some quarters, particularly in the business community and the media since the Washington Summit, an inordinate degree of enthusiasm has been expressed about near-term growth in U.S.-Soviet trade, buoyed by more than a touch of "Gorbamania".

The U.S. government is uniquely vulnerable to intense lobbying by special interest groups, among them business. Often policy is adjusted too rapidly, due to intense lobbying, especially of Congress. Under such conditions, ill-considered regulations and policy choices are made, with adverse consequences only recognized much later. In the short term, excessive enthusiasm over prospects for U.S.-Soviet trade may lead to a LTGA that offers too many concessions on the American side and insufficient sanctions for a Soviet

---

[32] See especially hearings on bank lending to Warsaw Pact nations Chaired by Rep. Robert Gracia (D-NY) of the House Banking Subcommittee on International Finance, Trade, and Monetary Policy (September 22, 1988), and Hearings on "Changing U.S.-Soviet Economic Relations and Their Impact on Small Business", by Congressman John J. LaFalce, Chairman of the House Committee on Small Business (September 23 and September 30, 1988).

refusal to adhere to the terms of the agreement. In addition, it might lead to a too-rapid push for excessive public or private credits, or an ill-conceived rush for joint ventures. Credits are currently controlled at $ 300 million, but there is some movement in Congress to make it easier for the President to offer more credits.

Much enthusiasm for joint ventures is clearly premature. No more than several dozen currently exist between the Soviet Union and Western companies, compared with more than 7,000 now operating in China. Even among these few, West Europeans and Japanese far outpace the United States. About 20 U.S. firms are "actively discussing joint venture projects with the USSR, 15 of which have submitted proposals,"[33] but as of April, 1988 only one large U.S. firm (Combustion Engineering of Stamford, Connecticut) had signed a joint venture. Energy, agricultural equipment, transportation, and pharmaceuticals all seem of interest to the Soviets. The Soviets are only beginning to issue the regulations necessary to make these a reality throughout their industries and foreign trade ministries, and virtually all of the tax and investment data necessary to handle repatriation and investment of profits as well as taxation and insurance issues is just now being investigated. The early evidence is not encouraging. Combustion Engineering must take its profits primarily in gasoline and diesel fuel, not in hard currency, and try to sell it for dollars outside of the Soviet Union. Roma Food of Piscataway, New Jersey hopes to build 25 pizza parlors in the Soviet Union, but will have to acquire its profits by selling Soviet champagne, cut glass and mushrooms in Europe first.

Even with reasonable expections regarding the scale of likely investments, U.S. government officials frequently remind eager business leaders that this is but the third wave of U.S. investment in the Soviet Union, and that the previous two led to major and uncompensated business losses.

---

[33] John P. Hardt and Jean F. Boone, "U.S.-USSR Commercial Relations: Issues in East-West Trade", (Washington, D.C.: Congressional Research Service, November 25, 1987), p. 2.

The Jackson-Vanik amendment

The Jackson-Vanik amendment to the 1974 Trade Act is perhaps the most symbolic expression of America's concern for human rights in the Soviet bloc. Currently, major attacks are now being mounted against it, including requests for a one-year waiver or an outright repeal.

Sections 401 - 409 of the Act deny "eligibility for nondiscriminatory [trade and tariff] treatment and for U.S. government credits and credit and investment guarantees, and prohibit U.S. commercial agreements in respect to any non-market economy country (Poland and Yugoslavia excepted) denying its citizens the right or opportunity to emigrate or to join permanently through emigration a very close relative in the United States, or imposing in general, on such emigration or emigrants more than a nominal tax or fee. Current full compliance of each nonmarket economy country with these requirements must be reported by the President to Congress initially before the Most Favored Nation (MFN) status is extended, and semiannually while nondiscriminatory treatment is in effect."[34]

Although the Soviet Union has always reacted adversely to Jackson-Vanik, and Romania, Hungary, and China have reacted positively, key questions now need to be resolved as emigration totals from the Soviet Union continue to rise.[35] For example: should the United States continue in principle its discriminatory overall treatment of trade with communist countries? If discrimination is to be abolished, should this be done, as thus far, on a country-by-country basis or should it apply to all communist countries without exception? If the former, what criteria would determine that eligibility, especially on waiver assurances? Would the purpose of the Jackson-Vanik waiver not be better served if the requirement of emigration assurances is replaced by one calling for the president's determination of the country's satisfactory emigration performance? Are political, rather than purely economic, criteria appropriate or advisable in deciding whether discriminatory treatment is to continue or to cease? As a reciprocal granting of MFN by a communist and a free-economy state does not bestow on the latter as large benefits as on the former, should the granting of MFN be contingent on some additional concessions granted by the communist state? If so, should they be limited to trade? Should the

---

[34] Vladimir N. Pregelj, "Most-Favored-Nation Policy Toward Communist Countries" (Washington, D.C.: The Congressional Research Service, June 30, 1987), p. 8.

[35] Ibid., pp. 24-25.

freedom-of-emigration requirement for the extension of MFN status be broadened to include human and religious rights in general?

The GATT, IMF, the World Bank

As part of the "global trade offensive" launched by the Soviets over the past two years, a major new focus has been evident. In 1986 the Soviets made an abortive effort to participate in an unspecified status in the General Agreement on Tariffs and Trade (GATT) world trade negotiations at Punta del Este. Apparently, this was a preliminary step in an effort to gain GATT membership. By substantial lobbying of the Japanese, the Soviets also secured limited representation at the Pacific Economic Cooperation Council meetings in 1986 and 1988, as well as observer status at the Asian Development Bank meetings in 1987 and 1988. In addition, they have also surprisingly joined the Common Fund for Commodities, although a high cost. They are also exploring the possibility of membership in the IMF and the World Bank, and in offering the first Euronotes and bonds since the 1917 revolution. To that end, they "participated in an international debt offering for the first time by underwriting a part of a $ 97 million Eurobond offering by a Finnish bank. This action has been viewed as a first step toward a bond offering by the Soviets themselves to finance their own debt."[36]

There are two perceived dangers that lie in this new Soviet initiative: one, the Soviets may disrupt or hamstring key organizations that are crucial to free trade and Western industrial societies, and two, in the absence of advance planning and proper consultations, the West may allow itself to be manoeuvred into letting the Soviets gain access by the back-door "observer status" route.

There are clearly two schools of thought as to whether the West, especially the United States, should allow Soviet membership in key international financial and trading institutions. Some argue that Soviet attempts for membership "suggest a long-term strategy of greater integration in world trade". They argue that the political implications of such an attempt are not necessarily dangerous.[37] By contrast, the United States and the GATT's trade ministers opposed the Soviet effort to joint GATT in 1986 based "on the incompatibility of Soviet centralized trade practices with those of market economy coun-

---

[36] Hardt and Boone, "U.S.-USSR Commercial Relations", p. 7.

[37] Franklin, "Soviet Trade", p. 88.

84

tries."[38] They argued that although some non-market states have joined the GATT, including Yugoslavia, Hungary, Poland, Czechoslovakia and Romania, "their foreign trade practices conform more closely to those of capitalist countries, and as small economies, they have little impact on the organization as a whole."[39] In addition, some worry that the Soviets would at least rhetorically champion the plight of debtors, and thus make rescheduling considerably more difficult. Although the Soviets have denied any intention of seeking membership in the IMF and the World Bank, the Reagan administration opposed such admissions.[40] The key policy question for the United States is whether the costs of increased Soviet influence in the world economy, and lessened U.S. influence, outweigh the benefits of greater international cooperation.

5.5 Should the United States bank on Gorbachev's reforms?

The Soviet Union is "a superpower with a 'one-crop' export structure more commonly associated with Third World economies."[41] As such, Gorbachev has the deck stacked against him. His dilemma is that he has to show successes, or at least progress, in the short run; yet, the problems he faces are solvable only in the long term, if then. He's a remarkable man and a unique politician for staking his short-term political career on long-term remedies that may be beyond his grasp. What are the most important constraints that he faces? How much economic manoeuvring room does he have?

The most serious problem that the Soviet Union faces is its reliance on petroleum and petroleum products for over half of its hard currency earnings, and for the majority of its exports to the West. By the early 1980s, oil and gas accounted for nearly four-fifths of total Soviet exports to OECD countries.[42] Every one-dollar decline in the price of oil per barrel reduced Soviet earnings by about $ 500 million annually, and the reduction in oil prices to date may have cost the Soviets $ 5 billion or more. As gas prices are pegged to oil, and

---

[38] Hardt and Boone, "U.S.-USSR Commercial Relations", p. 7.

[39] Ibid.

[40] Ibid.

[41] Franklin, "Soviet Trade", p. 76.

[42] Ibid.

as they are sold on the spot market denominated in dollars, gas prices eventually fell too. The sharp depreciation of the dollar also affected the Soviet Union's terms of trade.

As a result, the Soviets boosted the quantity of their energy sales to the West by one-fifth, and made a big effort to expand manufactured exports, including a one billion dollar increase in arms sales. Nevertheless, the Soviet trade deficit with the West rose from $ 1.2 billion in the first nine months of 1985 to $ 3.5 billion in the first nine months of 1986.[43] In 1986, it was also estimated that the Soviets' current account deficit reached $ 3.0 billion and there was evidence that its net debt doubled over the previous two years in order to make up for lost earnings.[44] The Soviet's total estimated hard currency earnings in 1986 amounted to about $ 26 billion, or less than one-third of General Motor's total revenues for 1986.[45]

By contrast, the world demand for other Soviet raw material exports, such as metals, timber, and other industrial materials, will grow slowly in qualitative terms. Thus, Soviet hard currency earnings are likely to adjust by a function of price changes in key commodities, including oil. That is a shaky foundation to base any industrial development program on, especially a reform process as ambitious as Gorbachev's.

Gorbachev needs high technology inputs for his reforms, but foreign exchange for imports will be tight for the foreseeable future. His options are limited. He has to pay for his economic development program through oil and gold sales, expanded manufactures that may be a decade or more away, or by borrowing. That is why the Soviets find credit so important. A high level of annual borrowing may continue for several years, depending upon world oil prices. Some analysts expect that the Soviets may borrow $ 2 to $ 3 billion each year through the mid-1990s, even though they have sold gold heavily since 1986 (about $ 4 billion in 1988). PlanEcon, Inc. has estimated that the total gross debt of the Soviet Union will increase from $ 29 billion in 1985 to $ 53 billion by 1990.[46]

---

[43] Ibid., p. 80.

[44] Hardt and Boone, "U.S.-USSR Commercial Relations", p. 7.

[45] Robinson, "The Security Dimensions", p. 95.

[46] Ibid., p. 96.

Soviet academician Oleg Bogomolov has stated that the Soviet state budget deficit could double in 1990 to about 100 billion roubles.[47] The Chernobyl clean-up, the 13 billion rouble or more price-tag for the Armenian earthquake, and the Tadzhikistan earthquake in January, 1989 have all combined to exert substantial unexpected pressure on the Soviet budget. In addition, losses from alcohol sales of some 35 billion roubles in the last three years have also drained the state's treasury, leading to a deficit of some 11 per cent as a percentage of total national income. Many of the recently announced plans to cut subsidies on food and other consumer goods, as well as planned reductions in military spending and state investment, can be attributable to the growing budget deficit. The Soviets also remain concerned that there may be adverse economic consequences as a result of rapid scientific innovation, and their concerns may well affect prospects for trade.

What if the reforms do not work? How will that affect the evolution of trade? Gorbachev has apparently done the right things, but most experts conclude that he has not gone far enough. He has decentralized trade enterprises, made a move toward equitable rouble exchange rates, and offered considerable financial resources for export-increasing investments through the Foreign Trade Bank. As of April 1, 1989, virtually all Soviet business organizations have the right to engage in foreign trade. However, enterprises cannot get greater import allocations of foreign exchange unless they earn them. Moreover, the state's monopoly on foreign trade is not being totally broken, it's only been relaxed. Commodities such as oil, gas, food, timber, and about 60 per cent of machinery imports will continue to be traded by the Foreign Trade Organizations. The State Foreign Economic Commission may also suspend import and export operations in cases "involving unfair competition", or where "the activities harm the interests of the state". The Council of Ministers can also ban the import or export of certain goods, and the December 2, 1988 decree limits the right to purchase consumer and related products to 10 per cent of an enterprise's hard currency fund.

Furthermore, we do not know what forces hinder or propel reforms in the Soviet Union. The flood of trade in the 1970s allowed for import substitution, not reform. Poland is a good example of what the Soviets want to avoid. It was flooded with Western credits, more than it could use efficiently, and that allowed the government to avoid reforms through consumerism.

---

[47] See *Argumenty i fakty*, no. 3 (1989).

The U.S. government also remains concerned about an attendant problem: that joint ventures might become an active technology transfer mechanism, particularly in the area of computer technology, with subsequent military gains. Deputy Assistant Secretary of Defense David Wigg told the Joint Economic Committee of the U.S. Senate that "the opening up of East-West commercial ties would provide a windfall for the Soviet and East European intelligence services and their technology acquisition programs".[48] Government officials cite the Soviet Chamber of Commerce and Industry, and state that some one-third of the Chamber's 140 employees are known or suspected Soviet secret service officers. Declassified portions of a recent CIA investigation state that the Soviet Chamber of Commerce and Industry is a center of Soviet industrial espionage "while acting as a trade promoter and facilitator with excellent access to Western firms".[49]

The most recent data available in the West suggests that Gorbachev's reforms may already have stalled.[50] If so, the priority on acquiring technology from the West, legal or illegal, is likely to be heightened. Perennial difficulties caused by bad weather and transportation bottlenecks combined with some-times severe disruptions born of the economic reforms to drag real GNP down below 1 per cent in 1987, and 1.5 per cent in 1988. A firm foundation has not yet been developed for Gorbachev's economic reforms: shortfalls in machinery output limit the pace of modernization, worker motivation and productivity is undercut by reduced job security, shortages of consumer goods, and fears of price increases, and key enterprises are still confused by contradictory guide-lines. Furthermore, performance in the key machine-building complex was not nearly as impressive as in the fuel and energy complex in 1987. The output of high technology products was especially disappointing, with more than two-thirds of the quotas remaining unfulfilled. U.S. government projections for the rest of the Soviet Five Year Plan (1988-1990) predict annual GNP growth of 2 per cent or less. Consumer dissatisfaction born of shortages and disruptions is growing more pronounced as a result.

---

[48] See U.S. Department of State, *Intelligence Collection in the USSR Chamber of Commerce and Industry*, 1987, for an analysis of Soviet methods of technology acquisition.

[49] Ibid.

[50] "Gorbachev's Economic Program: Problems Emerge" (Washington, D.C.: A paper prepared by the Central Intelligence Agency and the Defense Intelligence Agency for the Sub-committee on Economic Resources, Competitiveness and Security Economics of the Joint Economic Committee, Congress of the United States, March 24, 1988.

Foreign trade turnover in 1988 amounted to some 132 billion roubles, or about 2 per cent over 1987, but Soviet terms of trade worsened considerably. The value of Soviet exports dropped by 1.9 per cent to 67 billion roubles, even though the volume of exports increased by 4 per cent. By contrast, the value of imports increased by 6.5 per cent, even though the volume only increased 1 per cent.[51] Trade with Socialist countries rose to 65 per cent of total foreign trade.

As we have seen, whole economy reforms are notoriously difficult to achieve on will alone. Most take an exogenous variable like a revolution, a defeat in war, the opening of a new frontier, or the discovery of a major new natural resource. None of these cataclysmic changes is affecting the Soviet Union now, so Gorbachev is pinning his hopes on some big "ifs": many, profitable, and varied joint ventures in the near term; good prices for his exports; few, if any, sudden drains like bad harvests or the $ 900 million Chernobyl clean-up; no more work stoppages due to social unrest, such as occurred in the Baltic and the Caucasus during 1988; speedy, accurate, and sufficient enabling legislation for his reform decrees; overcoming his moribund system's inertia; big trade increases without a convertible currency; no more debilitating economic sanctions imposed by the West; and sufficient, sustained lending or credits from Japan and Western Europe.

Finally, although Gorbachev is, by most accounts, the undisputed leader of the Soviet Union, his policies are certainly not undisputed. This remains the case even though he was able to oust Brezhnev holdovers such as Grishin, Romanov, and Tikhonov and promote his own reformers such as Ryzhkov, Zaikov, and Yeltsin into top leadership positions. Most of the top Soviet leadership wants to reduce the military burden on society, but most also disagree on the methods to accomplish that goal without compromising security. Likewise, at this early stage in technological acquisitions, with a major foreign exchange constraint, a few costly mistakes might undo production goals for entire sectors. Will Gorbachev be given enough rope to weave through these and other obstacles, or will his many rivals in the realm of practicality sweep his options away, and with them, perhaps, the last Soviet chance to meet the 21st century on Western terms?

---

[51] John Tedstrom, "Recent Trends in the Soviet Economy: A Balance Sheet on the Reforms", RL Report on the USSR, 1, no. 5 (February 3, 1989), p. 17.

5.6 High stakes for the Bush administration

Despite its small volume, U.S.-Soviet trade is a national security issue deserving of reasoned and sustained attention at the highest levels of Administration policy. The lack of such careful attention, and past wild swings in U.S. policy, have repeatedly strained key allied relations and caused severe domestic controversy. This dissension is needless, and can be prevented. American policy can be clear and well-articulated, balanced, and acceptable to Republicans and Democrats alike. The United States can meet its varied goals and still offer a blue-print for allied unity on East-West trade.

The issue has never been more pressing, for the Soviets are poised at the beginning of a sustained push for Western investments, Western Europe is crying out for markets, and even the giant American industrial machine is seriously weakened by trading problems. To avoid disunity, the United States must make and market the basis for unified Western policies on trade with the Soviets, particularly in terms of military technology security. It remains crucial that the United States promote its own interests, and those of the West. It can stress and encourage business development, but never at the cost of national security. It must intelligently balance foreign policy and economic returns over the long term, and remain sensitive to West European concerns, while acknowledging unique aspects of U.S. politics, such as human rights concerns. The United States must remain vigilant. Gorbachev's reform program may be a positive phenomenon for the United States, as well as for the West, but it will not necessarily make a stable security balance easier to achieve.

The West's foremost safeguard is a coordinated, updated, and flexible COCOM process. "Higher fences" around fewer products should continue to be our goal, as should greater cooperation with America's allies. Japan must be brought more firmly into the process, as well as other non-COCOM states that serve as technology conduits, and COCOM surveillance of exports to third countries must be updated.

A successful U.S.-Soviet trade relationship can only be built if the United States gets its own house in order. It must ensure that the differences within the Departments of Defence, Commerce, and State on technology security controls are resolved in a coherent and timely fashion. High-level oversight and direction must also be introduced to reduce unclear and often conflicting policies. Similarly, legislative and executive cooperation on these often divisive issues must be enhanced in terms of policy formulation and implementation;

U.S.-Soviet trade policy cannot be left to the business community. Even the human and religious rights activists who influence Congress - no matter how deserving their petitions - should not be allowed to dictate U.S-Soviet trade policy.

The primacy of American and Western interests must be maintained, with policies designed to promote our own interests, no matter how Soviet behaviour and goals may evolve. U.S. policymakers should remember that the Soviets' core political interests have not changed, although they may have changed the means of achieving them. The key problem for designing a U.S.-Soviet trade policy may be in defining and implementing the United States' own interests; until this is done, it risks entering into agreements that could jeopardize U.S. long-term interests and those of the West. In addition, the United States must astutely balance foreign policy, allied concerns, economic returns, and human rights over the long term.

A fundamental improvement in the U.S.-Soviet relationship is a requirement for substantially more normalized economic relations. Yet, until that occurs, there is still room for the development of more predictable and profitable trade. However, new enthusiasm for expanded U.S.-Soviet trade must not conflict unduly with other important policy goals. West-West trade must not be damaged, for open scientific communication and trade are crucial to maintaining the West's lead over the Soviet Union in science and technology, as is the overall economic health of Western Europe. As a champion both of Western strength and world trade, the United States must clearly demonstrate how to enhance and preserve Western economic vitality, without either unduly freezing the Soviets out or allowing them to meddle with international financial or trading institutions.

The best U.S. approach is a cautious one - watching for the Soviets to display their cards more openly, and waiting for Soviet reforms to go beyond the theoretical stage, particularly with price reform, the key to the entire process. For foreign trade reform, crucial for expanded U.S.-Soviet trade ties, is inextricably linked to domestic reforms, and these may already be in trouble. Over the long term, the United States should be able to reap political gains from encouraging Soviet economic reforms, more pluralism, and a better economic lot for the Soviet people. However, it must not abridge its own interests in doing so, or invest too much in a ship that may sink. Similarly, it would be unwise to appear to be freezing the Soviets out of the information and technology revolution, for a hungry and isolated Soviet Union would be exceedingly dangerous.

In this process, the United States should not expect major changes to occur too quickly. However, if perestroika succeeds, interdependence with advanced industrial economies, including joint ventures, science and technology exchanges, and participation in the international economic system will become more relevant for Gorbachev. The United States and West must be cautious, however, for one long-term goal of the Soviets is the renegotiation of the world's trading relationships, and the playing of a key role in that renegotiation. The United States must take the lead in ensuring that the Soviet Union does not disrupt through future membership bodies such as the IMF, the World Bank, and the GATT, where at least a modicum of consensus reigns. The West has no obligation or incentive in giving the Soviets a key role as an independent actor in international economic relations; they must earn it.

Similarly, joint ventures should not be pushed too rapidly. Current Soviet law is vague and imposes restrictions on Western equity holdings and profit repatriation. The U.S. government could facilitate investment by clarifying the following: control of U.S. equipment and the quality control process, access to domestic markets, ability to repatriate profits in hard currency, assurance of supply and work environments conducive to quality and timely deliveries, and access to foreign supply and market networks and systems.

In terms of trade and finance, the United States can negotiate effectively with the Soviets by offering economic incentives. In principle, U.S. trade with the Soviet Union should, as much as possible, promote a linkage between economic reform and political liberalization. Likewise, the United States should concentrate on promoting trade as a means of improving human and religious rights performance in the Soviet Union, and Eastern Europe, using both bilateral ties and the CSCE process. The time is certainly ripe to move on key trade-related legislation such as the "Slepak Principles"[52] and import controls on goods produced by slave labour. The United States should also respond

---

[52] The Slepak Principles urge that American companies engaged in commerce with the Soviet Union: will not produce goods or provide services that replenish the Soviet military; will not use goods or products manufactured by forced labour in the Soviet Union; will safeguard Soviet employees prone to dismissal based on politics, religion, or ethnic background; will decline to participate in a commercial transaction if the place of work is a Soviet-confiscated religious edifice; will ensure that methods of production do not pose an irresponsible physical danger to Soviet workers, neighbouring populations and property; will refrain from making untied loans to the Soviet government which may be used to subsidize Soviet non-peaceful activities; and, finally, will attempt to engage in joint ventures with private cooperative rather than institutions connected directly to the Soviet state.

aggressively to Soviet efforts to defuse criticism of their religious performance by highlighting a "Millennium of Christianity" in Russia.

Given the Jackson-Vanik amendment's central role in U.S. human rights policy, the United States must be prepared to rebut a Soviet push for a one-year "trial" waiver of the Jackson-Vanik and Stevenson amendments to the Trade Act of 1974 (despite low levels of emigration) to secure MFN status and renewed access to U.S. EximBank credits unless high levels of emigration are sustained and guaranteed in Soviet law.

Americans must also be prepared to deal with what may be the "pipeline controversy of the 1990s": U.S. government and commercial credits that subsidize Soviet trade with the United States. The debate over extending credits to the Soviets is a hot one, but it must be resolved before we can move forward in bilateral trade relations. Given the Soviets's ample gold reserves and excellent credit status, as well as human rights issues such as slave labour and emigration, the U.S. government should not subsidize Soviet trade. Current U.S. government credit limits under the Jackson-Vanik, Stevenson, and Byrd amendments should be retained.

The only exception to subsidized Soviet credits might be the Department of Agriculture's Export Enhancement Program (EEP). However, priority should be placed on securing long-term, stable, and favourable markets without heavy subsidies. In order to avoid farm market price disruptions and conflict with our allies, the United States should not sell grain to the Soviets on a non-discriminatory basis without first obtaining Soviet crop forecasts, advance warning on future grain needs, and penalties for Soviet contract abridgement. Moreover, U.S. agricultural policy must not be held hostage by hopes for arms control agreements.

A heightened focus on U.S.-Soviet trade must go far beyond the next Administration and the next Summit; it must focus on a series of summits and administrations. U.S. policy needs to be as subtle and as sophisticated as recent Soviet policy development has been, preferably more so. A bold U.S. strategy must also be informed by a much greater investment in studying the Soviet Union.

Trade relations may not be large in the short term; they may never be great. However, if these recommendations are taken, at least bilateral trade will be informed by a more realistic and pragmatic policy on the American side, emphasizing U.S. and Western goals, not just reacting to Soviet initiatives.

Chapter 6

U.S. FOREIGN ECONOMIC POLICY TOWARDS EASTERN EUROPE

Urszula Plowiec[1]

According to widespread American opinions[2], three basic factors have shaped U.S. policy toward Eastern Europe since World War II: first, the critical position of Eastern Europe in the global superpower confrontation, including its direct relationship to the security and political orientation of Western Europe; second, the influence of organized ethnic groups representing immigrants and their descendants from Eastern Europe; and third, the idealistic pursuit of the universal desiderata of national self determination and respect for human rights. The first is by far the most important.

American policy toward Eastern Europe has always been set within the broader East-West context of U.S.-Soviet relations. Sometimes it is said that American policy towards Eastern Europe has merely been the side effect of American policy towards the Soviet Union.

The basic principles of American East-West policy were formed at the end of the 1940s and the beginning of the 1950s in the climate of political changes in Czechoslovakia in February 1948, the proclamation of the People's Republic of China in October 1949, the Berlin Blockade of June 1948, and the outbreak of the Korean War in June 1950.

American policy took the form of "containment". Its main elements were the Truman Doctrine of March 1947 (defence bases in Greece and Turkey), the Marshall Plan of June 1947, the North Atlantic Treaty of April 1949 and support for Yugoslavia after Tito's break with the Soviet Union in 1948.

The basic American preoccupation of those years was with the fear that Soviet influence might be extended to Western Europe and Asiatic countries either through communist party successes or by other forms. Thus, the important goal was to encourage countries on the borders of the Soviet Union to resist Soviet overtures. This function was played among others by Radio Free Europe, established in 1950.

---

[1] Professor, Foreign Trade Research Institute, Warsaw, Poland.

[2] See Lincoln Gordon with J.F. Brown, Pierre Hasner, Josef Joffe, and Edwina Moreton, *Eroding Empire* (Washington, D.C.: The Brookings Institution, 1987), p. 67.

In consequence, U.S. East-West trade policy was highly politicized and became an economic instrument of U.S. national security policy. The following rules were, therefore, binding in principle: not to allow socialist countries to sell commodities in a rentable way (i.e. not to allow them to have enough free currency); not to allow them to buy strategic commodities; and not to finance exports to these countries. These principles have persisted without substantial changes over the last 40 years.

6.1 Import Controls

Making it more difficult for Eastern countries to acquire free currencies is achieved by denying most of them MFN status and imposing other strict import regulations to prevent them from developing their exports to the United States. Between August 1, 1951 and June 5, 1952 the MFN status was lifted successively from: Lithuania, Latvia, Romania, the GDR, Bulgaria, Czechoslovakia, Poland, the Soviet Union, and Hungary. In principle the U.S. president could grant MFN status to any Eastern country, but the political climate of the 1950s in East-West relations made it impossible. However, since 1962 even this was no longer possible because of new legal provisions instituted by the United States.

In 1975 it became possible to grant this treatment to Eastern (non-market) countries except in cases when such country: 1) denies its citizens the right or opportunity to emigrate; 2) imposes more than a nominal tax on emigration or on the visas or other documents required for emigration for any purpose or cause whatsoever; or 3) imposes more than a nominal tax, levy, fine, fee or other charge on any citizen as a consequence of the desire of such citizen to emigrate to the country of his choice. These conditions (the Jackson-Vanik amendment requirements) are clearly of a non-economic nature.

MFN status is very important but at the same time of limited value for the permanent development of bilateral trade relations. It may be obtained only on the basis of bilateral agreement, not through the participation of interested countries in the GATT. This agreement, binding for three years, must encompass, among others, discriminatory provisions concerning market disruption. This agreement must be approved by the U.S. Congress and the MFN status included in it is granted only for one year and is subject to renewal by the president, if there is no opposing resolution taken by Congress. Romania obtained such conditional MFN treatment in 1975 and Hungary in 1978.

Countries having MFN status pay, at present, an average of 20 per cent of the duty at the 1930 tariff level, while others pay 100 per cent. Lack of MFN status is an important obstacle to the development of exports of processed goods.

Moreover, countries which do not have MFN status are ineligible for U.S. government credits, credit guarantees, or investment guarantees. MFN status is viewed by the United States as a privilege, as a sign of friendly relations, and not as a result of trade negotiations based on the respect of comparative cost principle or any other economic one.

There have always been two requirements for more favourable tariff treatment: East European foreign policies at variance with those of the Soviet Union and favourable to Western interests; and a measure of domestic economic, political, and cultural liberalization, including freedom of emigration for dissidents. Romania was an example of the former, and Poland and Hungary of the latter. This policy of "differentiation" was initiated in the second part of 1950s and remained the characteristic mark of U.S. policy towards East Europe until Reagan administration.

However, besides the partisans of differentiation policy there are many U.S. policymakers who argue that any form of Western support for improved economic conditions in Eastern Europe entails a counterproductive easing of the burdens of the Soviet Union, as well as legitimation of unsavoury regimes. They favour a policy of the-worse-the-better and generally oppose differentiation.

Consequently, liberalization in Eastern Europe is not always, and not always quickly rewarded, although such is the official long-term declared goal. Medium and short-term objectives prevail quite often over the long-term ones and, in practice, it is revealed as a passive U.S. policy toward Eastern countries.

This passivity might, to some extent, be ascribed to the small share of U.S. exports to the Eastern countries compared to total U.S. exports. In 1985-1987 it ranged between 0.36-0.29 per cent. The political importance of these countries far surpasses their economic importance in U.S. trade.

The events in Poland in 1956, and especially the "rightist" deviation represented by Gomulka, have been interpreted by the United States as a promise of desired changes, (i.e., political and economic liberalization, achieved through peaceful means). To encourage these changes, Poland was granted economic assistance beginning in 1957.

On November 16, 1960 President Eisenhower restored MFN status to Poland in the climate of improving bilateral relations, caused by the coincidence of such events as: the signing of an agreement to repay indemnities totalling $ 40 million to American citizens caused by nationalization, the declaration of Poland's access to the GATT, and the anniversaries of Chopin's 150th birthday and Paderewski's 100th birthday. The strenghtening of these bilateral ties was, of course, supported by the Congress of American Polonia.

Thus, Poland regained unconditional MFN treatment and at least until 1989 was a unique socialist country in this respect. [Editor's note: Romania renounced renewal of its MFN status in 1988 and Hungary received "permanent, non-waiver" MFN status in 1989.]

Poland's MFN status was suspended in November 1982, as one of the sanctions introduced after the imposition of martial law on December 13, 1981. The initial sanctions rapidly imposed at the end of 1981 were relatively moderate and did not include either suspension of MFN status or blocking Poland's admission to the IMF. The formal reason of the MFN suspension in 1982 was the delegalization of the Solidarity union and the unsatisfactory fulfillment of Poland's obligations towards the GATT. At the same time, three desired changes in Poland's behaviour were specified as conditions of lifting the sanctions: the termination of martial law; the release of political prisoners; and the renewal of dialogue among government, church and Solidarity officials.

Some years later (on February 19, 1987) unconditional MFN status was again restored because of economic and political liberalization in Poland. How much influence these sanctions exerted on the government behaviour remains a matter of dispute. It is widespread opinion in Poland, that they were too severe and too long lasting. They destroyed America's positive image in Poland which had been so persistently and successfully cultivated from the mid-1950s. Moreover, there was widespread opinion that the real reason for the U.S. sanctions was not the situation in Poland but rather the construction of the Urengoi natural gas pipeline in Western Europe.

Other regulations concerning imports from all of Eastern Europe have a rather discriminatory character. Provisions concerning the concept of market disruption, as well as those concerning procedures of investigation and counteracting measures, discriminate against East European countries in comparison with the provisions relating to market economies.[3]

The anti-dumping provisions, based on the concept of surrogate country prices or constructed value, also contain the assumption that merchandise from the state-controlled country cannot be the least costly. However, it is not always easy to properly evaluate the margin of dumping in the case of imports from non-market economies (NMEs).[4]

Although they are not currently used against NMEs, provisions concerning countervailing duties are potentially very discriminatory. Since these countries are not signatories to the GATT anti-subsidy code, investigations toward them can be conducted without proving the existence of injury test.

6.2 Export Controls

There are also a variety of U.S. export controls which are used to protect national security, promote foreign policy goals, and guard against short supply. The controls seek to classify exported merchandise into strategic and non-strategic categories of goods.

The provision of economic aid to Western countries in the form of the Marshall Plan of 1948, the formation of COCOM in November 1949, and the Battle Act of October 1951 permitted American export control regulations to be extended to the Western allies and, in consequence, exports of weapons and munitions, nuclear materials and goods of strategic importance were included in COCOM lists and multilaterally embargoed to Eastern bloc countries. In addition, the United States maintained unilateral controls including (since 1980) militarily critical technologies. Moreover, since the early 1950s the resale and transhipment of goods included on COCOM lists, as well as exports of these goods produced by U.S.-owned firms located outside the United States have also been controlled.

The ending of Marshall Plan aid in 1954 allowed a gradual relaxation of the multilateral embargo towards Eastern Europe but did not affect the main line of American export control policy. The apogee of warfare in export controls came in 1962 (the Cuban crisis) when, according to the Export Control Act of 1962, the president could ban any export promoting even the "economic potential" of the Eastern bloc countries. Export control policy was somewhat relaxed with

---

[3] Sec. 406, Trade Act of 1974.

[4] Sec. 773 Tariff Act of 1930, amended.

the 1969 and 1979 Export Administration Act. In the 1980s, however, regulations concerning exports of militarily critical technologies, as well as dual-use goods (i.e., those with both civilian and military applications) were tightened considerably in line with the Reagan administration's hard line against communism.

For most of the post-war period the president had practically unlimited freedom to impose sanctions for foreign policy reasons. This was highly criticized inside and outside of the United States. Economic sanctions were easily imposed in 1980 and in 1981-1982 (and not only on the socialist countries), destroying economic ties between the United States and some Eastern bloc countries. This policy of using the export ban to punish the trade partner and neglecting the importance of East-West trade development was termed "lightswitch diplomacy".

Sanctions were imposed at the expense of American as well as other Western producers. In 1981-1982 some compensation for farmers and contract sanctity provisions concerning agricultural products were legally assured. Later on, according to the Export Administration Amendments Act of 1985, exports of agricultural commodities were further protected from national security export controls.

6.3 Credit controls

The financing of exports to Eastern Europe has been strictly regulated during the post-war period. From 1945 to 1967 there was no U.S. governmental financing of exports to the socialist countries because of the cold war climate, even though there were no legal prohibitions. During this period only Poland obtained some credits from the Eximbank for agricultural products.

Legal limitations were in force from 1965 to 1967 and a legal ban was binding from 1968 to 1971. Under the regulations of 1971, exports to all socialist countries could be financed, and from 1972 to 1974, for instance, the Soviet Union obtained about $ 1 billion's worth of government credits, that financed some 43 per cent of its purchases during this period.

Conditional export financing to Eastern Europe was introduced by the Jackson-Vanik amendment which stipulated that only countries having MFN status could obtain U.S. government credits, credit guarantees and investment guarantees. As a result, since 1974 only Poland (until 1982), Romania (until 1987) and Hungary could obtain credits.

In the beginning of the 1980s these three countries had problems repaying their debts. In the case of Poland, the United States, as part of the sanctions package, made the rescheduling of goverment-backed debts in 1982-1983 more difficult, and even complicated their future repayment by opposing Poland's admission to the International Monetary Fund and its ability to obtain IMF credits. The financing of exports to Eastern Europe by private banks was limited during the whole post-war period by the Johnson Debt Default Act.

6.4 Overview of U.S. policy

Looking at U.S. trade policy towards Eastern Europe one should emphasize: one, the cold war origins of legislation that has permitted the United States to conduct a range of policy between selective detente and limited cooperation; two, the partial imposition of U.S. export and credit policies towards Eastern Europe on its Western allies; three, a distinct differentiation of East-West economic policy after 1974 largely based on the granting of MFN status; four, a clear avoidance of mutual economic interdependence between East and West; five, an emphasis on economic "sticks" as opposed to "carrots"; and, finally, the creation of some myths, such as the utility of economic sanctions, which only served to undermine U.S. East-West trade policy.

In the present period, a policy of competitive coexistence would be much more desirable. Such a policy would require a complete review of existing U.S. trade laws in order to base East-West trade on the principle of comparative advantage.

6.5 Change in Poland

In the second half of the 1980s [before the series of revolutions at the end of 1989] at least two East European countries, Hungary and Poland, had substantially transformed their economic, social, and political systems. The pace of further changes is significant.

In Poland's case we may distinguish three main waves of economic reform. The first started in 1981-82 and included significant changes, such as the abolition of central directives in planning, the initial liberalization of enterprises, the introduction of freely determined categories of prices, the enactment of uniform commercial exchange rates, and the mergers of some branch ministries.

The second was introduced in 1986 when radical changes were made in the organization of the central authorities. This period was characterized by an elaboration of large reforms in the economic sphere and some in the political sphere. In the former, the reforms further liberalized enterprises, stimulated entrepreneurship, increased the scope of the market, and aimed to convert the zloty. At the same time it became clear that economic reform had to be followed by political reform, and changes were made by establishing a State Tribunal, a Constitutional Tribunal, an ombudsman's office, and some advisory bodies (in the Sejm, the State Council, and elsewhere).

The third wave of reform, thus far, was initiated at the end of 1988 and involved the process of "deep reform of the party itself", and forming a "pluralistic society" and a "socialist market economy".

The roundtable process started in 1989 will most likely result in the legalization of Solidarity; new elections to the parliament with a controlled move to democracy (about 40 per cent of seats would be allocated to the opposition parties); depoliticization of the economy and society; an independent judiciary; free registrations of associations respecting the constitutional order (there are already about 2,500 registered associations); freedom of publications; and the creation of self-governing local councils.

In the economy the general idea is to introduce as much market as possible and as much planning as necessary (especially strategic planning). Much has already been done. At the end of 1988 the so-called economic constitution was adopted. This law equalized legal treatment of all sectors of the economy (state, cooperative, private) in terms of taxes, material supply, credits, etc. This law permits citizens to undertake an economic activity, private enterprises to employ unlimited number of workers, and (with some exceptions) foreign trade to be freely undertaken; meaning the abolition of the foreign trade monopoly.

The zloty is to be made convertible in stages by limiting the central financing of imports from the hard currency areas (35 per cent of imports in 1989) and by a foreign currency auction system now being used to set a free exchange rate. The banking system has been separated from the Finance Ministry, and nine new commercial banks have been created which will start to compete and offer a variety of services. Interest rates have been increased to the level of planned inflation (40 per cent at base). The foreign investment law allows foreigners to set up 100 per cent foreign-owned joint stock companies or a joint venture with a Polish state or private partner, and engage in any business with the same rights as a Polish enterprise. In short, the free market has become the new orthodoxy, even with some exaggeration and excessive glorification of market forces.

The transition from a centrally planned to a market economy engenders high inflation, and requires some reserves of hard currency and support for the best enterprises. At the same time foreign debt service constitutes too big a burden for the economy (in 1988 the hard currency debt service ratio was 17 per cent), especially since imports from hard currency areas must grow.

The promotion of market forces in Poland requires a new Marshall Plan or new forms of assistance in the realization of a policy of differentiation. First, Western governments under the aegis of the United States could consider debt relief in the context of far-reaching reforms in some socialist countries. In Poland's case, reducing interest rates on old debt and further restructuring of debt owed to the Paris Club governments would be useful.

Second, the IMF, World Bank and other financial institutions could make credits conditional on specific reforms, for instance: reducing the central bureaucracy, promoting largely independent market (goods, capital, foreign exchange, labour) mechanisms, liberalizing rules for foreign investment (direct and portfolio), and developing the banking system. Loans could be smaller, granted to specific pro-export, pro-market projects.

Third, there is an enormous need in Eastern Europe for training in industrial management, bank management, and English and other Western languages. Western societies, foundations, banks, enterprises, and private citizens could significantly assist in these matters.

6.6 The prospects for policy change

The new situation in Eastern Europe is undoubtedly a challenge to the United States and other Western governments. Are they adequately prepared to cope with it? What are possibilities and prospects for constructive change?

Eastern Europe has only been ranked high among Western policy concerns in times of crisis, and even then not for long. Besides, there is a bitter conviction among the people of Eastern Europe that, in spite of political declarations, Western governments appreciate changes in the formal international status of governing elites while insufficient attention is paid to the evolutionary transformation of these societies and their changing aspirations. The liberalized passport policy of Polish authorities, for instance, caught Western countries completely unprepared. The danger exists that a similar situation may occur regarding economic reform. Are Western countries prepared to facilitate and encourage the transition to a market economy? Are their economic policies towards Eastern Europe cooperative or conflictual? The Western countries should consult regularly to make a joint assessment of the conditions and prospects in Eastern Europe in order to coordinate their policies.

Finally, what of America's leading role among Western countries in this crisis situation? At present there is opportunity to play this role in a positive, new way. The United States may need to develop special guidelines to normalize its economic relations with those East European countries reforming their structures; especially for participation in large investment projects.

Formal revision of American foreign economic legislation towards Eastern Europe is also necessary. For instance, at the time of writing, the Jackson-Vanik amendment remains in force while there are no barriers to emigration from the currently reforming socialist countries. The temporary granting of MFN status for one year periods stymies the permanent development of foreign trade. It is not right that imports from all socialist countries are submitted to the same regulations while the functioning of their economies is so different.

Chapter 7

U.S. EAST-WEST ECONOMIC POLICY: A SOVIET VIEW

Nikolai Shmelev[1]

Entering the last decade of the 20th century, both East and West face a choice which is no less momentous (if not more momentous) than that they were confronted with after the end of World War II. How should they conduct their economic relations in an interdependent world? What guidelines, principles and mechanisms will best serve their long-term national and international interests as the world economy burdened by the weight of global problems undergoes profound technological change? The solution of these problems would to a large extent define the world economic order of the next century and the prospects for military confrontation being superseded by the binding forces of the international division of labour.

The United States, being the military and economic leader of the West, has to make an important choice too. The four decades that have elapsed since the end of World War II have shown that a bipolar world based on superpower confrontation offers too few opportunities for productive East-West economic relations. Of course, the fundamental differences between the market economies of the West and the administrative economies of the East also impeded progress. And it is true that the policy of military-strategic competition has left a deep imprint on the modus operandi of both the United States and the Soviet Union regarding trade and technological cooperation.

However, one cannot be blind to the fact that, with rare exceptions, American policy towards East-West economic cooperation has been devoid of constructive objectives, leaving no room for mutually acceptable compromises. "The worse it is for the East, the better it is for the West" type of thinking has dominated American policy both during the times of a relative improvement in East-West economic relations and during the times of crises unrelated to economic cooperation. The United States has made trade hostage to its military and political interests in their relationship with the East.

The steady decline of bilateral trade has been largely the result of such an approach. Trade is mostly limited to our purchases of American grain. Exports and imports of other types of products remains at a level which is more like a

---

[1] Institute of U.S.A. and Canada Studies, Academy of Sciences of the USSR, Moscow, USSR.

de facto cessation of trade. The United States accounts for no more than 1 per cent of Soviet trade, while the Soviet Union accounts for just 0.5 per cent of the American turnover.

The general environment of East-West economic relations is not much better. Socialist and capitalist countries account for three-quarters of world industrial production, while their bilateral trade is just 4-6 per cent of world commerce. The United States accounts for less than 10 per cent of Western turnover with CMEA countries.

However, the East-West climate is changing rapidly; indeed, in many important respects it has changed already. The transition to a multi-polar structure of the world economy and politics, and less emphasis on military capability as a factor of a country's power are coupled with an increasingly evident trend both in the East and in the West towards a more open economy and a greater integration of economic resources and factors of production. Both East and West are increasingly often making a choice in favour of the entrepreneurial initiative of enterprises, whereas the rigid administrative methods of organizing national and international economic relations are justifiably rejected as antiquated.

Transnational entrepreneurship is increasingly superseding simple and short-term forms of economic relations between independent parties in different countries. East-West interdependence is acquiring a new dimension. It is defined not only by the existing economic relations but also by a growing similarity between economic priorities and methods of organizing the economy. The growing opportunity costs of foregone economic opportunities, which take the form of a slower adjustment of national economy vis-à-vis the internationalization of science, technology, information and social flows are another dimension of interdependence.

Perestroika, which is based on a realistic analysis of both national and international trends, is creating tangible conditions for a breakthrough in East-West economic relations. First, the economic reforms in the Soviet Union make its national economic priorities and organizational structures more like those of the West. These changes are especially apparent in the Soviet foreign economic sphere as enterprises are getting new freedoms to do business autonomously in internationally recognized ways. The December 1988 Council of Ministers guidelines abolished ceilings on Western participation in the capital of joint ventures created in the Soviet Union, gave every competitive enterprise, organization and cooperative free access to world markets, outlined a stage-by-stage introduction of rouble convertibility, and adopted internationally recognized methods of conducting trade and foreign economic policies. This is a major step in the right direction. The Soviet, Hungarian, and other national models of transition from the administrative-type to a market-type economy reduce economic incompatibility as a barrier to expanded East-West economic relations.

Second, perestroika leads to a serious re-appraisal of the Soviet Union's national security doctrines, primarily that of its central military component. It has resulted in agreements on medium-range missiles and Afghanistan, unilateral Soviet cuts in military forces, and a number of other well-known Soviet proposals aimed at lowering East-West military confrontation.

Third, the movement towards greater democracy in Soviet society has broken down the wall of East-West misunderstanding regarding humanitarian issues which the United States and its allies used to employ as pretext for restraining economic relations.

Fourth, the Soviet Union and other socialist countries have clearly stated their intent to become involved in the activities of international economic organizations which are dominated by the United States and their Western allies. This is not intended to drive a wedge between the participants but, rather, to look for new constructive solutions to problems which burden the world technological, trade, and financial regimes today. This is the spirit in which one should view the establishment of a dialogue between the CMEA and the EC.

Thus, the Soviet Union and its allies have made practical rather than rhetorical steps towards erasing the "enemy image" in East-West relations. But is the United States prepared to meet it halfway?

Indeed, some positive developments are already evident. But, with rare exceptions, they have not involved East-West economic relations as U.S. policy is dominated by old stereotypes rather than by the seeds of new thinking. If one looks exclusively at the facts, then one is bound to see that today the U.S. export controls remain in place the way they were during the crisis period of the early 1980s. Moreover, the scope of the Western export control regime has even broadened as the newly industrializing countries (NICs) are pressured to join it.

The Soviet Union and a number of other socialist countries continue to be discriminated against in terms of trade and credit regimes. The United States continues its old East-West "containment" policy in economic relations which is even directed against U.S. allies which are ready to respond to opportunities offered by the economic and political change in the East.

For now [April 1989] the official choice of Washington in terms of East-West economic relations gravitates towards the old pattern which is the legacy of the confrontation period; the "stop and go" policy is highly probable to survive in bilateral economic relations. It looks like West European and Japanese governments which are tied to the United States commercially, financially and technologically are closely watching the U.S. lead.

No wonder American business has adopted a "wait-and-see" stance in the absence of a clear lead from Washington. Right now, as in the past, U.S.-Soviet trade is limited to a single commodity, while the United States stands as low as fifth on the list of the Soviet Union's trade partners. American firms are playing second fiddle to those of West Germany, Finland, Italy, and Austria. Even in such a promising field as joint ventures, they have fewer projects going. One can understand Soviet businessmen and officials engaged in planning foreign trade who view with anxiety the prospects of developing full-fledged economic relations with the United States. Commercial risks because of possible discriminatory actions on the part of the U.S. government are much higher than is the case of the more predictable West European partners.

One could continue looking for more or less plausible arguments which explain the United States' reluctance to take the lead in normalizing East-West economic relations. Of course, one could continue waiting for more serious breakthroughs in arms control and for better results of the economic reforms in the Soviet Union and in other socialist countries. But the favourable climate which has developed in international relations in the late 1980s may never occur again. No one can guarantee that the momentum in arms control negotiations can be sustained. The rapid development of East-West economic ties through greater trade, technological and industrial cooperation and through joint ownership of assets could preclude possible crises in non-economic East-West relations. Past experience shows clearly enough that political relations cannot become stable unless there is also simultaneous economic rapprochement and a greater degree of cooperation in solving world economic problems.

One cannot help agreeing with the noted American expert John Hardt:

If the United States and the Soviet Union begin, for the first time, to place East-West commerce in the framework of a global commercial policy viewed as critical to the domestic performance of each economy, the superpowers may move with their allies toward a trend of long-term commercial normalization... For the United States the questions of trade, credit and technology transfer may be taken off the agenda of divisive policy issues in COCOM, NATO and the OECD.[2]

Hardt notes with justification the beneficial impact of trade normalization on arms control and on lowering tensions in the Soviet and U.S. relationships with their respective allies.

What is the realistic alternative to current U.S. East-West economic policy? The time has come for economic relations to no longer be completely subordinate to political relations. The objective should be to make economic relations into a separate, independent component of U.S.-Soviet relations and to depoliticize economic relations. This implies that the United States should no longer use economic relations to gain unfair advantages and concessions and should give up using embargoes and sanctions for political purposes.

Thus, there is an imperative need to put trade issues on the agenda of Soviet and American government leaders; issues which have not been discussed at a sufficiently high level since the 1970s. Unlike other spheres of the bilateral relationship, there are not even the beginnings of a common intergovernmental approach to the future of economic and technological relations.

Of course, such an approach should be built on the principles of reciprocity. Since the Soviet Union is going to introduce tariff and non-tariff instruments of regulating trade, the Soviet Union, the United States, and their allies could immediately start work on granting each other MFN status. One tends to agree with American experts who say that MFN would not lead to a rapid growth of Soviet exports. However, such a step would radically change the general climate of the trade and political relationship and create a basis for a future economic rapprochement.

There is a perceived need to create a long-term legal framework which would protect the interests of businesses that conduct joint activities and invest capital in the economy of the other party. A special system of mutually agreed safeguards would be needed in order of liberalize technological transfers and joint R&D activities.

As a rule, East-West technological exchange is viewed in the United States in the context of export controls on high technology transfers to the Eastern bloc. There seems to be a bias in favour of U.S. government intervention in

---

[2] John P. Hardt, "Perestroika and Independence: Toward Modernization and Competitiveness". Comments for Panel of the U.S.-USSR Trade and Economic Council Meeting, Moscow, April 1988, p. 18.

terms of national security, foreign policy, and so on. Such an approach could hardly be called constructive from the point of view of stimulating the development of world science and technology.

Only the United States and the Soviet Union possess R&D capabilities which make it possible for them to conduct R&D in all the spheres of global scientific and technological problems. Despite serious obstacles in the way of scientific contacts, Soviet and American scientists and engineers are generally familiar with the main patterns of research done in both countries. In this connection, ongoing information flows would be highly desirable for mutual scientific advancement. However, this is a passive process and does not preclude duplication of R&D and does not create conditions for joint work.

The U.S. curbs on technology transfers lead to a inadequate functioning of inter-firm and inter-governmental technological cooperation mechanisms. The participants in these projects always face the danger that the U.S. government can arbitrarily annul all this. The U.S. ban on the use by General Electric and General Motors of Soviet rockets to launch communications satellites and other non-military hardware is a recent example of this. The growth of the international division of labour in science and technology is an objective trend. One cannot ignore this fact. On the other hand, one cannot ignore the complicated nature of the relationship between the superpowers. This is why scientific and technological interaction must be based on a most important principle: the technologies transferred and the results of joint R&D activities must stay within the civilian economies. Mutual commitments based on a mutually acceptable inspection regime do not sound too far-fetched now in the light of the procedures involved in the medium-range missile treaty.

The initiatives of businessmen alone may be not enough to give an impetus to East-West economic relations. The inertia of the confrontation period may be too great. Businessmen who are getting involved in East-West trade for the first time know too little about the peculiarities of the two economic systems and of their commercial practices. It would be difficult to break down these barriers without judicious government support. This is why economic and psychological support on the part of governments of both domestic and foreign companies who are newcomers to East-West economic relations is especially necessary.

All these efforts can bear fruit only when East-West economic relations are freed from ideological prejudices and cease to be hostage to military confrontation. The choice which the two systems face would define the future degree of bilateral openness of their economies. This choice would depend to a large degree on America's priorities in its economic relations with the East.

One has to reiterate that the economic reforms conducted in the Soviet Union would accelerate its movement towards an open economy and a more active integration into the world economy. But conditions for a secure and mutually beneficial economic cooperation of all states can be created only by joint efforts. This is why assistance for the Soviet Union's integration into the world economy is in the national interests of the United States and all the countries of the world.

The scale of possible changes which can be caused by the Soviet Union's integration into the world economy bears absolutely no comparison to the subordinate status of the economic issues in the bilateral relationship. The dominant attitude in the United States is to treat economic issues as something of secondary importance, although not everyone shares this approach.

It is becoming increasingly imperative to treat economic issues as a separate and highly important aspect of the East-West relationship. This in- volves beginning a serious dialogue on the main political and organizational issues of the Soviet Union's participation in the world economy. In other words, good political conditions for an economic rapprochement must be created. This is true both of bilateral and multilateral cooperation.

For instance, changing U.S. attitudes towards possible Soviet participation in the IMF, GATT and the World Bank are highly important. Up until now, the U.S. attitude has been a negative one. Three reasons are given for this: first, the Soviet Union is bringing politics into such organizations, which make it more difficult to deal with substantive issues; second, if the Soviet Union joins these organizations, it will gain unfair advantages; and third, the Soviet economic system is incompatible with the principles of the organizations' operations.

This attitude can be partially explained by Soviet actions in the past. How- ever, the most important factor is the entrenched idea that isolating the Soviet Union from the world economic system is the best policy. The continuation of mistrust and animosity would be the most likely outcome of this policy. But this is not in the national interests of the United States.

There is another approach, which is little different from total rejection. It is based on the traditional notion that the normalization of bilateral relations and changes of attitude towards cooperation are a kind of American favour to the

Soviet Union which has to be paid for in military and political coin. First, such a policy is counterproductive not only towards a greater power but also towards the overwhelming majority of the nations. Second, Western support for the changes in the Soviet Union can facilitate these adjustments, (although this is not the decisive factor that determines the economic situation of the Soviet Union). Third, all countries will equally benefit from the integration of the Soviet Union into the world economy.

One cannot ignore the existence of very real and knotty problems and objective difficulties which impede our progress towards a mutual economic rapprochement. A serious and unbiased analysis of the attitudes of the parties and a gradual removal of mutual misunderstanding and a search for compromise would be most advantageous. The logic of growing international interdependence demands increasing a search for ways to make the world trade and financial systems more homogenous and to mould its institutional underpinnings in a way which would take into account the interests of the whole of the world community.

A search for new approaches to the solution of the major international economic problems in terms of the new level of interdependence is in order. It is clear that the world economy increasingly needs effective inter-governmental coordination. But it is equally clear that such regulation cannot be based on restrictive agreements or involve only a limited number of nations.

One has to balance different conflicting but, nevertheless, quite genuine interests of the international economic actors, without this one cannot hope to achieve a stable and harmonious development of the world economy. More and more American experts and politicians share this view. For instance, New York Governor Mario Cuomo stated that:

> To survive and prosper in the years ahead we must understand the diversity of ways in which nations organize their economies and conduct trade; ways markedly different from our own.[3]

As economic problems become increasingly global in scope, the dialogue aimed at a joint search for a mutually acceptable way of solving them should also become more global. This dialogue should be as intensive as those on military and political issues.

In this regard it would appear worthwhile to conduct annual summit meetings involving representatives of all groups of states in addition to the

---

[3] *The Cuomo Commission Report* (New York, 1988), p. XXIII.

summit meetings of the seven leading capitalist countries. Thus, it would appear important to determine the actual contribution of individual countries to world economic stability and to discuss collectively the domestic economic problems which acquire an international dimension.

Regardless of the policies of the United States, the Soviet Union's position in the world economy will not change rapidly. However, the upshot of closer political cooperation will be felt immediately. This would make a strong positive impact on the complex of factors which determine the development of modern international relations.

We must think together about ways of adjusting to the changes in the structure of international economic relations. No single state can halt the objective flow of events. In any case, the openness of the Soviet economy will increase. However, unless there is political support, this process can be full of conflict and pain. Thus, the creation of a firm political foundation for new mechanisms of economic interaction, mechanisms that would allow the world community to face the 21st century in a civilized way, is becoming a practical issue.

COMMENTS ON PART II

Friedrich Levcik[1]

Two U.S. authors and two economists from the Soviet Union and Poland have prepared chapters on U.S. East-West trade policy. It is obvious that the two Eastern papers are critical of U.S. government policies on East-West trade while the U.S. papers concentrate on explaining U.S. governmental attitudes. Even from a West European vantage point some aspects of U.S. policy leave one unsatisfied and puzzled. To some extent past U.S. policy has simply been a reaction to events in the East but what is particularly puzzling is the persistence of old thinking in the face of unprecedented new developments in some CMEA countries, including the Soviet Union.

The papers by Hansen and Kaufman cover largely the same ground. They give a detailed and well-informed description and analysis of the ways in which U.S. East-West trade policies have been and are being shaped. The analysis of

---

[1] Professor of Economics, University of Vienna and Consultant at The Vienna Institute for Comparative Economic Studies, Vienna, Austria.

the interplay between the Administration and the Congress, the often differing attitudes and policy positions among principal government agencies, and the dependence of Congress on its constituencies and lobbies was very enlightening to me and to other European participants at the Workshop. However, the U.S. authors did little to come up with some forward-looking, fresh ideas about possible U.S. policies in the face of new developments in the East.

Shmelev's short paper does not provide a thorough analysis of past U.S. East-West economic policies and the Soviet Union's responsibility for these developments. It discusses present U.S. East-West trade policies in a cursory and naturally critical manner, and concentrates mainly on normative issues: how U.S.-Soviet trade and overall economic relations could be normalized in view of new developments and government attitudes in the Soviet Union. In this part of his chapter Shmelev comes up with some interesting suggestions which warrant further discussion.

Dr. Plowiec from Poland pays more attention to past developments. She adds useful information on the U.S. policy of "differentiation" towards individual Eastern countries. East European foreign policies at variance with those of the Soviet Union, or domestic liberalization measures, including freedom of emigration for dissidents, were and are rewarded; compliance with Soviet policies are punished. Her main thrust is to plead not only for a normalization of U.S.-East European trade policies but specifically for a new "Marshall Plan" or some other new forms of assistance for the reformed economies of Eastern Europe and mainly for Poland in the pursuit of a differentiation policy.

The two American authors will probably agree on the following crucial issue: how to balance the possible economic and perhaps even political benefits of normalized East-West trade for the United States with the risks for Western security. According to general opinion in the United States, as reflected by the authors, East-West trade is not to be judged solely by the mutual economic advantage gained; it has to be assessed together with the need to protect militarily significant technology, to secure some foreign policy aims, and to gain concessions on human and religious rights in the Soviet bloc. To be sure, all three issues are important not only to the United States but also to her allies and to the free world at large. In the CSCE Final Acts the three elements of security and disarmament, of trade and cooperation and of human rights form a whole but are being treated each on its individual merits. In U.S. East-West trade policy "linkage" and "leverage" prevail with the other elements. As one cannot immediately achieve all aims in the field of disarmament and in the liberalization process according to one's own wishes, trade and financial relations with the East must, for the time being, be discriminated against, restricted or even embargoed.

In a way the United States is economically hurt most by this insistence on "linkage" and on the broadest possible interpretation of national security. Dr. Hansen poses the question why U.S.-Soviet trade is so limited. But she sees the fault mainly through restrictions and impediments on the Soviet side. She maintains that the Soviets deprive themselves of imports. But her approach cannot explain why, with all the impediments governing East-West trade for all trade partners, Soviet trade with various West European countries is several times larger than U.S.-Soviet trade.

By the mid-1980s the United States became aware of the risk of unilateral action and tried to strengthen allied support for controls. It succeeded in tightening the enforcement of multilateral (COCOM) export controls, but had to back down on the extensive interpretation of the so-called "dual-use purpose" technology by agreeing to an export control policy of "higher fences" around fewer products. The United States also came to the conclusion that proposals to control with the allies general purpose commercial lending by Western banks to the CMEA countries would be unenforceable and therefore counterproductive. Also earlier attempts to extend unilateral export controls extraterritorially (in the pipeline controversy) had to be given up in the face of stiff opposition from the European allies. While Kaufman and Hansen generally agree in the descriptive and analytical parts of their chapters, one can discern a difference in approaches and attitudes when they come to the point of possible new U.S. policies on East-West trade in the face of the striking new developments in the Soviet Union and Eastern Europe. Hansen sticks to the old arguments and prejudices of the past by either disregarding new developments in the East or interpreting them in a way which justify an unchanged attitude of U.S. government policies. Kaufman sees "the need to rationalize and contain export controls, and to respond appropriately to Soviet actions and signals".

The difference in outlook becomes most obvious in the interpretation of the ongoing debates on keeping or waiving the Jackson-Vanik amendment to the 1974 Trade Act linking the acquisition of the MFN status and access to government credits to the right of citizens to emigrate from an Eastern country. In Hungary and Poland emigration is practically unrestricted; in the Soviet Union there has been a visible liberalization of emigration practices. Kaufman notices with satisfaction that the U.S. government has thus far responded correctly to signs of change in Soviet emigration policy by indicating a willingness to consider waiving Jackson Vanik. Hansen however advocates that "the U.S. must be prepared to rebut a Soviet push for a one-year trial waiver of the Jackson-Vanik and Stevenson amendments ... until and if sustained high levels of emigration are guaranteed".

Coming from Austria, a country directly bordering on several East European countries, and being confronted in everyday life with the problems of emigration from the East I should like to warn my American friends from continuing a policy of linking the permission of normal trade practices with the demand for "sustained high levels of emigration". As I had to emigrate twice in my life from my native land I have great sympathies with those who emigrate today. But Jackson-Vanik and similar trade restrictions connected with human and foremost with emigration issues are raising false hopes in the hearts of citizens in the East that the United States as the true champion of freedom is inviting all those willing to emigrate to come over and find there an open and secure refuge. By continuing the Jackson-Vanik amendment the United States is, however, neither able nor willing to absorb the growing stream of refugees from the whole world. In Europe resistance is also growing against an unmanageable flood of emigrees not necessarily persecuted but tired of the dreariness of life in a country of "real socialism". Austria is continuing its liberal and broad-minded policy of offering shelter to genuine refugees who have been forced to flee from political persecution. These refugees are receiving public support, permission to work, and will be fully integrated if they choose to stay. Austria also recognizes the right of all citizens to emigrate for whatever reasons but as a small country, with its own economic problems, it cannot support all who are leaving their country only for the reason to better their lot.

These people, not considered to be genuine refugees according to the Geneva Convention, are left without any public support. It is Austrian policy not to send back anybody to his native land against his wishes. But without public support these people are staying on without work permission and are forced either to work illegally or at cut-rate labourers wages, without health insurance and social security coverage, or else become objects of private or religious charity. Other European countries, larger and richer than Austria, have similar problems.

Is there an alternative to sitting on the fence, preserving or even tightening trade and credit restrictions, insisting on "sustained high levels of emigration", and waiting to see if and when reforms in the East are going to succeed? The opinion is growing in Europe that it may be in the interests of the West to support not only by words but by deeds the ongoing economic and political reforms in the East.

Nobody is suggesting that the West gives presents to the reforming Eastern countries. However, the giving up of discriminatory trade practices--with the exception of narrowly and well-defined export controls for security reasons-- debt relief and new credits for projects restructuring the economy, cooperation in science and technology, transfer of managerial skills with the help of joint ventures, training schemes, and similar measures could all help in strengthening the forces of reform and in overcoming the economic crisis. Such measures would also further the process of political reforms, and level the road towards freedom and democracy. It would give to the citizens of Eastern Europe new hope in finding a worthy destiny for themselves and for their children in their own country instead of seeking salvation abroad.

The West, and particularly the United States, should also facilitate the Eastern countries' integration into the world economy by allowing them to join the GATT, IMF, and World Bank, with the necessary safeguards. One could expect that by such a process the Eastern economies would become more open to world trade and to the rules of market economy coordination which also would support the social forces of reform. Obviously the Soviet Union should participate in such a general East-West rapprochement. Is there a risk in such an alternative policy? Nobody can give a guarantee that the political and economic reforms in the Soviet Union will succeed, but certainly they have a better chance in a setting of friendly cooperation than in one of animosity and of making things more difficult for them.

PART III - EASTERN EUROPE

Chapter 8

FOREIGN TRADE STRATEGIES IN EASTERN EUROPE: DETERMINANTS, OUTCOMES, PROSPECTS

Paul Marer[1]

This chapter has several purposes: to discuss the fundamental political, ideological, and systemic determinants of East Europe's foreign economic policies and outcomes; to provide an overview of East Europe's post-war economic relations with the West; to analyze developments in the CMEA and how they are linked with East-West economic relations; to call attention to major changes in East Europe's external economic environments, East as well as West; and to speculate about the future of the East European economies and of East-West relations to the year 2000.

East Europe is defined here as the six Central and East European members of the Council for Mutual Economic Assistance (CMEA): Bulgaria, Czechoslovakia, East Germany, Hungary, Poland, and Romania. An occasional reference is made to Yugoslavia.

8.1 Basic determinants of foreign economic policies and outcomes

Three of the fundamental determinants of the foreign economic policies and outcomes of the East European countries are: 1) the international political environment; 2) their leaders' set of beliefs, conditioned by historical traditions and experiences; and 3) the economic system and economic strategies.

---

[1] Professor of International Business, Indiana University, Bloomington, U.S.A.

The international political environment

The two main influences on East Europe's post-war foreign economic policies and outcomes have been politics in the Soviet Union and the status of East-West political relations.

After a brief period of normalization of Soviet relations with the West after World War II came the Cold War. The Soviet Union, preparing for the possibility of war with the West, was determined to extract maximum resources from Eastern Europe. Therefore, it forced the East European countries to devote immense efforts to defence production, which required building up their heavy industries. Heavy industries were also regarded as the unconditional bases of socialism. At the same time, the West, also preparing for the possibility that the Korean War might become a general war with the communist world, maintained strategic controls on a substantial part of East-West trade. Consequently, the East European countries, with the notable exception of Yugoslavia, had no choice during the Cold War but to orient practically all their trade to the Soviet Union and to each other, and to pursue domestic and regional autarchy.

Political relations between Western Europe and the Soviet Union began to gradually improve in the mid-1950s and U.S.-Soviet relations began to improve in the mid-1960s. Although there have been numerous ups and downs in those relations since then, the long-term trend has been one of improvement. That, in turn, has facilitated the normalization of commercial relations between the West and East Europe. On the one hand, the Soviet Union became gradually less concerned about the political implications of East Europe's expanding trade with the West. At the same time, the West also became less worried about the military implications of liberalizing trade with East Europe. In fact, improved economic relations with certain East European countries has been relied on by some Western countries either as a lever for normalizing political relations with those countries (an important motive, for example, for the FRG), or as a lever to try to loosen the Soviet hold on Eastern Europe (the main political motive of the United States).

Although even now, in 1989, political relations between the East and the West are not yet fully normal, since the early 1970s, they have been sufficiently normal for the level and composition of trade since then to be shaped largely by economic forces.

Economic system and strategies

During the 1950s, the external political environment (and assumptions by the East Europeans about the external environment) largely determined East Europe's foreign economic policies and outcomes. Since the early 1960s, the economic system and economic strategy variables have gradually become much more important.

The main *systemic* determinant of CPEs' foreign trade policies and outcomes has been the state monopoly of foreign trade which insulates domestic producers and consumers from foreign markets. As a result, the East European manufacturers' standards of innovation, quality, and service are determined largely by the requirements of the domestic "market". And since the actions of enterprises on the domestic market are driven largely by vertical dealings with a cumbersome bureaucracy rather than by horizontal, market-driven negotiations with customers and suppliers, the standards of quality, modernity, and service on the domestic market tend to be poor. Consequently, the East European countries are not, as a rule, very competitive with their finished manufactures on Western markets; they often have difficulty selling at competitive prices even semi-manufactured products. Initial gains of Western market shares by East Europe during the second half of the 1950s and during the 1960s - from an exceedingly low base, to be sure - were reversed during the 1970s and the 1980s. East European manufacturing and product standards have been falling further and further behind those of the market economies.

The so-called "comprehensive system reforms" introduced in Yugoslavia in 1965, in Hungary in 1968, and in Poland in 1982 have not yet altered the economic systems and policies even of these countries sufficiently to reverse their declining market shares and competitiveness in the West. Consequently, the East European countries were able to enlarge their capacity to import from the West only as long as they could increase the export of primary products and simple manufactures, or obtain credits.

The main *economic strategy* influences on CPEs' foreign trade policies and outcomes are: 1) maintaining growth rates that overheat the economy; 2) deploying a disproportionately large share of investment resources to mining, metallurgy, and other basic and heavy industries, at the expense of the infrastructure, manufacturing, the service sectors, and (in certain countries) agriculture; and 3) pursuing extreme versions of import-substitution. (In recent years, servicing the large external debt has also become important.) The economic strategy and economic system features are mutually determined and interacting.

These economies are pushed by the authorities toward unsustainably rapid rates of economic growth that *overheat the economy*. The main motives behind this strategy are a desire to catch up with the more advanced economies and the dependence of the regimes on good economic performance for political legitimization. The chief manifestation of this "rush for growth" is overly ambitious investment plans. That, along with the inefficient use of resources by enterprises, creates and maintains shortages. Shortages, in turn, swell the import bill and constrain exports. Setting overly ambitious growth targets at every level in the economy is one of the main causes of the sustained tensions in the convertible-currency balance of payments.

Investment allocation is not based on present-day realities. Just as military leaders often prepare to fight the last war, the authorities in Eastern Europe have worked hard to construct an economic structure similar to that erected by the main capitalist countries during the second half of the 19th and the first half of the 20th centuries. They gave sustained high priority to basic and heavy industries. Although Marxist ideology and Soviet-inspired military considerations have played an important role, especially during the 1950s, much of the blame for maintaining and enlarging an increasingly outdated and inefficient industrial structure lies with the authorities in Eastern Europe. Poor understanding of the forces that determine economic performance in the long run, the inertia that besets most large bureaucracies, unwillingness to tolerate temporary unemployment, and (probably most important) the lobbying muscle on behalf of basic and heavy industries of powerful vested interests (an alliance of union leaders, industrial workers, enterprise mangers, regional party leaders, and branch ministries) are among the main reasons for this state of affairs. The two main implications of an industrial structure that is increasingly out of date for foreign trade are a voracious appetite for energy, raw materials, intermediate products, and capital goods imports; and a loss of export competitiveness in Western and to some extent Eastern markets.

Import substitution is a reputable economic strategy under any economic system, unless it is extreme in scope and sustained for too long. The basic (and generally valid) idea is to provide *temporary* import protection to those *selected branches* of the economy where the country has a prospective comparative advantage, to enable infant industries to develop and eventually become competitive on the world market. At that point, protection is to be removed. But if a high wall of protection is built around the entire economy

122

and protection remains permanent, eventually costs will sky-rocket, enterprises become inefficient, exports lag, the balance of payments suffer, and the economy turn sluggish.

An economy that clings to extreme import substitution, sooner or later finds itself in a double catch-22 situation. Its balance of payments problems will become so severe that the authorities feel compelled to cut all but the most essential imports, typically using inefficient, bureaucratic methods. Hence, the economy remains protected and its growth constrained by perennial shortages and import bottlenecks. These may be temporarily alleviated through credits. But as the capacity to increase manufactured exports lags, the country's creditworthiness declines. At some point, the country will become insufficiently creditworthy to borrow abroad on the scale needed to modernize its outdated economic structure. This is exactly the story of each and every country in Eastern Europe (and in many countries in Latin America and elsewhere).

One of the main consequences of these systemic features and strategies is the persistent and growing tension in the East European countries' convertible balance of payments.

Another, much less visible consequence is that they are foregoing potentially large "static" as well as "dynamic" gains from trade. ("Static" gains are obtained when imports replace more expensive domestic substitutes and when export specialization reduces the unit cost of production; "dynamic" gains are long-term improvements in efficiency triggered when domestic producers are exposed to foreign competition and gain ready access to information as well as high-quality and cheap inputs.)

In CPEs, gains are foregone because imports are decided by the authorities (in the reformed economies, in part by enterprises) not mainly on the basis of what would be cheaper to purchase abroad than to produce at home but, rather, on the basis of shortages. The shortages are often the result of systemic and policy mistakes, not the country's comparative disadvantage. Many imports are purchased to obtain the investment resources needed to build and the inputs required to operate the large number of often uneconomical investment projects, decided upon by the bureaucracy and powerful lobbies, without anyone being accountable for the outcome. When the balance of payments constraint becomes binding, periodic export campaigns occur, disregarding costs of production as well as the resulting disruption in the domestic economy.

For these reasons, the static gains from trade are almost certainly much smaller in a CPE than in a market economy of comparable size and development level. And dynamic gains from trade are not realized at all. Foregoing potentially large gains from trade is a greater problem for the relatively small economies of Eastern Europe than for large economies, such as that of the Soviet Union or China.

8.2 Economic relations with the West: an overview

Main long-term trends

One must go back to before World War I to find "normal" East-West trade relations. During the inter-war period, East-West (as well as Soviet-East European and intra-East European) trade declined much more than world trade, owing to political considerations, the devastating effects of the Great Depression, and the unusually high level of import protection that the countries erected. During the 1930s, East European trade levels were, therefore, considerably below normal. East Europe conducted two-thirds of its trade with West Europe, exporting mostly primary products and importing manufactures.

East-West trade spurted briefly after World War II. During the first half of the 1950s, the Cold War reduced trade to insignificant levels. Intra-bloc trade, especially Soviet-East European trade, surged.

During the 1960s and 1970s, East Europe (as well as the Soviet Union) increased trade with the West faster than trade with each other. However, one must consider the low base from which the growth of East-West trade had begun.

Dollar trade values and shares

Table 8.1 juxtaposes East European and Soviet trade (exports plus imports) with the developed West. In 1987, the combined export and import trade of East Europe with the developed West was $ 47 billion, the same as in 1980. Whereas until the mid-1970s, East Europe's trade with the West was significantly larger than that of the Soviet Union. During the next decade Soviet trade became larger, owing to the rapid rise in energy prices, a commodity that dominates Soviets exports. But by 1987, Soviet trade with the West shrank to about the same level as that of East Europe's, this time owing to the decline in world fuel prices.

For the developed West, trade with East Europe accounts for about 2 per cent of total trade (another 2 per cent is with the Soviet Union), although for select countries (e.g., Austria and Finland) the shares are substantially higher.

124

Table 8.1

**East European and Soviet trade (exports plus imports)
with developed market economy (OECD) countries:
selected years 1950-1988**
(billions of current dollars)

	Eastern Europe	Soviet Union	Ratio: Eastern Europe/ Soviet Union (1):(2)
	(1)	(2)	(3)
1950	1.6	0.5	3.2
1955	2.0	1.1	1.8
1960	3.4	2.1	1.6
1965	5.2	3.1	1.7
1970	8.9	5.3	1.7
1975	26.7	22.2	1.2
1980	46.9	48.9	1.0
1981	40.2	50.3	0.8
1982	35.2	52.1	0.7
1983	34.5	50.4	0.7
1984	35.7	50.7	0.7
1985	37.2	47.3	0.8
1986	41.6	44.1	0.9
1987	46.9	45.2	1.0

Source: PlanEcon, *CPE Foreign Trade Data Bank*; United Nations, Economic Commission for Europe, *Economic Survey of Europe, 1987-1988* (New York: United Nations, 1988), p. 358; United Nations, Economic Commission for Europe, *Economic Bulletin for Europe*, 40, p. 99.

For CPEs, the trade shares accounted for by Eastern and Western trading partners cannot be accurately computed. This is because identical goods are traded at different prices on the two markets. Moreover, the prices in trade with the East and with the West move in divergent patterns, exchange rates are arbitrary and several cross-exchange rates are inconsistent.[2] In addition, accurate information on the quantities, the quality, and the prices of the goods traded is often not available. Nevertheless, it is not likely to be far off the mark to state that in recent decades, on average, approximately half of East Europe's trade has been with the East and about half with the West (defined here as including the developing countries.)

Romania was the first CMEA country to stake heavily on the West, back in the 1960s. Romania's decision was motivated by fear of excessive dependence on the Soviet Union under the CMEA integration formula proposed by Khrushchev. At the other extreme, Bulgaria has remained the most heavily dependent on the CMEA (especially on the Soviet Union), with which it has been conducting more than two-thirds of its trade. The divergent trade policies of Romania and Bulgaria may in part be traced to the fact that Romania historically has had an adversary relationship with Russia, whereas Bulgaria has always looked to Russia as a friend and protector.

Commodity composition

Chart 8.1a presents the commodity composition of East European exports to West Europe for 1955, 1973 and 1983. About half of what East Europe sells is comprised of manufactures (the share is greater for the more developed and smaller for the less developed East European countries), mostly semi-finished goods and standard, non-sophisticated industrial and consumer items. Primary products used to dominate the other half of exports (vide the bar charts for 1955 and 1973), more recently, fuel has become dominant (bar chart for 1983). The rapid rise in the share of fuel in East Europe's exports is accounted for not just by Polish coal or by the rise in fuel prices. Also important is that each East European country has felt compelled to export or re-export substantial quantities of energy - a commodity in which most of them do not have a comparative advantage (Polish coal being an exception) - because of the lagging competitiveness of their manufactures.

For the sake of comparison, *Chart 8.1b* depicts the commodity composition of Soviet exports to West Europe for the same years. The share of Soviet

---

[2] That is, the dollar-rouble cross exchange rates implied by an East European currency's exchange rates vis-à-vis the dollar and the rouble, respectively, may differ substantially from the official dollar-rouble exchange rate maintained by the USSR. This creates a host of difficult problems in bringing to a common dollar denominator the Eastern and Western trade flows of the individual CMEA countries.

manufactured exports declined from about one-third of the total in 1955 to about 10 per cent by 1983. At the same time, the share of fuel rose from one-fifth to four-fifths because both the export quantities and their prices rose rapidly. (Because fuel prices have declined since 1983, the share of fuel in the total must have declined, too.)

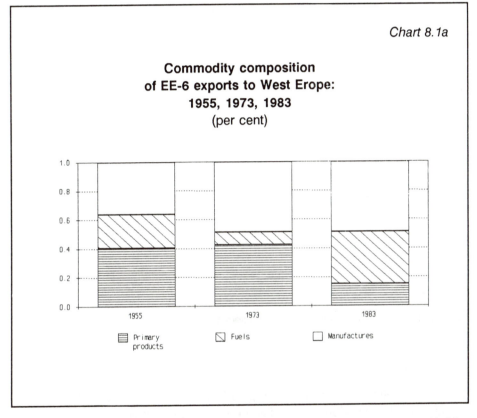

Source: Maurice Ernst and Paul Marer, *The Substitutability of Eastern Europe's Trade with Other Soviet Bloc Countries and with the West* (Indianapolis, IN: Hudson Institute), Charts V-1.

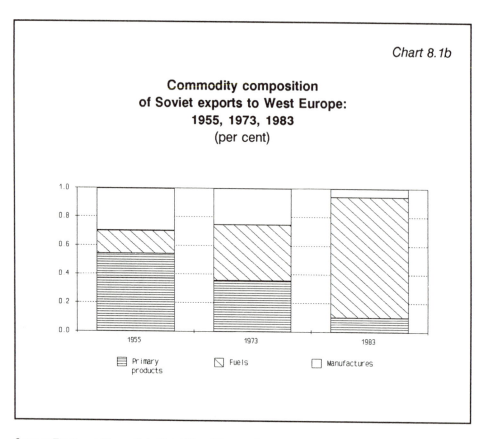

Chart 8.1b

**Commodity composition
of Soviet exports to West Europe:
1955, 1973, 1983**
(per cent)

Primary products   Fuels   Manufactures

Source: Ernst and Marer, *Substitutability of Eastern Europe's Trade*, Charts V-1.

Balance of trade, payments, and debts

To ascertain trends in East Europe's financial situation vis-à-vis the West, it is desirable to focus on "convertible currency" transactions, irrespective of the trade partner with which such transactions occur. Although most convertible-vertible-currency transactions take place with the OECD countries, substantial hard-currency balances are generated also in trade with the developing and the socialist countries. For example, since the 1970s, a significant share of Hungary's trade with the Soviet Union has been settled in dollars, with Hungary running large (though in recent years rapidly declining) positive balances. Most (perhaps all) East European countries settle their trade balances with China in Swiss francs.[3]

Table 8.2 presents the convertible-currency trade and current account balances of the six East European countries combined. Comparable figures for the Soviet Union also are shown. The balance on the current account is the best statistic on a country's balance of payments. A current deficit means that, in the given year, the country was a net borrower from the rest of the world; a surplus, that it was a net lender. The current account includes, in addition to exports and imports, trade in services (e.g., tourism, shipping), interest payments on foreign loans, as well as dividends and other remittances.

During the 1950s and the 1960s, the CPEs were not in a position to obtain large, long-term loans in the West; they had access only to short-term trade financing. Their access to credit improved dramatically as a result of detente, the willingness of the CMEA countries to settle outstanding financial claims against their countries, the need of the large commercial banks after 1973 to find new borrowers to recycle the OPEC surplus, and the desire of Western governments and businesses to promote exports by providing credit support. During the 1970s, the East European countries were considered highly creditworthy, based on two assumptions that lenders made. One was that since the money was borrowed or guaranteed by the governments, which were stable and in full direct control of their economies, there was no danger of default. The other assumption was that the Soviet Union (possessing vast and readily marketable natural resources and gold) would come to the aid of an ally in debt-servicing difficulties. This assumption was known as the "umbrella theory".

Between 1972 and 1980, the countries of East Europe were running large trade deficits, annually in the $ 2.2 to $ 5.4 billion range (column 1). Until 1979, current deficits (column 2) were smaller than the trade deficits because net revenues on the service account exceeded interest payments on the debt outstanding. But the debt was building up rapidly, making the East European countries highly dependent on the continued availability of large new loans, and exposed them to the risk of interest rate fluctuations. During the 1970s, the East European countries became "hooked" on credits. As with any addiction, the substance is enjoyed but eventually a price has to be paid.

---

[3] Details and computations can be found in Paul Marer, "Ungarns Außenhandel, Zahlungsbilanz und Schuldenentwicklung, 1970-1990", *Europäische Rundschau* (Summer 1988).

Table 8.2

**Convertible-currency trade and current account balances
of East Europe and the Soviet Union:
1970-1987**
(billions of current US dollars)

	East Europe		Soviet Union	
	Trade balance	Current account balance	Trade balance	Current account balance
	(1)	(2)	(3)	(4)
1970	-0.2	-0.4	0.4	0.9
1971	-0.3	-0.4	0.5	0.8
1972	-0.7	-0.5	-0.4	-0.2
1973	-2.2	-0.8	0.5	1.1
1974	-4.6	-2.7	1.6	2.4
1975	-5.4	-2.6	-4.5	-4.2
1976	-5.4	-2.6	-4.5	-4.2
1977	-4.4	-2.8	1.9	1.9
1978	-4.4	-3.2	0.9	0.8
1979	-5.0	-4.1	4.2	4.0
1980	-2.8	-6.6	3.4	2.8
1981	0.8	-5.1	-0.7	-1.7
1982	5.2	0.7	4.3	3.5
1983	5.7	2.2	6.2	5.9
1984	7.1	3.7	6.7	6.6
1985	4.0	1.3	0.7	0.6
1986	2.0	-0.9	1.4	0.9
1987	3.3	1.3	8.1	7.8

Sources: United Nations, *Economic Survey*, p. 359; United Nations, *Economic Bulletin*, p. 101.

Between 1980-1982, world interest rates rose dramatically. This affected not only new loans, but payments on total loans outstanding from commercial banks. In 1981, as Poland - and subsequently other major borrowers in other parts of the world - could not make the required payments and asked for rescheduling, a global debt crisis was triggered. That, in turn, closed for several years East Europe's access to new credits.

The East European countries, therefore, had no choice but to substantially reduce their imports (mainly by large cuts in investments) and to undertake campaigns to push exports. The export campaigns centered largely on drawing down stocks and diverting resources from the domestic market. As a result, East Europe was able to convert a $ 5 billion trade deficit in 1979 into a $ 7 billion trade surplus by 1984 (*Table 8.2*, column 1), a dramatic, $ 12 billion adjustment relative to a total convertible-currency import bill of about $ 30 billion.

During the 1980s, East Europe's balance of payments constraint became the visible cause of their deteriorating economic performance. But the balance of payments problem was only a symptom. Its main underlying causes were the reckless borrowing policies of the 1970s and the inefficiencies resulting from the economic system and strategy factors mentioned earlier. The sudden deterioration in the availability and cost of credits was not the fundamental cause, only a contributing factor.

The convertible-currency trade and current balances of the Soviet Union (*Table 8.2*, columns 3 and 4) reveal both greater year-to-year fluctuations and, on balance, relatively much less borrowing than by Eastern Europe.

Table 8.3 presents series on net convertible-currency debts and net debt-to-export ratios for each East European country, for the six combined and for the Soviet Union. Net debt is defined as gross debt (i.e., total borrowing) less gold and other convertible assets (mostly East European deposits in commercial banks located in the West). Net debt-to-export ratios are computed by dividing net convertible debt outstanding into convertible exports of the corresponding year. These ratios standardize the debt burdens of the individual countries, making it easier to analyze developments in a given country over time and to make inter-country comparisons.

A country's stock of net debt usually increases when it runs a current deficit (which must be financed via new loans) and decreases (or its foreign assets increase) when it generates a current surplus. But the current balance may not match changes in net debt if a country is adding to (or running down) its "reserves" (mainly gold and currency on deposit), exports on credit, or cannot collect on a timely basis the credits it had granted. Also important is the "foreign exchange rate adjustments". Since debt is expressed in U.S. dollars but some portion of it may in fact be denominated in other currencies, an "exchange rate adjustment" has to be made if the exchange rate of any of the other currencies moves against the dollar. For example, if debt is denominated in DM and the dollar declines against the DM (that is, one DM becomes worth more dollars), then the country's total debt expressed in dollars increases. Because during the 1970s and between 1985 and 1988 the dollar trended downward against many of the major currencies, many debtors, including those in Eastern Europe, had to make precisely this kind of an adjustment in reporting their total debt. (Between 1980 and 1985, during which the dollar appreciated, the adjustments were in the opposite direction.)

Table 8.3

Convertible-currency net debt and debt-to-export ratios of the individual East Europe countries and the Soviet Union: 1970-1987
(billions of current US dollars)

	Bulgaria	CSSR	GDR	Hungary	Poland	Romania	EE-Six	USSR
	(1)	(2)	(3)	(4)	(5)	(6)	(7)	(8)
Net debt								
1970	0.6	0.0	0.9	0.6	0.9	1.0	4.0	0.6
1971	0.7	0.1	1.2	0.8	0.7	1.2	4.8	1.4
1972	0.9	0.1	1.2	1.0	0.8	1.2	5.3	2.3
1973	1.0	0.2	1.9	1.1	2.0	1.5	7.7	3.4
1974	1.4	0.6	2.6	1.5	4.7	2.4	13.2	4.6
1975	2.3	0.7	3.6	2.2	7.7	1.4	17.9	12.2
1976	2.9	1.3	5.2	2.8	11.3	2.4	26.0	16.1
1977	3.3	1.9	6.6	4.1	14.5	3.4	33.9	18.3
1978	3.8	2.3	8.0	6.7	17.7	4.8	43.4	18.3
1979	3.9	2.8	9.2	7.1	22.6	6.9	52.3	17.3
1980	2.9	3.3	11.6	7.7	23.5	9.3	58.2	16.6
1981	2.4	3.0	12.3	7.8	25.2	9.9	60.6	20.5
1982	1.9	3.0	10.7	7.0	24.9	9.5	56.9	18.4
1983	1.2	2.6	8.7	6.9	25.1	8.4	52.9	16.0
1984	0.7	2.1	7.1	7.3	25.4	6.6	49.0	14.2
1985	1.4	2.3	7.1	9.5	28.1	6.3	54.6	18.3
1986	3.5	2.7	8.6	12.9	31.8	5.8	65.4	22.6
1987	5.1	3.5	10.2	16.2	36.2	4.3	75.6	25.3

Exchange rate adjustments as well as the other factors mentioned account for the fact that while between 1970 and 1980, the East European countries had a combined current deficit of $ 20 billion (*Table 8.2*, column 2), in the corresponding period, their net convertible indebtedness increased by $ 54 billion, from $ 4 to $ 58 billion (*Table 8.3*, column 7).

Table 8.3 (continued)

**Convertible-currency net debt and debt-to-export ratios
of the individual East Europe countries and the Soviet Union:
1970-1987**
(billions of current US dollars)

	Bulgaria	CSSR	GDR	Hungary	Poland	Romania	EE-Six	USSR
	(1)	(2)	(3)	(4)	(5)	(6)	(7)	(8)
Ratio: net debt to export								
1970	1.5	0.0	0.7	0.7	0.7	1.4	0.7	0.1
1971	1.4	0.1	0.9	0.9	0.5	1.5	0.7	0.3
1972	1.5	0.1	0.8	0.9	0.4	1.1	0.7	0.4
1973	1.4	0.1	0.9	0.7	0.8	0.9	0.7	0.4
1974	1.4	0.2	0.9	0.7	1.2	0.9	0.9	0.3
1975	2.3	0.3	1.2	1.0	1.8	0.5	1.1	0.9
1976	2.6	0.5	1.5	1.2	2.5	0.7	1.5	1.0
1977	2.4	0.6	1.9	1.5	2.8	0.9	1.8	0.3
1978	2.2	0.7	2.2	2.1	3.1	1.2	2.0	0.8
1979	1.6	0.7	2.1	1.7	3.4	1.3	1.9	0.6
1980	0.9	0.7	2.0	1.6	3.3	1.4	1.8	0.4
1981	0.7	0.6	1.7	1.6	5.0	1.4	1.9	0.5
1982	0.6	0.6	1.3	1.4	4.5	1.5	1.7	0.4
1983	0.4	0.5	1.0	1.4	4.8	1.4	1.6	0.4
1984	0.2	0.4	0.8	1.5	4.6	1.0	1.4	0.3
1985	0.4	0.5	0.8	2.1	5.4	10	1.7	0.5
1986	1.4	0.5	0.9	3.1	5.7	1.0	2.0	0.7
1987	1.8	0.7	1.1	3.2	5.7	0.7	2.1	0.6

Source: United Nations, *Economic Bulletin*, Appendix Tables 10 and 11.

During 1982-1984, when new loans were not generally available to the CPEs and East Europe could not refinance the debt that was maturing, debt levels did decline (with assistance from the exchange rate adjustment), from $ 61 to $ 49 billion. Thereafter, debt levels rose rapidly again, at the end of 1987, standing at $ 76 billion. By contrast, the Soviet Union - which has about the same level of convertible exports as the East European countries combined (*Table 8.1*) - had a 1987 level of debt only one-third as high as East Europe, $ 25 billion (*Table 8.3*, column 8).

These generalizations about Eastern Europe hide substantial and fascinating differences among the countries. The tabulation on net debt-to-export ratios (lower part of *Table 8.3*) - which are less affected by exchange rate adjustments because the denominator (export earnings) is also adjusted - reveal the following:

Poland is in a class all by itself. It has the largest debt burden by far. Its debt is still growing, not because the country is obtaining new money but because the unpaid interest is capitalized.

Czechoslovakia has followed the most conservative borrowing policies throughout this period, and its debt ratio has been of the same order of magnitude as that of the Soviet Union.

Bulgaria had the highest debt-to-export ratio between 1970 and 1977. Thereafter, it made a spectacular voluntary adjustment, reportedly with Soviet assistance: obtaining from the Soviet Union and then reexporting substantial quantities of "hard goods", mainly fuel. This assistance must have ended by the mid-1980s. Between 1984 and 1987, Bulgaria's net debt increased seven-fold (from $ 700 million to $ 5.1 billion), with a corresponding rise in its debt ratio.

Between 1970 and 1981, Romania increased its net debt from $ 1 to $ 10 billion. Thereafter - angered by the constrained availability and increased cost of credits, as well as by IMF "conditionality" on new loans - Ceaucescu responded by pledging that he would repay all of the country's debt. He then proceeded to make good on the promise, pursuing an extremely severe austerity program at home, which created shortages resembling war-time conditions. By 1987 Romania's net debt was reduced by more than 50 per cent; by early 1989, all of its debts to commercial banks paid off in full. This is a record that no other heavily-indebted country in the world has matched.

The GDR was heavily into debt during the 1970s. However, it also made a rather impressive adjustment during the 1980s, bringing its debt ratio down to manageable levels.

Hungary's performance is surprising. Between 1973-1978, the authorities allowed debt to increase six-fold (from $ 1.1 to $ 6.7 billion), where the debt stayed until 1984. Between 1984 and 1987, net debt as well as the debt ratio more than doubled, partly as a result of exchange-rate adjustments. As a consequence, Hungary had become the region's second most heavily indebted country, and by a substantial margin, after Poland. Hungary's large debt hangs like the sword of Damocles over the country, hurting seriously its economic performance and reform prospects. Given the weakness of its economic base and export capability, paying in full the interest on the debt has required a decade of austerity, and no relief is in sight. That, in turn, is increasingly undermining, in the eyes of Hungary's population, the "reformist" course pursued by the leaders. The alternative would be to reschedule, which would also discredit the "reform" course, this time also abroad. While during the 1970s, excessive foreign borrowing (which can occur irrespective of a country's economic and political system) appeared to have boosted economic performance, during the 1980s, it has pulled it down, thereby discrediting Hungary's positive reform achievements.

8.3 Intra-CMEA economic relations

An understanding of the forces that shape East-West trade requires an analysis of how developments in the CMEA affect East-West economic relations. This section highlights relevant arrangements and outcomes in the CMEA.

Institutional role of the CMEA

As an institutional force, the CMEA is not really important. It has no supranational powers like the European Community. It has no authority to make or interpret rules (as does the Commission in Brussels). It has no financial institutions that have independent command over resources (as does the European investment Bank, for example). Its bureaucracy cannot wield influence over the economic decisions of the member countries. The CMEA is mainly a forum for largely public discussions, a platform for promulgating and administering rules and policy decisions that have been agreed upon previously and bilaterally. The term "CMEA" is, thus, merely a convenient designation to refer to the core group of its seven European members, and to the rules that the member countries have agreed to observe for conducting economic transactions with one another.[4]

Prices and gains from trade

Most important among the rules are those that concern the setting of prices for intra-CMEA transactions. Because the domestic prices and exchange rates

---

[4] A comprehensive description of how the CMEA operates can be found in Jozef van Brabant, *East European Cooperation: The Role of Money and Finance* (New York: Praeger, 1977) and *Socialist Economic Integration* (Cambridge: U.K.: Cambridge University Press, 1980). For an "insider's" view see Kalman Pecsi, *The Future of Socialist Economic Integration* (New York: M.E. Sharpe, 1981).

of the member countries are arbitrary and their currencies inconvertible, no CMEA country has been willing to accept the domestic costs or prices of its trade partners as the basis for setting intra-CMEA foreign trade prices. Instead, average world market prices of an agreed earlier period are used. The formula is periodically changed; currently it is a moving average of world prices of the previous five years.

To the extent that foreign-trade prices are adjusted in accordance with the agreed price formula, intra-CMEA prices and terms of trade follow, with a substantial lag, price developments on the world market. No comprehensive information is available on the details of how intra-CMEA prices are negotiated and adjusted or what they actually are, commodity by commodity and year after year, in the various bilateral relations.[5] But most experts will agree with the following generalizations:

The prices of primary products (fuels, raw materials, and standard agricultural products), whose Western prices can be determined quite unambiguously, are generally set and adjusted on the basis of prices and trends on the world market.[6] Therefore, large changes in world market prices and terms of trade, triggered by fluctuations in energy, raw material, and agricultural prices, are reflected, with a lag, in intra-CMEA prices and terms of trade. This is an important link between developments in the West and in the CMEA.

The prices of manufactured goods, especially those of complex or unique products, are much more subject to bargaining. Since the negotiations are not between supplying and customer firms but between the authorities, prices are primarily determined not by supply and demand forces, but by other considerations such as how a price change of one commodity would affect the prices or the quantities of all *other* commodities traded. During the late 1950s and early 1960s, intra-CMEA prices of manufactured goods were relatively high (as compared with intra-CMEA prices of primary products, taking price levels and price ratios on the world market as the base). Since then, however, the prices of many manufactures traded in the CMEA have not kept pace with

---

[5] This is one reason why there is much controversy in the West about the facts and their interpretation. Another reason for the disagreement is that different specialists in the West apply various standards to assess who gains and who loses, and how much, by trading at prices at which a given expert *assumes* that the CMEA countries are trading.

[6] To be sure, "special deals", such as fixing future prices on deliveries made to repay certain loans or foreign investment, can distort prices estimated on the basis of computed unit values (value divided by quantity).

price changes of similar products on the world market. Some of the lag can be accounted for by the deteriorating quality of intra-CMEA manufactures. Whether the prices of manufactured goods are still relatively high or whether they have by now become relatively low (as compared with price levels and ratios on the world market) is not clear; there is evidence to support either position. Most likely, sweeping generalizations about the relative prices of manufactures can no longer be made; prices now "depend" on a host of factors that may be specific to a given industry, product, bilateral relations, and time period.[7]

In any event, there is a consensus that even if intra-CMEA prices followed world market prices faithfully - which they do not - they would still not be equilibrium prices based on regional supply and demand pressures. This is one reason why prices do not - and cannot - serve as the basis for deciding which goods and what quantities should be traded in the CMEA.

Since prices do not equilibrate supply and demand pressures, other mechanisms had to be found to achieve balance. One is that each country places all tradable goods into various categories of "hardness" and "softness". The hardest goods are those that have large convertible-currency import content and for which there is excess demand in the CMEA (in most cases these are the goods that can be readily sold on the world market). The softest goods are those that have low convertible import content and in which there is large excess supply (because they are not readily marketable in the West at a good price or for hard currency). In most cases, countries are willing to export hard goods only against "payment" in other hard goods, and to import soft goods only against goods of at least equal softness.

Specialization and trade decisions

Prices in the CMEA do not as a rule reflect scarcities and are not the main basis for decisions on speicalization and trade. On what basis, then, are those decisions made?

---

[7] The most authoritative and detailed "inside" account of how prices are negotiated and what they are in Soviet-Hungarian trade can be found in Andras Inotai, ed. *The Hungarian Enterprise in the Context of Intra-CMEA Relations* (Budapest: Hungarian Scientific Council for the World Economy, 1986).

Specialization and trade decisions appear to be based on a combination of: resource endowment (e.g., oil and gas in the Soviet Union, coal in Poland, bauxite in Hungary, tobacco in Bulgaria); engineering considerations (the CMEA electricity grid and oil and gas pipelines); shortages (an eagerness to import from a CMEA partner any basic input or finished product that is domestically in short supply); a desire to achieve economies of scale (which often requires exports to other countries); and efforts to balance the bilateral accounts, (the import of almost any product being preferred over the granting of credits because interest payments are nominal and especially because, in a world of inconvertible currencies, the future purchasing power of the asset represented by a loan is uncertain).

Specialization based on resource endowment is a sensible basis for trade or import substitution. But CPEs have difficulty identifying the point at which 1) the marginal cost of, say, selling an extra ton of oil by the Soviet Union or ton of coal by Poland exceeds the marginal cost of some potential other export, and 2) the point at which the marginal revenue of importing, say, Soviet oil or Hungarian bauxite falls below the marginal revenue of importing some other product or producing import substitutes.

There are relatively few projects which can be decided on engineering considerations alone, so that it is generally not a good basis for trade.

Alleviating shortages is the main criteria for imports. But if the decisions that caused the shortages in the first place were economically unsound, then the gains from imports to meet those shortages will also be limited and in many cases may generate apparent rather than real gains.

The desire to achieve economies of scale is an excellent basis for specialization and trade, especially in manufacturing, provided that it involves products in which the country does not have a permanent comparative disadvantage. For the small and medium-sized economies of Eastern Europe, economies of scale requires sufficient foreign demand for their exportables within the CMEA. Such demand can be generated only if a prospective trade partner is willing to tolerate foreign competition; willing to give up domestic production of the item; or if it does neither, has a large enough domestic market to accomodate domestic producers as well as imports.

Large gains from *West* European integration after 1958 were generated by increased intra-industry specialization in parts and components, subassemblies, differentiated final products, and services. In most cases a firm in Western Europe chooses from among domestic and foreign suppliers on the basis of cost, quality, and other economic considerations. Not so in the CMEA, where a host of considerations constrain dependence on suppliers located in other CMEA countries. These include the methods of CMEA price formation (which do not facilitate exporters sharing with importers the gains from increased scales of production); the arbitrariness of prices (which does not permit ready calculation of the potential gains from trade that cheaper imports would yield); the inability of the authorities who make the deals to have sufficient information and effective instruments to micromanage this process. At the same time, enterprises have neither the incentives nor the opportunities to make strategic business decisions, since they depend more on the vagaries of vertical regulation than on the acumen of their horizontal dealings with customers and suppliers.

There are additional and perhaps even weightier reasons: intra-CMEA specialization and trade decisions are made when the five-year plans are negotiated. Given the time it takes to negotiate and implement an agreement, specialization decisions may have to be reached up to seven years in advance; an impossible task in most cases.

Probably the most important constraint on specialization and trade is past experience, which has shown that suppliers from other CMEA countries often deliver components that do not fit, ship products whose quality leaves much to be desired, and offer delivery terms that often leave the customer stranded. Although there are similar problems with domestic suppliers (which in part explains why enterprises in the CPEs tend to be highly vertically integrated, one of the main causes of their inefficiency), problems within a country are easier to manage through the bureaucratic channels. Since, as a rule, there is no effective recourse against suppliers located in other CMEA countries, it is best not to depend on them in the first place.

These are the reasons why such a small share of intra-CMEA trade is comprised of parts, components, and subassemblies. Instead, trade involves mainly an exchange of fuels, raw materials, and standard semi-manufactures that can be stockpiled or obtained quickly from the world market; and finished products where supply disruptions are more easily managed.

Obstacles to intra-CMEA trade in manufactures are greater among the East European countries than between each of them and the Soviet Union. The Soviet market is so huge that even when the Soviets maintain a large domestic production in the products imported from CMEA partners (as the Soviets customarily do), East European exporters are able to realize economies of scale. An example is IKARUS buses, Hungary's single most important export (by value) to the Soviet Union. Although the Hungarian firm is one of the world's largest producers and sells to the Soviet Union more than half of its output (14,000 buses a year), the product is readily absorbed by the Soviet market, along with the products of several large bus manufacturers located in the Soviet Union. At the same time, however, the economies of scale, both in assembly and in component production, remain limited. One reason is that because product standards and quality requirements are different in the Soviet Union than they are in the West, Hungary cannot export similar buses to the Soviet Union and to the West. The buses sold on the two markets use different components and, in terms of workmanship, are assembled differently. Even so, the buses that the Soviets import from Hungary are acknowledged to be much better than those produced in the Soviet Union. The same is the case for most light industrial goods and a portion of heavy industrial products.

Bus production in Hungary is much more vertically integrated and autarkic than are the operations of its counterparts in the West. Few bus components are produced on a scale sufficient to generate full economies of scale. Numerous attempts to enter into specialization agreements with CMEA partners to produce certain of the components have failed because of the unwillingness or inability of the prospective partners to meet required specifications. And no component that a Hungarian firm is able to manufacture in "reasonable" quality can be imported from the West, irrespective of costs, owing to Hungary's convertible currency constraint.

For all these reasons, IKARUS (and other manufacturers in the CMEA) gains less from being one of the world's largest bus producers than it would do if it did not face the pervasive constraints enumerated. This typical example shows why the gains from intra-CMEA trade are considerably less than in trade among market economies.

Commodity composition

Chart 8.2a presents the commodity composition of Soviet exports to East Europe; *Chart 8.2b*, that of East Europe's exports to the Soviet Union; *Chart 8.2c*, that of intra-East European trade. About half of Soviet exports to East Europe represents manufactured goods, the other half mostly primary products in the 1950s and mostly fuel by the 1980s. Although the share of fuel in the total has fluctuated as world fuel prices go up and down, during the last four decades, there has been a substantial shift, also in real terms, away from primary products and towards fuel. By the 1980s, more than 80 per cent of

Soviet imports from East Europe are manufactured goods (*Chart 8.2b*); about the same proportion as in intra-East European trade.

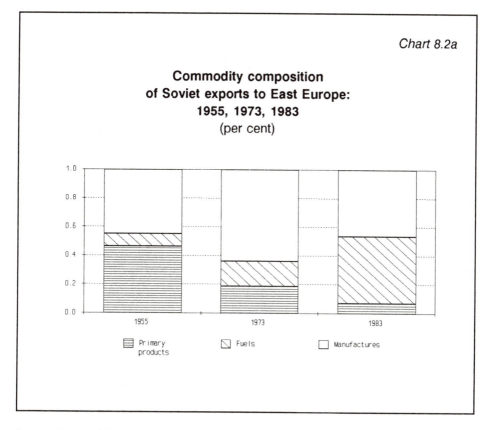

Source: Ernst and Marer, *The Substitutability of Eastern Europe's Trade*, Charts V-1.

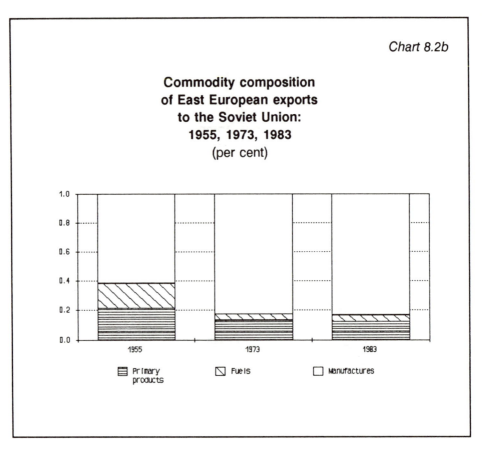

Chart 8.2b

**Commodity composition
of East European exports
to the Soviet Union:
1955, 1973, 1983**
(per cent)

Source: Ernst and Marer, *The Substitutability of Eastern Europe's Trade*, Charts V-1.

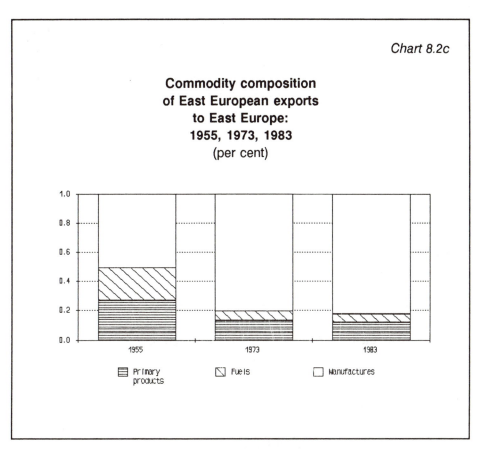

Chart 8.2c

**Commodity composition
of East European exports
to East Europe:
1955, 1973, 1983**
(per cent)

Primary products   Fuels   Manufactures

Source: Ernst and Marer, *The Substitutability of Eastern Europe's Trade*, Charts V-1.

CMEA integration: definition and motives

Integration in the CMEA has meant mainly each East European country specializing for the Soviet market, exporting (mostly) manufactured products in part for other manufactured products and in part for fuel and raw materials. During the 1950s, this pattern of trade was largely imposed by the Soviet Union, which specified in great detail the products it wished to purchase. East Europe was relied on to provide the Soviets the products they could not obtain from the West because of the embargo. Many were goods considered strategic at the time - ships, railroad stock, machine tools, instruments, engineering goods, telephone systems, special metal alloys - to mention but a few. The Soviet Union often provided the blueprints, the technology, and some of the inputs needed for their production.

During the past three decades, a subtle shift has taken place in Soviet-East European relations. Overall, imports from East Europe have declined in relative importance. At the same time, for decisionmakers in Eastern Europe, trade with the Soviet Union has remained at the centre of their economic development strategy. This shift in emphasis does not mean that in certain branches and for specific products, the Soviet Union does not remain heavily dependent on supplies from its CMEA partners or that it does not have strong preferences concerning what each East European country should specialize in.

The change has been one of emphasis and degrees of dependence. Ever since the 1950s, the East Europeans have been pressing the Soviets to export growing quantities of fuel, raw materials, and fuel and raw material-intensive semi-manufactured products, in exchange for standard quality, mass-produced finished manufactures. (East Europe has been much less enthusiastic about increasing the import of Soviet manufactures because much of what has been available is not the type or quality of product that is needed.)

Planners in East Europe have been motivated by the presumed large benefits of a continued rapid expansion of "their" type of trade with the Soviet Union. Such trade would provide much of the energy and material inputs required to build and operate the new industrial capacity that was being erected. The resulting products would be shipped mainly to the Soviet, East European, and domestic markets. This trade strategy was complementary to the economic strategies pursued by Eastern Europe. It was thought that the expansion of trade with the Soviets would help maintain impressive growth rates and full employment. Increased purchases of Soviet energy and raw materials would also support East Europe's Western exports, which had increasingly taken the form of standard metallurgical, chemical, textile, and other semi-manufactured products, with relatively low value added. In the 1970s, the rapid increase in world energy prices and subsequent recession in the West reinforced East Europe's commitment to this strategy because fuel and raw material imports sourced from the Soviet Union could, for a time, be obtained relatively cheaply and then reexported to the West (with some value added), at attractive prices.

These motives prompted East European planners and political leaders to exert maximum pressure on the Soviet Union to supply growing quantities of fuel and certain other basic products. Until the debt crisis of the early 1980s, annual and five-year plans for East Europe's domestic economies were "driven" by Soviet export commitments, which in large part shaped investment decisions, capacity utilization, exports to the West, and the rate of economic growth. (As other authors in this volume point out, several East European economies are now "driven" by their debt-service requirements and the need to maintain minimum living standards.)

CMEA integration and East-West commerce

This strategy and pattern of integration with the Soviet Union did not displace trade with the West. On the contrary, it increased rapidly East Europe's demand for complementary convertible currency imports. Much advanced technology, including a significant share of the machinery needed to build the new industrial capacity, had to be obtained from the West.

Paradoxically, more and more of the inputs needed to operate the new capacity also had to be purchased outside of the CMEA. In addition, growing quantities of grain and other agricultural products as well as high-quality consumer goods were sourced largely outside the CMEA. The convertible currency intensity of East Europe's light industry products (e.g., shoes, textiles, clothing, food products) - a significant share of the output destined for the Soviet market - has also been rising rapidly. To make matters even more difficult, during 1975-1985, East Europe's terms of trade vis-à-vis the Soviet Union deteriorated very substantially, as the 1973-1975 and 1978-1981 increases in world energy prices were passed through into CMEA prices. Although the Soviet Union did grant the East European countries terms of trade credits, the largest part of the terms of trade decline was financed by increasing the quantities of exports to the Soviet Union more rapidly than the quantities of imports. This increased further East Europe's demand for Western imports. During the 1970s, East Europe's lagging capacity to expand the export of high-value manufactured goods to the West was bridged by credits.

Consequences of the integration strategy

The consequences for East Europe of this pattern of integration in the CMEA were quite different in the short and medium run than in the long run. For some years, integration with the Soviet Union supported impressive rates of (what might be called) "quasi-growth": the expansion of production capacity and living standards that were not sustainable in the long run because of a rapidly growing and (by the 1970s) extremely high degree of dependence on both the Soviet Union for essential imports and markets and on the West for other essential imports and credits.

Excessive dependence means vulnerability to changes in the external environment. The degree of vulnerability is measured by the ease or difficulty with which an economy can adapt to inevitable changes in its environment.

8.4 Changes in the external environments and the consequences

During the 1980s, the East European countries had to contend with dramatic changes in their external environments; in the West and in the CMEA.

External environment: the West

In the West, one major change was the ending of easily available and large credits at negative real rates of interest.[8] This change - though perhaps not its suddenness - should have been foreseen by prudent policymakers, but most of them did not adequately prepare for it. The forced adjustment since 1982, impressive as it was, has clearly undermined the East European economies' long-term prospects.

Another major development in the West has been the accelerating pace of technical change, shortened product life cycles, and increased competition from Japan and the newly industrializing countries (NICs). Meeting these challenges requires flexibility and adaptability in economic structures and decisions at the macro as well as micro levels; the exact opposite traits, in fact, that characterize the economies of East Europe. The main culprit, of course, is the economic system. But the pattern of integration with the Soviet Union has made it possible for policymakers as well as enterprise managers to disregard developments on the world market and thus to fall further and further behind in their economies' ability to compete in the West. And since their economies' dependence on imports from the West was increasing, they became more and more vulnerable. The trends, clearly, could not continue.

---

[8] Real interest rates are nominal interest rates adjusted for average price changes in the debtor's convertible-currency exports.

External environment: the East

In the East, the major shock has been the change in Soviet foreign economic policy toward Eastern Europe. A brief background discussion will show why and how this came about.

The cost of producing fuels and raw materials in the Soviet Union has increased rapidly in recent decades relative to the cost of manufactured goods.[9] At the same time, as its trade with the West grew rapidly, the Soviet Union relied predominantly on fuel exports to finance needed imports (*Chart 8.1b*). As long as world energy prices rose rapidly, as they did between 1970 and 1981, the Soviets were in a position to increase imports from the West at a fast clip. Consequently, the *opportunity cost* of supplying growing quantities of fuel to East Europe remained reasonable, in spite of increased production costs. Between 1960 and 1980, the *volume* of Soviet fuel exports to East Europe increased by about 50 per cent every five years, almost 10 per cent per annum; exports to the West grew even faster.[10]

But when world energy prices declined (by about 50 per cent between 1981 and 1987), the Soviets were forced to accelerate the growth of fuel exports to the West (even so, they could not earn enough to maintain the volume of imports from the West). The combination of rapidly increasing costs since the mid-1970s and the need to increase exports to the West after 1981 greatly increased the opportunity cost to the Soviets of supplying additional fuel to Eastern Europe. As a result, Soviet fuel (as well as total) exports to East Europe have stagnated during the 1980s, except for the additional quantities sold to certain countries for convertible currency. The Soviets have stated publicly and clearly that this is not expected to change.

Gorbachev would also like the East Europeans to supply more consumer goods as well as investment goods that support new Soviet priorities and to pay for machinery imports from East Europe not with fuels and materials but with machinery exports. Paradoxically, while East European planners would often be willing to acquire Soviet investment goods, East European enterprises tend to resist such purchases because the items offered typically do not meet their requirements.

---

[9] Fuel production costs increased substantially in the mid-1950s, declined in the 1950s, declined in the 1960s and early 1970s as new, low-cost gas and oil deposits were developed, and increased greatly again since the mid-1970s.

[10] Ernst and Marer, *The Substitutability of Eastern Europe's Trade*, ch. V, section D.

147

At the same time, Gorbachev wants an across-the-board improvement in the quality of the goods the Soviets import from Eastern Europe. In most cases, this does not mean insistence on Western standards, but meeting more consistently the quality, delivery, and service aspects specified in the contracts. And, as the Soviet terms of trade with East Europe have declined (owing to the delayed effects of price developments on the world market), there are also pressures to lower the prices of East Europe manufactures.

The East European countries are generally not in a good position to comply with these demands, just as the Soviets are not in a strong position to enforce them. There are several reasons why the new Soviet demands appear to have no "teeth". First, East Europe is not in a position to rapidly increase the export of consumer goods because that would require large new investments and a great deal of convertible imports; their economies are too weak to carry such additional burdens. Second, East Europe does not need additional quantities of the kinds of manufactures that the Soviets are able to offer. Third, the quality, assortment, modernity, timeliness of delivery, and servicing of current Soviet exports leave a great deal to be desired. Hence, the Soviets are not in a position to point fingers. Fourth, the CMEA pricing mechanism rewards neither the improvement in the quality and customer-orientedness of current deliveries nor the introduction of new products. Finally, and perhaps most importantly, the economic and related political weaknesses of Eastern Europe constrain Gorbachev from employing the Soviet Union's considerable economic leverage to try to enforce these new demands.

In sum, the outcome of the continued CPE strategy of "integration" with the CMEA has been to reduce East Europe's gains from trade and to make their economies exceedingly vulnerable. The cost of this strategy became obvious during the 1980s; the large "bill" for it will continue to be paid by the East European populations until comprehensive reforms fundamentally change the CPE model, including the foreign economic strategies vis-à-vis their CMEA partners.

Another important change involves intra-East European relations. Since each East European country faces similar problems and intensified balance of payments pressures, importing "hard goods" and exporting "soft goods" from/to each other has also become much more difficult recently. This exacerbates pressures on the balance of payments as well as the problems of capacity utilization because certain inputs previously purchased from East Europe have become unavailable and markets for output have also been lost.

The CMEA environment for East Europe, clearly, has changed. Most important, the Soviet Union is no longer willing to support the kind of "quasi-growth" in Eastern Europe that it had underwritten for decades.

8.5 Prospects

Let's consider the most likely external scenarios East Europe will be facing during the 1990s, in the CMEA and vis-à-vis the main Western partners.

The Soviet factors

Conventional wisdom says that the key external factor for Eastern Europe is the fate of Soviet political and economic reforms. However, from the point of view of East Europe's external economic environment in the East, it will not matter a great deal whether Gorbachev and his reforms survive and move forward or whether he is replaced and the reform process is halted. This is because the relevant aspects in Soviet policy are likely, in either case, to remain on a predictable course.

It is highly probable that the Soviet Union will not return to a trade policy vis-à-vis East Europe similar to that it pursued during the 1960s and 1970s. Its fuel and raw material reserves are not abundant and their location is increasingly in remote, inhospitable regions. Production costs are rising and internal economic pressures are growing. These are all objective constraints, irrespective of who leads the Soviet Union and the policy priorities that are pursued. Furthermore, under any reasonable political scenario, Soviet trade with the West will continue because imports from the West are essential for the Soviet economy. But even if the Gorbachev reforms continue to move forward, it is unlikely that during the next ten years the Soviets can replace fuels, their main earner of convertible currency, with manufactured exports. This is another objective constraint on what they might be willing to do in Eastern Europe. To be sure, one of the big unknowns is world energy prices: a substantial and sustained rise could ease the constraint but would hurt East Europe in other ways.

These objective factors suggest the high probability that changes in the Soviet environment and in policies that occured during the 1980s will remain irreversible during the 1990s. Paradoxically, while this situation has created problems for the East European economies in the short run, they are positive for them in the long run because it is forcing their policymakers to rethink their foreign economic strategies; indirectly, these developments intensify pressures in East Europe for market-oriented reforms.

It is most likely that during the 1990s, the rate of growth of the volume of Soviet-East Eurorpean trade will increase little and may even stagnate or fall. There will be a gradual change in the commodity composition, in the direction desired by the Soviets. The present strict partitioning between the type and quality of manufactures sold to CMEA and Western partners, respectively, may be eased; this would benefit all trade partners. Thus, it is possible for the *growth of trade* to slow, stagnate, or decline and, at the same time, the *gains from trade* to rise.

Recent "reforms" in the CMEA, such as the promotion by the Soviets of direct enterprise-to-enterprise relations, are not likely to fundamentally alter CMEA's present institutional arrangements. The reason is that the essential preconditions of meaningful direct links between enterprises - namely, well-functioning domestic markets in the member countries and the convertibility of their national currencies - are reforms that are still a long way off.

The Western factor

Given that Soviet foreign economic policies are not likely to support con-tinued "quasi-growth" in Eastern Europe, the main constraint on East Europe's economic performance will be the shortage of convertible currency, as has already been the case during the 1980s. Whether any East European country can break this constraint will depend, first and foremost, on whether it will implement domestic reforms and policy changes that would eventually yield sustained increases in export capability in accord with the country's compara-tive advantage. While export campaigns and isolated reform steps (such as introducing a domestic foreign currency auction market or permitting equity foreign investments) can yield modest results in the short run, sustained im-provements in export capability will require comprehensive, far-reaching, market-oriented reforms. This means reforms not only or even mainly in the so-called "second" (private) economy, but reforms that improve the efficiency and export competitiveness of the "first" (socialized) economy, which after all is the dominant sector.

The economic environment in the West is likely to become even more diffi-cult for Eastern Europe. The rate of change will continue to accelerate and competition will become tougher.

The European Community (EC) and its member countries are likely to pay frequent lip service to the desirability of increased East-West commerce. But they are not likely to be able and willing to do much that will affect East European policies and outcomes in the long run. The main economic interest of the EC is to improve export opportunities for its firms in the CMEA. To promote this - and to obtain cooperation on environmental protection issues - large new credits may occasionally be provided to Eastern Europe. But without fundamental reforms, credits can provide a temporary boost, not a sustained expansion, of East-West commercial relations. Joint ventures and other forms of foreign direct investment will increase, but not near as much as it is hoped by those East European countries that permit them because of two constraints. One is the poor economic environment relative to many developing countries and the less developed Southern members of the EC. The problems include an underdeveloped infrastructure, lax work ethic, too much bureaucracy, and the uncertainties of how the system and the frequently changing regulations work. The other constraint is the new possibility of entering the Soviet Union directly, through trade and joint ventures, which diminishes the attractiveness of investing in Eastern Europe, to serve as a possible bridge to penetrating the Soviet market.

The one significant policy step that the EC could offer to one or more East European countries is associate or full membership in the EC, in return for substantial progress in moving toward market-oriented reforms and political democratization. But such a step is not likely to be taken by the EC before, say, the year 2000. During the 1990s, the EC will have to "digest" both the new members it recently admitted and the set of internal liberalization measures that are to take effect by the end of 1992. Moreover, certain EC members would consider this kind of conditional membership offer unwarranted "interference" into another country's internal affairs; certain EC members would be concerned about antagonizing the Soviets; and some would worry about its implications for West German-East German rapprochement.

Conclusion

East Europe's external environments will become economically more difficult and politically more permissive during the 1990s. It is largely up to each East European government to decide how it will respond. Although each will face similar fundamental pressures and changed external environments, there are large differences among the countries, in terms of their domestic economic and political situations and external political relations. These can be decisive in shaping the policies and the outcomes in these countries. In the future, East Europe will act less and less as a bloc.

One common denominator is that they all face pressures to reform their economic systems and foreign economic strategies. But the pressures are not of equal strength in every country. Moreover, pressures by themselves are not sufficient for governments to change course. Major changes in policy are usually triggered by some dramatic event, such as an economic or political crisis or a change in leadership.

Chapter 9

THE ROLE OF GOVERNMENTS IN FOSTERING EAST-WEST ECONOMIC COOPERATION

Tamás Bácskai[1]

9.1 East-West differentiations and common interests

The fast and growing diversification of both political and economic institutions and legislation in the East and the membership or non-membership of Western countries in the EC makes it difficult to formulate a general recipe for both groups of countries today, and even more in the mid-1990s. With these two kinds of differentiations every government's "first port of call" is, to a varying degree, different. Beyond this reality there is also a psychological factor. Just as every single person wishes to be treated as an individual, so does every nation wish to be treated as an individual, unique entity.

In the East, three different types of socio-economic political models have arisen with existing or envisaged new political patterns matching the socio-economic changes:

a) pluralistic mixed economy;
b) neo-Stalinist; and
c) classical Stalinist.

Hungary, Poland, China, and the Soviet Union are striving toward the pluralistic, mixed economy model with varying degrees of progress. In Hungary, Poland, and China there is a relatively strong, predominantly small-scale private sector. The same sector in the Soviet Union is based on a leasehold (arenda) relationship. Actual Hungarian legislation stipulates privatization (Company Law, Law on Investments by Foreign Investors, Law on Transformation of State-Owned Companies). There are differences in import liberalization among these reforming countries. Hungary liberalized about 40 per cent of her imports from convertible currency areas in 1989. In all the countries concerned there is a trend towards raising the competences of the parliaments and courts at the expense of the executive branch of government. While Hungary and Poland belong to the GATT, the IMF and the IBRD, the

---

[1] Professor of Finance, Karl Marx University of Economics, Budapest, Hungary.

Soviet Union does not. The Western trade of these countries varies widely and, accordingly, so do their foreign policy options.

The second group of countries, which currently adhere to a neo-Stalinist model, include: the GDR, Czechoslovakia, and Bulgaria. Here, too, there are differences in the proportion of Western trade and, hence, in international trends and interest in the CMEA. In the political field, differences are slight but may soon become of more importance.

Romania and Albania currently adhere to a classical Stalinist economic model. Again, in certain respects there are big differences between the two countries: Romania is a member of international official financial and trade institutions, Albania is cautiously improving certain new paths leading to better bilateral relations. Having made these differentiations, it should be made clear that they may well be rendered invalid if the reform movement catches on throughout Eastern Europe.

The decisive line of differentiation in the West is membership or non-membership of the EC. This is a major problem of international economy in general and not only of East-West economic cooperation. It is also a matter of strong disputes within the boundaries of the EC. Every country outside the EC is concerned about a protectionist single European market from the United States of America to Hungary. While there are minor differences among countries with or without a publicly subsidized export credit and exported capital guarantee system, this mostly affects the modus operandi and not the substance of East-West economic cooperation.

The aforementioned differences on both sides of the fence - and not an iron curtain - dividing East and West mean that there are different tasks to be fulfilled by governments in almost every East-West bilateral relationship. These tasks even differ to a certain extent on the Western and the Eastern side. In many cases, for example, certain institutional changes in an Eastern country are traded off against some pecuniary advantage offered by the Western partner.

Nevertheless, it is possible to arrive at a number of useful generalizations in these relationships.

First, the confrontation between the two systems is being mitigated, leading to a significant decrease of the role of the military factor in the East-West relationship as well as the possibility of trade-offs wherein military concessions are demanded or offered by one of the trading partners.

Second, interstate, or rather intergovernmental, relationships are going to shred ideological, a priori judgements widening the scope of rationality or policy decisions and improving the international atmosphere.

Third, international interaction will gradually go radically beyond the boundaries of blocs in all walks of economic, cultural, and scientific activities.

Fourth, a mutual interest exists in the stability of the "other" side, excluding attempts at mutual destabilization.

Finally, though in the present state of affairs, economic interest in the development of East-West relations is asymmetric (the West is both a quantitatively and qualitatively important business partner for the East, whereas the share of the East in Western trade is negligible), the potential Eastern market, factors of production, manpower and research capacity makes it a worthwhile target for Western businessmen and, hence, for government promotion.

9.2 Governments' roles in fostering East-West economic cooperation

Governments' roles in multilateral diplomacy (in international and regional organizations) should include: dismantling barriers hindering mutual access to markets; getting equal treatment for the other side's countries; and paving the way for membership in international trade and financial organizations for non-member CMEA countries on the basis of symmetrical concessions (that is, not necessarily in the same field. For example, a lowering of tariffs on the Western side is not reciprocated by a similar step in a country with non-liberalized imports).

Governments' roles in bilateral measures include expanding the sheer physical facilities for cooperation. Specifically, this means: opening more transit facilities (roads, railroads, ports) if countries are neighbours; facilitating the flow of manpower (working permits, scholarships, visas); creating off-shore zones between neighbouring countries; concluding treaties on the avoidance of double taxation, investment protection, intellectual property, etc.; mediating the settlement of debts which have arisen between the two world wars, unsettled nationalization claims, and the like; and extending export credit guarantees and exported capital guarantees to the CMEA countries.

There are some things that East European governments can do unilaterally, such as reducing the enormous amount of red tape and government interference that hinders economic relationships. The measures enumerated below are first and foremost in the interest of the socialist countries themselves.

First, gradual import liberalization and steps toward the establishment of a convertibile currency can make the biggest contribution both to trade and capital imports. Second, business should be deregulated to allow the widening of the competence of business firms in decision making and a sizeable reduction of state intervention (licensing, permits, etc.). This is a necessary prerequisite for revitalizing economic cooperation.

Third, a mixed economy should be established, allowing private initiative, risk-bearing, and responsibility to play a much bigger role. Except for key branches, ownership should tend to take into consideration this experience.

Finally, establishing certain constitutional safeguards in economic life is crucial. Either the constitutions or special legal documents should give guarantees to domestic and foreign proprietors of business, should limit the role of the executive branch of power in economic life, should exclude any levying of taxes by decree, and so on. The above described "model" is in fact the Hungarian model, partly as realized already, partly as an endeavour on which there is a wide consensus in the country among different political forces.

156

Chapter 10

THE ROLE OF THE HUNGARIAN GOVERNMENT IN EAST-WEST ECONOMIC RELATIONS

Laszlo Lang[1]

10.1 Economics versus politics: some general reflections

Had the liberal perspective of the early 1970s on international political economy proved right, we would now be witness to a world economic theatre in which "coalitions are formed transnationally and transgovernmentally, [and] the potential role of international institutions in political bargaining is greatly increased".[2] Had the neo-realist perspective of the early 1980s come to predict correctly what we were facing, we would now be enmeshed in various kinds of economic warfare waged by desperately mercantilist states, small and large. Both perspectives were mistaken and yet, paradoxically, both of them were able to depict substantive parts and trends of the economic world which we are heading for towards the end of this century. It would be both commonplace and euphemistic to suggest that this will be one in which the relevant processes are contradictory and rarely unidirectional.

One fact, however, is clear. The clash between the integrating forces of the world economy and the centrifugal forces of the sovereign state[3] will be with us for a long time to come. As global market integration (horizontal and vertical) proceeds, states will find it increasingly difficult to sustain the effectiveness and autonomy of their domestic policymaking. At the same time they may show increasing reluctance with regard to inter-state policy coordination; that is, to subordinate what they think to be their sovereign privilege to some larger decision-making and rule-enforcing entity whether in form of economic

---

[1] Deputy Director, Hungarian Institute for International Affairs, Budapest, Hungary.

[2] Robert O. Keohane and Joseph Nye, Jr., *Power and Interdependence: World Politics in Transition* (Boston: Little Brown, 1977), p. 35.

[3] Richard Cooper, "Economic Interdependence and Coordination of Economic Policies", in Ronald W. Jones and Peter B. Kenen, eds., *Handbook of International Economics*, vol. 2 (Amsterdam: North Holland, 1985), pp. 1220-21.

summitries, international institutions, or norm-governed regimes.[4] Deregulation in some issue areas will result in more regulation in others; calls for free trade here may cause claims for fair trade there; the expanding license of multilateral institutions will lead, by definition, however paradoxically, to the expanded reliance on state intervention, and so forth.

As a rule, dialectics lies alarmingly close to sophism. One could discuss which of these contradictory trends causes which, and although I may have some definite perceptions about the "salient side of the coin", there is no room to elaborate on them here. Suffice to say that nation-states and their governments will continue to be the major actors on the international political economic scene. Their interests may be fragmented and their powers may be decentralized. Yet they are the only ones who can make valid decisions about socially acceptable levels of economic "deregulation", and who will try to further their peoples' interests, as perceived or misperceived, to the best of their ability, whether through cooperative international arrangements or competitive national or regional neo-mercantilism.

For states, unlike for political theories, there is rarely a major difference between the "low politics" of, say, economic cooperation and the "high politics" of national security. As early as 1972 Richard Cooper declared and demonstrated that "trade policy is foreign policy".[5]

10.2 Economics and politics: the East-West dimension

For obvious reasons, this separation between low and high politics has never existed in East-West relations. There, everything and anything that could be associated with the inter-system confrontation had long been regarded as high politics, be it trade, human rights, or military security. Hence, the role and input of governments in East-West economic relations had been pervasive. State trading, featuring the East bloc economies, had to be reciprocated in kind on the Western side. Security-motivated controls on technology flows were imposed by both sides. Economic relations were, more often than not, practiced as either carrots or sticks, and governments yielded to particularistic interests and pressures within their own countries.

---

[4] Robert Gilpin, *The Political Economy of International Relations* (Princeton, NJ: Princeton University Press, 1987), pp. 380-81.

[5] Richard Cooper, "Trade Policy is Foreign Policy", *Foreign Policy*, no. 9 (Winter 1972-73), pp. 18-36.

If the relationship is, as it indeed has been, perceived in zero-sum terms, it is evidently up to the governments to provide for the necessary trade-offs. Small country governments, in such an environment, have a limited range of choice. Their foreign trade may become just one of several means of validating a particular security relationship. Their trade patterns will be skewed to reflect the pattern of their overall security alignment, and attempts to deviate from those patterns (to maximize economic opportunities) may lead to intra-bloc friction, crises and, eventually, hierarchical solutions.[6]

The hierarchy of intra-bloc structures, however, has continuously been eroded since the mid-1950s (with the emergence of a special European interest within the overall East-West relationship) and particularly in recent years. Security interests and security constraints are being redefined reflecting a cautious shift away from the strictly military interpretations. This increases the nuisance value of the conduct of East-West economic relations. Nevertheless, these relations are a derivative of "grand politics" only to the extent that they are sensitive to the downward cycles of the overall relationship. They do not have a constant "hidden momentum" to react with immediate booms and expansion in the upward cycles. Politics can be a constraint on but not, on its own, a momentum behind trade. It is in the periods of receding security constraints that the structural and institutional handicaps of East-West economic ties are best revealed. These handicaps lie, for the most part, in the anti-trade biases inherent in Eastern Europe's economic systems. These biases (such as protectionism, persistent excess demand, unconditional safety nets for loss-making enterprises)[7] can only in part be explained by "pure" economic or even ideological factors; their persistence is accounted for by "pure" politics; namely the interests of the party-state and its major actors. Consequently, unless an economic restructuring based on radical political reform is pursued and implemented in these countries, East-West economic relations are doomed to give rise to recurrent frustrations. These frustrations, in turn, are bound to result in the rise of security considerations, and hence bloc hierarchy, in East-West economic relations.

---

[6] Karl J. Holsti, "Politics in Command: Foreign Trade as National Security Policy", *International Organization*, 40, no. 3, (Summer 1986).

[7] Ed A. Hewitt, "East-West Economic Relations: Obstacles to Change", (unpublished) paper presented to the Annual Conference of the Institute for East-West Security Studies, June 1988, Potsdam, GDR.

What then if these reforms are in fact implemented in parts of Eastern Europe and especially in the Soviet Union? Will governments simply "walk out" from East-West business and leave it to the pro-market actors of both sides? To put it bluntly, no way or (to hedge a little!) very unlikely. First, bloc-tied security perceptions will continue to work and strongly impact upon economics so long as the loose bipolar structure of the politico-military world continues. Second, at the heart of the reforms which are claimed to be pre-conditions for any change there lies the "self-restraint" - another euphemism - of the respective states, parties and governments. Of course, the "self-restraint" of the Western governments may be inevitable. One is therefore faced with a long transitional period in the course of which governments continue to be stars in the the East-West economic theatre.

From a broader political economic viewpoint, even the most optimistic scenario would involve a level of politization of East-West trade, finance and investment approaching the level of politization of other international economic interactions where states seize or forego emerging external economic opportunities, observing both their national security interests and international obligations and where they try to continuously reconsider, reestablish and institutionally globalize the norms and rules of the inter-national political economic game. If this is the case, East-West economic relations would be "normalized", to use a worn out phrase, to the extent that they are progressively multilateralized and involve a rich variety of international political economic linkages.

10.3 Security, politics, and economics: reflections on Hungary's case

Over the past 15-20 years, the economic role of the state has been viewed with increasing scepticism. Failure has become virtually synonymous with the expanded economic undertakings of state. At the same time, however, substantial historical evidence has piled up suggesting that in several industrial late-comers in Southern Europe, Latin America, and the Far East, national development strategies have had a substantive role to play in forging structural change, industrial competitiveness, and modernization. The obvious technological take-off of the Far Eastern economies has been the result of, inter alia, very conscious developmental and foreign trade strategies on the part of their respective governments. Hence, the issue of state versus corporate actors in economic development is clearly not one that can be defined in "whether...or" terms but rather one of correct proportions; a rational division of labour.

All this is not meant to be an apologetic for the pervasiveness of state inter-vention in Hungary's post-war economic history. Admittedly, Hungary, an underdeveloped country on the European periphery has consistently failed to find the correct proportions, for reasons which ranged from external con-straints to domestic vested interests, from a pre-capitalist legacy to normative ideological schemes, and reasons which combined all these and other elements. Politics and economics have become indivisible. The monopoly of political power gave birth to the monopoly of economic power, and vice versa. The lack of competition in the political sphere was simply paralleled by the lack of competition and the persistence of protectionism in the economic arena. The "division or labour" between government and (state) economic actors rested on a simple principle: companies were to become "efficient" and the government was to provide for full employment. The inevitable outcome has been to tax those who in fact became efficient and save those who con-sistently failed, leaving little margin for social welfare gains and a large one for political voluntarism, inter-personal "live and let live" associations, and cor-ruption.

Of course, it would be inaccurate to say that this model piled up only failures, immoralities, and no results. After all, accelerated capital accumulation may temporarily "legitimize" mobilizing regimes such as the command-type, overcentralized political economic structures of Eastern Europe. Hungary went through not only an accelerated post-war reconstruction under this kind of regime but also succeeded in converting its agrarian underdevelopment into an industrial-technological underdevelopment which raises qualitatively diffe-rent implications and challenges, though invalidating the model which led to it.

The foreign economic factor in Hungary's post-war development has always been of crucial importance. Due to its size, development level, and limited natural resources (which constantly need foreign inputs for their ex-ploration), the economy is highly vulnerable. Its export competitiveness defines its equilibrium conditions whereas its industrial-technological underdevelop-ment determines its export competitiveness. The balance of payments constraint is, thus, structural and it is aggravated, eventually to intolerable levels, by the anti-trade features inherent in the long sustained political eco-nomic model.

Vulnerability, as perceived and misperceived, has been the alleged reason underlying the recurrent subjugation of economic opportunities to security constraints. It was certainly "pure politics" that caused a full-scale reorientation of Hungary's historical trading pattern in the immediate post-war period. The

Cold War, the isolation from the new multilateral setting of the international economy, the rejection of the Marshall Plan, the war reparations and then the Soviet-led codification of the existence of "two world economies" overturned the relative balance of historical trading patterns. Hungary, for reasons which lie partly in its historical roots, partly in the trauma of 1956, has never been an enthusiastic supporter of the concept and practice of "two world markets" originally conceived by Stalin, but unhesitantly preserved by most of his successors. The concept implied not only that the "socialist world market" worked on different principles than its counterpart, but also that it had to achieve "invulnerability" vis-à-vis the other with no regard to the opportunity costs. In the case of Hungary, these opportunity costs materialized not only in terms of economic gains foregone but also and primarily in a peculiar structural maldevelopment. This implies not only a marked dualism of Hungary's trading patterns vis-à-vis its CMEA and Western partners, but also that the CMEA partnership has helped to sustain large production capacities, or rather a full economic structure which is increasingly dependent on inputs from outside the CMEA whereas its output is becoming increasingly irrelevant, in competitive terms, in Western markets. Understandably, there have been substantial domestic industrial interests which sought to preserve this pattern so long as the CMEA outlet was artificially made "profitable" by governmental policies for the involved corporate actors.

Hence, the highly unbalanced trading pattern has been sustained for decades for reasons of politics, security, and ideology as well as, and increasingly, economics. There is no room here to analyze in detail how these various factors have forged and hampered the shifts which have progressively come about in this trading pattern. The general state of East-West relations has always been a major factor. Hungary's attempts at a "re-opening" towards the West in particular, and in re-nationalizing its economic interest in general, could not but sensitively and sensibly react to what was happening in the larger political and security theatre. Ideological fears of run-away changes have been less decisive though recurrent and rhymed, as a rule, with the tones in the larger international setting. Economic structures and interests have worked more as a constraint rather than a driving force in Hungary's reintegration into the world economy. It was not only Hungary's case that demonstrated that an accelerated "world economic integration" on the basis of neo-Stalinist central planning was bound to result in a stop-go process at best and is likely to cause mutual frustrations on both sides of the East-West divide. Eastern countries may find that this integration comes to reinforce their structural disequilibria, while only marginally enhancing their modernization efforts. Western business and governments may realize that promoting this kind of integration may result in what can be perceived as an attack against the "liberal" economic order of the West in terms of enhanced monopolistic or monopsonistic powers, spreading countertrade and bilateralism, dumping, and the like while not yielding the promised fruits of access to large untapped markets. Hence, the process has been cautiously managed by both sides if only for economic reasons.

Thus economics and politics interacted harmoniously and clearly regressively. Hungary first wished to break this vicious circle from the economic side, initiating from the top down a comprehensive economic reform as early as the mid-1960s. As a result of these reforms it could accede to the GATT in 1973 on market economy principles. The domestic reform slump from 1972, then the adverse international economic conditions in the post-1973 era and finally the new cold war period from the late 1970s set back the re-integration process and shifted the priorities back to the political level. It was in the early 1980s that Hungary, under undisputable economic duress, made a major attempt to refute the adverse international political climate; to delink economics and politics, now primarily from the foreign policy side. Hungary applied for and received IMF and World Bank membership in the politically least conducive years of the post-Cuban crisis East-West relationship. Relying on its "small country doctrine" it also undertook considerable political confidence- and bridge-building activities in the same period. Simultaneously, however, a reborn complacency in domestic politics set in with clear implications as far as the resumption and resolute pursuit of the economic reform drive were concerned. As a result, by the late 1980s it has become clear that the relatively good credit rating in Western capital markets, which reflected professional economic and non-economic diplomacy rather than the real state of the economy, was not sufficient in itself to sustain a political economic model that has progressively discredited itself.

To sum up, bloc-level security constraints have not been the only factor that circumscribed the room for manoeuvre in Hungary's post-war external economic decision-making. They have been ever present, and occasionally decisive; yet perceptions of domestic systemic security proved to be no less constraining. Combined, the two circumscribed economic reform which has been and continues to be the single major factor of positive change in the East-West economic relationship. Despite all the constraints, Hungary has pursued a strategy of incremental economic opening towards the West since as early as the mid-1960s. However, this strategy is bound to be handicapped and produce mutual frustrations unless the confines of domestic political economic reform are stretched over the conventionally acceptable lines. It follows, that this necessitates a thoughtful reconsideration of the requirements of domestic systemic security as well as external obligations.

10.4 An international economic strategy: Hungary's options, hopes, and doubts

East-West economic relations came to a virtual deadlock in the late 1980s. Despite the conducive political climate, powerful economic constraints hampered the resumption of the earlier dynamics. Growing confidence and selectively improving political good-will can not, on their own, do much to remove the obstacles to change. The danger is that emerging economic regionalism in Europe and elsewhere will push the CMEA economies to a sub-peripheral position, fostering a revival of "offensively-defensive" political and security considerations.

Governments will have a crucial role to play in preventing this gloomy scenario from becoming reality. Hungary's government can contribute to this effort in several ways. It should, first and foremost, go resolutely on with its own recent reform enterprise. By doing so, it may decrease the number of permanent crisis- and instability-prone economies of the East by one, and increase the numbers of those who can participate in the international economic game on a norm and rule-governed basis. Second, it should continue with re-Europeanizing its political approaches, innovatively fostering the CSCE process, and restoring the East-West balance in its external economic patterns. Third, it must work for change in its own alliance and, from an economic viewpoint, particularly in the CMEA, recognize that the rigidities of that organization adversely affect both its own reforms and the general improvement of economic relations between East and West. Fourth, as a small country which has much to lose from a disintegration of international economic arrangements and which favours multilateral approaches to conflict resolution [8], it should actively work in international economic regimes and trans-bloc coalitions to facilitate more inter-state economic cooperation.

---

[8] See Gerald K. Helleiner, "An Agenda for a New Bretton Woods", *World Policy Journal*, 1, no. 2 (Winter 1984), pp. 373-74.

In more programmatic terms, Hungary's pluralizing governmental structure will be faced with five major issues where resolute and immediate action will be needed in terms of the country's norm-governed and irreversible re-integration into the international economy, and East-West trade in particular.

Deregulation and liberalization

The lack of competition in Hungary's economy has been a significant constraint on economic modernization. Deregulation would remove most of the institutional and administrative obstacles that have hampered the efficient and continuous reallocation of the factors of production within the economy. The deregulation of exports would mean abolishing all sectoral or subsectoral foreign trade monopolies as well as governmental intervention in the marketing process. Export subsidies can be maintained only to the extent that is justified by the "subsidy-competition" in certain international market segments. Imports, primarily those from the West, must be progressively liberalized as the single major tool of forging market economy conditions. Access to Western imports cannot be dependent on traditions or personal political influence. In the not too distant future, imports should be regulated only through the monetary and fiscal tools of macroeconomic demand-management. In the short term, however, the deregulation of imports raises the dangers of both the aggravation of the balance-of-payments difficulties and a fall in corporate export performance as earlier administrative export pressures diasppear. Therefore, besides a massive devaluation of the country's currency, a temporary regime may be needed which links corporations' import budgets to their export performance.

No one in Hungary believes that a wide-ranging economic deregulation and trade liberalization could be devoid of social tensions or political implications (and political preconditions, for that matter). After all, there is no such thing as a free lunch. Deregulation will not work unless it provides for equal treatment for the economic actors irrespective of their ownership pattern.

Convertibility

Hungarian economists are heatedly debating whether the convertibility of the forint is the ultimate goal of or the magic key to liberalization. As usual, economic history provides contradictory evidence. Clearly, the full convertibility of Hungary's faltering currency has a long way to go. Even external convertibility, however, seems to necessitate controlled inflation and interest rates that do not lag behind those in other countries. For the moment, neither of these prerequisites holds true for Hungary. Others, however, would posit that there is nothing psychologically as effective in rearranging a hot-house economy as is the external convertibility of its currency. If so, then the success of such shock treatment needs foreign therapists; for instance, a currency market intervention facility sponsored and set up by West European central banks as a part of a hypothetical financial package for Hungary.

The CMEA connection

Evidently, no changes in Hungary's Eastward-looking economic system can be achieved unless the current pattern of its economic relations with the CMEA, and the Soviet Union in particular, is radically altered. After all, as a result of policy pursued over the past 40 years, the "international competitiveness" of a large part of Hungary's industry and agriculture is confined to Soviet and East European markets. Hence, the country cannot just leave the CMEA; Hungary is not only rhetorically or wishfully a bridge between the two parts of Europe; it is indeed a bridge that needs solid legs on both banks. Hungary has been voicing the need for change in the CMEA since the early 1960s. A strategy of "concerted unilateralism" would provide several options, including: planning all bilateral exchanges on a convertible currency basis, and separating trade in mutually "hard" commodities from trade in anything that is "softer", while keeping the rouble as an accounting unit. With the first option, inter-governmental clearing could be maintained, while with the second, direct inter-enterprise deals could be concluded with the reservation that the Hungarian corporations involved must either spend their rouble surpluses for their needed inputs or reexports, or sell them in a supply-and-demand managed domestic rouble market; perhaps with considerable discounts. Another option would be to continue trading in the frameworks of long-term and annual inter-governmental agreements without undertaking state obligations to sell or purchase certain products. It would be only the interested companies which would venture into mandatory annual and longer term contracts after having agreed with their Soviet partners. Exchanges would continue using the transferable rouble as a unit of accounting, yet, the annual deficits of either side would be discharged in convertible currencies.

Economic unilateralism, whether concerted or not, implies considerable risks. In our special case, one cannot discount (nor confirm) the possibility that Soviet fuel and raw material deliveries to Hungary would substantially decrease. If so, the additional short-term costs must be discounted against the payoffs that may arise in structural terms over the longer haul.

The EC connection

Hungary's 1988 agreement with the EC stipulates that only by the mid-1990s will Hungary be treated by EC standards no worse than other GATT member countries that are at a similar development level. In that sense, it provides a reparation rather than any special privilege. After that happens, however, the baseline will be reciprocity, in the truest sense of the word. The question of any quid pro quo between a dynamic economic power centre and a peripheral economy will not even be raised unless the weaker actor adjusts to the standards (technological, legal, etc.) of the stronger partner. This is a minimum requirement not only for any accession to or close formal association with but for normal co-existence with the emerging West European economy. The short-term costs of trade-offs that a small outsider, such as Hungary, must accept cannot be evaluated at face value; they must be again discounted against the historical costs of a squeeze-out from the secular process of economic Europeanization. What can be the outcome of the unilateral adjustment effort Hungary is determined to accomplish vis-à-vis the EC? The eventual outcome can be a formal association with the Community, implying generalized preferences, or an incremental, informal accession with or without generalized preferences. Be that as it may, Hungary ought to beware of illusions. For economic, as well as political and security reasons Hungary is not an overly attractive partner for the EC. Raising illusions that conceal these facts of the day would be as irresponsible as failing to point out that adjustment to the emerging single West European market is in Hungary's best national interest and that the EC will need a viable hinterland. Certainly, as a function of the general evolution of East-West and East-East relations, one could also conceive some bolder patterns of a potential *Ausgleich* between Hungary and the Community. However, this presupposes, among many other things, that the Community will resolutely resist the temptation of creating a Fortress Europe.

Debt service management

Debt servicing is the weakest link in this strategic chain. Deregulation and liberalization may simply not work under a permanent liquidity crisis. Pressures to maintain uncompetitive, and therefore subsidized, exports and to restrict imports through administrative means in order to produce the necessary surplus on the current account may be too large to resist. Similarly, fears that a "concerted unilateralism" within the CMEA may endanger the availability of the resource basis on which a substantial part of the convertible exports rely, may soften the resolve to pursue such a strategy. Also, capital market pressures to preserve a good credit rating, i.e., the image of the "eminent debtor", may divert resources and political will from a liberal reform course. One cannot start a rapprochement towards the EC if one is forced to dump exports and restrict imports for balance-of-payments reasons.

A formal rescheduling is hardly a way out. A squeeze-out from the voluntary credit markets would be too high a price to pay for temporary relief in servicing the amortization. A reliance on FDI-inflow rather than financial markets is a visionary goal, however popular in Hungary these days; it is no panacea for the immediate future. Consequently, one is bound to search for other, non-conventional solutions which, in principle, should imply substantial, conditional debt relief effected through voluntary capital market means with the concerted involvement and guarantees of Western governmental actors. The feasibility and/or desirability of a package like this should be given urgent consideration.

I suggested earlier that political neo-detente increases the nuisance value of economic relations. This, on the one hand, implies that the key to change is with the East through launching, accelerating, or radicalizing domestic political economic reforms. It also follows, however, that the West cannot sit idle as long as the countries of the East convert themselves into democratic market economies. The increased nuisance value means that economic contacts between East and West progressively gain in their political importance for the West. Consequently, it might turn out to be in the West's best self-interest to tailor economic relations with the countries of the East so that they be structurally consistent with the intensity of reforms growing out from the domestic environment of these economies. The practice of "structural reform consistency" may range from conscious withdrawal from specific interactions in certain cases to outright relief packages in others. Such a strategy of "differentiation" would reflect the objective differences in the individual countries' potential contribution to lowering the level of East-West confrontation.

Chapter 11

THE IMPACT OF GOVERNMENTS ON EAST-WEST ECONOMIC RELATIONS: THE CASE OF POLAND

Aleksander Lukaszewicz[1]

11.1 Transition

For many years we have been accustomed to governments having monopoly control over foreign economic relations in centrally planned economies. However, the rapid reforms sweeping Eastern Europe are eroding this monopolistic control there, and substituting more conventional, liberal forms of foreign economic policy making and conduct. The formal abolition of foreign trade monopolies is simply a matter of time, although this timing will vary from country to country depending on the state of the national economy, particularly the balance of trade and level of indebtedness. Poland's reforms of foreign economic policy are typical of the reforms taking place all over Eastern Europe.

11.2 Determinants of the changing role of governments in Eastern Europe

In general terms, the economic reforms taking place in Eastern Europe represent an effort to: improve economic efficiency, meet growing domestic consumer demand, and respond to and thus be competitive on world markets. These objectives are, of course, far-reaching and time-consuming. They require enormous efforts to restructure production capabilities, property relations, resource allocation, capital formation, to strengthen market forces, and to create capital and money markets. All of this requires vigorous technological and organizational change (both indigenous and imported) in virtually all parts of the economic process. The shift from one economic system to another is complicated by the fact that Poland, like other East European countries, is not fully industrialized nor is its agricultural sector fully modernized. This means problems with labour skills and infrastructure, in addition to industrial bottlenecks. And, of course, the political panorama is changing; some-

---

[1] Professor of Economics, Warsaw University, Warsaw, Poland.

times the political changes precede new economic institutions and arrangements, and sometimes they follow them.

Given these tremendously complex challenges, the question that arises is: if the government leaves its command posts in the economy, who takes on the brunt of these challenges? A reduced role for government in the economy means that market forces take over. This is facilitated by granting more autonomy to public and cooperative enterprises and to the mushrooming private and mixed enterprises (including public and foreign-financed joint ventures).

The economic and institutional reforms have recently begun to profoundly reshape ownership relations in Poland. Most importantly, the tenet that state ownership is synonymous with social ownership is being rejected. Instead, state ownership should be socialized in various new forms which should dominate the economy. Among the forms already applied or conceptually prepared for implementation are: factory self-government, workers renting factories and enterprises, property sharing in the form of bonds and stocks sold to enterprise employees, and the restoration of communal property managed by territorial self-governments. The socialization drive also is manifested in the creation of many new cooperatives and injecting renewed cooperative spirit into existing large cooperative organizations.

All of these developments are taking place in circumstances of high inflation and foreign debt (to mention but two) which are unfavourable to economic progress. While the reforms are the necessary long-term solution to put the economy on an even keel, they have a destabilizing impact in the short and medium term. In a sense, Poland is paying a double price: correcting past blunders in economic and social policies, and creating new systemic conditions to prevent their recurrence.

The complexity of the current situation and of the future challenges elicits a variety of viewpoints concerning the methods, measures, and pace of reform implementation. However, there is consensus in Poland on the need to: balance the national accounts; reduce inflation from two- to one-digit; restructure and modernize the industrial base using indigenous and foreign technological means; remove the administrative rationing of industrial inputs and foreign currency (thus strengthening enterprise autonomy); and to increase exports to fully service foreign debt and to regain creditability on the international financial markets.

There has been some progress on the last of these interwoven objectives. The government's export promotion policies, in particular the far-reaching liberalization of export licensing procedures, have helped to increase exports. These policies have been strengthened by legislation enabling foreign capital to invest profitably in Poland, especially in the production of exports. However, despite its importance to national economic recovery, the export measures have encountered serious obstacles. Most importantly, the short supply of goods in the domestic market creates a kind of resistance to exports on the part of a population motivated by a vigorous defence of personal consumption levels. This is but one of the many issues pushing various political forces, including labour unions, to the negotiating table.

11.3 Government approaches and options

While there may be some consensus on what needs to be done, getting there requires the selection and application of a set of carefully chosen policies. (This process is one of the main causes of disagreement among the various political actors.) This calls for a proper assessment of realistic possibilities and a due judgment of what little room there is for manoeuvre.

Some of the domestic constraints have already been described. The external constraints may be roughly divided into two categories: relations with other CMEA countries and relations with the West; the two of which account for the bulk of Poland's foreign trade.

Although trade with CMEA countries has systematically grown over the years, there are a number of constraints such as: the inherent rigidity of barter, an inefficient pricing system, and the prevalence of inter-government contracts. The CMEA is subject to sharp criticisms by most of its members (including the Soviet Union), resulting in a vigorous search for new organizational, managerial, and procedural methods and rules. Some measures have already been taken to reform the terms of trading and cooperation and to totally reshape the organization in the future. These measures include: developing direct relations among the relevant economic agents, widening the use of inconvertible, national currencies to settle accounts, forming joint ventures, and trading consumer goods surpluses among neighbouring regions.

Like other CMEA countries, Poland's economic relations with the OECD countries, and particularly the EC, are heavily overshadowed by indebtedness. Poland has been unable to service its foreign debt, and negotiations to restructure the debt have been problematic to say the least. Government attention and activity has been focused on two interrelated solutions: first, export promotion in an effort to service debt in the shortest possible time; and, second, foreign capital investment in joint ventures and the creation of special or custom-free zones. There has been some progress on both solutions. Indeed, Poland is now fully competitive with the Soviet Union, Hungary, and China for foreign capital with the legal and organizational framework (including a gradually adapting banking system) being established.

The problem of foreign debt has been given top strategic and political priority in Poland; not only because of internationally accepted rules of economic relations, but also because the solution of this problem is in the interests of national economic development, social well-being, and a minimum of internal social harmony. (This is because balance of payments surpluses used for debt repayment contribute heavily to domestic inflation.)

The effort to cope with indebtedness is related to the next strategic and political priority; that is, technolgical progress (which is necessary to meet Poland's critical ecological needs). Imports of technology and technological know-how are indispensable, especially for smaller countries, yet they encounter constraints already discussed and, of course, COCOM restrictions. These constraints mean a growing emphasis on indigenous technology which, in turn, means greater R&D outlays. This is not enough though. At least equally important is the need to strengthen the technology absorption propensity of domestic economic agents who will react accordingly if they permanently feel the pinch of economic compulsion. The economic reforms give rise to such compulsion. The greater the openness of the economy, the greater the impact of this compulsion borne by competition. The influx of foreign capital is supposed to invigorate competition in the domestic market and fortify the competitiveness of domestic industries on world markets. One may also assume that the presence of foreign capital in the national economy (if significant enough) may contribute to the export of indigenous technologies.

11.4 Conclusion

Three major points can be made in conclusion:

First, the dismantling of the foreign trade monopoly means a growing degree of free access of foreign capital to the Polish market, and of Polish economic agents - public, cooperative, and private - to foreign markets. Of particular importance is the opening of channels for capital interflow. Obviously, the measures taken must be balanced with the basic principles of national economic sovereignty and economic security.

Second, although there has been an opening to market forces in the economies of Eastern Europe, the role and impact of governments in foreign economic relations remains predominant, even though it is visibly different from the recent past. The legal and economic institutions and instruments of foreign economic relations continue to change: state trading companies, limited in the past to the trading area, are changing their status into joint stock companies with industrial, transportation, and other activities; and cooperatives and private enterprises are vigorously entering the foreign trade arena. In short, Poland and other East European countries are looking more and more like mixed economies in their foreign economic relations, and the traditional image of centrally planned economic agents acting on the world markets is gradually disappearing.

Third, the reforms in the economy and polity create a system profoundly different from that labelled "real socialism". This is problematic. A dramatic movement from administrative command rules of resource allocation to market rules inevitably means substantial shifts in the distribution of national income. This often results in labour unrest, particularly under inflationary conditions. Consumers can readily support the reforms so long as their real incomes are growing or at least untouched. A deeply felt, almost primitive sense of egalitarianism may also obstruct the progress of reform. While these impediments, constraints, and contradictions are not insurmountable in the long term, they exert an adverse impact on the government's expansionist foreign economic policies in the shorter term.

Chapter 12

EAST-WEST ECONOMIC RELATIONS AND NATIONAL INTERESTS: THE CASE OF THE GDR

Peter Sydow[1]

12.1 Determinants of national interest in East-West relations

Government policies are a function of national interest, and their goals, scope, and effectiveness can only be measured using the yardstick of national interests. This is the same for all countries no matter their social systems.

The policies, and hence national interests, of diverse countries meet in the international realm. There are inevitable conflicts; some transient, some apparently permanent. Whatever the case, two things need to be considered: first, the national interests of some powerful countries may "dominate," although they do not render the national interests of other countries ineffective; second, the interplay of national interests of countries with different social systems hinges very much on the kind of relationship that exists between these systems; which at the extremes can be hostile and confrontational or cooperative. The development of bilateral and multilateral relations between countries is certainly important in containing, mitigating, or reconciling conflicting national interests.

There are quite a few trends which suggest that national interests are becoming less important as we move on to the next century: the gross product of big corporations was larger than the GNP of small countries; the widening gap between developed and underdeveloped countries made the interests of the latter a permanent plaything of the former; most governments had neither the potential nor the interest to effectively contribute to the solution of global problems; the utilization of the scientific and technological revolution by major Western countries was leading to a multipolarity of the world economy and diminishing the clout of groups of countries, including that of the countries of Eastern Europe, in global economics; and the necessary creation of an "open world economic system" required abandoning national interests in order not to obstruct "the social progress of the world community".

---

[1] Professor of Economics, Academy of Sciences of the German Democratic Republic, Berlin, GDR.

Though such perceptions may be realistic they tend to disregard the durability of national interests; that is, the interests of states and peoples. They confound the changing international environments for the operation of national interests with the latter's permanent existence. This perspective appears particularly relevant to East-West relations for a number of reasons.

First, Europe was the starting point and a theatre of two world wars. That historical experience has generated an overriding national interest of both the German Democratic Republic and the Federal Republic of Germany to work for a permanent state of peace on German soil. This interest is vital, and is being shared with other European nations. It determines the GDR's willingness to be actively involved in cooperation with other European countries in all fields.

Second, Europe consists of peoples and states which show major distinctions in age and in historical and ethnic experiences and which, more important, have chosen and represent differing social and economic systems. It is the national interest of the GDR to develop a modern socialist society whose essential objective consists in further raising the material and cultural living standards of the people on the basis of a rapid tempo in the development of socialist production, increasing efficiency, scientific-technological advancement, and growth of labour productivity. Its foreign policy serves socialism and peace, international understanding, and security.

Finally, the international pressures for a safer peace and further effective measures of disarmament, the increasing impact of other global concerns, and the progress of the scientific and technological revolution pose great challenges for the states and governments in Europe, with inconsistent implications for the living conditions of their peoples. Consequently, national interests are subject to a diversity of modifications. While the general international setting has a bearing on national interests and on the latter's complexity and structure, the way in which these national interests are pursued in the given circumstances entails consequences for Europe, indeed for the world.

The genesis of the national interests of European countries and their future evolution in East-West relations, just like those of these countries' major partners outside Europe, have therefore been an important subjects of multidisciplinary research.

The national interests of states in East-West relations are determined by *socio-economic* facts. As a whole, they are an outflow of the character and the political objective of the society in question, of its prevailing ideology, of the type of ownership, of the key means of production, and of the resulting way of appropriating the results of production. At the same time, national interests are determined by economic capacity, natural wealth, the level achieved in productivity, and the overall ranking of the state in the international community. This is why the national interests of the states participating in East-West relations on objective grounds are different and even contrary to one another. These differences of interests, however, need not hinder the dynamic evolution of these relations; indeed, they can promote and sustain mutual cooperation under the right circumstances.

Effective steps of arms limitation and disarmament, renunciation of the use and threat of force (military and economic), non-recourse to spiritual aggression, and a variety of mutual information and monitoring as elements of confidence-building and an atmosphere of equal partnership and peaceful competition are basic factors indispensable for the positive development of East-West relations.

The national interests of states are multidimensional in nature. They are essentially a set of political, social, economic, military, cultural, and scientific and technological interests which are susceptible to evolution while remaining basically constant and durable.

The sum total of national interest determines the policy of every state, with states playing an active rather than a passive role in the interplay of national interests. A further contribution to healthier East-West relations can occur simply by governments changing the pattern of pursuing their multidimensional national interests: from attempts to obtain military superiority to the assurance of common security; from motivations of hostility and distrust to friendship and trust among peoples and states; and from leitmotifs of confrontation to those of cooperation.

The basic structures of the national interests of socialist and capitalist countries seem to be undergoing objectively conditioned shifts, which can only be sketched out here, but whose detailed analysis might produce many positive options for achieving a greater dynamic in East-West relations. Parallel tendencies are discernible in this regard.

First, in the general set of national interests those of a domestic nature retain a dominating role which has even been increasing in certain areas. They are related to the development of the social system, the preservation of state sovereignty and territorial integrity, the safeguarding of national security, and the protection and enhancement of the national wealth and of cultural and spiritual values.

Second, the weight of the social, economic and techno-scientific forces behind domestic interests is mounting under the impact of the technological revolution in its emergent new phase and on account of the growing social needs of the working people. National wealth, social security for all citizens, a high standard of living, productive sciences and a developed level of education are all hallmarks of internationally respected states. A modern socialist society is not achievable without sophisticated productive forces and an efficient economy. For this reason socialist countries need favourable international environments without military threats to be able to earmark a maximum of resources for the satisfaction of material and cultural requirements at home, with minimum economic resources diverted for defence and protective purposes. In this respect they can take advantage of their type of society in which the production of military means yields no particular economic or financial gains for any social class or group of people.

Finally, in both evolutionary processes in national interests, the correlation of domestic and international components is coming to the fore. The main reason is that the pursuit of domestic interests is more and more pervading the fabric of countries' international interests while international elements are more and more permeating their domestic interests.

In socialist countries it is the people's desire to live in peace, plus the endeavour to ensure social welfare, social security, and a safe future that determine their fundamental national (and necessarily international) interest in detente, disarmament, prevention of military conflicts of any kind, and common security.

Within their domestic interests, there is a reinforcement of those elements which reflect the objective processes of an internationalizing economic, cultural and social life, with its attendant global problems. These elements symbolize a willingness to engage in mutually beneficial, equitable and contractually assured economic, commercial, scientific and technological cooperation upon whose progress the economic, scientific and technological performance and ecological safety of the states of Central Europe are becoming increasingly dependent.

In view of their geographical situation at the divide between the two social systems in Europe, their historical experience of the Cold War, the size of their territory and the heavy foreign-trade dependence of their economies these nations are extremely vulnerable in a physical, social and economic sense. Therefore a concept of deterrence, no matter how it is presented, will generate opposition.

Any argument that national security needs to have precedence over trade and cooperation appears inconclusive, to say the least, as long as the volume of such exchanges amounts to fractions of one per cent of the gross national product. (By comparison, the share of the GDR's trade with capitalist countries in its net material product is at present over 15 per cent.)

Surprisingly, there is a simultaneous clamour for a modern United States global commitment, for a "newly defined internationalism", whose essential aims are seen to consist in strengthening Western unity on defence issues and in accelerating the establishment of an open global economic system.

Considering the high degree of foreign-trade interdependence that has meanwhile been reached, any emphasis on national security by Western countries logically leads socialist countries to the conclusion that their own concepts for the conduct of East-West relations must continue to consider all the aspects of economic stability, solvency, and scientific and technological capability in strategic fields as a vital priority.

12.2 Structures and instruments of national economic interests in the GDR

The German Democratic Republic is one of the technologically well-developed industrial nations. It ranks 96th in territory, and 27th in population, 14th in industrial output (by volume), and, in 1987, 18th in international trade.

Being a highly developed industrial nation with significant foreign trade activity (with nearly 50 per cent of its net material product traded in the global marketplace) the effective conduct of its foreign trade operations and external economic dealings in general are a basic condition of an intensive pattern of growth on the national economic scale.

The GDR's strategy for developing its national economy works on employing and using its external economic links to ensure sustained growth and a high level of efficiency. The GDR has 4-5 per cent of its scientific personnel employed in research and development facilities (including manufacturing industries). Its material expenditure on research is 7-8 per cent of the Soviet Union's expenditure. In 1988 the GDR spent over 12,000 million marks (about 4 per cent of its net material product) on science and technology purposes.

Combining the various elements of the national economic and social structures, the hard core of its social strategy, and implicitly of its economic strategy, consists in harnessing economic performance for social welfare. In the social and economic interest, this policy is planned to be continued

179

beyond the year 2000 because it is believed to be an essential component of socialism, in fact one of the appealing hallmarks of socialism in the colours of the GDR.

This policy has been and is marked by continuity and renewal as the mainspring of ever new resources for greater economic achievement and productivity. In practical terms this requires a 4 per cent rate of growth of the net material product annually; a target that is achievable through the intensive pattern of developing and utilizing the productive forces by the most advanced standards.

A central factor is the development of key technologies, in particular microelectronics, without the economically effective use of which it is impossible to operate a state-of-the-art engineering industry which turns out internationally competitive manufactures. Modern structures must be put in place in other industrial sectors. Another prerequisite is close interaction of science and production. The immense inputs for the development of key technologies and the sweeping rationalization and streamlining of production presuppose an expansion of accumulation in the productive sectors.

In its external economic dealings, the Soviet Union is and remains the GDR's chief partner. The quality of this mutual relationship is not only determined by the extremely high volume of trade between the two countries. More important, they share common forward-looking interests aimed at increasing the efficiency of their cooperation, inclusive of progressive forms of direct links at decentralized levels, in strategically important fields. This will enable them to step up the yields of their scientific and technological cooperation, of specialization and cooperative ventures in the productive sectors, notably in the engineering and electrical electronics industries. The Soviet Union's market assures stable sales for many of the GDR's major industrial producers for many years ahead. The GDR imports essential shares of its raw material needs, but also of required manufactured goods from the Soviet Union and other CMEA countries. Last but not least, the GDR is an active partner in the implementation of the CMEA's Comprehensive Programme of Scientific and Technological Progress.

As the GDR sells over 50 per cent of its net material product in foreign markets, it is evident that those markets are determinant on this scale for the actual growth of that product. Consequently, the unity of economic and social welfare policies presupposes effective measures to improve the cost-benefit ratio, naturally by the standards of the international markets.

It is in this sense that the principle of self-generation of funds, which was experimentally launched in the country with good results in 1988, is going to be extended gradually to the entire economy. This principle means, in essence, that the head of each industrial combine is expected and has personal responsibility to generate the funds necessary for the development of the public assets he has to manage and to use these resources with maximum economic benefit.

Four principal indicators to evaluate the performance of industrial combines - net output, cost-cutting, finished products for sale to private consumers on the domestic market, and exports - ensure an efficient economic management. The appraisal of working tools, materials to be processed, and labour has been modified in recent years in a way that any increased expenditure becomes visible and alterable in the only sphere where it can possibly be reduced: that of material production.

Looking back on the GDR's record of successful economic development and resulting social stability, it is obvious that its national system of socialist economic planning and management has been functionally effective. At the same time we have seen since the 1970s an ongoing evolution consistent with the country's national (social and economic) interests which has ensured adjustment to changing external economic environments. This process of *real reform* has demonstrated that a continuity of economic development can only be maintained if changes in the instruments of the planned economy and in means of economic policy correspond to the producers' social expectations, to national conditions of production, *and* to the challenges of modern productive forces.

Speakers at international conferences (including the one in Athens, Georgia) keep arguing that central state planning and observance of the state's foreign trade monopoly were hindrances to effective international economic and scientific ties. It is beyond question that the scientific-technological revolution, competition in the world marketplace, preparations for the single EC market of 1992, but also the required qualitative advancement of socialist economic integration in the CMEA are important causes for a further perfection of the modalities of employing those instruments of the socialist planned economy.

Moreover, one should not lose sight of the fact that central state planning balances national economic developments and ensures solvency and the proper repayment of all due external liabilities; a crucial factor of sound, mutually advantageous economic dealings. This kind of planning makes it possible to set targets for overriding national economic projects and to earmark the required resources. And such projects provide opportunities for long-term economic agreements with foreign partners which enable contracting parties to make anticipatory arrangements in terms of their respective production development.

The organization of the foreign trade monopoly has for many years ensured that foreign trade earnings are included in the accounts of industrial combines and thus become economically effective, and that world market challenges are used as the basis for combines' R & D activities and innovation of their products. These merits are to remain basic tenets of the socialist planned economy when the introduction of self-financing in a greater number of industrial combines in 1990 will extend the material and financial responsibility of their general managers on the basis of long-term, stable normatives.

12.3 National economic interests in East-West relations

On account of its social and economic strategy, the GDR has an abiding interest, independent of the generally prevailing economic situation, in playing an active part in East-West trade and economic relations. This interest is not confined to preserving the level and stability of its commercial relations as they currently exist. Mutually advantageous trade and production cooperation is viewed as a vital field of international activity whose development can promote the process of easing tensions, strengthen the climate of confidence, and support normalcy in international affairs in general. Therefore the GDR's foreign policy seeks to encourage trade and production cooperation on the basis of further normalized and organized bilateral relations with all capitalist states.

Out of national interest the GDR desires, moreover, that the potential of economic relations be turned to account for a peaceful international situation through agreed political measures, both at the bilateral and multilateral levels. To this end its government has been making a number of contributions such as unilateral disarmament moves without conditions and establishing political relations with the EC and opening an official mission. It is safe to assume for the 1990s that the GDR government will continue to look after its political and economic interests in this dual, dialectical way.

But trade and economic relations have not only an essential political and ideological dimension, and they are not merely something that will grow through international political dialogue and normalcy, and may be adversely affected in periods of international tensions. Trade and economic relations have a momentum of their own which is supported by the commercial, technological and scientific interest of the parties, reflects their capabilities, complementarities and interdependence, and is determined by a shared preference for peaceful economic competition. The more powerful these specific economic and social dimensions of East-West cooperation, the greater will be the commercial benefits for those involved, the more diverse can be really workable forms of international division of labour, and the fewer will be negative repercussions like those which continue to arise from strategies of superiority, deterrence, and technological division and from the ongoing modernization of certain military arsenals.

These determinants of East-West economic relations are likely to become more powerful in the 1990s; not least because these relations tend to expand the material resources required to satisfy the needs of the communities concerned. The GDR will surely enhance its means for consumption and accumulation. Yet considering the current high intensity of the country's external economic ties, they will not be just a complementary, additional source of growth and improved material living standards, for the volume, structure and economic results of its trade and economic links are operative already as an element of its economic strategy, one that is a yardstick of national performance and is included with foresight in the projected evolution of sustained economic growth.

This concerns, first, the GDR's criteria for national scientific and technological development deduced from top standards in the conception and implementation of key technologies; second, the principal lines of structural adjustment with emphasis on the modernization of the engineering and electrotechnical industries and the refinement of raw materials and primary commodities while maintaining the highest reasonable level of food self-sufficiency; third, costs per product which need to be oriented on the international average determinant (that is, world market prices); and, fourth, the size of production and the effects of manufacturing techniques on product quality and functionality where flexible supply capacities and sustained competitiveness plus high foreign currency earnings in the final analysis must reflect the economic viability of those standards.

A diversity of structural adjustments to modernize industry, extensive rationalization of productive capacities, development and application of material and energy-saving technologies, the design and use of integrated machine systems, and collaboration in the introduction of environmentally sound technology are the directions in which the GDR is ready to engage in a broader international cooperation for the sake of greater competitiveness of its economy, greater export capabilities, and an increased openness to imports. In this context the GDR is also interested in cooperation in the development and introduction of high technologies.

It is logical that the pursuit of these economic interests will have to embrace all effective forms existing in world economic relations. Effective in a sense that there need to be attractive benefits for both of the sides, that these forms would be compatible with the economic systems that vary greatly between socialist and capitalist countries, and that the rights and duties of both sides would be clear-cut.

Current experiences indicate for the 1990s that next to foreign trade, scientific-technological and production cooperation (based on commercial contracts and, more broadly, on long-term inter-state trade agreements) will offer the greatest potential. Giving further concrete content to that kind of cooperation and deriving additional experiences from it so as to deepen and expand it is a major area for theoretical discussion and practical activity. That cooperation can, of course, be effective only if it is market-oriented and takes account of market conditions. Yet recent international discussions furnish indications and evidence that Western politicians and theoreticians advance propositions that go much further. Divorcing the governing political parties, the state and the economy, reprivatizing public property, developing a political opposition modelled on bourgeois democracy, and even abandoning principles of pricing policies that have been geared to social welfare standards - to mention just a few such political demands - run counter to national interests since they add to the risks of political erosion. It would be wise to stop attempting such political adventures, while it remains useful for scholars holding diverging or even contradictory views to analyse and to generalize determinants, concepts and strategies, circumstances and affects of East-West economic cooperation. This can only be helpful in working against the existing asymmetries in thought and trading patterns, in accommodating conflicting interests, and in encouraging realistic trends and processes.

Chapter 13

EAST EUROPEAN GOVERNMENTS AND EAST-WEST ECONOMIC RELATIONS: THE CASE OF CZECHOSLOVAKIA

Váltr Komárek[1]

As of early 1989, it was still debatable whether or not fundamental economic reform would be realized in Czechoslovakia. However, a number of steps were taken towards reform and as a result of the Institute for Forecasting's report, "Czechoslovakia 2010", the question of economic reform received serious attention by the country's leading economic and political authorities. More than a prognosis, the report amounted to a program for economic reform.

After many years of discussion it is now more and more clear that the negation of the law of value and suppression of the market mechanism is among the greatest economic mistakes in the history of socialism. This recognition has to some extent been rectified by introducing some elements of the market mechanism, yet only in a very limited sense.

From a prognostic point of view the movement of the Czechoslovak economy towards optimal, really effective and dynamic development involves market-oriented economic reforms as well as the opening of the economy and its full participation in the international division of labour, especially with developed market economies. At the same time it is necessary to establish the common market of the CMEA countries and to connect it more and more effectively to the unified European and world market.

To return the Czechoslovak economy to a sound path of development it is thus necessary to abandon the bureaucratic manipulation of people. The detailed central planning and administrative control of enterprises must be replaced by a market regulation of economic activity of enterprises while retaining social control over the market. It is obvious that these insights are facing some incomprehension as well. But it is unlikely that some economic and political circles that have not yet understood the necessity of an economic reform might restrain it in the long run. The rather less dramatic start of the

---

[1] Director, Institute for Forecasting, Czechoslovak Academy of Sciences, Czechoslovakia.

reform process is probably influenced also by certain peculiarities of Czechoslovak economy.

The economic situation in Czechoslovakia is probably more in equilibrium than in some of its neighbouring countries. The foreign debt of the country in convertible currencies is for the time being negligible with much higher outstanding credits among the developing countries and some of the socialist countries. Moreover, there is a relatively consolidated domestic market, with fairly stable retail prices and savings by the population.

At the same time, however, there are some significant problems in the Czechoslovak economy and destabilizing trends are reaching new levels; this should not be underestimated. Czechoslovakia's national markets are losing contact with the developed world markets. Under the pressure of perestroika and economic reform, the demand for Czechoslovak products in socialist countries is declining, so that from a long-term point of view and in an increasingly apparent manner, its share of world trade is declining markedly. This represents a serious problem. Unless the structure of the economy changes in the future Czechoslovakia shall have increasing problems selling its products and with unemployment aggravated by the relative decline in the competitiveness of its products and the general efficiency of its economy in relation to the rest of the world, with negative consequence for the country's terms of trade and living standards. Therefore, even in Czechoslovakia the reform has no alternative and its realization is inevitable.

The Czechoslovak economy is highly specific; its most typical characteristic is a high level of industrialization. Even during the Austria-Hungarian empire, it was as industrialized as France. After the monarchy disintegrated, the newly created Czechoslovak republic was left with approximately two-thirds of all manufacturing capability, which had originally served an extensive domestic market of 60 million inhabitants. In the first decade after World War I this industry greatly expanded its potential. Beside the important consumer goods and food industries, basic industries developed, especially engineering; at this time Czechoslovakia represented 26 per cent of world exports of arms technology. In the second half of the 1930s the Czechoslovak economy attained positive economic results on a world-wide scale:

Thus Czechoslovakia entered the post-war period of building socialism with a developed manufacturing industry, with a highly developed intelligentsia and working class, and with a rich cultural and historical tradition. A large-scale program of socialist industrialization led to the further strengthening of heavy industry and engineering. At this time industrial output increased twice as fast as in the Western European countries and it would be difficult to find parallels of such advances in the developed countries.

Table 13.1

**Real per capita domestic product
in current U.S. dollars in 1939**

U.S.A.	518	Netherlands	262
Great Britain	405	France	255
Switzerland	388	Czechoslovakia	220[a]
Canada	356	Belgium	220
Sweden	330	Italy	140
Norway	319	Japan	90
Denmark	311	Greece	79

[a] After subtracting data for the economically underdeveloped sub-Carpathian Ukraine.

Source: Calculations based on data from *Statistical Yearbook of the League of Nations 1938-1939*, Publications of the Czechoslovak State Planning Commission, 1947; and Colin Clar, *The Economics of 1960*.

According to official statistics, the physical volume of industrial output in Czechoslovakia during the first three decades of the post-war period increased 2.5 to 3 times; and according to corrected indices (adjusted for hidden price increases), it increased approximately 1.5 to 2 times more rapidly than in the majority of industrialized countries. Comparisons of capital output with the 10 most developed Western countries in 15 key industries put Czechoslovakia first in seven cases, second in two cases, and third in one case. Such rapid development and favourable comparisons are typical for other important sectors of the national economy such as the construction industry, and especially agriculture. Moreover, the general infrastructure (including housing, urban facilities, education, and health care) has kept pace with the expansion on industrial and agricultural production.

In the mid-1980s, Czechoslovakia's per capita GDP was between U.S. $ 8,000-9,000 per annum. And, on the basis of the parity of purchasing power of national currencies in current prices, Czechoslovakia most closely approaches the level of Italy and is 10-15 per cent below the level of countries like Britain, Austria, and Belgium. The less developed European countries - Greece, Portugal, and Ireland - with which Czechoslovakia is sometimes compared are actually some 30-40 per cent below Czechoslovakia.

By virtue of its size, accumulated national wealth, production levels, and educational and cultural indicators Czechoslovakia belongs among the economically industrialized countries. However, while Czechoslovakia's quantity of production compares it to the industrialized countries, the quality of production most certainly does not. This is the downside of centralized economic planning, and it has not been corrected because Czechoslovak products have generally been sold on the domestic and CMEA markets where they have not been subjected to the rigours of intense competition. Thus the imposition of centralized economic planning at first led to an impressive acceleration of economic growth due to the existence of large markets, including the Soviet Union, with demand that far exceeded Czechoslovak industrial capacity. With such large markets with no competition, it was inevitable that the quality of Czechoslovak products should decline to the point where they were practically unable to compete in the more realistic, Western markets.

In the present historical context, the task of the Czechoslovak government is to redress the balance between the quantity and quality of the social product, and to thus increase the competitiveness and value of Czechoslovak goods in Western markets. Of course, far-reaching structural change is necessary to adjust to these new competitive conditions.

Czechoslovakia's geographical position in the centre of Europe gives it some advantages when it comes to developing economic relations with the West. Moreover, although the cost of labour is 1.6 to 1.8 times higher than in the Soviet Union and generally higher than in the rest of Eastern Europe, it is still lower than in West European countries. In comparison to an average of U.S. $ 5-9 per hour paid in Belgium, France, the FRG, the Netherlands, and Denmark (calculated in terms of parity of the 1986 purchasing power of national currencies), hourly wages in Czechoslovakia were U.S. $ 3-3.5. (Of course, Czechoslovakia's high employment rate should be kept in mind; consumption by the population or the GDP would be influenced by this.)

It follows from these general observations, that Czechoslovakia should export labour-intensive products rather than energy and other raw materials. It should export products involving highly technologically qualified and relatively expensive national labour to the Soviet Union and other East European countries, and products involving low to medium levels of technologically qualified labour to the West. Of course, with the continued rapid growth of wages and living standards, which forecasts predict, Czechoslovakia's comparative advantage at the lower end of technological sophistication will decrease, making it necessary to place more emphasis on exports involving still higher levels of technological sophistication.

Different international markets will make different demands on the structure of Czechoslovakia's economy and its output, and so the exact nature of structural changes towards an economic optimum will depend on how different Czechoslovak exports fare in different international markets. Practical solutions will depend on how competitive "inconcerto" Czechoslovakia will be. Consequently, forecasts can only formulate some preliminary hypotheses on the basis of a number of assumptions.

The territorial structure of Czechoslovak foreign trade has achieved extreme values, which are not consistant with the requirements of a rationally functioning economy. The generally positive orientation towards decisive CMEA markets led to a situation where enterprises seeking "soft markets" raised the share of the socialist countries in Czechoslovakia's foreign trade to 80 per cent and the share of Western countries decreased to a mere 16 per cent. If Czechoslovakia in the long-term is to maintain its lead in relation to the majority of other CMEA countries in a more effective manner than has been the case until now and develop scientifically and technologically highly demanding products made by highly skilled labour, then it will have to systematically develop a substantial volume of continuous imports of high-level modernization technology.

According to detailed international analyses, as well as forecasts of planned modernization programs, on a preliminary basis it seems that adequate imports of high technology from the West to Czechoslovakia should, in the next several years, be in the vicinity of 3 billion U.S. dollars annually. To this should be added imports of other kinds of advanced machines and components of about 3 to 4 billion U.S. dollars (imports of electronic components in particular should be increased), as well as necessary increases of imports of chemical specialities and new materials, high-quality consumer goods, food, and some services. It is necessary that imports from the West increase from about $ 4.5 billion to $ 12 billion by the year 2000. This would increase the West's share of Czechoslovakia's foreign trade to about 40 per cent.

This rough outline, however, indicates the order of the changes which will have to be carried out during the 1990s while Czechoslovakia modernizes its output and revitalizes its domestic market. This assumes that a turnabout will occur towards the production of convertible commodities, validated by conditions on the most demanding markets. At the same time the world socialist market, above all the Soviet market, will continue to be of cardinal importance for the development of the Czechoslovak economy. We should, however, expect a fairly rapid reversal in the quality of demand on the Soviet market towards higher quality consumer goods, including consumer durables, as well as towards services, highly sophisticated engineering products for the modernization of Soviet industry, as well as a whole complex of deliveries for the large-scale restructuring and modernization of Soviet rural areas, including telephones and the development of the infrastructure in general.

In relation to the West, Czechoslovakia probably will not have any opportunity to make a mark in the area of top-level technology nor in the mass-scale production of products made by above average skilled labour at adequate prices. It will be better to concentrate on the complementary supply of a broad assortment of products: on the one hand the existence of a world-wide assortment of goods offered on Western consumer markets always makes it possible to offer some attractive products made in Czechoslovakia; in the area of engineering technology it is always possible to penetrate markets with highly individualized, made-to-order products and/or in cooperation with our main suppliers. Czechoslovakia must also strive to make use of fluctuating markets and to sell large quantities of its typical products with a traditionally good technical quality and competitive prices, which include for instance machines for the textile, shoe-making, and typographical industries. Generally, it is true to say that Czechoslovakia shall not be able to successfully export without importing electronic components, especially active components which now represent an obligatory standard on Western markets. Czechoslovakia should also strive to expand to a maximum degree active tourism, where it has substantial comparative advantages and a number of attractive historical monuments, and relatively lower prices on its domestic markets.

The existence of opportunities for improving performance in convertible currency areas can also be documented by the fact that Czechoslovakia's present exports to the majority of the developed capitalist countries represent only a fraction of these countries' total imports. For instance, Czechoslovak imports represent only 2.1 per cent of total imports in the Netherlands, 3.2 per cent in Denmark, 2.1 per cent in Norway, 5 per cent in Finland, and 1.4 per cent in France. Similarly, Czechoslovakia's participation in the largest and most dynamic market among the developed capitalist countries, the U.S. market, is negligible. Czechoslovak exports to the United States equal approximately $ 70 million annually and account for only 0.2 per cent of total U.S. imports. In comparison to some socialist countries which have, however, been granted MFN status, such as Hungary and Poland, U.S. imports from Czecho-slovakia are only one-fifth or one-third in size. Yet U.S. imports from the small Western European countries - from Belgium, the Netherlands, Sweden, and Switzerland - are thirty to forty times greater than those from Czechoslovakia.

The relatively small scope of Czechoslovak exports to the West indicates that this is not only a problem of technical level or quality but also the outcome of trade policy. The production of convertible commodities for Western markets also requires learning how to do business there and how to adequately take into account the demanding methods by which modern markets function, including the complicated mutual interaction of commodity, service and financial flows, the export and import of capital, and the role of associated operations and joint ventures. But at the same time we should not ignore the sensitive political aspects of East-West trade; we should all actively strive to find friendly solutions.

It will evidently be necessary to carry out far-reaching changes in the thinking and practical implementation of solutions to problems concerning cooperation between Czechoslovak enterprises and Western firms, not only in the sense of simple contracts but also the development of much more demanding forms such as joint ventures and participation on the basis of in-vested resources.

A turnabout of the Czechoslovak economy towards producing more goods for sale on convertible currency markets will require far-reaching structural changes. The share of agriculture and construction remains high, especially in comparison with the share of these sectors in the West. Heavy industry, which in Czechoslovakia swallows up over half of the productive resources of in-dustry as a whole, is also too large (see *Table 13.2*).

Specifically, the exceptionally large size of the Czechoslovak iron and steel industry should be pointed out. The present annual output of approximately 15.5 million tons of steel approaches the absolute peaks of output in Britain and France, and about one-fifth of U.S. production. If calculated in terms of per capita output of tons of steel, then Czechoslovakia produces 2 to 3 times more than the majority of Western European countries, and in terms of U.S. dollars of GDP, 2.5 to 4 times more. Moreover, by extracting more than 8,000 kilograms of coal per capita Czechoslovakia exceeds the average of those countries which extract coal several times over. (It should be noted that the majority of Western European countries do not extract coal at all.) The number of people employed in the extraction industry (including petroleum, gas, and ores) also shows that Czechoslovakia exceeds all West European countries.

The relative size of the heavy engineering and machine producing industry in general is especially noteworthy: 1.2 million people work here, which is approximately half of all those employed in British or French machine production, three times as many as in Sweden, 3.5 times more than in the Netherlands, 4 times as many as in Belgium, five times as many as in Austria, and about the same number as in Italy.

Table 13.2

**The share of heavy industry
(including heavy engineering)
in national economic indicators**
(per cent)

	Czechoslovakia	The West[a]
Total GDP formation	20.0	12.1
Total investments[b]	24.0	10.1
Total employment	17.5	8.9

[a] Includes an average of the following countries: Austria, Belgium, Denmark, Netherlands, France, FRG, Japan.

[b] Excluding investments in agriculture.

The exaggerated dimensions of industry are not only connected with a hypertrophy of heavy industry. Other industrial sectors, such as textiles, wearing apparel, leather goods, and construction materials, represent too large a share of output and employment. On the other hand, progressive product lines such as paper products and printing, specialized chemicals, and instruments and measurement technology represent a sub-optimum share when international comparisons are made.

The tertiary sector in Czechoslovakia is undersized by approximately 0.5-1 million employees and by about 20-30 billion Cz. crowns of annual investments. In the future, the need to reallocate resources will increase. These restructuralization and reallocation processes will extensively influence the further development of the economy, employment, living standards and social policy. This whole concept is aimed at accelerating both growth and qualitative changes in living standards.

192

Table 13.3

**The structure of employmet and investments
according to sectors**
(1985 per cent)

	Share of employment			Share of investments		
	I	II	III	I	II	III
Chechoslovakia	12.5	47.0	40.5	15.3	44.5	40.2
The West	6.0	32.1	61.9	4.8	25.5	69.7

Source: Calculations by Institute for Forecasting.

A more detailed analysis of problems concerning future social development would require an analysis of many other aspects of the problem, such as the status of the young generation, the role of the family and the education of children, problems connected with pensioners and old-age benefits policy in general, the high employment rate among women, and so on. Other problems which should be mentioned are the need to increase the quality of freely provided services, such as health care and education, and certain environmental problems. However, it is not possible to deal with all of these issues here.

The above cited opportunities which exist for developing the Czechoslovak economy and its living standard depend on the implementation of economic reform. In this specific historical context, there is no alternative to reform. This reform should change not only the economic mechanism in the narrow sense of rules according to which enterprises function, but also economic policy as a whole, including the broader context of social and political change, which is clearly connected to this. It would be incorrect and naive to assume that such reform can be achieved merely by new legislation, by issuing new rules and regulations concerning planning methodologies, and so forth which would liberalize entrepreneurial activities. This is in fact a highly complicated and mutually linked economic and political complex of problems, the solution of which require a combination of circumspection and consistency.

One of the most important problems is the still open question of competition. It offers a variety of opportunities in the form of small-scale individual businesses, especially in the area of services and crafts, or by opening up the hitherto unaccustomed area of competition between industrial enterprises which would be differentiated objectively according to the nature of the industry or branch. Product lines which are directly connected with consumer demand could make it possible to rapidly open a broad spectrum of small or medium-sized enterprises, competing with each other. Although in heavy industry, where Czechoslovakia has large, concentrated enterprises with many thousands of employees, it will probably be more rational to turn to forms which exist in multinational firms, whose competitive edge is aimed at international markets. At the same time it would be beneficial if in the top management of such firms, the government and or its bodies were represented by outstanding specialists, such as economists and specialists in financing.

Thus Czechoslovakia's whole concept of industrial entrepreneurship is open to change. The problem is whether and where it should turn to small-scale and intermediate size enterprises and where to large and huge multinational enterprises, whether and where enterprises should remain fully national, where foreign capital participation should be permitted in certain enterprises and where completely foreign firms should be allowed to function, and so on.

At present competition can be weakened or strengthened and also effectively simulated by various interventions and measures taken by banking, government, financial or foreign trade bodies. But all this is connected with an opening up to world markets of commodities, currencies, capital, and with regulating the degree of their impact on domestic output. Making it possible for the mechanism of competition to function also requires the legislative and practical solution of many problems, especially those connected with enterprise adaptability and flexibility, the occupational and territorial mobility of the labour force, the organization of requalification and social programs for preventive reactions to the risk of more extensive losses of employment in dying industries, and the closing down of inefficient enterprises.

Even more complicated and demanding will be the solution of another key condition for rational entrepreneurial activities on the basis of the market mechanism, that is, the renewal of economic equilibrium. At present, a marked degree of disequilibrium and deficits are typical. The background to this disequilibrium is not only the current mechanism of a supplier's economy, but also the real structure of the national economy with its marked hypertrophy of heavy industry, which by its high capital-output, material-output and energy-output ratios and its self-reproduction of interests and inertia creates an extensive demand for investment goods and supplier capacities in construction and engineering, and of basic materials and energy. This industry does not face strong international competition and works for relatively easily attainable

194

orders from domestic customers and/or from other East European countries (or else for orders financed by loans to developing countries), which according to valid domestic criteria are profitable and even if consistent self-financing were to be introduced, would not necessarily have payment problems. We realize that this "speeding train" continues to go on and on. New large nuclear power plants costing hundreds of billions of Cz. crowns are under construction; the same is true of new coal mines and quarries, new large-scale heat-supply plants, large de-sulphurisation plants, new parts of petrochemical combines and ambitious programs for the reconstruction and modernization of the iron and steel industry which will preserve its overinflated size.

Thus it becomes clear that the problem for the Czechoslovak government is not only a transition from direct management and control to indirect economic management, but also the creation of a different economic reality. This different economic reality will come about only when enterprises' resources for investments will come only from income which enterprises receive in excess of their costs, from increments in the output of convertible commodities and convertible currencies, and from government purchases financed from the state budget under the pressure of objectively measured efficiency and hard restrictions.

The artificial prosperity Czechoslovakia has been experiencing, pulled along by a self-moving heavy industry which feeds production for the sake of production and investments for the sake of investments, which creates an easy and extensive market for heavy industry, objectively represents a continuation of existing trends in a supplier's economy with a seller's monopoly, in a new version with a stronger market environment. Economic equilibrium and the new decisive status of the customer will hardly be possible under such conditions.

From what we have said it becomes clear that what is needed is an extensive economic and political complex of mutually linked measures, whose execution and implementation still awaits us. Such particular measures at the government level and at the level of its authorities (such as the Finance Ministry, the state planning commission, the Labour Ministry, and the Ministry of Foreign Trade) are being brought forward in Czechoslovakia now.

There should be no doubt that all of this involves new possibilities for strengthening and improving East-West economic relations. The key conditions for such an improvement have been created by perestroika in the Soviet Union, and the reform movements in Eastern Europe, especially in Poland and Hungary. However, the complicated processes taking place cannot be achieved unilaterally. Considerable East-West economic cooperation will be necessary; indeed, a certain amount of dependence on the West, including the United States and Japan, will also be necessary. But for such cooperation to take place, the mutual economic benefits must be clear to all involved. This sets a responsible and constructive task for leading economists from East and West to continue to meet to discuss not only theoretical issues but also projects aimed at the development of East-West economic cooperation.

Chapter 14

THE REFORM OF SOCIALISM AND EAST-WEST RELATIONS: THE YUGOSLAV EXPERIENCE

Dragomir Vojnić[1]

14.1 Institutional constraints on the development of East-West economic relations

Recent discussions in international academic circles on the problems of perestroika and reforms have undoubtedly highlighted a great interdependence between these reforms and overall East-West relations with a special emphasis on economic relations. This was clearly seen at the 12th international Workshop on East-West European Economic Interaction whose principal subject was "The Impact of Governments on East-West Economic Relations".

The very poor results achieved in East-West economic relations in the postwar period can best be illustrated by the following data. The socialist and developed capitalist countries account for approximately three-quarters of the world industrial production. However, trade between these two groups of countries amounts only to 4-6 per cent of total world trade.

This is predominantly caused by a fundamentally different approach to the economic and development policies by the governments of East and West. The most conspicuous differences are in the economic systems themselves, in the concept and strategy of development, and in long-term development policies. Based on the centrally planned systems, most governments of the socialist countries adhered (until recently) to the model of the closed economy and to the concept of autarchic development.

Such features of the economic systems and development policies were a great barrier to the development and intensification of East-West economic relations. As a feedback effect, they were also responsible for the overall retardation of East-West relations in such areas as science and technology and the political realm. The consequences of this situation are well known and will not be further elaborated.

In fact, the fifteen-year activity of the international Workshop on East-West European Economic Interaction has demonstrated both the basic problems of

---

[1] Professor of Economics, Zagreb University, Yugoslavia.

these relations and the possible directions of their development. In this connection there is no doubt that the reforms which are under way in different socialist countries provide a sound basis for improving economic and overall East-West relations.

As far as perestroika and reforms are concerned, particularly those in the second half of the 1980s, it may be emphasised that they involve radical changes. They are in fact dealing with the reform of socialism. Some theoretical and practical questions concerning a new model of socialism may be raised in this connection. These questions have been quite normally and spontaneously raised in the framework of the activities of the Workshop on East-West European Economic Interaction, including the session at The University of Georgia.

14.2 Historical problems: the case of Yugoslavia

A synthetic expression of the crisis of socialism appears in all socialist countries in the form of the two main phenomena: a low and unsatisfactory level of economic efficiency and a low and unsatisfactory level of political democratisation. In actual practice, these are two sides of the same coin since economic efficiency and political democratisation are mutually connected and interdependent. This can be deduced from some constant features of historical development. That is why these two phenomena and criteria have always been used in analysing and evaluating the success of any socio-economic and political system. Socialism is in crisis because it has not been able to satisfy these two criteria. As a consequence, the reform of socialism has to be directed towards increasing economic efficiency on the basis of an overall democratisation of the economy and society.

One of the fundamental errors which led to the crisis of socialism consisted in underestimating the role of commodity production for the market and of the market mechanism in the organisation of the socialist economy and society. This error was especially pronounced at the time of the third technological revolution. The classical model of socialism has proved to be unable to make the necessary structural changes and adjustments.

In the period preceding the technological revolution the weaknesses of socialism appeared mainly (owing to defects in the motivation system) in the field of acquiring its own fundamental knowledge and its own technology and products. Up to the technological revolution, however, socialism had succeeded in following the development of science and technology through the creative transfer of technology. But in the technological revolution this transfer was thwarted as a result of the defects of the classical model of socialism, especially because of its inability to make rapid structural adjustments. It was this fact that pushed and accelerated the processes of reforms in different socialist countries. The historical interdependence between commodity production and the market in the organisation of the socialist economy and society on the one side, and their economic efficiency and political democratisation on the other, can be clearly shown in the case of Yugoslavia.

A third large-scale reform is now under way in Yugoslavia. The first reform started in the beginning of the 1950s with the introduction of the workers self-management in the Yugoslav socio-economic and political system. The second reform set out in the mid-1960s, and the third large reform began in 1983 with the acceptance of the long-term programme of economic stabilisation.

The common features of all these reforms are: the importance of the role of commodity production and the market, and the model of the open economy and the democratisation of the economy and society. All reforms devoted special attention to the increase in economic motivation and to the enhanced autonomy and freedom for the enterprises in their decision making.

For an evaluation of the problems of reforms it is of special interest to analyse the problems and reasons which caused the reform of 1965 to be abandoned. The abandonment of this reform is very often connected with the student demonstrations of 1968. Though it cannot be denied that these events were a contributing factor, their significance was only marginal as can be concluded from the corresponding investigations of the underlying political forces.

The essential problems lie in the political sphere, in the relations of political power in the society and, consequently, in the ideological setup itself. The Yugoslav economy and society at the time of the 1965 reform were already thoroughly ripe for the fundamental changes in the direction of overall democratisation. However, the relations of political power in Yugoslav society and the structure and movements in the ideologial sphere did not provide a favourable framework for such processes. As a result, the reform was given up. The reformist trend did not reappear until 1983 when the long-term programme of economic stabilisation was accepted.

The socio-economic relations, installed in Yugoslavia in the 1970s, were pejoratively dubbed a "contractual economy". It would be more adequate, however, to describe them as an attempt to establish an economic system without any coercion, either economic coercion emanating from the market, or administrative coercion as in the centralised planning model. Such an attempt was a mere utopia and, as such, doomed to collapse.

This period was characterised by great distortions in the economy which gave rise to the high social costs of development and which resulted in low competitiveness of the economy. Further consequences were a decline in the external liquidity of the economy, inefficient investments, a surge in inflation, and a particularly big increase in foreign indebtedness.

The fall in overall economic efficiency was especially evident in the increased social costs of development. In the fifteen-year period, 1956-1970, it was necessary to invest 2.9 dinars in fixed assets in order to attain an increase in the gross product of 1 dinar. The same increase in the gross product could be achieved in the ten-year period, 1970-1980, only by investing 4 dinars of gross investments in the fixed assets of the economy. Together with the fall in economic efficiency, all processes of democratisation were slowed down adversely affecting the development of self-management.

A comparative analysis of the social costs of development measured by means of the capital coefficients indicates that Yugoslavia lagged far behind some other countries. If these costs had been the same as in countries such as Greece, Spain, Portugal, and Turkey between 1960 and 1980, or at least similar to them, the Yugoslav gross product would have attained an amount twice as big as it actually was by 1980. It should be pointed out here that Yugoslavia, due to its existing structural characteristics, can be compared with these countries.

Such a situation has necessarily led to the current crisis. However, no solution of this crisis can be found without an overall democratisation of the economy and society. But this is just the domain where the fundamental and most difficult problems arise. As a result of the indecisiveness and the ensuing vacillations, the long-term programme of economic stabilisation, accepted in 1983, was not seriously implemented until 1988.

A political consensus, reached in the meantime, has underlined that reform must encompass all spheres of socio-economic and political life. This consensus has put a special emphasis on three kinds of pluralism as a foundation of the development of the Yugoslav society: a) pluralism of markets, b) pluralism of ownership and c) political pluralism.

Market pluralism means the overall market valuation of the prices of goods and factors of production (including financial markets with the corresponding instruments such as different kinds of stocks and bonds). The pluralism of ownership means that all forms of ownership are equally treated in market competition. Political pluralism is not a priori identified with party pluralism but first of all with the demonopolisation of the League of Communists of Yugoslavia in every respect. An orientation towards political pluralism in Yugoslavia started three decades ago when the name of the Yugoslav Communist Party (CPY) was changed to the League of Communists of Yugoslav (LCY). These changes were meant to put the LYC on an equal footing with the Socialist League of the Working People, and with the Youth and the Liberation War Veterans organisations. A special position was foreseen for workers unions bearing in mind the important role of their autonomy in the development of self-management under market pluralism, especially of the labour market.

Despite a long-standing orientation towards political pluralism very little has been accomplished in this area up to now. It may be expected therefore that political reforms in the sense of the political pluralism and the reform of the party will be most difficult to carry out in practice. The same is true not only of Yugoslavia but of the reform of socialism as a whole.

This reform is, however, indispensable. It is one of the greatest challenges to contemporary socialism. Without facing and successfully solving this challenge the LCY would have great difficulties in trying to keep its position in the political scene with the same degree of influence and significance as in the past. In a somewhat longer term perspective this can again also be said for the overall reform of socialism.

14.3 Prospects for the reform of socialism

Based on the experience of reforms of socialism in the international scene, and particularly in Yugoslavia, some generalisations can be made. Such generalisations may be important for visualising the main directions of the reform of socialism and for determining some principal assumptions for more intensive economic and overall East-West relations.

The first thing to be stressed in this connection is that the starting point of the reforms in the majority of socialist countries consists in increasing the role of the market, in greater freedom for economic enterprises, in enhancing economic motivation, and in adopting an open economy model. Such an orientation, by its inherent properties, destroys numerous barriers which have thwarted a more intensive development of East-West economic (and other) relations.

Furthermore, such an orientation of the reforms means that the ideological indoctrinations and prejudices concerning the role of commodity production and markets in the organisation of the socialist economy and society must be abandoned. Historical experience has undoubtedly demonstrated that commodity production and markets are a priori neither socialist nor capitalist. On the other hand, however, these institutions represent an essential precondition for an efficient functioning of both socio-economic and political models.

In this sense it might be said that these institutions belong to history and civilisation. In the history of our civilisation it is not possible to find a socio-economic model that was efficient without being based on the institutional framework of the market mechanism and commodity production. In analysing and evaluating the efficiency of these models it is necessary to apply the two criteria which have already been mentioned: economic efficiency and political democracy. All contemporary socialist reforms have to be interpreted as the end of a relatively inefficient (basically Stalinist) model of socialism and as the beginning of the development of a new model of socialism. The historical justification of this new model of socialism lies in the affirmation of those values that make the life of man richer and give him more political freedom. Operational conditions in the economy should incite people to maximal efforts in order to contribute, according to their capabilities, to the maximisation of the social product. Using the instruments of its economic policy and its development, taxation and social policies, the socialist state must determine the limits of the possible and acceptable social differences with the highest consideration for work efforts and work motivation. Hence it is essential for the new reformed socialism to emphasise the individual man with all his economic, democratic, and human motives, preferences, and priorities.

Reformed socialism ought to do away with the fear that the individuals may get rich and in doing so to enlarge the differences that exist in the society. What it has to be afraid of instead is the existence of misery, poverty, unemployment, underemployment, bribery, corruption, work evasion, lack of motivation and so on. It must also break decisively with the so-called "uravnilovka". This egalitarian principle amounts to such relations in income distribution in which those who do work are exploited by those who do not. In such a situation the prospects for any progress are severely hampered.

The theory, philosophy, ideology, as well as the practice of socialism must accept the differences (even big ones) produced by the market valuation of the results of work. Equality in socialism must relate to those welfare areas where in addition to market criteria, and due to their intrinsic nature, the criteria of solidarity have to be applied. Such areas are health care and social welfare, and, to a lesser extent, education, cultural life, and so on.

The equality in socialism will have to be attained through the toleration of differences. If the social conscience in reformed socialism accepts the historical necessity of the equality in differences it alone will give a positive impetus to the long-term tendency that will gradually result in less differences and more equality for all. Such changes in the development of socialism will undoubtedly have a many-sided impact on the totality of relations in the contemporary world. This is especially true of the overall economic, political, and other East-West relations.

COMMENTS ON PART III

Christopher Saunders[1]

The movement of capital and technology from West to East has been much discussed. But little has been said of how progress can be stimulated by movement of *people*. Throughout history the intake of qualified and enterprising people from other countries - some pulled, others pushed - has been a vital element in the transformation of national economies and societies. Examples are the beneficial influence of the flight of French Huguenots after the revocation of the Edict of Nantes on early industrialisation in Britain, the Netherlands, and Germany; of the influx of Europeans and Asians into North America; of Scottish engineers all over the world; of central European and Spanish Jews in establishing the great merchanting and financial networks. Increasing facilities for free movement within the European Community is showing useful results. (In international football or soccer the concept of "national" teams is becoming a joke.) The earlier history of the East European economies and the Soviet Union is no exception to the fertilising effect of foreign innovators; and there are welcome signs that doors are now being opened somewhat more widely. But if this path of modernisation and intensive growth is to be followed effectively, I suggest that it is for the socialist governments to take much more active measures than at present exist to cut down the bureaucratic and other obstacles to the pulling in of productive "human capital".

---

[1] Science Policy Research Unit, University of Sussex, United Kingdom.

Andrzej Rudka[2]

Within the broad spectrum of questions brought about by the topic of this workshop and ensuing publication, there is one fundamental issue pertaining to the role of individual governments in the East and West in fostering or hampering the development of East-West economic relations. It has generally been assumed for years that East European governments' influence on their countries' East-West economic relations has always been relatively bigger than the impact of Western governments. This disparity in kind has been largely justified by systemic political and economic differences between both groups of countries. The predominantly high level of concentration of central decision making (with a state monopoly of foreign trade as an important principle) has allowed East European governments to make arbitrary decisions concerning their economic relations with the West, often irrespective of their economic justification and to the detriment of those relations and East European economies themselves. On the other hand, although Western governments have a relatively smaller direct impact on their countries' business engagement in East-West economic relations, history has shown that Western governments have had the power to restrict or even sever East-West economic relations.

Therefore, besides all the existing and well known asymmetries in East-West economic relations, we can identify yet another asymmetry concerning governments' role in their development. For the governments of both sides so far it has generally been much easier to restrict these relations than to promote them. And there is no doubt that until now the former possibility has been much more effectively used than the latter. As Professor Lang stated in his paper, "politics can be a constraint on, but not on its own a momentum behind trade".

In a period of vastly growing interdependence between East and West, it is worth considering whether the pattern of governmental activities in this area should not be reversed due to the fact that the economic aspect of East-West relations has always been regarded as "high politics".

After the discouraging results of East-West cooperation in the 1970s and completely discouraging experiences of the early 1980s, some East European governments have taken relatively radical steps to reverse the above mentioned pattern. They did it by introducing deep economic reforms backed by important internal political changes; the most comprehensive ever under-

---

[2] Professor of Economics, Foreign Trade Research Institute, Warsaw, Poland.

taken in Eastern Europe. These reforms are directed at increasing overall effectiveness, opening up the economies, making them more competitive, and more integrated into the world economy (no more "export campaigns and isolated reform steps" as Marer characterized earlier attempts at reforming socialist economies).

As a result of more decentralized economic decision-making (even a far-reaching erosion of the state's monopoly over foreign trade in Poland) the role of East European governments in East-West economic relations becomes more indirect, and its main goal becomes the creation of the necessary economic and organizational conditions for enterprises to engage in East-West trade. Lukaszewicz states that a "reduced role for government in the economy means that market forces take over".

It does not mean, however, that East European governments will quickly and easily deprive themselves of all means of directly influencing the foreign activities of their enterprises, especially considering their economies' problems (including high indebtedness). Taking all this into account, East European governments will go through a transitional period in which they will have to closely monitor economic events and adjust (or stimulate the adjustment of) different economic parameters. At the same time they have to create or properly reshape the legislative basis for the development of foreign economic relations, including those with market economies. As Lang puts it, "one is therefore faced with a long transitional period in the course of which governments continue to be the stars in the East-West economic theatre".

We cannot forget the important and indispensable role of governments as observers and protectors of the national economic sovereignty and security. This is especially valid in the context of experiences of some socialist countries (mainly Poland and the Soviet Union) in the early 1980s. The problem for East European governments is how to reconcile national economic security with greater involvement in East-West economic relations. On the other hand, taking into account U.S. export control policy and the view expressed by some American participants at the Workshop on possible COCOM-type financial controls, one may wonder who is more preoccupied with security concerns; the United States or East European countries?

Throughout the turbulent post-war history of East-West economic relations, we have noticed periods of both Eastern and Western governments' domination in laying out the main directions of these relations. In the early 1990s, it is generally assumed in the West and largely accepted in the East that the overall impact of Western governments on East-West economic relations is practically and potentially smaller than that of underlying factors in Eastern economies; namely the endeavours of some of their governments to introduce market-oriented reforms backed by radical political changes. Does this mean that Western governments cannot influence the final outcome of the economic (and finally political) reforms taking place in Eastern Europe? Of course, this is not so. Western governments can have a very significant influence on East European reform and the future course of East-West economic relations. The question is how should Western governments act to strengthen current processes in Eastern Europe in the interest of global East-West relations and international cooperation as a whole. One thing is clear. They cannot allow emerging new economic regionalist trends in Western Europe and elsewhere to push the CMEA economies to a marginal position, fostering again domination of political and security considerations in East European countries' attitude towards the West.

In conclusion, one can easily agree with Lang that the key to changes in East-West economic relations is now with the East through accelerating and radicalizing domestic political and economic reforms. The West, however, cannot sit idle until East European countries convert themselves into democratic market economies. Some assistance, but not charity, is needed from the West. And the West has to act quickly because the environment in the 1990s will most probably change for the worst for the socialist countries. If the West confines itself to theoretical discussions on what can be done, one cannot exclude the possibility that we may lose the "window of opportunity" for normalizing East-West relations and integrating Eastern Europe into the world economy.

Jean Tesche[3]

The chapters on the role of East European governments address several important issues. One main issue is the need for freer, less managed foreign trade both within CMEA and the West. At the same time Western countries, particularly the EC and the United States, seem to be moving in the opposite direction. This move includes the possibility of increased protectionism as well as increased use of trade for political purposes. Other common themes in the chapters are the sense of reform as a process rather than a single goal and

---

[3] Assistant Professor of Economics, Emory University, Atlanta, Georgia, U.S.A.

the social implications of economic reform. After a brief overview of the chapters, the major points will be summarized.

Marer's chapter provides a good, detailed overview of historical trends and future prospects of foreign trade in Eastern Europe. The main changes in Eastern Europe's external environment are the end of easy credits from the West and of increasing fuel and raw material imports from the Soviet Union. The Soviets are also increasingly demanding better quality imports from Eastern Europe. Marer does not feel that the effects of political and economic reforms in the Soviet Union will have a large impact on Eastern Europe's external environment. The above changes will hold true, regardless of whether the reforms succeed in the Soviet Union. The major external problem for Eastern Europe is the convertible currency shortage and, therefore, the need for economic and political reform to increase export capacity. The main issue in East-West trade is the degree of protection in Western countries.

The remaining chapters deal with specific countries: Poland, Hungary, and Czechoslovakia. Lukaszewicz's chapter points out that Poland faces two main problems: reform, to create a more efficient economy and competitive trade and, at the same time, the need to correct past economic and social mistakes. He recognizes the need for more flexibility in CMEA trade, including increased multilateral trade and more direct relations between enterprises. He agrees with Marer that the main problem in Eastern economic relations is the large amount of debt and, therefore, the need for increased exports of foreign investments to service the debt. Lukaszewicz makes two very important points: first, economic reform is a long process; second, besides increased economic efficiency, the transition to a market-oriented economy implies increased income differentials, inflation and possible labour unrest. Economic reform is only popular as long as real income is increasing. When incomes stagnate or fall there can be problems.

Lang's chapter on Hungary also points out that reform is a process, not a fixed goal. Lang feels that the role of governments is pervasive in East-West trade. However, he notes that the issue is not just that all government intervention is bad, but how much intervention and what type. Is it control over the type of output or export promotion? The two major problems in East-West trade are how protectionist the EC will turn out to be and the large amount of East European debt. The main problem with CMEA trade is its rigidity. He feels that after 25 years with little change in CMEA trade, unilateral action may be necessary. He admits that neither increased foreign direct investment in

Hungary nor possible currency convertibility are "magic keys" that can save the economy, however desirable they may be.

In his chapter, Komarek notes that Czechoslovakia differs from Poland and Hungary in two main ways. One is that it is only beginning to consider the kind of reforms that the other countries are in the process of implementing. He notes the need for Czechoslovakia to implement deep market-oriented reform and to increase foreign trade. However, he also feels that social control over the market is necessary. It is not clear what this is to be and how much control is intended. In Hungary social control over the market has sometimes meant, in fact, very little market. The other main difference is that Czechoslovakia is closer to both internal and external balance, with a small amount of foreign debt. However, in the long run it is losing competitiveness and facing the problems of lack of innovation and efficiency inherent in command economies. He points out that Czechoslovakia should use its competitive advantage, a skilled, educated labour force, to compete at a medium level of technology. Czechoslovakia has neither abundant natural resources nor low wage rates to compete with low cost producers or enough high technology to compete with Japan, for example.

All these authors agree on the need for economic reform, although they differ in degree. In Poland and Hungary, with their longer reform experience, it is recognized that economic reform is a long process with social and economic implications. There is no magic, quick solution. The rigid, bilaterally balanced trade within CMEA is seen as a major constraint to increased trade overall. East European countries are no longer able to increase production with cheap, abundant fuel and raw material resources from the Soviet Union. The current Soviet reform efforts may add to the impetus to change the rigid CMEA trade system.

There is some recognition that East European countries must find their country's comparative advantage to compete on world markets. An increased role of the market is the best step in this direction. Poland and Hungary are constrained by their high amount of debt servicing. Overall, there is a desire to increase convertible currency trade and to increase participation in international organizations. The goal is a reorientation of trade to increase the importance of Western trade, but not to the exclusion of CMEA.

There is general acknowledgement that Eastern Europe cannot rely on either the Soviet Union or the West for help to improve economic performance. One way Eastern Europe can increase trade is by making CMEA trade more flexible. Another is by advocating free trade in the face of increasing protectionism in the West. Promoting economic reform is the best way to increase exports (and foreign investment) in order to deal with the high levels of debt in Poland and Hungary and in order for Czechoslovakia to become more competitive.

As the West encourages political and economic reform in Eastern Europe in the direction of increased market mechanisms, it is important to remember that without continued access to Western markets, there is a limit to the amount of market-oriented liberalization possible in Europe.

Jozef M. van Brabant[4]

Some of the chapters by Eastern Europeans provide us with a remarkable illustration of the depth and range of social, political, and economic probing, socio-political concerns, and hard questioning that has been coming to the fore during the past few years in Eastern Europe. Whereas one could detect some dissent on this or that issue on the official policy agenda, and therefore propounded with a certain "view", before the ascent of Gorbachev to power, the independent observer is now confronted with an exceedingly diverse spectrum of far-reaching questions. This ongoing debate may in a short period of time fundamentally alter the way in which outside observers of the centrally planned economy (CPE) scene have traditionally approached the economic paradigm of these countries individually and in their CMEA concert.

I have no major disagreements with the authors of chapters in this section. At least, I see little reason to dissociate myself fundamentally from the main thrust of the positions advocated. But I do have some divergent views on imputations, suggestions, and recommended streamlining advocated particularly in the chapters by Lang, Lukaszewicz, and Marer.

Komarek's paper candidly underlines the mistakes and other drawbacks that Stalinist-type economic policies entailed for a rather highly developed country such as Czechoslovakia and the legacies that the country's current and prospective leaderships will have to come to grips with. I doubt that any serious observer would challenge his interpretation of Czechoslovakia's need to regain greater competitiveness through economic reform, through bold exploitation of trade opportunities in all components of the global market, and

---

Staff member, International Economic and Social Affairs, United Nations Secretariat, New York, U.S.A.

through a measurable increase in technology inflow from industrial countries. He also suggests that there is an urgent need to adopt a constitutional compact that would legally circumscribe the area for decentralized decision making in a thoroughly reforming Czechoslovakia. This all sounds fine with me.

Bacskai's observations on the role of governments in one type of socio-political system with respect to facilitating changes in another are interesting. A typical suggestion, which also crops up in Lang's report, is the need to facilitate access of CPEs to the international economic system and the concomitant international economic organizations in place without insisting upon any kind of very specific reciprocity. Reciprocity in the post-war international economic regimes, particularly the trading regime, has been rather diffuse in the sense that the counterbalancing of reciprocal gains in a specific category of international relations, such as merchandise trade, is computed over the long haul and imprecisely at that. At least with respect to the reforming CPEs, Bacskai, Lang, and Marer would all like to change the kind of diffuse reciprocity we have known since the mid-1940s. In its stead, they argue for the introduction of a much more general type of diffuse reciprocity. I disagree with this. I have much more sympathy for Bacskai's emphasis on the need for Eastern European governments themselves to undertake most measures required to facilitate greater participation in the international economy.

Lang's paper is very much in the spirit of what I perceive as the core of the ongoing debate in Hungary on what needs to be done to enhance that country's strategic long-term economic development. I can well understand his concern about the real possibility of Hungary, and perhaps the rest of Eastern Europe, being increasingly marginalized in Europe. This is a certain undercurrent that the chapter by Marer shares. I disagree with of the positions that both authors put forth, however.

Marer's chapter amounts to a very broad, rather general, overview of post-war East-West economic relations with a good deal of historical CMEA and CPE development weight thrown in for goods measure. While there are many points on which I would like to challenge Marer, I stumbled over three items, particularly in his outlook section, that I find very difficult to subscribe to.

First, he is apparently prepared to absolve or nearly exonerate East European governments for the prevailing economic disarray. I for one would argue that, beginning with the mid-1950s, the East European leadership has to bear a good deal of the blame for the protracted economic and socio-political mismanagement as well as the shortsighted output gains obtained by taking advantage of Soviet raw materials and willingness to absorb below-standard manufactures. To take but one example: Gierek's dash for growth and all around modernization through reckless foreign borrowing in the 1970s or the decision of many CPEs to postpone structural adjustments after the first oil crisis cannot be attributed to Soviet policy impositions. They stem squarely from the inability of the governments in place to conceive of and put in train actions consonant with well-argued economic points. Surely, in some cases, as Gierek's demonstrated so overwhelmingly, unsound economic advice was heeded. But this occurred in most cases because the views of other factions in the development debate that were less inured by what the leadership wanted were ignored in this extraordinary process.

Second, Marer argues that Soviet reform will not exert any measurable change in Eastern Europe; but it may offer opportunities for each Eastern European government individually to formulate its own remedial course, as opposed to previous decades when presumably the Soviet dictate inhibited such experimentation and reflection within East Europe. Although there is undoubtedly a grain truth in this contention, I feel that Soviet perestroika, if adhered to in the 1990s, will exert a measurable influence not only on the room for manoeuvre in East European economic policies but also in the design, scope, and speed of implementation of economic and socio-political reforms, and their related societal transformations. These direct and indirect influences are bound to emerge even if Gorbachev in the end were to fail grandly.

Finally, Marer contends that nothing much can happen with CMEA integration to alleviate Eastern Europe's lingering growth constraints. Of course, I cannot see any immediate and grand takeoff in CMEA economic integration solely because of the permission in principle to allow microeconomic entities to make deals themselves. Nonetheless, we need to remind to ourselves that such decisions are influenced not only by microeconomic parameters, such as prices and conditions of delivery, that are within the bailiwick of the entrepreneurial sphere for which experience is lacking as a guideline. They are also determined in a non-trivial way by environment, including (as Marer puts it) experience with wholesale trade and foreign parameters such as exchange rates and settlement conditions. The latter two are within the competence of central governments. The streamlining of this environment depends eventually on the political will to introduce such changes, monitor the behaviour of agents, and fine-tune according to experience. Currency convertibility could be instrumental in spurring on inter-enterprise transaction. But it is certainly neither a sine qua non nor a panacea for Eastern Europe's economic ills. Convertibility is in any case not something that can be put in place in the very near future. Western European experience after World War II once again offers food for sobering thought and realism.

Finally, I share most of the thoughts in the chapter prepared by Lukaszewicz. But I should like to advance two cautionary comments on the state monopoly of foreign trade and payments (MFT) that, after digestion, may well indicate that I do have more fundamental disagreements on a number of topics to be raised with our Eastern European colleagues.

I should like to group my specific comments under six headings.

Reform and the role of the MFT

Lukaszewicz make no bones about the erosion of the MFT. I have no qualms with his observation that foreign trade institutions in many CPEs, including Poland, are being replaced by more conventional commercial policy instruments and a corresponding infrastructure. But I fail see how this cold signal the beginning of the end of MFT.

To my mind, the MFT essentially consists of two components. One refers to the authority to decide over trade and foreign exchange matters. The other revolves around the way this authority is exercised in practice; that is, in the conduct of foreign economic transactions. These have traditionally bee managed through institutions that, with the help of the budget, are instrumental in separating domestic from foreign markets. The principal purpose is to maintain the substantial degree of domestic price-determination autonomy so much prized by the traditional central planner. Under such conditions, there is need for a comprehensive, active foreign exchange policy for that is fully embedded in the central plan. This aspect of the MFT has undergone considerable revision, first in the late 1950s in some East European countries, beginning with Hungary and Poland, and since the 1960s in virtually all East European countries; the Soviet Union has now joined the group and Lukaszewicz is right that there is a serious erosion of the MFT taking place in some sense postulated in his chapter.

Whether this will in lead to "the formal abolition of the foreign trade monopoly" is more questionable, however. Even the shock treatment advocated by Lang does not strike me a very constructive, that is, realistic proposal at this juncture of Eastern Europe's economic woes. But I shall deal with that particular problem in the last section. If by MFT we mean indeed the authority vested in central decision makers to intermediate in trade and foreign exchange matters in the pursuit of some goals (not necessarily confined to economics), then I believe it would be erroneous, in fact dysfunctional, to call for the abolition of the MFT or the "shock treatment".

The authority to decide over trade and foreign exchange matters, which was traditionally absolute in the orthodox CPE, is admittedly being devolved to individual economic agents. But their microeconomic actions are being decisively shaped by the macroeconomic policies set at the central level. This will certainly remain the case for as long as full current account convertibility will not be a feasible policy objective. Central intervention continues to be very powerful as far as international exchange matters are concerned; that is, the acquisition and disposition of foreign exchange, at what price, and through which organs. Even as far as merchandise trading matters are concerned, central authorities are having and will continue to exercise a very powerful voice in shaping the level, commodity composition, and geographical distribution of trade without necessarily having to disaggregate this particular aspect of the MFT to individualized "from-to" commodity flows. But for that to work properly, there is a need to develop commercial and foreign exchange policies in their own right rather than as one element of traditional central planing.

As elaborated upon below, the reforming CPE has essentially entered a long drawn-out process aimed at producing an economic structure that in time will differ radically from the one that typically emerged under traditional central planning. This calls for imposing structural adjustments through some kind of centrally regulated economic mechanism. Short of simply opening up CPE markets to unbridled competition, the adjustment process will have to be chaperoned to ensure not only that it in fact takes place, but also that its costs are contained close to the necessary and distributed according to some acceptable equity rules.

Coordination during the reform process

Perhaps a more fundamental point is the issue, as Lukaszewicz puts it, of "control and coordination measures" that are "either left as they are or liberalized depending on the general situation of the national economy". In my mind, there are several ways to pursue the reform process. Some are feasible in theory and others may be set as an objective for practical action.

The range of alternatives is determined by two extremes. One could be seeking measurable structural change in the CPE through full-fledged market mechanisms, except perhaps in some spheres in which the prerogatives of socialism remain very strong indeed, as detailed below. This is presumably a format that would respond to some of Lang's "shock treatment" thesis.

Substantive structural change could also be sought as the outcome of an adaptational process. This would seek gradualism in introducing changes in economic structures with two purposes: one, the need to cushion palpable social and economic costs associated with structural adaptations over time; and two, to ensure that the costs are distributed equitably, by some standard of measurement.

Whichever way decision makers may seek to go, progress with economic reform will almost inevitably be conditioned by and anchored to incremental changes in development strategy and, more important, in the economic model of the CPE. Under the latter I include all the policy instruments, institutional infrastructure, behavioural rules, and short-term macroeconomic policies required to steer an economy. Many issues could be tabled here. In what follows, I shall try to clarify some aspects of economic coordination, the objectives and means of economizing that are typically socialistic, and the transition phase of moving from an existing social organism to an economic arrangement where coordination is organized indirectly. I shall do so largely from my perspective on reform in existing CPEs.

Indirect economic coordination

One of the more striking features of the reform process in Eastern Europe is the rather casual way in which the problem of coordinating decisions, including their institutional infrastructure and requirements on policy instruments, has traditionally been treated. Even at the height of the reform debates of the 1960s, how to ensure proper coordination of decentralized decisions was rarely examined comprehensively. Moreover, the leaders of reforming East European countries have rarely deliberated about these topics in an ex ante fashion either conceptually or in a coherent technical framework. Inasmuch as reform is by definition a process spread out over time and therefore associated with a protracted transition period, how to ensure coordination during that fluid phase may require different answers from what is needed to design and implement a coherent coordination mechanism for the reformed CPE.

Yet, coordination is central in devolving decision making from the higher to the lower tiers of the economic hierarchy in the expectation of thereby enhancing the efficiency of resource allocation. This entails, among anothers, moving away from rather inflexible, if not necessarily rigid, central planning to an environment that is expected to correct the perceived shortcomings of implementing the "centrally planned" design. In the former system, a triad of hierarchical operational levels was in fact postulated, namely: one, a nucleus at the political apex to set priorities in various socio-economic, political, and strategic spheres; two, a small group of highly qualified planners brought together under the roof of the planning centre as one critical component of the governmental bureaucracy; and three, economic agents in the production sphere that simply carry out centrally set directives and concrete input and output targets according to a highly mechanistic view of the clock-like central regulation of economic processes. All those assumptions have to some degree been removed from reality both when the CPE is examined with respect to its evolution over time as well as in cross-country comparisons. It was precisely these gaps in the coordination mechanism entrusted to the central planning agency that first called for innovating structural change.

On the transition phase

The post-war track record on modifying CPEs is unambiguous: reforms are rarely viewed holistically, formulated into a clear blueprint and then implemented by the political leadership according to a set schedule, and invariably face opposition as well as internal and external obstacles that were not or fully heeded when the reform was conceptualized. Instead, a reform is essentially a process of learning even at the highest level of the Communist Party and government. Hence the prevalence in reforms of instability and sometimes outright vacillation in rules and regulations; disagreement or divergent views on what is to be done and how changes should preferably be carried out; and willingness quickly to intervene in the direction of recentralization rather than tolerance for the zigzagging that may be unavoidable, which provides a learning process in itself, in any societal transformation process. In any case, there appears to be one constant: regardless of the ambitious nature of the reform, it invariably falls short of the goals envisioned at its inception.

In appraising the consistency and potential of moving meaningfully toward economic decentralization and evaluating the reform's performance, it is essential to gain a proper perspective on the evolution of how the tasks of coordination are being viewed by agents and the degree to which measures are taken to correct outcomes that do not correspond to the reform's intentions. This may require frequent socio-economic engineering; that is, the periodic fine-tuning of policies, institutions, and instruments in response to assessments of performance with a view to guiding the reform back on track. By advocating such professional and technical appraisals, I am not positing that politics should be subservient to economics or even that all technical economic details can be realized at a cost inferior to pursuing another reform format. All I desire to point out is that it is incumbent upon the economist concerned about the reform process to clarify technical matters pertaining to the inevitable disruptions and adjustment costs implied in such a decision. Whether these are acceptable is a matter that derives importantly from political precepts. But technically competent advice phrased within the context of decentralized coordination is something worth striving for in itself. It should in principle constitute one critical input into the decision making of the socialist political leadership.

In this connection, the question arises of what state-wide economic policy in a reformed CPE should be all about. Clearly, differences between social and private preferences need to be bridged by "guiding" or "intervening" in purely privately motivated decisions; socio-political preferences need to be safeguarded centrally, though implemented according to new (reformed, possibly market-type) rules of the game; the non-material sphere remains largely under central control; and certain infrastructural and large-scale projects need to be initiated at the top level, though certainly not in an economic vacuum. More on this issue is provided in the next section. There may be wide agreement about this division of priorities and responsibilities. But rarely is it realized that such a new constitutional arrangement has to emerge from the economic structures, institutions, and policy instruments (the economic model, if you wish) in place, rather than in a vacuum.

In this respect, it is critical that those managing the transition toward a reformed setup institute comprehensive monetary and fiscal policies to steer the behaviour of individual agents. In addition, the leadership needs to impose proper incomes and price policies with a view to enhancing the realization of social priorities. In economies that wish to integrate themselves into the global economy to strengthen the degree to which wants can be satisfied with given limited means, these macroeconomic policies will need to include active foreign exchange and commercial policies. All this may sound easier than it really is. In fact, instituting coherent macroeconomic policies in lieu of traditional central planning is an exceedingly complex assignment if only because the traditional CPE has not been very much concerned about this particular macroeconomic infrastructure. Macroeconomic policies and institutions in the economies that adopted the CPE model after World War II or the 1930s in the Soviet Union were shoved aside or their range of activity was narrowed considerably by central planning and its associated institutions and behavioral requirements.

Ownership and property rights

The original raison d'etre of socialism was to overcome exploitation of labour by owners of the means of production without overly encroaching upon economic efficiency. In the traditional CPE, this dilemma was invariably solved in a preemptory fashion by full socialization. From a technical economic point of view, however, full socialization is neither necessary nor sufficient for proper resource allocation. But neither am I aware of a sound technical economic argument that justifies privatization as a better alternative to social ownership. In this connection, it is useful to distinguish between ownership and property rights. For all practical purposes, the capital stock in place in virtually all CPEs at the inception of market-oriented reform is state ownership. Whether this should be maintained is a contentious matter, however. Several of the East European contributions argue that it should not be. But it would be useful to base the argument in the first instance on technical economic grounds or at least to distinguish those from the more emotional, political, and ideological obiter dicta so pervasive in the recent literature on reforms in socialist economies.

There are probably instances in which it would be advisable to encourage private ownership, if only because the cost of ensuring proper allocation of user rights associated with state property would be horrendous. On the other hand, precepts on income and wealth distribution and access to a certain social dividend, as the "scientific socialists" referred to it, may well counsel for rather than against maintaining state property of basic sectors of economic activity. But that does not necessarily mean that it would be justified to have the state exert its property rights directly through central planning.

Custodial rights over the use of social property could be traded in functioning capital markets. Can such a market for the usufruct of capital be entertained and, if feasible, can it possibly be efficient? In other words, can it lead to a more effective allocation of scarce resources than attainable under the traditional CPE system? An answer can usefully be formulated by first looking at the stationary state and then at one where there is positive growth of the capital stock, possibly combined with shifts in its structure.

With a stationary state, macroeconomic policy needs to ensure that capital use does not eat into the social capital stock through proper charges and safeguards. In principle, it is entirely feasible to let economic agents bet on the right to access society's capital, to institute a control mechanism (for example, a mandatory insurance scheme) to ensure that the capital stock is kept intact out of the profits that the usufruct's rent yields over and above the charge to be paid to society, to let firms fail when unable to pay the net charge for the usufruct, and to ensure that bankruptcy does not entail the destruction of society's wealth by having in place a broadly based mandatory insurance scheme. Of course, a social safety net needs to be developed and maintained.

In a growing economy, questions of how additions to the capital stock and its replacement are decided upon loom large. These problems revolve around the issue of how best to facilitate exit and entry as well as the steady upgrading of the capital stock. Both additions to and replacement of the existing capital stock could be handled through exit and entry by entrepreneurs bidding on access to future assets. This can be organized in two conceptually different ways. The preferred one would involve the development of full-fledged capital markets, including forward transactions. Entrepreneurs would simply explore with commercially viable financial institutions how best to allocate society's savings, including amortization funds and state savings proper. There is plenty of room for the purely technical exploration of the alternatives from which society may then choose without raising objections to social ownership of the means of production provided. The focus of attention could usefully be directed at the critical assumption to the effect that proper capital markets, including forward markets and insurance schemes to guarantee risk, can be instituted in a relatively costless fashion.

Given the complexity of ensuring such efficient markets even in mature industrial market economies, it is hard to see how the reforming CPE could institute fully functioning capital markets within a comparatively brief period of time. In fact, multiple ownership forms in combination with the gradual emergence of capital markets for the bulk of society's capital may well be the more desirable way of proceeding. Private or cooperative ownership under some conditions can internalize coordination at a very small cost that would be hard to defray through full-fledged capital markets. But such dilution of property rights would be based on technical economic grounds within the given environment rather than on the ideology of the distribution of material wealth.

On CMEA reform and socialist integration

Lang's chapter devotes considerable attention to what he calls the sub-peripheralization of Eastern Europe in general and Hungary in particular, and how to forestall the outcome of this potentially disastrous scenario. He advocates "concerted unilateralism", which would move Hungary into the "hinterland" of the EC, and perhaps eventually into membership thereof, as argued by Marer and at times by Bacskai, and away from deliberations that aim at strengthening integration within the CMEA. I disagree with this diagnosis and certainly with the remedial action that is being advocated.

I very much doubt that without active efforts, including on the part of Hungary, to "harden" from within the CMEA's capacity to gain a more competitive position in world markets the socio-economic adjustment cost of the shock treatment, including convertibility and all that, is bound to be horrendous. If so, it is most likely to prove unacceptable from a socio-political point of view. Although remarkable changes in the climate for such deliberations have been crystallizing over the past several years, I still feel that the fragile socio-political and economic constructs in place would not be able to sustain a serious cut in levels of living in a comparatively short period of time.

Perhaps a small footnote in this connection, but one that has surfaced in a number of recent reform debates in Czechoslovakia, Hungary, Poland, and the Soviet Union, revolves around how to attain convertibility and what it may mean. Lang leaves no doubt that he favours the shock treatment. But he would like to have this cushioned through a financial support scheme put in place by West European central banks.

Convertibility is by definition a category that makes sense only when it is associated with the automatic and anonymous clearing of all or some classes of transactions. For that, it is necessary to create the fundamental preconditions. One cannot start convertibility through some support scheme when the preconditions for maintaining access to some markets in an anonymous and automatic fashion are not yet in place. This is a fortiori the case when there is not as yet policy agreement on what can realistically be put in place. In my view, those conditions can only be created by the countries directly suffering from the lack of convertibility. Measures need to be embraced in Eastern

Europe. This can be done by countries individually or by the group in concert perhaps with some outside support as a palliative. I still believe that the latter is a more realistic and promising alternative than anything else I have seen in the recent literature.

I have a small footnote also with respect to the conditional debt relief, which, although Lang does not fully sketch it, appears to smack of some kind of latter-day Marshall Plan assistance, this time forthcoming chiefly from within Western Europe. Once again, that is not very likely to materialize, certainly not from within Western Europe. This position can be further amplified by thinking beyond the surface of the advocated strategy that Hungary become the EC's hinterland. That can bring profitable opportunities only if the hinterland is, first, allowed to emerge and, second, becomes genuinely integrated with the rest of the "land", that is the EC for now. Lang is sufficiently aware of the pitfalls that are involved here, though I find the suggestion for an *Ausgleich*, apart from the ill-chosen terminology, not very attractive. Neither of the two alternatives sketched above seems very likely and I hope that the Hungarian leadership will not be willing to fall by the wayside in this matter. Instead, it should act to further socialist economic integration, for example, through a Central European Economic Union.

PART IV - WESTERN EUROPE AND JAPAN

Chapter 15

THE ROLE OF THE EC IN EAST-WEST ECONOMIC RELATIONS

Klaus Schneider[1]

This chapter points to the movement of the EC towards a unified market in 1992 and the creation of a European Economic Space covering Western Europe, and, against the background of increased economic cooperation in Western Europe, it summarizes the present state of economic relations between the EC and the East European countries.

15.1 The Community's new attractiveness

The European Community is undergoing profound and far-reaching changes. Past weaknesses were overcome and the Community is now moving steadily towards the single Community market and European Union, the ultimate objective of the Single Act. Decisions have already been taken on many of the measures needed to create the single European market; and the route for the remainder has been clearly mapped out. This will remain the Community's key priority in the years to come. But, the Twelve are only part of Europe. What about the "other Europeans"? How can the successful integration of the Twelve be reconciled with the wish of these "other Europeans" for closer cooperation or even membership? Many believe that any further enlargement of the Community is unlikely in the immediate future because internal development must take priority over enlargement. But the Community

---

[1] Commission of the European Community, Brussels, Belgium.

certainly welcomes its neighbours' increased interest for more cooperation. The President of the European Commission, Jacques Delors, recently urged the Twelve to develop what he termed "flexible proximity policies" tailored to a wide variety of situations. Different spheres of cooperation in Europe, more or less intensive, have developed and will be pursued in future. These include: EC-EFTA cooperation; increased cooperation with the EC's Mediterranean neighbours (Cyprus, Malta, and Yugoslavia) and with Turkey which has applied to join the Community; and emerging cooperation between the EC and its East European neighbours.

This chapter will focus on the development of the European Community's relations with Eastern Europe. It is evident that the community's new attractiveness can also be seen in the historic breakthrough in its relations with the East over the last four years, with the establishment of diplomatic relations with the Soviet Union and five other countries, the parallel opening of official relations with the CMEA, the conclusion of bilateral agreements with Hungary and Czechoslovakia, and the prospect of a network of bilateral trade and cooperation agreements with all the European members of the CMEA. But it should also be stressed from the outset that the substance of economic relations between the EC and most of its East European neighbours will be significantly weaker, for quite some time, than cooperation on a West European scale.

Economic integration/cooperation can be seen in three areas: the completion of the EC's internal market; the parallel creation of the EC-EFTA European Economic Space; and East-West (or "pan-European") economic cooperation.

15.2 The EC's internal market

The Community's internal market 1992 project is an acceleration of a process which started in 1958 with the creation of the EEC. At that time the Community was assigned the tasks of achieving "four freedoms": the unhindered movement of goods, services, capital, and persons. Much has been achieved over the past 30 years but the original objectives have not yet been fully attained. Hence, the Community's decision to set a time limit (the end of 1992) to do the job.

Looking to progress achieved in direction of the single, frontier-free Community market, what is most striking is the new qualitative change: there has been an immense leap forward with the harmonization of technical regulations and standards, simple mutual recognition sometimes taking its place. Public procurement accounting for a large proportion of economic activity in the Community is still often restricted to within national borders. They will soon become more open. And the days are gone when it took eighteen years to adopt a directive on the free movement of architects. Moreover, the directive on the mutual recognition of diplomas will eventually ensure that holders will be able to exercise their profession anywhere in the Community. This is a clear sign of the Community's changing economic and social dimension, leading eventually to a Community labour market.

All the measures required for the liberalization of capital movements have been adopted, thus ensuring that a genuine Community financial services market can be created. It ties in neatly with the need to bring tax systems closer into line and to improve monetary cooperation in the Community.

The impetus of change has caught on in every sphere of Community activity. There will be a single market for everything from transport to energy to spin-off products from scientific advances. The result of these changes will be a wider choice for the 320 million consumers and a major boost to the Community economy, a boost which will have favourable repercussions both inside and outside the Community.

The external impact

Ever since the Community was established there has been a common external trade policy, as provided for in the Treaty of Rome. Now that the Community is intensifying its internal integration, it is natural that its external policy should keep abreast.

Three different classes of external policy measures in connection with the single market can be distinguished. Some are indispensable if internal barriers are to be removed, many are covered by the existing international obligations of the Community, others represent virgin territory with respect both to Community policy and to international rules.

The best example of external policy measures which are indispensable are the gaps which still exist in the common commercial policy itself as a result of the current divergences among the import regimes applicable in individual member states. The most important are quantitative restrictions with regard to imports of certain products from, for example, Eastern Europe and the limits fixed for individual member states within the Community's quotas under bilateral textile agreements and for sensitive products in its Generalized System of Preferences for developing countries.

Such measures will make no sense when frontier posts disappear between the member states because they will no longer be policeable. After 1992 the Community's rules on imports from third countries will need to be fully unified. In many cases the national restrictions will simply be eliminated, although this may require Community assistance to restructure certain sensitive sectors.

It cannot be excluded, however, that by the end of 1992 there will still be a limited hard core of products where particular economic difficulties in some member states may require the replacement of national protective measures by appropriate measures at the Community level. Any such measures would, of course, have to be in conformity with the Community's international obligations. With respect to this class of measures, the final effect of an extension of Community external policy is unambiguous. The Community market as a whole will have a lower level of protection than it does now.

A second class of measures concerns those many areas in which new external action will be fully subject to the Community's existing obligations, whether these be multilateral (GATT, OECD, etc.) or bilateral (EFTA, Lomé, Mediterranean countries, etc.). These agreements are already based largely on procedures directed towards the progressive liberalization of world markets, and the extension of the scope of Community action within them will thus result, once again, in a world-wide decrease, not an increase, of protection.

Finally, a number of measures will break new ground by extending Community external action to fields not covered by international rules such as the GATT rules. Here the same logic applies; the same objective of world-wide market opening will be pursued. In these areas the EC may give non-EC firms access to the benefits of 1992 conditional on a guarantee of equivalent or, at least, non-discriminatory access in those firms' own countries for EC firms. As Jacques Delors has said: "the single market will be open, but it will not be given away".

The Community is finalizing its strategy for external economic and commercial policy on the basis of the European Council's approach (as defined at its meeting in Hanover, 1988): "The internal market should not close in on itself. In conformity with the provisions of GATT, the Community should be open to third countries, and must negotiate with those countries where necessary to ensure access to their market for Community exports. It will seek to preserve the balance of advantages accorded, while respecting the unity and the identity of the internal market of the Community".

15.3 EC-EFTA cooperation

With the abolition, in early 1984, of the last remaining tariff barriers and quantitative restrictions affecting their bilateral trade in industrial products, the Community and the EFTA countries have attained the goal set in the 1972 Free Trade Agreements. EFTA is the EC's main trading partner, more important than the United States or Japan. In fact, EC-EFTA trade has become vital for both groupings and amounts to over 25 per cent of world trade. Since the April 1984 Luxembourg ministerial meeting, EC-EFTA cooperation has become more systematic. Concrete results are the two novel, multilateral conventions on the Single Administrative Document and transit procedures in force since the beginning of 1988. Negotiations for the elimination of export restrictions in EC-EFTA trade will shortly be concluded. EC and EFTA countries are now engaged on a necessarily rather long-term exercise to eliminate technical barriers to trade.

One of the key conclusions reached at Luxembourg in 1984 was that there should be continued pragmatic and flexible cooperation beyond the framework of the Free Trade Agreements. The goal is to create a dynamic European Economic Space covering the whole of Western Europe. There has been considerable progress towards that goal: EFTA participates in a number of Community research and development programmes; there are framework agreements with most EFTA countries in the field of science and technology; the EC and EFTA, in September 1988, adopted a convention on the jurisdiction and enforcement of civil and commercial judgements, thereby taking an important step towards the strengthening of the legal framework of EC-EFTA cooperation; the EC and EFTA are examining the possibilities for mutual cooperation on the environment, in the fields of financial services, road transport, civil aviation, product liability, indirect taxation, counterfeit and intellectual property; and various other possibilities for mutual cooperation are being explored, such as education, new technologies, statistics, and tourism.

As to future prospects of EC-EFTA cooperation, it is clear that the Community process of achieving the single market by 1992 provides both an incentive, and an opportunity for greater EC-EFTA cooperation in many fields covered by the 1992 White Paper. In his statement at the European Parliament of January 17, 1989, referring to the prospects of EC-EFTA cooperation, President Delors offered the following reflections:

> With each step we take the slope is getting steeper. We are coming up to the point where the climber wants to stop to get his breath, to check that he is going in the right direction and that he is properly equipped to go on. There are two options; we can stick

to our present relations, essentially bilateral, with the ultimate aim of creating a free trade area encompassing the Community and EFTA; or, alternatively, we can look for a new, more structured partnership with common decision-making and administrative institutions to make our activities more effective and to highlight the political dimension of our cooperation in the economic, social, financial and cultural spheres. It would be premature to go into the details of this institutional framework. I have my own ideas, but they need to be discussed by the new Commission and then informally, without obligation, with the countries concerned.

At the same occasion, however, President Delors also made it clear that there are important differences between the single Community market and the European Economic Space. There are clear limits to "picking and choosing" certain types of benefits of the frontier-free Community market. First, the single market is first and foremost a customs union. Are EFTA partners prepared to abide by the common commercial policy that any customs union must apply to outsiders? Second, the single market also implies harmonization. Are EFTA partners willing to transpose the common rules essential to the free movement of goods into their domestic law and, in consequence, accept the supervision of the Court of Justice? And third, the Community is much more than a large market. It is a frontier-free economic and social area on the way to becoming a political union entailing closer cooperation on foreign policy and security.

Future discussions of EC-EFTA cooperation will be a major challenge for both parties. This process gained new impetus with the Oslo Declaration of March 1989 of the Heads of Government of the EFTA countries envisaging negotiations with the Community "which would lead to the fullest possible realization of free movement of goods, services, capital and persons, with the aim of creating a dynamic and homogeneous European Economic Space". One week after the Oslo meeting an informal joint meeting of EFTA and EC ministers took place in Brussels to discuss future steps towards a more structured and more global approach for future EC-EFTA cooperation. The aim of proceeding on a two-tier track - achieving further progress under the Luxembourg Declaration while at the same time laying the basis for an additional dimension in EC-EFTA relations - was confirmed by both sides in June 1989.

The Community's internal integration and joint EC-EFTA efforts to promote cooperation on a Western European scale are, of course, important contributions to the aims of the current Uruguay Round of multilateral trade negotiations (i.e., the maintenance and strengthening of the liberal world trading system).

15.4 East-West (or "pan-European") economic cooperation

Compared to EC-EFTA trade flows, the two-way trade flows between the Community and the European CMEA region are much less important. Community exports to just one of the EFTA countries, Switzerland, are by far larger than Community exports to all East European countries, including the Soviet Union. In recent years, the share of EC trade with the Eastern regions in the EC's total world trade has amounted to about 6-7 per cent. These shares for the United States and Japan are 1 per cent and 2 per cent, respectively. It should be remembered that focusing on the OECD countries' trade with the European CMEA region one is looking at a very small slice of the total trade of the Western world, about 3 per cent. But it is also true that 60 per cent of Western trade with the East European region is channelled through the European Community. The recent normalization of relations between the EC and its Eastern neighbours can thus have a positive impact on East-West trade and East-West economic relations in general. Whether this development will actually lead to increased trade flows is largely a function of the domestic economic conditions in Eastern Europe. This is especially so for the Soviet Union which in recent years accounted for about three-fifths of total East-West trade and whose policies have a strong influence on the trading activities of its East European allies.

The systemic incompatibilities between Eastern and Western economies are the most fundamental impediment to East-West trade. It is encouraging that the socialist countries of Eastern Europe seem to have accepted the need for economic reform for the sake of economic performance in general and competitiveness in manufacturing exports in particular. This is not to say, of course, that the reforms in question will be implemented, or that they will necessarily deliver the goods. But this is another theme.

The legal framework of EC-CMEA trade

In 1974 the trade agreements of the Community's member states with the East European countries expired, since authority on external trade matters passed over to the Community. The Community offered to replace these with agreements with the Community itself, but none of the East European countries responded to this offer at the time. The other non-European state trading countries also failed to respond.

As of January 1, 1975 the Community had to set up *autonomous measures* in its trade relations with the state trading countries, including the European members of the CMEA. Imports of products from these countries became subject to special reglations. The large majority of products listed in the Community's external tariff were liberalized and they were not subject to any quantitative restrictions throughout the whole of the Community. A small number of remaining products were subject to quantitative restrictions inherited from, and therefore varying among the different member states of the Community for which quotas are opened each year by decision of the Council of Ministers of the Community, and which also vary in relation to each of the state-trading countries concerned. Amendments are made to these arrangements throughout the year either by the member states alone, within certain margins, or through a Community procedure which is used on numerous occasions, almost always to expand the import possibilities rather than to restrict them.

A number of autonomous import measures of the Community were suspended over the years by *bilateral agreements*. During the second half of the 1970s the Community, in fact, concluded various agreements with East European countries in specific sectors, namely in textiles, steel and agriculture.

In the *textile* sector, the conclusion of the first Multifibre Arrangement (MFA) within the GATT framework led to the conclusion in 1976-81 of a series of bilateral agreements between the Community and CMEA countries, both members of the GATT, Romania, Hungary, Poland and Czechoslovakia and a non-member, Bulgaria. Further to the renewal of the MFA in 1986, twenty-six bilateral textile trade agreements have been renegotiated and applied de facto since January 1987, which again include the five above-mentioned CMEA countries. The export licences foreseen in these agreements permit the exporting country to control the allotment of export possibilities more efficiently than a system of import quotas would allow. The flexibility concerning advance use and overruns of permitted amounts enhances these possibilities, while the consultation arrangements permit problems to be dealt with as soon as they arise. For the duration of these agreements the quantitative restrictions of the autonomous system are suspended.

In the *steel* sector, arrangements with the above-mentioned CMEA countries have been concluded by the Coal and Steel Community. Since 1978, in fact, imports of steel products into the Community have generally been subject to a system of basic prices or to special arrangements with supplier countries. The five East European countries thus undertook to restrain their exports to the Community in return for price concessions. These arrangements also provide a framework for consultations should any problems arise and have generally led to a satisfactory chanelling of trade in these products.

Finally, arrangements on imports of specific *agricultural products* provide that certain supplementary levels of the Community's Common Agricultural Policy would not be applied on condition that the countries concerned respect the sluice-gate prices. In addition, self-restraint agreements concerning exports in sheep- and goatmeat from these five East European countries to the Community have been concluded since 1981; the last one with the German Democratic Republic in 1987.

For two state trading countries the Community's autonomous system of quantitative restrictions lost further importance (China in 1978 and Romania in 1981) when these countries accepted the Community's offer of 1974 to negotiate *general trade agreements*. An agreement on trade in industrial products, and another one on the establishment of a Joint Committe between the Community and Romania came into force in 1981. A number of quantitative restrictions were abolished immediately, others were suspended, and yet other quota amounts were opened or increased. Increases in quotas are proposed and discussed within the annual meetings of a Joint Committee.

As demonstrated below, the partial or complete abolition of remaining quantitative restrictions was made possible for the Community once all other East European countries had shown interest in general, contractual trade relations with it.

In the *tariff sector* the Community autonomously grants most favoured nation treatment to state trading countries irrespective of whether they are entitled thereto as members of the GATT. In addition, within the Community's generalized preferences, Romania is one of the developing countries which benefits from the tariff preferences concerning industrial, agricultural and textile products.

In accordance with Articles VI, XVI and XXIII of the GATT and in particular of GATT Anti-Dumping Subvention and Anti-Subsidy Codes concerning their interpretation, the Community has established a system of protection against dumped or subsidized imports from non-EC member countries. However, the special economic system of state trading countries has to be taken into account and some rules are therefore modified with respect to them. Anti-dumping rules may be taken as an example. Dumping is deemed to occur when the export price of the goods is lower than the normal value of a similar product. The concept of "normal value" is based on the premise that a free and open market exists in the exporting country with prices being fixed by factors of supply and demand. Since it is considered that prices in state trading countries do not result from this market process, Community regulations lay down special rules to calculate normal value by referring to production costs and prices in a market economy third country. Many complaints of dumping by state trading countries are received from Community producers.

Like all other decisions and regulations of the Community institutions, those taken in the anti-dumping procedures are open to review before the Community's Court of Justice, and it is interesting to note that Soviet trading bodies have taken advantage of this opportunity on more than one occasion. A ruling given in one case concerning imports of Soviet products imposed specific obligations on the Commission of the EC concerning the method of establishing an equivalent normal value for dumped imports from state trading countries. These applications to the Court were of course of political as well as legal interest since they implied the recognition by Soviet exporters of the Community's powers in this field and in particular the competence of the supreme organ of Community law.

There are many other Community instruments which conern trade with East European countries (e.g., the Common Agricultural Policy with its various mechanisms on levies and so on). As these concern third countries in general, they will not be dealt with here.

Apart from the autonomous regulations, the various sectoral agreements and arrangements, and the emerging general trade agreements, the Community has relations with the countries of Eastern and Central Europe in various *multilateral* organizations.

The GATT is the most significant convention governing international trade and lays down detailed rules with regard to most favoured nation treatment in the tariff sector, the administration of import quotas, payments for imports and exports, subsidies, dumping, and many other subjects. Czechoslovakia, Poland, Romania, and Hungary are parties to the GATT, but in the cases of Poland, Romania, and Hungary, it must always be remembered that their obligations are modified by protocols allowing the accession of these countries to the GATT which take into account the particular nature of their economic systems. In two cases, Poland and Romania, specific import obligations were assumed in view of their tariffs and in all three cases, specific safeguard provisions, allowing protective measures to be taken under conditions less stringent than those of GATT rules, are foreseen.

Another important multilateral trading framework is constituted by the Multifibre Arrangement, renegotiated within the GATT Textile Commitee and renewed for five years in 1986. This lays down detailed rules for the conduct of trade in textiles, for differentiated treatment of different groups of suppliers (with particularly favourable treatment for the LDCs), and for special rules for the imposition of safeguard measures. In particular, it foresees the conclusion of specific bilateral agreements within its framework (see above for the sectoral agreements concluded between the Community and East European countries).

There are a number of other multilateral links between the Community and certain member countries of CMEA. Various relevant topics are discussed and examined at the Economic Commission for Europe of the United Nations.

The formal framework of EC-CMEA trade

The long-standing main aim of EC policy has been to normalize EC-CMEA economic relations. This means, for example, being able to discuss common problems, to negotiate agreements, to have formal relations through accredited missions to the EC, and to end efforts to hinder normal EC participation in international organizations and conventions. A turning point in this respect was the signing on June 25, 1988 in Luxembourg of the EC-CMEA Joint Declaration. It marked the establishment of official relations between the European Community and the CMEA and the recognition of the Community's identity, both in terms of its competences and its territory. At the same time it gave the impetus for the normalization of bilateral relations between the Community and the individual East European members of the CMEA. The importance of this recent development can only be understood against the background of the "failures of the past".

The history of Community relations with Eastern Europe can be summarized as follows. For many years after the creation of the EEC in 1958, the Eastern European countries, and particularly the Soviet Union, adopted a hostile attitude to the EEC as "the economic arm of NATO". Although, the Community had long been ready to normalize relations with its Eastern neighbours, little progress was made. In November 1974, the EC Commission proposed to all state trading countries an outline of an overall trade agreement but they ignored this initiative. Their reaction was to propose in 1976 a draft agreement to be concluded between the Community and the CMEA, as well as the member countries on both sides. It laid down principles for the development of trade relations between the Community and the individual CMEA member countries: MFN treatment, the removal of obstacles to trade, non-discrimination, etc. According to this draft, bilateral agreements between the Community and CMEA member countries would only be used for the solution of "certain particular concrete questions" and the Joint Committee, as proposed by the 1976 draft, would have the right to "contribute to the solution" of these questions. The Community saw this draft agreement as intended to play down the significance of bilateral relations between the Community and individual East European countries, to lay down guidelines for these relations in a "bloc-to-bloc" agreement, and to submit the bilateral agreements to the control of a "bloc-to-bloc" body, the EEC-CMEA Joint Committee. For the Community, the inclusion of EC member states in the proposed agreement was evidence of the CMEA (Soviet) wish to ignore and by-pass the Community's exclusive powers over trade policy matters and to compel the EC to conduct its trade relations not directly with individual CMEA countries but in a framework in which the CMEA would play the role of a kind of intermediary. The CMEA, however, had no common commercial policy towards Western countries, and no trade agreements, as an organization, with any Western industrialized country (with the exception of Finland).

In short, the second period of relations between the Community and Eastern Europe was a period where, mainly due to the Soviet Union's wish, the CMEA refused to recognize the Community's identity as it was, and even tried to change it.

Despite the Soviet policy line of avoiding direct dealings with the Community, and despite the spreading of a network of cooperation agreements with EC member states, most of the East European countries nevertheless found it useful to conclude sectoral agreements with the Community as such. These agreements were, apparently, consistent with the overall line agreed within the CMEA whereby member countries were allowed agreements with the Community on "concrete questions". Even when Romania concluded a much broader agreement with the EC in 1980, covering trade in all industrial products, it was intended to be regarded officially as a sectoral agreement of the same kind; this was the reason why the Romanians insisted that the agreement on the creation of a Community-Romania Joint Committee, which was negotiated and concluded simultaneously with the industrial product agreement, should be kept separate from it.

After the first period of hostility and the second period of limited contacts with stress on the CMEA as intermediary, there followed the present period of "normalization" of relations. The first signs of a more open and flexible attitude to the EC came in 1983-84 with approaches by Hungary and Czechoslovakia seeking wider trade links than the sectoral agreements they already had. Also the CMEA began to send signals that it was time to take up again the dialogue suspended in 1980. However, a recognition of the true nature of the Community as an economic and political entity had to await the imprimatur of Mr. Gorbachev given in a May 1985 meeting with Mr. Craxi, then President of the EC Council. Less than a month later the CMEA proposed to establish official relations between the CMEA and the EC, no longer by the conclusion of a full-scale agreement but by the adoption of a Joint Declaration.

Nearly three years were to go by before the declaration could be signed. This may be surprising in view of the brevity of the text, which in substance simply announces the establishment of official relations between the two organizations and provides for subsequent contacts to work out possible areas and forms of cooperation between them. However, two problems had to be resolved: first, the Community found it unreasonable to establish official relations with the CMEA without also normalizing bilateral relations between the Community and the individual East European countries (i.e., the "parallel approach"); and second, the Community had to make sure that the CMEA agreed to the territorial application of the Treaty of Rome which included West Berlin.

The first problem was resolved by May 1986 when all East European countries had reacted positively to the Community's "parallel approach". The second problem was resolved only in May 1988 when it became clear that for the Commission and the member states the territorial application clause was a sine qua non for the signing of the Joint Declaration.

The significance of the Joint Declaration, then, lies less in its content than in its existence which symbolizes the normalization of East European relations with the Community, opens the way for diplomatic relations and the conclusion of bilateral trade and cooperation agreements between the EC and individual CMEA member countries, and represents recognition of the Community's identity both in terms of its territory and of its competence. The Joint Declaration clearly limits EC-CMEA cooperation to areas where both partners have powers and where they have a common interest. The EC's powers are wider than those of the CMEA as an organization; and the willingness of the CMEA countries, and notably the Soviet Union, to negotiate with the Community on trade and a wide range of other areas of cooperation recognizes this.

In short, a long-standing dispute over the Community's exclusive power to negotiate on trade matters with the East European countries has thus been resolved in favour of the EC.

From a general framework to real substance?

The bilateral agreements already concluded between the Community and East European countries have a common characteristic: they are or will be non-preferential agreements. The extent to which it will be possible in the long term to extend to Eastern Europe the network of specific agreements which the EC has with its West European neighbours will very much depend on how far the process of modernization and economic reform goes in Eastern Europe. The idea of an EC-CMEA free trade area would for the foreseeable future come up against the problem of the differences between economic and trade policy systems. It is hard to see how such a free trade area could be put into effect without a complete revamping of the Eastern economic systems. The removal of customs barriers would not make trade in a state-trading country any more "free". The only really trade-creating device in these agreements are, on the Community side, the (full or partial) abolition of the so-called discriminatory quantitative restrictions which only covered a small portion of Community imports from these countries in recent years. On the Eastern side, hope is expressed that concessions in the form of "commercial cooperation" (i.e.,improved business facilities, better economic information, etc.) may improve export opportunities to East European countries.

Despite the numerous limiting factors these trade agreements are a necessary (but not sufficient) condition for a future expansion of East-West trade flows. They create a framework aiming to bridge the still largely incompatible economic and trading systems. As a result, the process of negotiation and exploration between East European countries and the Community on trade and cooperation matters has become particularly intense over the last year or two. The most important landmark to date in the process of developing Community agreements with Eastern Europe is the agreement on trade and commercial and economic cooperation with Hungary, which was signed on September 26, 1988 and entered into force on December 1, 1988. In the field of trade, this provides for the removal of Community quantitative restric-

234

tions (QRs), insofar as they are inconsistent with Article XIII of GATT (i.e., "discriminatory" or "specific" QRs). This removal will take place in three stages: the first, during the first year of the validity of the Agreement, will see the liberalization of non-sensitive products which have not been imported from Hungary during the last three years; in the second stage, up to the end of 1992, restrictions will be removed on a large number of imports which are not particularly sensitive; in many cases these have already been liberalized experimentally, or else the quotas allowed under the present "autonomous import arrangements" have not been fully used. Imports of sensitive products will be freed from restrictions during the third period from 1992-95. Until 1998 (the Agreement is a ten-year one) special safeguard measures will be in force to protect the particularly sensitive sectors of Community industry which might be affected by a rapid increase in imports of the products liberalized in the third stage. Besides agreeing to these safeguard measures, Hungary has also accepted, in the chapter on commercial cooperation, to give non-discriminatory treatment to Community firms in such matters as the issue of licences, the administration of Hungary's global quota on consumer goods, the facilities provided for businessmen who wish to set up representations or agencies in Hungary and the treatment of trading partners in matters of intellectual property. The part of the agreement concerned with economic cooperation mentions such areas as industry, agriculture, science, transport, tourism, the environment and energy. All those are areas where Community specialists who have studied the matter believe that there is an interest for the Community in cooperating with Hungary. The provisions on this cooperation do not enter into details on the exact fields to be covered or methods to be used. These will form the subject of bilateral discussions later, particularly in the Joint Committee set up by the agreement which can discuss practically an economic subject which concerns the two parties.

The agreement with Hungary, therefore, has a substantial section on economic cooperation and, as far as the trade aspect goes, it represents what is in effect the limit of the trading policy possibilities of the EC vis-à-vis a state trading country. In negotiating this agreement great attention was paid to the particular situation of Hungary: for example, its status in GATT, where its Protocol of Accession of 1973 recognizes the economic validity of the Hungarian Tariff, and also provides for the removal of discriminatory quantitative restrictions, in principle by 1975. Then again, Hungary has gone further than other East European countries in certain aspects of its economic reform movement (e.g., in the monetary and fiscal areas). This has attracted the interest and goodwill of the EC and its member state governments and has also improved the possibilities for cooperation with Hungary by Community firms.

The trade agreement between Czechoslovakia and the Community signed on December 19, 1988 entered into force on April 1, 1989. It only covers industrial products, it has no element of economic cooperation, and it is a relatively short-term agreement (four years). It grants increased quotas for products of interest to Czechoslovak exporters and commits the latter country to take appropriate measures to encourage imports from the Community through positive steps in the field of commercial cooperation and the supply of relevant economic information. One of the tasks of the "Consultation Body" set up by the agreement (a kind of Joint Committee) will be to examine the possibility of negotiations of a successor agreement. Czechoslovakia has already signalled interest in further economic cooperation with the Community.

Formal negotiations for trade and cooperation agreements with Poland and Bulgaria began in March and April 1989, respectively. Negotiations with Poland were favourably influenced by internal developments there, both in the political and economic spheres. On April 24, 1989, the Community's Foreign Affairs Countil welcomed the advances towards democracy which were made as a result of the "Round Table" meetings between the Polish government and opposition, and expressed the wish to assist Poland in overcoming its economic difficulties. On May 22, the Council expressed the wish to interpret flexibly the negotiating mandate in order to take account of the progress in political liberalization and economic reform intentions and steps in that country. Measures discussed included further liberalization of quantiative restrictions, concessions in the field of agricultural products, and an examination of possible action by the European Investment Bank. As of July 1989 the chances looked good for a far-reaching agreement between the Community and Poland.

Negotiations with Bulgaria will, no doubt, be complicated by its efforts to join the GATT and its wish to tailor the envisaged agreement with the Community in the perspective of its eventual GATT-membership. The question, currently, is whether the rather cautious moves towards economic changes and the absence of political reforms will create enough Western goodwill to envisage far-reaching cooperation with this country.

Negotiations with the Soviet Union on an extensive trade and cooperation agreement began in July 1989. The Soviet Union was the only East European country which had not yet concluded any sectoral agreements with the

Community, although negotiations and contacts are now underway for the conclusion of such agreements in the field of fisheries and textiles.

The first exploratory contacts for a possible general agreement took place between experts of the Commission and the Soviet Union early in 1988. In line with the Community's traditional policy towards state trading countries, the Commission negotiators offered an agreement covering trade only. The Soviet Union sought an agreement which would cover not only trade but also a wide range of areas of economic cooperation. Explorations on such a wider agreement only became possible after thorough Council discussions of the content of future agreements with East European countries, in particular the Soviet Union, which on July 25, 1988, led to the broadening of topics to be explored and which included commercial and, in particular, economic cooperation.

The Council's decision not only had a favourable impact on the exploratory talks with the Soviet Union but also on the exploratory meetings with Bulgaria and Poland. The discussions with these two countries led to the Council directives for negotiating an agreement with them on trade and cooperation in February 1989.

Radical political and economic reforms in the Soviet Union, as well as the turn around in Soviet attitudes towards the European Community, from hostility to a broadly realistic assessment of the Community and its identity, offer promising prospects for the future development of EC-Soviet relations. In June 1989 the Vice President of the Commission of the EC, Frans Andriessen, stressed that the EC-Soviet agreement will mark the culmination of the process of normalization of the Community's economic relations with Eastern Europe. It will be an ambitious agreement covering trade, commercial, and economic cooperation whose scope matches the importance of the two parties, their expectations, and the dynamics of their economic systems. It is envisaged that the agreement applies initially for ten years, a period which makes full allowance for the impact of perestroika and the single market on reciprocal trade. Industrial efficiency and diversification in the Soviet Union should benefit from management training, joint ventures, and other forms of business cooperation facilitated by the forthcoming agreement. Economic cooperation in fields such as environmental protection, the search for alternative energy sources and nuclear safety within the framework of the agreement will give a new sense of urgency to international action in areas of considerable public concern.

There has been a notable change in attitudes of the GDR to the Community. From having no contacts at all in the past, the GDR is moving towards broad interest in trade and cooperation with the EC. A first sectoral agreement on some agricultural products between the Community and the GDR was concluded in 1987. Exploratory meetings in the field of textiles and fishery were also held. In June 1988, a few days after the signing of the EEC-CMEA Joint Declaration, the GDR signalled interest in a broad, general trade agreement with the Community. Both parties made it clear that the special system of trade between the Federal Republic of Germany and the GDR should not be affected by a future EC-GDR trade agreement.

Compared to the radical internal reforms in Hungary, Poland, and the Soviet Union, the GDR has shown little enthusiasm for economic and political change of this kind. This, in turn, has not yet triggered much enthusiasm on the Community side for envisaging the broad cooperation it is willing to offer to the reforming countries.

Negotiations with Romania on a trade and cooperation agreement began in April 1987. It was intended to replace the existing 1980 agreement on trade in industrial products and to broaden the scope of cooperation. After a few rounds of negotiations in the same year, further negotiations were blocked due largely to the overall political situation in Romania. Negotiations were formally suspended in April 1989. In a joint Council and Commission statement of April 24, 1989 the Community and its member states repeated their deep concern at the Romanian government's continued failure to meet its commitments under the Helsinki process, in particular in the field of human rights. A resumption of the negotiations would take place only should clear evidence emerge of a significant improvement in Romania's respect for human rights and its observance of the commitments it had entered into through the Helsinki process.

15.5 Towards an EC "Ostpolitik"

Remembering that the Community at this same Council meeting welcomed the favourable turn taken by the process of political and economic reform in Poland, a specific pattern of the Community's policy towards East European countries clearly emerges. It is the principle of *specificity* in the Community's relations with these countries, the substance and intensity of which are shaped to be in line with the state of internal reform in the individual East European countries.

This policy was clearly expressed in the "Declaration of the European Council on the International Role of the European Community" in Rhodes,

December 2-3, 1988. It was here that member governments reaffirmed the Community's willingness to further economic relations and cooperation with the European members of the CMEA, taking into account each country's specific situation, in order to use the opportunities available in a mutually beneficial way. It is clear that the scope and intensity of present and future bilateral trade and economic agreements between the EC and the individual East European countries will necessarily be different from case to case.

Another element of the Community's "Ostpolitik" is the explicit linking of the external policies of the European Community and the policies agreed in the framework of the European Political Cooperation of the Twelve. Striving for coherence in this respect is based on an important provision in the Single European Act (Article 30 on European Foreign Policy). The European Community and the Twelve stressed their determination to make full use of this provision as spelt out in the "Declaration of the European Council on the International Role of the European Community". The Ministers of Foreign Affairs, at their Council meeting of April 24, 1989, stated that the aim of greater consistency between Community policies and those agreed in the framework of Political Cooperation is recognized as "being particularly desirable in the context of relations with the East European countries".

In short, the shaping of the Community's economic and trade relations with the individual East European countries will more and more be influenced by the political situation in these countries (political reforms, democratization, respect for human rights, etc.). This global approach is not only an additional challenge to Community/EPC decisionmaking, it also demonstrates that foreign policy and foreign economic relations between the EC and Eastern Europe are getting a much higher priority compared to only a few years ago when EC/EPC policy statements on the Soviet Union or other East European countries were almost absent.

Another challenge in the Community framework is the search for coherence between the existing cooperation policies of the EC's member states with East European countries and the cooperation which the Community is in the process of establishing with some of these countries in a number of areas. Community action in this field should be complementary to that of its member states, and not replace it. Community action should give cooperation with Eastern Europe a new dimension and should reflect the present and the future of the Community. In this context, the Council meeting of April 24, 1989 also emphasized the need for better coordination of the economic cooperation policies of the member states and the Community with regard to East

European countries and greater transparency and consistency of member states' export credit policies towards these countries.

The Community continues to give priority to relations with individual East European countries. It is prepared, however, to develop cooperation with the CMEA itself under the Joint Declaration signed in June 1988.

A first meeting of representatives was held in November 1988 in Brussels, and a second one in Moscow in April 1989. These meetings are examining the competences, working methods and activities of the two sides. Sectors for cooperation must be ones in which both sides have similar activities, and in which both have an interest. The EC and the CMEA today are still basically at the stage of "getting to know each other".

The CMEA has proposed eight areas for cooperation between the two organizations: environmental protection, statistics, standards and economic forecasting, transportation, nuclear energy, electrical energy, and science and technology. *Forms* of future cooperation also need to be discussed, they may range from a simple exchange of views to formal agreements in particular sectors.

It is difficult to foresee how cooperation between the Community and the CMEA may develop in future. A thorough exchange of information about what the two sides are actually doing in the areas mentioned or in other sectors, is certainly a useful first step. Much will, of course, depend on the future role the CMEA is asked to play by its own member countries, which not only include East European but also non-European countries such as Cuba, Mongolia, and Vietnam. A strengthening of the currently weak external role of the CMEA is not in sight.

15.6 Conclusions: a pan-European economic space?

The Community's relations with the Soviet Union and most of the other European members of the CMEA are in a process of fundamental change. A large gap in external relations was filled in 1988 when all these countries, with the exception of Romania, established diplomatic relations with the Community.

Bilateral agreements between the Community and individual East European countries are already concluded or will be concluded shortly. A process of cooperation in many sectors has begun. Without major achievements in Eastern economic reforms towards Western-style market economies, however, these agreements may well remain a dead letter.

The normalization of relations between the Community and its neighbours in Eastern Europe is an important step for overcoming the division of Europe. Two factors contributed to these far-reaching changes in Europe. First, the new dynamic created by the Community's progress towards a single market without internal frontiers, paving the way to increasing economic and political unity. Second, the bold initiatives in political reform and economic liberalization underway in the Soviet Union, Hungary, and Poland and the hope for similar reform intentions in other countries of the Eastern region.

It is true that much has been achieved in a short time compared to decades of ignorance and mistrust in relations between the Community and the European CMEA countries, and the CMEA as such. But the achievements today are only necessary, basic conditions for integrating the Eastern countries into the emerging West European economic space. The latter is based on common values and principles in political and economic terms. It is still uncertain whether the promotion of these Western values in the Soviet Union and her allies will be successful. The Soviet and East European societies will have to decide these issues for themselves. The sufficient conditions for a pan-European Economic Space will be fulfilled only in an environment of respect for human rights and fundamental freedoms, a free circulation of people and ideas, and the establishment of more open societies. A pan-European Economic Space between societies based on different social and economic systems would be an unattractive vision. Fortunately, the options are currently wider open than ever before. The Community's emerging Ostpolitik aims at mapping out the progressive reintegration of East European economies into the European Economic Space.

Chapter 16

EC-CMEA ECONOMIC RELATIONS: REALITIES AND PROSPECTS

Irène Commeau-Rufin[1]

16.1 Introduction

Mikhail Gorbachev's arrival has given a new impetus to East-West economic relations. The Soviet Union and the entire Eastern bloc have developed a new attitude towards international economic organizations and in particular towards the European Community (EC). The EC, on the other hand, has elaborated a unified European market which will necessarily affect the nature of the economic and political exchange within Europe. How will the European unified market affect the relationship between the countries of the EC and the rest of Europe? This question preoccupies the countries of the Eastern bloc. They are asking: what does the Single European Act imply; what are the economic realities of the CMEA and the EC; and what are the prospects for intensifying the relations between the CMEA and the EC in order to help overcome the division of the European continent?

16.2 The EC and the CMEA

The Single European Act has become an ideal in European affairs in the sense that it incites goverments and people to realize an ambitious task. Behind the construction of this large domestic market also lies an ideal of an organized economical whole, capable of participating in tomorrow's international competition.

Over the last 25 years Europe has set up a customs union, patiently constructed the early elements of a monetary organization, and has defined an external commercial policy. It has laid the foundations for a Third World aid policy focusing on those nations which had been European colonies in the past.

The process was slow but irreversible. Europe faced difficulties and as always showed herself the "daughter of necessity". Objective realities urge

---

[1] Researcher, French Institute of International Relations, Paris, France.

political decision making. Western Europe had a space where the industrial products freely circulated, but how could it remain partitioned regarding public service, while international public service exchange and especially financial exchange was expanding?

The unified European market consists in completing the free exchange zone with a free circulation of public services. In 1979, the European monetary system was created. The point was to determine a number of rules allowing the coordination of economic policies to eventually stabilize exchange rates.

The Germans were not convinced of this necessity in 1979. However, today Mr. Pachl says that his country is happy to benefit from a stable exchange rate with its EC partners. It is not possible to reach an absolutely stable exchange rate overnight, but relative stability can be achieved despite the monetary fluctuations that are typical in the international monetary system. This stability concerns not only the five EC members of the exchange system but also Switzerland, Austria, Sweden, and the other Scandinavian countries whose monetary rates follow the Deutschmark. This relative stability is one of the EC's most powerful assets in the present situation of monetary incoherence. The first task is to establish tighter relationships between the EC members' central banks.

The creation of a central Eurobank is improbable in the short run, but it appears that the central bank directors, by reinforcing their cohesion, may carry out a useful monetary policy on a world scale. The European currency unit's role in the international financial market must be reinforced. It can be developed in a distinct manner so as to stamp the EC's personality.

The ideal behind the European Common Market is the construction of an economic whole which is a commercial, monetary and technological area as well organized as possible. This organization will provide an integration or rather a redistribution of the productive forces in the Community: this in turn will translate into a specialization accomplished according to prices, economic criteria, and the running of national markets in relation to the international market.

All the protective partitioning established in the past must progressively be eliminated. In the years to come the main problem the Community will have to confront is tax procedures. During the late 1980s, the EC has increasingly reinforced its integration, whereas the CMEA had a tendency to maintain and even increase their internal divisions.

In the 1960s, the six East European countries still dedicated the major part of their GNP to the reciprocal exchange of merchandise, to a greater extent than Western Europe. This situation is changing today.

In the last 25 years, the EC has increased its external trade's share of GDP by 25 per cent, whereas the CMEA has only increased its share by 6 per cent. On the other hand, unlike the EC, the financial ebb and flow within the CMEA remains non-existent, as their currencies are inconvertible. The rumour that the Soviet Union and other CMEA countries will eventually make their currencies convertible is an important sign of change.

For now, the creation of a single market in the EC might well increase the gap already existing between the two halves of Europe. In commercial terms, the CMEA represents only 4 per cent of the EC's foreign trade, whereas the EC represents 11 per cent of the CMEA countries' foreign trade. Moreover, financial assets move almost one way, since the inconvertibility completely hampers the movement of assets from East to West. It consists essentially in public or private credits of a modest amount. The direct investment for the entire CMEA does not represent more than $ 200 million, whereas France's figure alone is of the order of $ 4 billion (20 times more); and France does not receive a particularly high amount of outside direct investments.

16.3 The expansion of EC-CMEA economic relations

These various observations suggest that there is plenty of room to expand the economic relationship between East and West Europe. This expansion could well happen, given the present changes taking place in the Soviet Union and the Eastern bloc.

The West has been able to develop and integrate making economic decisions on the basis of international prices. Western markets acknowledge and take account of the link between domestic and international prices. An expansion of East-West economic exchange could only take place in so far as the Eastern economies evolved towards this link.

It is important to consider the question of integration and specialization in the East and in the West because the forthcoming relationship between the two blocs depends on their mutual structural traits. The East and West distinguish themselves from one another very strongly in respect of specialization. In spite of the 1971 CMEA program's orientations, specialization takes place principally among different branches of activity: for example, the Soviet Union specializes in energy and raw materials; Romania specializes in consumer goods; and Bulgaria specializes in agricultural products. By contrast, specialization in the EC takes place within each branch of activity. The methods also vary. In the East, specialization takes place through centralized negotiation. In the West specialization is dictated by the market and, specifically, by the rules of comparative advantage, which lead producers to produce in areas where they are most competitive.

But the main difference between East and West is that, in the West, state intervention that is incongruent with the deep tendencies of the market will fail; whereas in the East, when there is such failure, there is still no change. In the West the penalty for failure will be immediate (i.e., bankruptcy). In the East, the poor use of scarce resources may continue for a long time.

There is another difference between East and West regarding the slowness and the difficulties of the adjusting mechanical process with respect to specialization. Monetary mechanisms such as devaluation and the movement of assets that allow the correction of the negative effects of specialization do not exist in the East: for example, the useless and hard to decrease commercial excess or the non-existent direct allowance for the evolution of production gaps.

Integration in the East is less intense, but the specialization it introduces draws a stronger interdependence. With perestroika's logic, the Soviet Union is attempting to correct its system's defects. In fact it leads the Soviet Union to specialize in one area: energy and raw materials (which is not particularly good news for the future because it does not allow the Soviet Union the experience of producing industrial goods for competitive world markets).

By moving towards Western methods of specialization, the CMEA countries will, however, face a major contradiction in the early 1990s: either integration will really take place on the basis of market mechanisms and worldwide prices, and CMEA will naturally be geared towards specializations in industries requiring strong manpower and less sophisticated technologies; or the introduction of market mechanisms in the CMEA will be limited and erratic, and the present shortcomings will last for a long time.

In other words, there is no possible middle path. In the West, we have chosen the price system and the logic of the market, along with all the amendments these latter systems and mechanisms hold in modern times. Unless the governments of the CMEA countries reform their economies to accept the logic of the market, the prospects for a significant expansion of EC-CMEA trade will be bleak.

Chapter 17

THE ROLE OF THE GOVERNMENT OF THE FEDERAL REPUBLIC OF GERMANY IN EAST-WEST ECONOMIC RELATIONS

Joachim Jahnke[1]

Because of its geographical position, its industrial strength, and its traditions, the Federal Republic of Germany (FRG) has always had a well-developed East-West trade. However, it should be borne in mind, that this trade has never been economically essential in the overall picture of the FRG's foreign trade. The volume of trade with all CMEA states, excluding the GDR, has amounted to only 5 per cent of all foreign trade for quite some time. This is about the size of FRG trade with Belgium. The share of trade with the Soviet Union, the biggest CMEA state, amounts to about Denmark's share.

The role of the FRG's government developed along two related lines of thought: foreign policy considerations on the one side, economic policy considerations on the other. The overall impact of the government's activity on the development of East-West economic relations is considered to be much smaller than that of other underlying factors in the Eastern economies.

17.1 Foreign policy considerations

The guidelines for economic relations with the East are still provided by NATO's Harmel Report of 1967, though more than twenty years have elapsed since then. According to this report, it is the Alliance's desire to maintain its necessary military strength while building a constructive East-West relationship through cooperation which benefits both sides. The principles of the Harmel Report have been confirmed on several occasions.

Security

The first pillar on which the Harmel formula is based is the compatibility of East-West policy with Western security interests. East-West trade must not be allowed to enhance the Soviet Union's military-strategic capability. The FRG

---

[1] Deputy Assistant Secretary, Ministry of Economics, Bonn, FRG.

fully shares the concern that there be no outflow of militarily relevant goods and technologies to the Warsaw Pact. The common instrument for this is COCOM. It is the conviction of the FRG that it is imperative for the COCOM lists to be efficient and realistic. The more the lists concentrate on the genuinely sensitive technologies, the more credible and enforceable they will be. The formula is "higher fences around fewer products". The FRG actively participates in keeping the COCOM lists up to date. This adds to the ongoing efforts to strengthen cooperation among the responsible authorities of all COCOM countries in order to harmonize national efforts in implementing COCOM decisions.

The COCOM lists provide guidelines for national regulations to prohibit undesirable and dangerous exports of technology to other directions. As a consequence of illegal deliveries to other parts of the world in the late 1980s, the FRG strengthened the whole system of export controls by introducing new regulations and much more manpower.

Another foreign policy consideration that stems from the Harmel Report sets specific conditions for economic cooperation: first, there should be no unacceptable dependencies and second, the benefits of trade should be balanced. "No unacceptable dependencies" is a constituent part not only of the FRG's East-West policy but also applicable to overall trade policy. Diversification of directions and origins of exports and imports is the prudent formula. The FRG's trade with the East is far from creating unacceptable dependencies. Discussion in the West has at times focused only on the energy sector, and particularly on natural gas. On the basis of solid work, the International Energy Agency in Paris has determined that none of the industrial democracies are threatened by the danger of becoming dependent on the East for energy supplies. Interdependence as such is a fact of international life; some elements such as the environment are to be discussed later in this chapter.

Trade should be balanced; that is, also benefitting the West. It should not be allowed to produce one-sided benefits for the Warsaw Pact countries. That is why trade with the East must be financed on commercial conditions. The government of the Federal Republic never accepted subsidized public credits as instruments to foster trade with the East. The appropriate instruments for financing are private credits that can be backed by export guarantees based on normal interest rates and normal fees for guarantees. Fees to the East are just the same as to other trading partners in the world.

Dialogue

The second pillar on which the Harmel formula is based is continuation of the dialogue with the East. This includes economic cooperation as an important element. The political framework is important here as trade based on long-term projects needs calculable conditions. The FRG supports the CSCE process and contributes actively to the work of the ECE in Geneva in an effort to improve the climate for East-West economic cooperation.

17.2 Economic policy considerations

As mentioned, economic policy considerations are not opposed to foreign policy considerations but are interlinked. There are mainly five elements to be elaborated.

Economic advantage

Economic advantage is to be derived from trade with the East as from all trade. The FRG builds its wealth to a large extent on foreign trade. Exports count for 30 per cent of GNP compared with only 7 per cent for the United States and 12 per cent for Japan. Trade with the East, though relatively small, is a contributing factor and a factor of diversification in the field of energy imports, for example.

The government of the Federal Republic of Germany does not believe in "fortress Europe". It is very much opposed to all tendencies to dismantle customs and regulations within the European Community (EC) when the single market will enter into force at the end of 1992 and to replace them by higher fences on the outside borders. The FRG cannot give up present economic links with the rest of the world and withdraw into part of Europe. The EC only represents little more than half of its foreign trade. Of course, the attractiveness of that large European market will be considerable, if we think of the unified legal, economic, and financial framework and its advantages to business in terms of conditions to rely on. If trade with the East is not to lose further importance it will have to become more attractive as well.

The government does not handle business

The government of the Federal Republic of Germany has never agreed to compromise with its own economic system in which the state has no say in individual trading contracts. In order to ease differences of systems, mixed commissions for economic cooperation have been created where the private sector is represented through its associations together with government representatives.

The concentration on central decision making in the East has always been one of the biggest impediments to the development of trade with the East. That is why reforms in the economic systems in the East now under way are vital. But these must be judged carefully without being overly optimistic. The FRG is supporting all the efforts of its Eastern trading partners to introduce market elements into their foreign trade systems. For instance, many seminaries for East Europeans on management and marketing are organized these days in the FRG, a quite new and interesting development.

Setting the conditions for trade

Trade policy matters are the competence of the EC. The FRG influences the decision-making process in Brussels in the direction of its general liberal position in trade policy issues. There are still about 1,000 national import quotas in the EC for goods from the East, not including the textile sector. It is hoped that within the framework of bilateral negotiations between the EC and the countries of the East, solutions can be found to phase out these quotas.

Agreement has been reached with Hungary to eliminate quotas by 1995. In exchange, Hungary has committed itself not to discriminate against firms from the EC and to improve working conditions for them. Another trade agreement was concluded in December 1988 between the EC and Czechoslovakia. It includes concessions in the field of import quotas and efforts of Czechoslovakia to increase imports from the EC. Negotiations are also underway between the EC and Poland, Bulgaria, the GDR, and the Soviet Union.

The importance of EC import quotas should not be overestimated. Outside the textile and steel sectors they only cover minimal parts of trade. Their reduction will not give rise to any spectacular development of East-West trade.

The FRG has supported the normalization of relations between the EC and CMEA. In June 1988 a joint declaration was signed. This was considered more of political than proper economic importance. The developing framework for trade between the EC and Eastern Europe should help to overcome possible effects of EC 1992.

Setting the conditions for cooperation

The bilateral commissions for cooperation supply fora to discuss better conditions for cooperation. Better working conditions for Western businessmen in Eastern Europe and better statistical and market information are among the fields under discussion. Joint ventures are specifically delicate operations and need a proper framework. Some bilateral framework agreements have already been entered into and others will follow. The success of joint ventures will finally depend on the outcome of the economic reforms in Eastern Europe. In the long run it will be essential to what extent Eastern Europe can be integrated into the free flow of currencies.

Global interdependence

There are some fields where West and East are becoming more and more dependent on each other, as are all countries of the world. Three examples are particularly prominent: the environment, energy, and the proliferation of dangerous technology. All countries of the world should unite not only to ban chemical weapons but to do their best to stop the proliferation of the relevant technology. The questions of the environment and energy are more complex.

Owing to geography, the countries in Europe have common environmental problems which can only be solved by common effort. Western Europe and the CMEA countries are, for instance, responsible for 37 per cent of global emissions of carbon dioxide due to the burning of fossil fuels (15 per cent in Western Europe and 22 per cent CMEA countries). An environmental conference held in Munich in 1984 at the initiative of Chancellor Kohl signalled the political start of his attempt to cooperate in this area. Since then, East and West have been working together to try to examine the causes of the environmental problems and particularly to overcome their impact by cooperation.

In the area of environment the FRG can offer technology to help prevent or eliminate environmental damage. Its technology is the more advanced as its problems are particularly big and thought to be so by the entire population.

The concrete efforts are concentrated in countries chiefly affected such as Czechoslovakia, Poland, and the GDR. The focus of cooperation is desulfurization, elimination of nitrogen pollution, treatment of waste water, and so on. It is obvious that such cooperation is not merely a business transaction; it is vital to the FRG's own environmental interests. This is why the FRG has entered into framework agreements with Eastern Europe concerning environmental protection.

In the field of energy, the nuclear energy sector requires specific treatment by governments. The nuclear disaster at Chernobyl shows that intensive cooperation among all countries is indispensable with regard to the safety of nuclear facilities. Once again, there is technology to be offered that has been developed because of the same needs.

17.3 Conclusion

It is very important to see the role of the government of the Federal Republic of Germany in its proper perspective. A generally favourable climate and an appropriate framework are necessary, but by no means sufficient conditions for the development of trade with the East. Insufficient diversification in the structure of Eastern exports and the current situation with respect to Eastern systems of foreign trade and internal economy are basic impediments to the development of East-West trade. In this respect the following commentary is neccessary in order to assess the impact of the government of the Federal Republic.

During past years, trade with the East has diminished because of the large share of energy products and raw materials in Eastern exports. The terms of trade have deteriorated specifically in relation to the biggest Eastern trading partner, the Soviet Union. At the same time most of the Eastern countries encountered internal economic difficulties that gave rise to efforts at structural reform. The future of trade with the East will depend to a large extent on the success of these reforms. Two examples concerning the Soviet Union illustrate this.

There are some questions now about the significance of Soviet reforms. Not long ago, Soviet firms were given the right to establish foreign trade operations. Though this was accompanied by big publicity, a study of the relevant legal text of December 2, 1988 shows that this is only true insofar as products are considered to be competitive. But the decision seems to be left to bureaucrats not to the markets, as all export-import operations are to be registered and licensed by the foreign trade administration. There is even another piece of bureaucracy: unjustified competition among Soviet exporters is to be eliminated.

The second example is that the general price reform has been postponed from 1990-1991 to the second half of the 1990s. Without prices determined by market conditions Soviet firms will not be in a position to calculate prices on their own responsibility, but will depend on the decisions of central administrations to attribute the necessary materials for production. A ministerial decree of end of January 1989 concerning "Measures for the Elimination of Deficiencies in the Formation of Prices", is now restricting the possibilities of cooperatives to handle their prices in order to eliminate "speculative tendencies". Public orders to firms that produce clothing for childen, for example, are to be made more stringent, even though it had been announced in 1988 that administrative controls would be reduced drastically.

Western estimates of the Soviet Union's inflation rate range from 6 to 10 per cent. The excess of demand seems to be in the order of 70 billion roubles, the budget deficit in the order of 100 billion roubles (11 per cent of GNP) according to Soviet studies. This indicates the order of problems if prices are to be administered and are not to react fully to the scarcity of supplies.

If the reforms under way should bring about the needed flexibility this will be a much more important step to the development of East-West trade than any action of Western governments.

The Federal Republic of Germany and its government has long had an interest in trade and cooperation with the East. But the extent of economic cooperation is relatively slight and will probably remain so as the underlying factors are not expected to change quickly.

The economic component is only one aspect of the matter for the FRG's government. It attaches not only economic importance but an even greater political importance to East-West economic relations. Foreign policy considerations are interlinked with considerations of economic policy. The impact of the government of the Federal Republic on the practical development of trade with the East should not be overestimated as the limiting factors lie to a greater extent with the situation of the economies in the East and the success of the reforms actually undertaken there.

Chapter 18

THE ROLE OF JAPAN IN EAST-WEST ECONOMIC RELATIONS

Issei Nomura[1]

The history of East-West relations (the term used to embrace all aspects of contacts and interchange among countries having very different social, political, and economic systems) has shown that relations in one area have never expanded or shrunk independently from relations in other areas. This is not a matter of theory but the reality of international politics. In the present international environment hopes for an expansion of East-West economic relations are growing because talks on arms reduction and control are being conducted between the East and West, particularly between the United States and the Soviet Union, and their political relations are shifting from confrontation to dialogue. At the same time, East-West economic relations have ceased to be totally dependent on East-West political relations and have become more independent and important. In such a context, the development of East-West economic relations would contribute to the long-term stability of East-West relations in general.

Japan has become an important factor in the world economy; it accounts for more than one-tenth of the total world product, it is the world's largest creditor country, and it possesses advanced technology in many key fields. Japan is thus expected to play an active role in the development of East-West economic relations. Put simply, Japan's role is to make an appropriate contribution to the establishment of a long-term stable relationship between the East and the West in various fields; first, by sharing the burden of Western security by controlling the export of strategically important advanced technology, and second, by considering deeply how its economic capability and resources can be used most effectively, particularly in such areas of East-West economic relations as trade, finance, and investment. In order for Japan to play this role, it is essential that it pays attention to the following points.

---

[1] Minister, The Embassy of Japan, Washington, D.C., U.S.A.

Coordination among the Western countries

Any leakage of strategically important advanced technologies will adversely affect the military balance between East and West. The Western countries should coordinate their policies to attain effective export controls. Japan should contribute actively to such coordination.

Policy coordination among the Western countries is necessary in order to avoid elements of confrontation or disturbance to the existing scheme of international cooperation. Japan should actively participate in such coordination which is necessary for the sound development of East-West economic relations.

Differentiated approaches to the East

In addition to policy coordination with Western countries, Japan adopts differentiated approaches to the Soviet Union, the East European countries, and China in its efforts to promote the sound development of East-West economic relations.

China has already established close economic relations with the West, including Japan, in the fields of trade, finance, and investment, and its interdependence with the Western economies is already quite considerable. China, a much less industrialized country than the Soviet Union and the East European countries, is still in the development stage. The present Chinese leadership is, however, boldly carrying out political and economic reform under the slogan of "Reform and Open-Door". That reform seems to be becoming an economic model for the Soviet Union and the East European countries. China seeks a peaceful international enviroment in order to carry out economic reform. Japan assists China's efforts for modernization because China's moderate and realistic policy to modernization will contribute to the stability of Asia. It is necessary for the West to further expand relations with China, supporting its modernization efforts and encouraging China to maintain its open-door policy.

East European countries seem to seriously desire to expand their economic relations with the West in order to revitalize their domestic economies. Relations between Japan and those countries were not very close in the past, for historical and geographical reasons. The growth of the Japanese economy has, however, increased the potential for closer economic relations with Eastern Europe. The basic policy of Japan, as a Western nation, is to promote its relations with the East European countries so as to contribute to stable overall East-West relations. Japan believes it desirable that its economic relations with the East European countries are based upon the principle of mutual benefit and commercial considerations. And Japan hopes that its economic relations with them would provide indirect assistance to their domestic reforms.

In the present situation, although both the West (including Japan) and the East have the political will to promote East-West economic relations, their economic ties have not yet progressed as expected. This is because East European manufactures are uncompetitive and the conditions are not right to attract foreign investment. It is to be hoped that the East European countries will make further efforts in their reforms and the rebuilding of their economies.

The Soviet Union is obviously a major factor in East-West economic relations. It can be appreciated that the Gorbachev administration has taken a positive attitude to economic relations with the West. It seems that the Soviet Union, following the example of China, wishes to promote an economic reform and open-door policy. It will provide an opportunity for the West to encourage the Soviet Union to open its economy and to persuade it to make its economy harmonious with that of the West. However, the West should be careful to ensure that expanded East-West economic relations be closely linked to improvements in its political relations with the Soviet Union. Progress in East-West economic relations without basic principles, as we saw in the 1970s, adversely affects efforts to build stable East-West economic relations on a long-term basis. We must adopt an approach that politics and economics are not to be treated in isolation from each other. In other words, progress in East-West economic relations should parallel progress in their political relations, for example, progress in arms reduction. In Japan's case, there is a very important political issue, the Northern Territories issue, pending with the Soviet Union. Japan's basic policy is that efforts to promote Japan-Soviet economic relations must be made in the light of the totality of our relations. In the Japan-Soviet relationship it is certainly not Japan's desire to see progress in the economic field, while allowing this important bilateral political issue to be left unresolved.

Chapter 19

THE ROLE OF THE AUSTRIAN GOVERNMENT IN EAST-WEST ECONOMIC RELATIONS

Fritz Gehart[1]

19.1 Introduction

The political organization of the world, which is the result of the conventions adopted within the framework of the United Nations since 1945, has given some reality to the idealistic principle "one country, one vote". Given a high degree of political culture, such as has been achieved by certain regions of the world, this principle enables small countries such as Austria to develop enough self-assurance to pursue active and sovereign policies. This may account for the fact that Austria's voice is heard in the concert of nations even though its territory represents only 0.05 per cent of the land mass, and its inhabitants make up no more than 0.15 per cent of the world population. And it explains why Austria, and the Austrian people, are masters in their own house even though the country finds itself in a highly complex and, as has again been demonstrated recently, most unstable geopolitical situation.

The situation is somewhat different in the economic sphere, which is largely governed by the variables of business activity. Business analysts describe the situation of a country such as Austria as that of a "small open economy". A share of 0.8 per cent of the world social product and 1.2 per cent of world exports and imports combine to make Austria highly dependent on foreign suppliers and markets (in the order of 70 per cent of GDP), which would make the idea of Austrian sovereignty in economic policies a mere illusion. There can be no doubt that in international commodity as well as service markets, and in particular in financial markets, Austrian businesses have to follow rather than determine price levels.

Austria's economic policy after the first petroleum shock demonstrates that it is perfectly possible to make a virtue of necessity by not even trying to uphold any illusions of economic sovereignty but rather by developing a pragmatic and realistic concept. From the economic, and especially the invest-

---

[1] Member of the Board, Österreichisches Credit-Institut, Vienna, Austria.

ment policy point of view, the creation of stable and calculable conditions is more valuable to business undertakings than the pursuit of "autonomistic" objectives per se. Faced with the alternative of upholding the sovereignty of the Austrian currency (which would have meant a freely floating schilling and, in consequence, erratic bouts of inflation and deflation) and the renunciation of monetary sovereignty (which constitutes an attempt to salvage, at least in part, the positive aspects of the Bretton Woods system), Austria opted for a linkage with the European hard currency bloc, which meant, in particular, the Deutschmark.

19.2 Austria's basic economic structures

It goes without saying that such a policy automatically exposes the economy of a country to a comparison with those countries to which its own currency is linked. Any "performance" deficits that may occur can be offset, in the short and medium term, by appropriate monetary policies (in other words, by offering higher interest rates than are offered abroad, as some sort of "risk bonus" for foreign investors). In the medium and long term, however, structural-policy considerations imperiously call for action. I should like to single out two elements which I see as particularly important and which have to do with the cost and product pattern of Austrian companies.

In a country that pursues a hard currency policy, businesses naturally have a narrow scope of action as regards pricing. Both in exports and in supplying the domestic market, they are at a competitive disadvantage vis-à-vis those countries whose currencies tend in the long run to become weaker than their domestic currency. Still, the advantages of a hard currency policy outweigh its drawbacks, as primary material prices and wage costs in particular tend to remain highly stable, with the latter rising only moderately since inflationary tendencies are not seen as a major threat. As regards long-term efforts to keep Austria's economy competitive, stability is of particular importance because workers and employees have made a major contribution to improving the cost pattern of businesses by not fully claiming the benefits derived from productivity increases. As far as labour's share in national income is concerned, the turning point came at the beginning of the 1980s. After an increase from originally 50 per cent of national income to a maximum of 76 per cent in 1981, the ratio of the total wage bill to national income has since dropped to 73 per cent.

This has not, at least not so far, been caused by any pressure due to high unemployment rates (at 5.4 per cent, Austria's unemployment rate is still clearly below the OECD average) but is due to a socio-political phenomenon commonly known as "social partnership". Since 1945 labour and management have consistently tried to steer a narrow incomes policy course that would guarantee the maintenance of mass consumption as a pillar of economic activity as well as the earning power of business enterprises and thus their readiness to invest.

In contrast to other industrial countries where governments have, at least from time to time, become hopelessly entangled in the net of wage and price policies to the detriment of their much more essential role in economic policy-making, the role of government in Austrian incomes policy has been virtually negligible. Despite close personal and informal ties between political and economic decision makers, Austria's incomes policy has remained outside the scope of government action.

Still, whether a country can remain competitive or not depends not so much on the cost element alone but more on the kind and quality of the products it has to offer. In this respect, companies are exposed to the massive pressure of hard currency policy, both in terms of foreign markets and with regard to the home market. At the same time, the hard currency policy has a predominant influence on the national budget which ought to create the best possible environment for constant technological innovation and reorganization in the light of product and market characteristics. I do not claim that Austria has been as successful in this field as it has been with regard to incomes policy. Again, reference should be made to the social partnership system, this time as a negative factor. It clearly has a tendency to preserve existing structures. While employers' associations are not particularly enthusiastic about new or progressive enterprises that do not logically fit into traditional patterns, the representatives of labour are unwilling to extend their solidarity to new vocational or professional groups whose ambitions and mobility make it difficult to fit them into established structures.

What is more, since approximately one-third of Austrian business is more or less under public control (though a strong trend towards privatization has recently tended to reduce government involvement), the role of the state as owner of nationalized industries generally limits the government's scope of action in structural matters. It should be clearly understood that the nationalization of a number of financial institutions and in particular of the basic industries, which took place after 1945, was not dictated by ideological considerations but was meant to protect enterprises that had been declared "German assets" from passing into the hands of the occupation forces. One long-term consequence of this policy is to be seen in the consistently large share of primary materials in the product range of Austrian industry and, until very recently, the national industries did not sufficiently adapt production patterns to world market requirements.

A structural problem of a different kind arises from the fact that another third or so of Austrian businesses are under foreign influence. Hopes that foreign direct investments would provide strong impulses for innovation have not always been fulfilled. Too often, Austria has been used as a "foreign-based workshop" for major industrial countries, and the value added by Austrian industrial activity has fallen short of what would have been theoretically possible. In concrete terms, Austrian subsidiaries of foreign business groups are largely used as suppliers of component parts while those steps which provide the lion's share of the value added, finishing and world-wide marketing, take place abroad. This means that Austria is often denied access to high-level know-how and technology. I should like to add that, in my opinion, the often expressed fear that Western technology is inadequately protected from "leaking" into Eastern Europe is but a marginal aspect that has been wildly exaggerated by the media.

For the sake of completeness, mention should be made of the remaining third of Austrian business, which is in private Austrian hands. With regard to the crucial question of Austria's competitiveness, these companies must clearly be seen as an important pillar of Austria's economic standing in the world since a prerequisite for their survival is that they adapt their processes and products to the requirements of the world market. They have no other choice, as they can neither rely on the same safety nets as enterprises under public influence nor on the diversification strategies of multinational groups.

19.3 The role of government in determining structural policy

I should now like to discuss the role of government in determining structural policy in Austria. Let me state first and foremost that although the Austrian economy has the typically tripartite structure which we have just talked about, goverment has nevertheless consistently devoted equal attention to all three sectors. In the 1970s and early 1980s, the hard currency policy was supplemented by an expansive budgetary policy which helped to offset a number of difficulties with which companies were confronted because of the hard schilling. The concept of what has been called "Austro-Keynesianism" is a highly complex system of economic policy measures best described as sophisticated public demand mangement which comprises: expansive budget policies; labour market and investment policies; a hard currency policy designed to ward off inflation; and, as flanking measures, labour management ("social partnership") agreements concerning incomes policy.

One may characterize this sample of economic policy instruments as a pragmatic but over a long time successful composition which highly differs from mere deficit spending on the one hand, and a mechanistic monetarist concept on the other. It was designed to allow for some political and economic transformation of society within a framework of maximum stability. In order to describe the effect of this concept on the non-monetary and financial patterns in Austria, I will have to outline, at some length, the development of the Austrian national accounts and national financial accounts. According to one theory, government deficits invariably entail current account deficits. As I see it, this is a gross over-simplification which leaves significant points out of consideration. The following might serve as a useful model: first, international financing and overall investments make up the change in the net financial position of the domestic economy vis-à-vis other countries, which, in turn, corresponds to the net current account position; and, second, a favourable current account gives rise to capital exports while a negative one results in capital imports irrespective of who is responsible for these capital flows.

Between 1974 and 1986 the Austrian economy accounted for AS 3,340 billions worth of investment in fixed assets and inventories as well as for AS 3,500 billion in financial assets. Of this total of AS 6,840 billion, 47 per cent was internally financed and 53 per cent financed through borrowing. More than 90 per cent of total capital formation was due to the private sector and as little as 9 per cent to the public sector while government had a 13 per cent share in the financing of total capital formation. This means that during the period under review private capital formation, both in terms of investment in assets and monetary wealth formation, was AS 290 billion higher than it would have been without governmental deficit spending. Thus, the government's strategy has been to convert its own debts into assets for Austrian companies and private individuals. The assumption was that in this way economic activity, which had suffered from the loss of purchasing power due to the first and second petroleum crises and to the disintegration of the system of fixed exchange rates, could be stimulated and, in particular, that the renewal (and, if possible, increase) of the capital stock available could be ensured despite liquidity shortages.

In terms of external economic relations, this meant that between 1974 and 1986 imports exceeded exports by AS 100 billion: a substantial amount in light of cumulative capital goods imports of AS 1,150 billion and a (cumulative) petroleum bill of AS 520 billion. The capital imports required to finance the current account were by and large effected by the public authorities, which, in view of the predominance of small and medium-sized enterprises in the country, proved the only sector capable of effectively utilizing foreign financial markets.

The foreign section of the national financial accounts of the period 1974-1986 shows this very clearly: 90 per cent of net capital imports (AS 100 billion) was effected by the public sector. However, Austria's rest-of-the-world account shows yet another striking feature which might elude the observer of the domestic section of the financial accounts. No less than 80 per cent of the cumulative 1974-1986 current account deficit of AS 100 billion was caused by the public sector on account of the rapidly increasing interest payments by the Austrian state to foreign countries.

Does this mean that what I said about the positive strategic objectives of "Austro-Keynesianism" was wrong? Did economic policy result in a giant circular movement of finance which took away as much as it contributed to the economy? The answer is yes and no, at least as regards Austria's external position. Between 1974 and 1982 the state compensated the loss of income due to higher petroleum prices and converted public debts into private wealth, while between 1983 and 1986 interest payments by the Republic of Austria to recipients abroad rendered the effects of capital imports ineffective.

In terms of Austria's external economic relations, this statistical "break-even point" of Austro-Keynesianism appears to have occurred around 1983 or 1984 at the latest, and it is no coincidence that at that time considerable concern was first voiced about the wisdom of continuing the economic policies of the 1970 and early 1980's. The dramatic growth of public indebtedness (20 per cent per annum from the end of 1973 to the end of 1986) and in particular the growth of the foreign debt (over 22 per cent per annum) rendered obsolete the role that the state had played up to that time in Austrian economic activity. It became clear that, in the interest of preserving Austria's excellent international credit standing and in order not to antagonize public opinion, the policy of incurring higher and higher debts could not go on indefinitely. The amount, composition, and time scale of the national debt has given rise to fervent discussion. However, none of these factors can be predetermined or predicted with any measure of certainty for they depend on the prevailing perception of the health of the domestic economic and its relative position abroad. This perception can change very quickly, causing previously effective economic measures to be no longer politically enforceable.

In its time, Austro-Keynesianism pursued a quasi-mercantilistic course. It pursued a "development policy at home" by granting non-recoverable subsidies for capital formation. Since the public sector lacked sufficient internal financing, these bonuses were financed through borrowing. However, a policy of incurring debts must pay its way, or in other words, the debt service must be covered by the return on investment.

Why was this no longer the case in Austria after 1983-1984 or even earlier than that? One of the reasons was the high interest rates prevailing in the early 1980s which made borrowing considerably more expensive. However, the most important reason lies in inadequacies inherent in the structural and economic policies pursued. Too little attention had been paid to the need to ensure the competitiveness of Austrian businesses in the longer term. While the unprotected sector of the Austrian economy had to stand up to keen international competition, economic policies failed to apply a sound measure of political pressure on the protected sector in order to motivate it to undertake structural changes and to adapt to the more exacting conditions of the world markets. There were (and still are) precious few concrete criteria for the promotion of individual activities but there are a great many government commitments laid down by law or resulting from political considerations. These are vehemently defended by the interest groups benefiting from them.

Structural sources of the deficit that cause a high degree of budgetary rigidity are: the administration with its rocketing personnel costs; the public pension system; the Austrian Federal Railways; the nationalized industries; and the high degree of government regulation of farming. All of these are, in fact, part and parcel of the protected sector as defined above since they would not be viable in their present form without public subsidies.

The present coalition of the two leading parties has made it its prime objective to introduce more flexibility into this situation and to reduce the net deficit ratio from 5 per cent in 1986 to 2.5 per cent by 1992. If we regard the net deficit ratio according to its mathematical definition (i.e., as the quotient of the net deficit and GDP), we see that a significant improvement is hardly possible via an increase in GDP, which means, in other words, that the deficit itself has to be brought under control. Even though the coalition parties have tended to concentrate on reducing expenditures, they have met with considerable resistance so that, for the time being, their efforts focus on providing government revenue through capital management (i.e., privatization). There can be no doubt that increases in ordinary revenue (for instance through the further reduction of tax exceptions) are no longer out of the question.

There is no escaping the fact that expenditures will have to be reduced (to the detriment of the traditional groups of beneficiaries) in view of the fact that the interest service of the public debt is consuming an ever growing portion of GDP and federal revenue. This trend can be offset only at the expense of other categories of expenditures since debt service through borrowing would clearly further increase the level of indebtedness. If we deduce the debt service from the above-mentioned 1986 net deficit (in the order of 5 per cent of GDP), we obtain a 2.5 per cent net deficit ratio adjusted for interest payments. This negative indicator will have to be turned into a positive one of the order of +1.5 per cent (i.e., converted into an interest-adjusted surplus) if an unadjusted net deficit ratio of 2.5 per cent is to be achieved by 1992, since the debt burden will by that time amount to 4 per cent of GDP.

Still, national budgets are not numbers games but economic policy concepts cast in figures. If, in its endeavour to consolidate the budget, Austria's fiscal policy gives rise to major adaptations, its prime objective is to do away with the widespread evil of individuals and businesses basing their microeconomic planning on expectations of government initiatives and public support. What the state wants to bring home to them is that, within the overall conditions offered by government action, it is indispensable for each individual to develop his own initiatives and to assume responsibility for his actions.

Austria's position in East-West relations

This rather detailed outline of the general economic conditions prevailing in Austria is intended to provide the necessary background for a discussion of East-West relations. Let me come back to the specific geopolitical situation of Austria, which is characterized not only by the typical problems facing a small country but also by its geographical situation at the periphery of the market economy countries, the result of the bloc formation after World War II. Austria's territorial integrity and sovereignty, formally regained in 1945 and fully achieved in 1955, was the product of the wish of the signatories of the Austrian State Treaty to have a calculable territorial entity in this part of Central Europe. While Austria's decision to opt for the status of permanent neutrality was an autonomous act in terms of international law, it is inseparably connected with the conclusion of the State Treaty from the point of view of realpolitik.

Even though Austria can, and does, claim to be part of the Western socio-economic system, its foreign policy (and thus its foreign economic policy) has to keep some equidistance from the two economic blocs in Europe. It would, indeed, be utterly unreasonable to turn exclusively to one side, and it would be absolutely wrong to believe that, because of its socio-political preferences, Austria "liked" exporting to the West and "disliked" exporting to the East.

The categories according to which foreign trade develops and takes place have, of course, nothing to do with such considerations. And it is equally clear that it has to be considered in a business-like way in Austria as well. It has to be guided by purely business-management considerations or a combination of these with economic policy criteria. I will come back to this later. For the time being I should prefer to dwell on the political and emotional aspects. Take the traditionally excellent relations between Austria and Eastern Europe. These relations are rooted in history but, today, they are even more due to factors of economic geography. These ties were severed by political turmoil in Central Europe but the specific security interests of the new Austrian republic made it imperative to pick them up again, while at the same time some of our East European neighbours were making similar advances.

From the very beginning it has been Austria's goal to ensure peaceful contacts between the different socio-economic systems and, if possible, to promote their convergence. For a long time it was considered illusory to believe that the social system of East European countries could be substantially changed by their adopting Western economic policy principles. Today such ideas do not appear unrealistic. In Eastern Europe and the Soviet Union, isolated attempts at marginal economic reforms, without even the slightest change in political conditions, have been replaced by the conviction that economic reform must always be preceded by the appropriate political reforms. And the fact that these ideas are now being promoted by the top echelon of the leading Eastern power suggests that the aim is not only to make the socialist system more efficient by putting it on a sounder economic basis but to open it to Western political concepts. The legislative efforts which are preparing the ground for a multi-party system in Hungary, are only the tip of the iceberg. Indeed, Moscow appears to have long tolerated the role of Hungary as a "test market" for pluralistic conceptions.

To come back to Austria's role in East-West relations, I do not wish to claim that Austria's foreign policy or foreign economic policy has ever been the mainstay or one of the principal elements of this process. Still, Austria's attitude of "talking to the other side while not identifying with its ideology" (an essential element of the fairly unheroic national character of this country) has somehow been a spiritual legacy to a divided Europe, something to give the world food for thought, along with the logistic opportunities for representatives of the two sides to take hesitant steps towards an understanding on neutral ground. Finding not only the lowest common denominator but the maximum consensus that can be achieved is a socio-political concept that has proved invaluable in resolving conflicts in Austria and which has resulted in the realization that, stripped of ideological trimmings, human needs are basically the same everywhere. From its rebirth as a sovereign state, Austria has always insisted that a greater measure of economic division of labour between East and West Europe might help ensure that the two sides think twice before they choose to interrupt the trade flows between them.

Austria's position in this context has not always been undisputed internationally. Just think of the need confronting Austrian foreign policy makers to take into account the diverging interests of the OECD countries on the one hand and the CMEA countries on the other. For a great many years, American administrations subordinated U.S. trade contacts with the East for strategic reasons and attributed low priority to economic issues. West European countries, on the other hand, adopted a somewhat different stand which varied from country to country and tended to change as political constellations in the world underwent modification. Nevertheless, from Austria's point of view, their attitude was somewhat more cooperative on account of their proximity to the East. On the other side, the CMEA countries originally steered an isolationist course guided by ideological considerations, and later on, at best, tended to move towards pronounced bilateralism. Here, the attitudes displayed were, in fact, the mirror image of those in the West, with the smaller countries favouring a certain economic rapprochement and the Soviet Union tending to put the brakes on East-West trade, which had not seen much dynamic growth until the 1970s and suffered a setback in the early 1980s that was due not only to economic but also to political factors: Soviet involvement in Afghanistan, martial law in Poland, and the international debt crisis (which started in Poland and other Eastern bloc countries), to name but the most important causes of this setback. Isolated incidents such as the shooting down of a Korean passenger plane furnished additional arguments to those who had traditionally favoured limitations of East-West economic relations. It was then that the U.S. administration began not only to tighten controls on the transfer of high technology to the East but also wished to extend these restrictions to non-strategic goods and to neutral countries. States such as Austria were forced to indirectly accept these moves in order not to be excluded from the delivery of such commodities but fervently rejected any such outside influence. To come back to the world-wide financial crisis, the situation was further aggravated by the growing awareness that the so-called "umbrella theory" (i.e., the assumption that the Soviet Union would underwrite its East European allies' debts vis-à-vis Western creditors) was untenable in practice.

Austria's trading position in East and West

In this situation, which was anything but favourable for neutral countries, Austria did not abandon its trade with Eastern Europe. Invoking in particular its unequivocal socio-political commitment to the West, with which it was linked by disproportionately strong economic ties anyway, it pleaded, on the contrary, for a continuation of mutual trade relations with the countries of the Eastern bloc. This policy was dictated not only by Austria's legitimate security interests, to which reference has already been made, but also by its specific foreign trade pattern which is not only the result of geopolitical constellations but also of important structural factors. Austria's relatively large economic sector, ranging from farming to construction and the nationalized primary industries, that had to be protected from unbridled international competition, has already been described in detail.

Eastern Europe presented a particularly attractive market for Austria's nationalized industries which could not be adequately protected from imports because of pressing domestic demand as well as customs agreements with the EC. The success of this branch of industry in exports to this market was on the one hand due to the somewhat lower level of technological and quality expectations but also to the support of a highly developed export promotion procedure, financial loans granted to East European countries and specific import regulations governing trade relations with the CMEA countries. In any case, this interaction worked well as long as the marginal operational weaknesses of the nationalized industries could be corrected by limited government subsidies. These were justified by the high priority that Austrian economic policy attached to full employment. And even in a phase of restructuring of the industries concerned, which has become indispensable on account of the excessive growth of financing requirements, the reorganized operational units of the government-controlled industries will certainly not be viable unless they acquire additional market potentials in Eastern Europe where standards are still less stringent than in the highly competitive Western European markets.

Austria's specific foreign trade position can best be characterized before the backdrop of some global key data of East-West trade. The share of East-West trade in world trade is very small indeed (only about 3 per cent) but varies in the importance it has for the various participating regions: at slightly more than 20 per cent, the relative position of OECD in CMEA trade flows is much better than the relative importance of the CMEA in OECD foreign trade with about 2.5 per cent.

By contrast, CMEA countries play a much more important role in Austrian foreign trade: on average, the share of CMEA in total Austrian exports has been three to four times as high as its share in total OECD exports, while the CMEA share in imports has been two to three times as high. However, there have been considerable fluctuations. Austria's exports to Eastern Europe reached their peak in 1975 at 17.1 per cent of total Austrian exports, and subsequently dropped almost continuously to reach 8.7 per cent in 1987; particularly in recent years this development has been largely due to the shortage of foreign exchange and the resulting import restrictions adopted in Eastern Europe. As regards Austria's imports from the Eastern bloc, the peak was reached as late as 1985 (10.7 per cent) and was followed by a relatively sharp decline to 6.8 per cent in 1987; this development was, however, largely due to changes in energy prices rather than in volume. These observations are borne out by a breakdown of exports according to types of product and trading partners.

Approximately 90 per cent of Austrian exports are industrial goods. With only a few exceptions, the structure of exports to the CMEA countries is not different from those to the OECD: exports to the East are below average in the fields of machinery and consumer goods but above the average of total exports in the field of manufactured goods and chemical products. By contrast, the share of more sophisticated goods in exports to the West (and in particular the EC) is above average, so that, in this respect, Austria's exports to the West are more significant and more future-oriented than its exports to the East.

The structure of Austria's imports from the East is strikingly different from the composition of total imports (and from the structure of exports to the East). Only 24 per cent of Austrian imports from the CMEA area (9 per cent from the Soviet Union and 32 per cent from Eastern Europe) are industrial products. The very high share of energy and raw materials, which may be partly explained by geographic factors, has a considerable statistical affect on the commodity structure of imports. Partly, however, it may perhaps be explained by the high Austrian external tariff vis-à-vis countries not belonging to the European Free Trade Area.

Austria's foreign economic policy

These facts give rise to the question of the importance of the individual trade partners (including the Eastern countries) for Austria and what economic policies it pursues with respect to these countries. Let me once again stress Austria's excessively strong dependence on foreign trade, while adding that the great political value attached to foreign trade (or rather, exports) has a long tradition in Austria and actually hails back to mercantilist times. In this way, Austria differs greatly from those countries which pursue policies of self-sufficiency, be it for geographic reasons, their raw materials, or their ideological orientation. Present-day Austria, as a successor state of the Austro-Hungarian monarchy, is not particularly blessed with natural resources and, despite its favourable attitude towards foreign trade, it has had its share of trade problems. To be more exact, Austria has been confronted with a structural trade deficit ever since 1918. While the remedy sought during the First Republic was chiefly import restrictions (hence the basically high customs tariffs operable even today), the preferred policy pursued since World War II has been that of export promotion. For the sake of completeness it should be noted that this change in policy was facilitated by the remarkable development of international travel and tourism and, especially since the 1950s, of mass tourism which is governed by completely different socio-economic conditions than those prevailing in the inter-war period, and which has substantially helped to improve Austria's foreign exchange position.

On this basis Austria gained sufficient time to develop an excellent and comprehensive system of export promotion which by and large rests on two pillars: export financing and underwriting by Oesterreichische Kontrollbank (which acts as a government agency in this field); and foreign trade information and logistic support provided by the Federal Economic Chamber.

It is in this governmental and quasi-governmental context that foreign trade should be viewed as part of Austria's general economic policy. In the medium term, Austria's hard currency policy presupposes a balanced current account, so that export promotion is a logical necessity. Furthermore, the exporting industries became an important factor in Austria's full employment policy in the 1970s, when domestic demand grew only moderately.

This is why Austria has no autonomously developed concept of foreign economic policy. Trade policies have always been derived from internal economic objectives or have, at best, consisted in ad hoc reactions to new international developments and problems. The motivation of Austria's foreign trade policy has been basically the same vis-à-vis Western and Eastern trading partners. Just as the government has no specific list of desirable industry and product patterns, there is no catalogue of priorities concerning specific foreign trade measures to be adopted in respect of specific countries or groups of countries.

Austria's trade policy vis-à-vis the West focuses on two things. First, it is important to prevent the discrimination of Austrian exports and to facilitate the access of Austrian firms to foreign markets. It is in this context that particular importance attaches to Austria's full participation in trade liberalization within the framework of OECD and the GATT and, naturally, its participation in European integration (EFTA and EC). And, second, Austria attempts to promote competition at home by liberalizing commodity trade and, to a lesser extent, capital movements. In this context mention should be made of the complete abolition of import duties and quotas for industrial products, initially vis-à-vis Austria's partners in EFTA (1960 to 1968) and subsequently vis-à-vis the European Community (1972 to 1977).

It goes without saying that this complete liberalization of trade in industrial products, which has been in operation for more than ten years with regard to most Western European countries, has accelerated the above mentioned structural adaptations in the unprotected sector of the economy. The problems of the nationalized industries apart, Austrian exports have gained considerable momentum and, with the liberalization of imports, Austrian products have seen less and less discrimination in foreign markets and have even gained access to new markets. Between 1977 and 1987 Austrian GDP grew by 2.1 per cent per annum (in real terms) while exports increased by 4.2 per cent, meaning that those parts of GDP which were not exported grew by only 0.5 per cent per annum. In other words, had it not been for the dynamic growth of exports, Austria's per capita GDP would not have amounted to AS 200,000 (about $ 16,000) but only AS 150,000 or less (if allowance is made for the multiplier effect).

This dynamic growth of exports can, in fact, be clearly attributed to geography. No less than 64 per cent of the overall growth of Austrian exports between 1977 and 1987 was due to deliveries to the EC, whose share in Austrian exports accordingly increased from 50 per cent in 1977 to 57 per cent in 1987. EFTA accounted for 11 per cent of the export growth during the ten-year period under consideration, the CMEA countries for 5 per cent, and the rest of the world for 19 per cent. This means that the absolute shares of the last mentioned areas in Austrian exports all declined. As all sides of the social partnership process agree, a favourable development of exports in the context of European integration is an indispensable prerequisite for a liberalization of imports. Since Austria's trade policy has been largely inward-looking, as I have already explained, the performance of exports to Eastern Europe has, from a purely economic point of view, been too poor to warrant equally extensive liberalization as has been considered possible vis-à-vis Western Europe.

Thus, while foreign policy considerations and the needs of Austria's full employment policy prompted Austria to make full use of its export promotion system, especially in relation to Eastern Europe and the Soviet Union, a distinction was made between the countries of Eastern and Western Europe in the field of import liberalization. The reasons were twofold: one, the countries of the Eastern bloc are seen as planned economies which normally do not operate according to market economy principles, even in foreign trade; and, two, Austria's export opportunities to the East have never been sufficiently substantial and safe to warrant incurring the risks of more extensive liberalization.

Studies of Austria's trade with Eastern Europe and the trade policies pursued vis-à-vis the individual countries concerned reveal the following principal features:

1. While, in formal terms, Austria's foreign trade policy is the same for East and West, there are, in actual fact, some differences in both export and import relations.

2. The Austrian system of export financing is mainly used to promote exports to Eastern Europe and developing countries.

3. Austria's involvement in the financing of CMEA countries is considerable. At 10-14 per cent of total Western bank loans to Eastern bloc countries (including financing credits), Austria's share is significantly higher than its share in foreign trade with the East (5 per cent).

4. Austrian exports to the East are supported by numerous intergovernmental cooperation agreements, cooperation at the company level, and flexible countertrade operations.

5. With just a few exceptions - especially with regard to Hungary and the Soviet Union - Austrian joint ventures with Eastern bloc countries have not developed as hoped for. While falling short of the original intentions, cooperation agreements have thus turned into instruments of export promotion.

6. In 1985 and again in 1988 Austria passed legislation to exercise supervision of high technology exports. The laws in question are formulated in a non-discriminatory way so that they could, if necessary, also be used to prohibit re-exports of Soviet high technology. In actual practice, the measures have of course been taken above all to prevent illegal exports of Western high techno-logy to the East, but they do not cover the export of products originally developed in Austria.

7. Imports from CMEA countries - like those from GATT members - are subject to most favoured nation treatment. In this context it should again be noted that Austrian basic duties are relatively high, so that there is some divergence, in respect of industrial products, between the situation of Eastern bloc countries and the duty-free entry of industrial goods from EFTA and EC countries.

8. In 1988, Bulgaria, Romania, and Hungary were granted the conditions of the General Preferences for Developing Countries, the relevant Austrian duties being 50 per cent of those operating under the MFN clause.

19.4 Summary

Finally, I should like to summarize what I regard as the most important aspects of Austria's relations to the East European countries. First, since the end of World War II Austria has always played an active role in promoting economic relations between East and West, and did not change its course even when the political confrontation between the superpowers made the policy pursued by Austria appear not only pointless but suspicious to certain observers. In so doing it was motivated by political considerations and economic utility which will be further discussed below. One motive, however, was certainly to maintain the close personal and cultural ties which have long been an important link between Austria and Eastern Europe.

Second, Austria has always regarded itself as a "Western" state on the basis of its democratic constitution and market economy, and its endeavours to promote positive relations with Eastern Europe have been pursued against the backdrop of growing cooperation with Western Europe. After the failure of negotiations to establish a wide European free trade zone, Austria became a member of EFTA in 1960 and a free trade agreement was also signed with the EC in 1972. At present Austria is exploring possibilities for extending free trade with goods into greater and, if possible, full participation in the European internal market. Austria has also been a member of the Council of Europe since 1956 and a member of the OECD since 1948 where it participates fully in the concerted work of the Western-minded countries.

Third, Austria has always been keen to see the dynamics of Western economic systems develop in the East, partly because of the market potential for Austrian products, but also for more specific political reasons. Austria has nothing to gain from a stagnating or backward economic area at its doorstep. Austria's special efforts to cooperate with Polish and Hungarian firms were certainly motivated in part by the impression that the internal revitalization process, which had in fact begun in those countries in the 1960s and which encouraged more market economy tendencies and individual freedom of action, was a most desirable way out of the social and economic stagnation engendered by the planned economies of Eastern Europe.

Fourth, Austria has always believed that economic cooperation with Eastern Europe should be undertaken with more than simply economic objectives in mind. Economic cooperation itself was expected to bring with it an increase in mutual dependence and thus also increased mutual concern for the well-being of the other country. The strenghtening of contacts at a personal and official level promotes the cultivation of cooperative relations amongst countries and helps do away with those structures that might give rise to disagreement and tension. It has been the declared objective of successive Austrian governments to promote this process. Austrian economic cooperation with its Eastern European partners was indirectly fostered through bilateral trade agreements, barter deals, cooperation in third country markets, tariff reductions, financing at favourable rates and, finally, through the personal commitment of leading politicians to the realization of promising and useful projects. However, the government seldom participated directly in carrying out such measures.

Because of its geographical proximity and the structure of its markets, Eastern Europe has always been important for Austria. This, coupled with the positive attitude of Austrian authorities towards Eastern Europe, has made Austria's volume of economic exchanges with the East relatively higher than that of any other Western country, with the exception of Finland. Austria's trade with Eastern Europe accounts for 7 per cent of its total exports and imports as compared with the OECD average of 2.5 per cent.

Austria's role in providing finance for Eastern Europe is of particular importance, and includes far more than only financing its own exports. For example, Austria accounts for 13-18 per cent of foreign borrowing by Poland, the GDR, and Hungary, whereas Austria's share in total imports of these countries is only 2.5-6.5 per cent.

Mention should also be made Austria's role in transit trade and as an intermediary in countertrade which is again becoming important due to the East's shortage of hard currency. The volume of trade via Austria is worth roughly AS 5 billion.

Fifth, Austria's commitment to fruitful cooperation between East and West, which goes beyond immediate political and economic concerns, is of course also determined by its geographic location at the border between East and West, its permanent neutrality and a realistic assessment of its potential in matters of economic policy. National security policy, while fully committed to military defence, also concentrates on creating favourable political and military conditions. Austria has consistently taken every opportunity to eliminate mistrust and bad feeling and in this way to encourage détente and disarmament. This is also reflected in Austria's endeavours to offer constructive solutions to East-West problems at different economic and political levels (e.g. the UN Economic Commission for Europe and the Conference on Security and Cooperation in Europe) as well as by its readiness to act as an international meeting-place and as the seat of various international organizations.

Finally, in view of current developments in Europe where, in the West, the EC is rapidly unifying into a single internal market and showing signs of concerted action in foreign policy and, in the East, long-standing structures are being toppled by market economy influences, decentralization, and greater individual freedom of action, Austria must seriously ask itself whether the structure of its East-West policy is still qualitatively and quantitatively relevant.

In my opinion, just as Austria is striving to strengthen its relations to Western Europe through participation in the European internal market, it should also examine whether and how its relations to Eastern Europe could be reconsidered and brought on to a new plane which is more in keeping with present economic and political conditions. That is, it should consider its possible contribution to the reorganization of the East European economies along market economy lines and to a reciprocal opening of markets.

276

Now is the time to think about models and conditions along which at least some sectors of the East European economies could participate in West European free trade. It is also the time to consider the best way to support and encourage the movement towards reform in the East. Finland's experiences with Hungary and Poland could provide valuable information in this respect.

Another way of actively promoting the new market economy orientation in the East would be by providing generous support for the development of training facilities for business management, marketing, and advertising, and by organizing exchange programmes for junior managers.

We may now have the unique opportunity of creating a better basis for permanent cooperation between the various states and economies of East and West; an opportunity that has arisen out of the increasing pluralism and market economy tendencies in the wake of present reforms in the East. If we let this chance slip by, we run the risk of a new and greater rigidity setting in.

I regard a new and intensified commitment on the part of Austria as the logical consequence of the foreign and foreign economic policy which it continued to pursue even when the East-West confrontation was at its height, and I believe that this will again place Austria in a position of political and economic initiative which will be commensurate with the times. In fulfilling this task, which for Austria, as a neutral country, is probably less difficult than for other Western countries, we would also be paving the way for the Western countries towards a goal which is ultimately in the interests of us all.

Chapter 20

THE WESTERN POLITICS OF EAST-WEST TRADE NEGOTIATIONS: EAST EUROPEAN COUNTRIES AND THE GATT

Leah Haus[1]

20.1 Introduction

One of the major changes occurring in the global political economy relates to the reintegration of the socialist countries. The importance of this topic has increased dramatically in the 1980s. Rapid changes in Soviet foreign economic policy confront the Western countries with a significantly altered situation that can be neither ignored nor wished away. These developments clearly call for an attempt to come to grips with the question of how East-West economic integration will proceed. As a contribution towards addressing this issue, this chapter focuses on the subject of participation by East European countries in the post-war international trade institution, the General Agreement on Tariffs and Trade (GATT).

The GATT was established in 1947 as part of the broader American designs to reconstruct a multilateral system of world trade. The General Agreement incorporated the main principles that were to guide trade relations in the post-war era. These norms and rules were geared towards ensuring the maintenance of an open, non-discriminatory market, where government intervention is minimized, and tariffs and prices guide the decisions of private firms. Thus, participation by the non-market economy East European countries poses an anomaly for the GATT. The functioning of non-market economic systems directly contradicts the market orientation of the neo-liberal trade institution.

Despite the systemic gap between GATT regulations and non-market economic systems, several East European countries are members of the institution, and others have shown an increasing interest in affiliation with the General Agreement. Poland, Romania, and Hungary became full members of the GATT in 1967, 1971 and 1973 respectively. Bulgaria became an observer at the GATT in 1967, and applied to accede to the GATT standards code in 1980.

---

[1] Assistant Professor of Political Science, New York University, New York, U.S.A.

Negotiations have recently officially opened over Bulgaria's request to accede to full GATT membership. The Soviet Union has expressed an interest in becoming an observer at the GATT since 1982 and officially requested to participate as an observer in the Uruguay Round. Soviet officials have conveyed that in 1991 the Soviet Union is likely to apply to accede to full membership. Negotiations are also currently underway regarding the full accession of China.

There has been extremely little written about the non-market economy countries' participation in the neo-liberal trade institution. The issue has been overlooked by two sets of relevant academic literature; namely, the international political economy literature and the East-West trade literature. The first objective of this chapter is to begin to fill this void, and to increase our understanding of a development that has important implications for both the future international political economic system, and for East-West relations.

The second purpose of this paper is to provide a structure for analyzing the Western policies towards negotiations between East European countries and the GATT. The study explores two broader themes: the relative influence of political-security considerations and trade policy considerations over foreign economic policy-making; and the relative influence of multilateral and bilateral approaches to foreign economic policy-making. I develop a framework that sheds light on the conditions under which these diverse considerations have had relatively more influence over the Western positions towards negotiations between East European countries and the GATT.[2]

20.2 The framework

The Western countries' policies towards negotiations between East European countries and the GATT have been influenced by a complex set of factors. Four primary issues have influenced the policy-making process during these negotiations: geopolitical goals, problems of obtaining effective reciprocity in trade relations between market and non-market economy countries, transatlantic conflicts over multilateralism and bilateralism, and European Community (EC) conflicts over integration and nationalism. An understanding of the conditions under which the diverse considerations have influenced policy making is facilitated by separating the negotiations into three categories.

---

[2] For a fuller treatment see Leah A. Haus, "The Political Economy of East-West Trade Negotiations: East European Countries and the GATT", (unpublished Ph.D. dissertation, Brandeis University, 1989).

The relative impact of the different factors has varied according to the stage of the negotiations. A disaggregation of the negotiations thus enables an assessment of the circumstances in which these different factors have influenced Western policies towards East-West trade negotiations within the multilateral GATT forum. The first phase of the negotiations relates to the question of whether or not an individual East European country was considered eligible to participate in the GATT; that is, the *criteria for reaching an agreement.* I argue that the Western countries have generally adopted a cohesive position towards this stage of the negotiations, and that this position has been primarily influenced by broader geopolitical considerations. Trade policy considerations had negligible impact over foreign policy-making under these conditions where geopolitical issues were a major consideration.

The second phase of the negotiations relates to appropriate *terms of agreement* for those countries that were deemed to be eligible candidates. The final phase of the negotiations relates to the *implementation of agreements* that were reached. These latter two stages were more directly concerned with the trade policy issues raised by the reintegration of the East European countries. Thus, although geopolitical issues remained an important background consideration, other factors also came to influence the policy-making process. It is at these stages that one can discern the beginnings of a normalization of trade relations with the East European countries in so far as trade policy issues surfaced. However, the additional influence of very diverse trade policy considerations and the continued backstage influence of broader political considerations leads to a less clear-cut picture of the second and third phases of the negotiations. In this chapter I suggest that an understanding of the Western countries' positions towards these more complex stages requires looking at three additional themes: trade policy dilemmas caused by the systemic gap between non-market economic systems and the neo-liberal trade institution, trade policy conflicts over multilateralism and bilateralism, and EC conflicts over nationalism and integration. These various issues had a different degree of influence over American and West European positions. This generated a certain degree of West-West conflict that was less apparent during the first stage of the negotiations.

Stage one: criteria for agreement

Since the late 1950s East European countries have put forward many applications to increase their affiliation with the GATT. Poland initially applied to participate in the Dillon and Kennedy Rounds, and subsequently applied for full membership in the trade institution. These moves were soon followed by requests from Romania and Hungary to become full members of the GATT. Bulgaria applied to join the GATT standards code, and to accede to full GATT membership in the context of the Uruguay Round. The Soviet Union has expressed much interest in obtaining observer status at the GATT, and officially requested to participate as an observer in the Uruguay Round. These applications received very different responses from the Western countries. Some applications were strongly encouraged, and others firmly discouraged. What were the major factors that determined the Western countries' positions towards the question of whether or not to accept an individual application?

The Western countries have generally adopted a united stance towards this first stage of the negotiations, and their positions have been overwhelmingly influenced by geopolitical considerations. Their policies have been motivated by a desire to further the foreign policy goals of containment of Soviet power and encouragement of diversity within Eastern Europe. The broader strategy of differentiation was applied to the specific economic negotiations within the GATT forum. In accordance with the strategy of differentiation, those East European countries that pursued domestic or foreign policies that differed from the policies of the Soviet Union were to be granted preferential economic treatment. Individual applications to participate in the GATT have consequently been supported or barred in accordance with these broader political objectives of the more dominant GATT members. Trade policy issues at times concerned those officials more directly immersed in GATT affairs. However, the overall impact of trade policy issues on the positions adopted by Western governments during this initial stage was negligible. This argument is supported by all the cases examined. This first part of the story was well explained by one former Western official interviewed, who stated that "The whole story is political... The political dimension was totally overwhelming. The trade policy people were out of the picture".[3]

The political goal of encouraging diversity within Eastern Europe led the Western countries to strongly support Poland, Romania, and Hungary's applications to join the GATT. Western governments employed the multilateral trade institution as a means to further their broader political goals. The fundamental

---

[3] All interviews were conducted on the condition that the anonymity of interviewees be preserved.

282

impact of political considerations was sufficiently strong that the Western countries' decision to conclude an agreement was decided *prior* to the opening of the formal accession negotiations. The desirability of these countries' accessions remained unquestioned throughout the subsequent discussions over terms of agreement.

Political considerations have similarly dominated the Western countries' responses towards Bulgaria and the Soviet Union's applications to increase their affiliation with the GATT. However, in these two cases the policy of differentiation has, to date, led to the opposite outcome; namely, no agreement. Many Western officials view Bulgaria as a close ally of the Soviet Union. Thus, Bulgaria has not been considered an eligible candidate for the preferential economic treatment granted to Poland, Romania, and Hungary under the strategy of differentiation. In addition, many Western policy makers have consistently and increasingly viewed the Bulgarian case as a precedent for the Soviet Union. They fear that concessions granted to the former could make it more difficult to devise an official argument to oppose the latter. The Bulgarian case has essentially become enmeshed in the Soviet case. The political considerations associated with the Bulgarian case have therefore grown to a size that is totally out of proportion with the country's position in the international system.

The Soviet approaches have raised some additional considerations that were absent in the cases of the smaller East European countries. The potential size of this non-market economy country's trading capabilities have generated a certain degree of trade policy concerns among some Western officials more directly immersed in GATT affairs. Some of these officials appear concerned that participation by a major non-market economy country may contribute towards a dilution, or erosion of the neo-liberal market oriented rules of the General Agreement. The official responses given to Soviet approaches are related to this concern and have focused on the lack of compatibility between the Soviet economic system and GATT regulations. However, official responses have largely omitted other political issues that have played a major role in influencing the Western countries' responses to the Soviet approaches. A large number of Western officials appear concerned that Soviet participation may lead to an "UNCTADization", or politicization of the GATT. It is this political issue, rather than concrete trade policy issues, that seems to have played a more significant role in the policy-making process. In addition, some officials continue to maintain an economic warfare attitude that dictates denying the

Soviet Union the preferential economic treatment granted to Poland, Romania, and Hungary under the strategy of differentiation.

It is currently somewhat difficult to ascertain precisely which of these considerations have had a significant influence over foreign policy-making. All the political and trade policy considerations dictate opposition to the Soviet approaches. It is therefore difficult to disentangle rhetoric from reality. However, it seems that trade policy issues have been exaggerated in official statements in order to provide a guise for the more fundamental political issues that fall outside the scope of the GATT. This argument also applies to the Chinese case.

Geopolitical considerations have overwhelmingly influenced the Western responses to the question of whether or not an individual East European country was considered eligible to participate in the GATT. Trade policy issues have had negligible impact over foreign policy-making under these conditions where political-security issues were a major consideration. In short, criteria for eligibility to participate in the GATT have been determined by geopolitical issues.

Stage two: terms of agreement

Political-security considerations deemed Poland, Romania, and Hungary to be desirable participants in the neo-liberal trade institution. The negotiations subsequently turned to the question of the terms on which these three countries should accede to the GATT. These discussions generated a substantial degree of conflictual and competitive behaviour between the Western countries, both across the Atlantic and within the EC. The negotiations led to numerous squabbles among the EC member states themselves, and between them and the Commission. This stage of the negotiations also led to a somewhat unusual alliance between the United States and the socialist countries in their common battle against the EC.

One of the major issues of dispute in all three cases related to discriminatory import quotas applied by West European countries against exports from "state-trading countries". The East European applicants requested that these discriminatory quotas be removed in accordance with the GATT rules on *non*-discrimination. This demand was adamantly resisted by those countries maintaining the quotas. These countries' representatives pressed for terms of agreement that would essentially provide them with an escape clause from the GATT rule on non-discrimination and would enable the maintenance of the discriminatory import regulations. This generated substantial conflict with the East European applicants and their supporters in the United States. An understanding of the factors that influenced the firm EC position towards this issue requires looking at two broader themes: trade policy dilemmas caused by the systemic gap between GATT regulations and non-market economic systems; and EC conflicts over nationalism and integration. An understanding of why the United States provided the East European applicants with significant support during this stage of the negotiations requires looking at a broader and historic transatlantic conflict over multilateralism and bilateralism.

The EC approach to the negotiations over the terms of agreement stressed the problem of how to ensure effective reciprocity from the non-market economy applicants. The systemic gap between non-market economic systems and the market oriented rules of the General Agreement creates substantial dilemmas when attempting to devise an appropriate entrance fee from the applicant in reciprocation for the benefits of GATT membership. The problems of bridging the systemic gap, which Jacob Viner has referred to as "the most perplexing question of all in the field of commercial policy", has a lengthy history.[4] The question was initially posed in the context of bilateral trade agreements with the Soviet Union in the late 1920s and 1930s. The method that came to be most widely adopted during that period required the Soviet Union to undertake a quantitative import commitment in exchange for obtaining MFN status. The second method, which was employed less often, came to be known as the commercial considerations clause. Each partner undertook to "be guided in regard to the purchase and sale of goods...by commercial and financial considerations only".[5]

The question of how to bridge the systemic gap reemerged in the 1940s, during the discussions over the Charter for the still-born International Trade Organization (ITO). Both of the previously employed methods were inserted into the Suggested Charter. Article 33 proposed that a state-trading country should undertake a global import commitment in reciprocation for obtaining MFN status. A commercial considerations clause was simultaneously inserted as Article 31 in order to attempt to ensure that the increased trade resulting

---

[4] Jacob Viner, "Conflicts of Principle in Drafting a Trade Chapter", *Foreign Affairs*, 25 (July 1947), p. 623.

[5] Cited in Martin Domke and John N. Hazard, "State Trading and the Most-Favored-Nation Clause", *American Journal of International Law*, 52 (1958), p. 59.

from the import commitment would be carried out in a non-discriminatory manner.[6] The Soviet Union's absence from the conferences where the Suggested Charter was discussed contributed towards a postponement of attempts to overcome some of the problems associated with the notion of a global import commitment. The proposed clause was subsequently entirely omitted from the final Havana Charter for the ITO, and from its offshoot the General Agreement on Tariffs and Trade. This omission left the problem unresolved at the time of the later negotiations over terms of agreement between East European countries and the GATT.

The dilemma of how to ensure effective reciprocity from the non-market economy applicants was emphasized by the EC during this second stage of the negotiations. This trade policy issue sheds some light on why the EC adopted a particularly harsh position towards the negotiations within the GATT forum. Some officials maintain that the problems of obtaining effective reciprocity explains why the EC member states were determined to retain the discriminatory import quotas. The dilemmas of devising a meaningful entrance fee in order to obtain increased market access in reciprocation for granting the non-discriminatory treatment associated with GATT membership are often said to account for the EC member states' firm attitude during the negotiations over terms of agreement between East European countries and the GATT.

Other officials and some observers suggest that the problem of obtaining effective reciprocity in the multilateral GATT context does not provide a comprehensive explanation for why the EC member states were so ardently opposed to eliminating the discriminatory quotas. These officials (including some from Western Europe) at times referred to the extreme emphasis placed on the problem of effective reciprocity as a "Community ideology" that should not be taken at face value. Many officials stressed that although there are commercial reasons for maintaining some of the quotas, these concerns have often been exaggerated. In some cases the geographical proximity caused a real fear of unfair import competition from the non-market economy countries' potentially heavily subsidized goods. However, the inclusion of a special discriminatory safeguard clause in the agreements ensures protection against unfair import competition.

---

[6] See Alexander Gerschenkron, "Russia and the International Trade Organization", *American Economic Review*, 37, no. 2 (1947).

These officials suggest that there is no clear-cut reason for the un-willingness to liberalize the quotas. The reasons have varied over time and among countries. The most general reason cited is that the quotas served as a means of national control in relations with Eastern Europe. They provide bargaining chips in bilateral negotiations with East European countries. This argument is supported by John and Pauline Pinder's observation that: "With President de Gaulle in hot pursuit of the leading role in detente, France also became, in 1966, the first member country to scrap a large number of its import quotas".[7] A desire to retain the quotas as a means to pursue national political-economic objectives is often said to explain the EC member states' unwillingness to liberalize the quotas.

The need to look beyond the argument that the EC member states' antagonistic position in the GATT forum was simply explained by the problems of obtaining effective reciprocity in the multilateral GATT context is sub-stantiated by looking at their positions towards similar discussions within the EC. The EC member states have also strongly opposed any interference with the quotas at the Community level where the issue of obtaining effective reci-procity is absent. The member states have traditionally firmly resisted the Commission's proposals to devise a common Community policy relating to the national discriminatory quotas imposed against "state-trading countries". Competing commercial interests and competitive diplomacy between the member states have led them to resist delegating authority to the Community.[8] As stated in a European Parliament report written in 1975:

> Although there have been signs, since last year, of a new readiness on the part of the state-trading countries to recognize the Community as an institution and perhaps as a negotiating partner, differing national interests on the part of the Member States of the European Community underlie the latter's hesitancy to surrender freedom in trade policy and political influence. For this reason the measures so far taken by the European Communities in the field of trade policy are basically confined to provisions for co-ordinating procedure in partial sectors without formulating a draft on a coordinated approach comprising all the trade policy instruments.[9]

---

[7] John Pinder and Pauline Pinder, *The European Community's Policy Towards Eastern Europe* (London: Chatham House, PEP, 1975), p. 19.

[8] See, for example, Werner Feld, *The European Common Market and the World* (New Jersey: Rowman & Littlefield, 1973), pp. 155-57; and Perre Hassner, "The Politics of Western Europe and East-West Relations", in Wils Andren and Karl E. Birnbaum eds., *Beyond Detente: Prospects for East-West Co-operation and Security in Europe* (Leyden: A.W. Sijthoff, 1976), p. 18.

[9] European Parliament Working Document, no. 425/74, (January 9, 1975,) p. 12.

The member states' opposition to the institutionalization of trade relations with Eastern Europe at the GATT level replicated this resistance to the institutionalization of trade relations with Eastern Europe at the Community level. In both cases they opposed expanding the scope of issues to be considered under the institution's jurisdiction. In sum, it seems that a comprehensive explanation for why the EC member states adopted a particularly harsh position towards the negotiations over the discriminatory quotas in the GATT forum requires looking at two issues: problems of obtaining effective reciprocity from the applicants in the multilateral GATT context; and a desire to retain a tool that provided a means to pursue national political-economic objectives in Eastern Europe.

The EC determination to obtain an escape clause from the GATT rule on non-discrimination generated much conflict with the United States. Once the United States had taken the political decision to encourage trade with a specific East European country, it then adopted the position that this trade should take place in a multilateral context. In other words, the United States favoured terms of agreement that would enlarge the scope of the trade institution's jurisdiction. The American position reflected a long-standing abhorrence for discriminatory quotas that had likewise contributed to the transatlantic conflicts during the negotiations over the ITO. A brief review of this broader historic dispute fills a missing link for comprehending the specific transatlantic battles during the negotiations over terms of agreement between East European countries and the GATT.

The broader conflict over multilateralism and bilateralism had dominated the discussions over the reconstruction of a post-war economic system during the 1940s. The designs for the post-war system included the construction of an International Trade Organization to oversee the implementation of a multilateral treaty on trade regulations. The post-war planners in the U.S. Department of State championed the goals of multilateralism and non-discrimination. However, this vision of the post-war economic order met with much opposition from other governments. West European nations were committed to ensuring full employment and avoiding a severe balance of payments crisis. Free trade and free enterprise were viewed as impediments to these objectives. These different priorities generated much resistance to the American crusade against any form of discriminatory trading practices, such as preferential trading agreements and discriminatory quotas. The irreconcilable views on the two sides of the Atlantic contributed towards the death of the envisioned ITO. As Richard Gardner has explained:

> The two major sponsors of the ITO sought to incorporate in the Charter a detailed state-ment of their favorite economic doctrines. The United States pressed formal under-takings for the elimination of Imperial Preference, quantitative restrictions, and dis-crimination of all kinds. The United Kingdom pressed equally detailed undertakings to protect domestic policies of full employment. The result was an elaborate set of rules and counter-rules...these rules and counter-rules satisfied nobody and alienated nearly everybody. They grew into such a mountain of complexity that the ITO finally collapsed of its own weight.[10]

The General Agreement on Tariffs and Trade - a multilateral trade agree-ment - was left to fill the ensuing vacuum, and came to assume a role that was not intended at its inception. However, the conflicting views towards multi-lateralism and bilateralism did not disappear with the death of the ITO. This broader transatlantic conflict resurfaced during the negotiations between East European countries and the GATT. One particular issue of dispute during the 1940s, discriminatory quotas, likewise generated much West-West conflict during the East-West negotiations within the GATT forum.

The two very different perspectives on the two sides of the Atlantic during the negotiations between East European countries and the GATT were well summarized by one former Western official who stated that "the U.S. approached these accessions as a multilateral exercise; it was a new experience for them to trade with East European countries, and they saw it in a multilateral framework. The EC saw the accessions as renewed bilateral negotiations".

American officials' preference for multilateralism led them to strongly support the socialist countries in their common battle against the EC member states' discriminatory quotas. The divergent views across the Atlantic first became evident at the early stages of the Polish accession negotiations.

The transatlantic conflicts became more pronounced as the negotiations proceeded, and a deadline for the elimination of the discriminatory quotas became the key U.S. objective in the Polish accession negotiations. The American determination to include a terminal date for removal of the quotas was at times even more pronounced than the Polish desire. American officials were instructed to urge the Polish government to take a strong stand on the issue when it became clear that the Polish resolve was weakening, and to

---

[10] Richard N. Gardner, *Sterling-Dollar Diplomacy: The Origins and the Prospects of Our International Economic Order* (New York: McGraw-Hill, 1969, expanded edition), p. 379.

convey that the United States was willing to intervene at a high level in order to try to resolve the issue. This pattern of alignment recurred during the Romanian and Hungarian accession negotiations. In all three cases the issue of discriminatory quotas became the main stumbling blocks to agreement.

Stage three: implementation of agreements

The final terms of agreement reached were somewhat ambiguously phrased, particularly those clauses relating to discriminatory quotas maintained against exports from the East European countries. The precise words of these clauses left much leeway for alternative interpretations during the subsequent implementation phase. One of the major disputes in the negotiations over the implementation of the agreements has centered on the issue of discriminatory quotas. The East European countries, particularly Hungary, have consistently maintained that the EC has failed to live up to the spirit of the agreement.

The agreements included a provision for periodic reviews of the protocols of accession. These meetings were transformed into a ritual series of arguments and counter-arguments between the Hungarian and Community representatives regarding the degree to which the signatories were complying with the agreement. The main target of Hungary's attack was the extremely slow pace at which the EC member states were removing their discriminatory quotas, and an increase in the discriminatory element of some quotas maintained against Hungarian exports. The Hungarian charge against the EC's failure to adhere to the clause on discriminatory quotas was consistently and increasingly supported by other GATT members, such as the United States and Cananda.

Despite the official defence put forward in biannual debates, a fairly large number of Community officials consider that the EC failed to live up to the terms of the agreement. Many Commission officials became increasingly embarrassed by the Hungarian publication of the dispute in the GATT forum. This embarrassment increased when the debate turned to the less ambiguously phrased part of the clause specifying that "Contracting parties...shall not increase the discriminatory element in these restrictions...". Commission officials were placed in a particularly awkward position when attempting to defend the increase in discriminatory quotas that occurred when Greece joined the Community, and when general quotas were removed against all GATT members except the East European countries. What accounted for this lack of compliance with the multilateral agreement?

The factors influencing the EC's position towards this final stage of the negotiations in part replicate the issues discussed in the previous section. The member states' unwillingness to liberalize the quotas was caused by a fear of unfair import competition, problems of obtaining effective reciprocity, and a desire to retain tools to pursue national foreign policy objectives. However, a more thorough explanation for the failure to live up to the spirit of the agreement requires expanding on the theme of the complex European Community.

The GATT regime's potential influence to encourage states to refrain from reneging on agreements in order to maintain creditworthy reputations was undermined by the institutional structure of the EC. It was the Commission, not the member states, that had to defend the Community's position in the GATT forum. However, the Commission held little power to resolve the issue which lay in the hands of the member states. The latter had little incentive to resolve the issue as it was not they but the Commission that experienced the embarrassment. The member states used the Commission as a "smokescreen". As one official from a member state explained: "We experience no feeling of embarrassment in the GATT as its the Commission that takes the embarrassment".

Many Commission officials were thus generally less opposed to the Hungarian demand that the discriminatory quotas be removed. This more forthcoming position also stemmed from the conflict between the Commission and the member states over the competence to determine trade policy towards Eastern Europe. The Commission's task of establishing a common commercial policy requires either abolishing the national quotas or developing a harmonized Community list of quotas. Thus, the Commission has consistently had a certain degree of interest in the elimination of the quotas in order to advance the broader goal of developing a common commercial policy. In direct contrast, the member states' interest in retaining the quotas was partially explained by a desire to retain national control over trade relations with Eastern Europe.

The American position towards the implementation phase was influenced by a combination of factors. The United States clearly demonstrated support for Hungary's demand that the discriminatory quotas be removed. Many officials' views on the reason for supporting the battle against quotas were succinctly summarized by one official who stated that: "It's a matter of principle". Other officials suggested that concrete commercial considerations caused the American opposition towards the discriminatory quotas. One gains the impression, however, that the degree of support was slightly more muted than that shown during the earlier Polish accession negotiations in the 1960s.

Several considerations dampened the extent of American support shown during the implementation phase. Some officials explained that there was a limit to how far the United States was willing to take action on the issue due to a fear of retaliation on other issues where America's own record might generate cause for debate. The more frequently cited reason was that there is a limit to how far the United States will antagonize its Western allies in order to support the cause of a country where the non-market economic system itself fails to conform fully with the GATT. The trade policy alliance between the United States and the socialist countries in their joint battle against discriminatory quotas was muted by the security alliance between the United States and Western Europe, and by the trade policy gap between non-market economic systems and the GATT. Many officials stated that although they considered that the Community had reneged on an agreement, its reputation had experienced negligible damage as the case involved a non-market economy country. If the Community had similarly failed to abide by the spirit of an equivalent agreement with any other GATT members, then the practical damage to its reputation would have been far more significant. As one Western official summarized: "The EC's non-fulfillment of the agreement had little practical impact simply because the East European countries are thought of as second-class citizens in the GATT. They have no standing".

20.3 Conclusion

The major lesson learnt from examining negotiations between East European countries and the GATT is not encouraging, and provides much support for the pessimistic outlook of a realistic analysis of world politics. Realism's focus on the primacy of political-security considerations in foreign policy-making provides much insight into the Western countries' positions towards the first stage of the negotiations. The conclusion this research conveys most strongly is that an applicant's eligibility to join the "private club" has been determined by the broader foreign policy goals of the more dominant GATT members. The Western countries generally adopted a united position towards this phase of the negotiations where geopolitical issues overwhelmed trade policy and commercial considerations.

This cohesive Western position disintegrated when the negotiations turned to the trade policy issues raised during the second and third stages. These parts of the negotiations pointed to divisive forces within the West. Many of the West European countries essentially opposed enlarging the scope of the GATT regime, particularly in the sphere of import quotas. Their positions amounted to a preference for retaining trade relations with Eastern Europe on a bilateral level. This generated much conflict with the United States. The American position displayed a preference for broadening the scope of issues to be considered under the multilateral trade institution's jurisdiction. The West-West disputes over these trade policy questions were often sufficiently strong to overwhelm or delay the development of a united Alliance and a united Community position towards these East-West trade negotiations.

Chapter 21

THE ROLE OF THE WEST EUROPEAN AND JAPANESE GOVERNMENTS IN EAST-WEST ECONOMIC RELATIONS: THE VIEW FROM EASTERN EUROPE

Dariusz K. Rosati[1]

21.1 Policy objectives of Western governments: economics versus politics

It is widely believed that East-West economic relations have always been heavily influenced by political factors. However, Western governments, even those following otherwise liberal and non-interventionist foreign economic policy, have tried to control the sphere of economic contacts with socialist countries, using various economic and non-economic tools. This tendency has been particularly visible in the case of the United States, although other Western countries have closely followed American political guidelines.

The foreign policies of Western governments have always been dominated by two fundamental objectives. On the one hand, it was recognized that expanding East-West trade and cooperation might bring about tangible benefits for Western societies in form of increased output and employment, access to new markets and sources of supplies, and the dissemination of Western cultural and social ideas. The economic and social motives for the development of economic relations with the East were therefore to maximize gains from trade and technical cooperation, based on geographic proximity, long established cultural links, and an abundance of cheap labour and raw materials. Thus, economic interests have played a stimulating role in the East-West trade.

On the other hand, political and military rivalry and confrontation between East and West have exercised an adverse impact on mutual economic relations. The political objective of the West was to restrict mutual trade and to maintain technological superiority over Eastern economies. Thus political considerations conflicted frequently with purely economic ones.

---

[1] Director, Foreign Trade Research Institute, Warsaw, Poland.

As a result, East-West economic relations have developed as the peculiar outcome of two contradictory tendencies, and have depended on fluctuations of the East-West political climate. One can identify several political cycles in the post-war period. (see *Table 21.1*)

Table 21.1

Political cycles in East-West relations, 1948-1989

1948-1955	Cold-war period (Korean war, Stalin's doctrine of self-reliance of the socialist "camp")
1956-1959	Temporary thaw (new leadership in the Soviet Union)
1960-1968	Period of increased tensions (U-2 affair, Cuban crisis, Vietnam war)
1969-1978	Gradual *detente* (Nixon's opening to the Soviet Union and PRC, Helsinki Accord, etc.)
1979-1985	Political confrontation (Afghanistan, Polish crisis, regional conflicts)
1986-	Towards disarmament and cooperation

Table 21.2 provides data on the trade dynamics of CMEA countries with EC countries and Japan. The figures indicate that the increase of mutual trade was in general faster in periods of reduced political tensions. However, more thorough analysis reveals that the impact of political considerations on economic relations has been of much lower singificance in the case of West European countries and Japan, than in the case of the United States. It seems that intra-European trade is either less politically sensitive or political objectives are more aligned with economic ones.

This very general overview is certainly not sufficient to examine the role of political factors in economic relations between individual countries. There were many nuances differentiating policies of Western governments towards particular socialist countries. There is no need to emphasize the special character of links between East and West Germany. Also, Poland enjoyed preferential political treatment in the 1960s and 1970s but lost this position to Hungary in the wake of political turmoil in 1980-1982. Similarly, Romania had received significant extra assistance and support from the West for many years, only to lose it in the 1980s when the West concluded that political benefits stemming from Romania's independent foreign policy no longer offset highly repressive internal policies, strongly criticized by the West. These sorts of discriminatory policies, however, do not alter the general tendency of attempting to strike a fragile and difficult balance between the contradictory tendencies of political confrontation and economic cooperation.

Table 21.2

Average annual rates of change of CMEA trade with the EC and Japan, 1955-1987

	CMEA exports to the EC	CMEA imports from the EC	CMEA exports to Japan	CMEA imports from Japan
1955-1959	17.2	13.3	66.0	16.1
1960-1968	12.2	16.3	36.3	36.1
1969-1978	25.4	24.5	12.6	33.6
1979-1985	10.2	0.0	1.8	0.6
1986-1987	-0.3	14.0	18.7	15.6

Source: Based on trade data from United nations *Handbook of International Trade and Development Statistics* (various years); and from Eurostat, *Commerce exterieur*, 1, (1989).

21.2 Policy instruments

Penetrating the post-war history of East-West economic relations one can safely conclude that, except for open military operations, all possible tools of government intervention have been used with various intensity and in various periods to influence the process of East-West trade and cooperation. The concept of "state trading", advanced by Western countries to describe the state monopoly of foreign trade form adopted in socialist countries in the late 1940s, was used to justify the much larger scope of Western governmental intervention in trade than otherwise could have been admitted as necessary in market-type economies. Apart from regular tools of commercial policy, like tariffs, non-tariff barriers (NTB), quotas, etc., numerous administrative restrictions have been widely used to tailor the level and structure of mutual trade and cooperation. Following the UNCTAD Trade Information System (TIS) all trade control measures can be classified as follows:

1) tariffs and subsidies (customs duties, fiscal duties, direct and indirect subsidies);
2) additional fiscal charges (excise duties, stamp tax, license fees, etc.);
3) service charges (statistical tax, transport tax);
4) internal taxes levied on imported and domestic products (sales tax, excise tax, value-added tax, turnover tax, etc.);
5) licensing and quantitative restrictions (restrictive licensing, quotas, prohibitions, automatic licensing, restrictions at the enterprise level);
6) monetary and financial measures (multiple exchange rates, foreign exchange licensing, permits and prohibitions, etc., financial and monetary preferences);
7) control of price level (custom valuations, anti-dumping measures, countervailing measures);
8) single channel for imports and compulsory national services (state trading monopoly, compulsory national insurance, transports, etc.);
9) preferential trading arrangements (multilateral and bilateral PTAs); and
10) special entry procedures (sanitary inspections, technical standards, packing requirements, etc.).

The measures enumerated above are applied by Western countries both to imports from the East and to exports. However, imports are regulated with a much larger variety of tools, with tariffs, quotas, price controls and special entry procedures playing the most prominent role. Western exports in turn are mostly influenced by licensing of high technology goods and by credit, insurance and financial measures. There follows a concise overview of government-imposed trade control measures in member countries of the EC and in Japan.

21.3 Trade control measures applied by the European Community in trade with European CMEA countries

The process of economic integration unfolding in Western Europe has led to the creation of a single European market, made up of 12 countries with a total population of more than 320 million and a combined GNP of more than $ 3.5 trillions. One of the main characteristics of this process is the ever-growing role of supranational bodies in determining the Community's economic and commercial policy. At the same time the decision-making powers of individual governments are being gradually reduced. At present, the EC Commission controls the most important trade policy instruments, like common tariff, bilateral trade agreements, non-tariff import restriction policy, preferential trading arrangements, and agricultural trade. Individual governments are still entitled to sign bilateral agreements on scientific and technical cooperation and co-production, to determine the rules of credit policy towards exports and imports, and to apply individual export promotion measures. As can be seen, the commercial policy of the EC countries towards socialist countries has since 1975 been determined neither by sovereign decisions of particular governments nor by bilateral intergovernment trade agreements but by unilateral actions of the EC Commission. This has produced a peculiar absence of any formal agreements because socialist countries, until very recently, have not recognized the EC as a supranational body, and insisted on bilateral negotiations with particular EC countries; and that, in turn, was consistently rejected by the EC. As a result, East European exports to the EC countries were restricted by a number of protectionist measures adopted at the Community level, not by individual countries. Western exports to the CMEA, in turn, were not so much influenced by unified trade policy as by political considerations, more or less common for all Western countries.

Tariff restrictions

After completing the Tokyo Round of GATT negotiations on the overall reduction of tariffs, the average level of the common tariff on imports to the EC has stabilized since 1987 at 2.4 per cent and is now lower than the average for all developed market economies (3.6 per cent). The comparative position of the CMEA countries can be assessed against tariff preferences granted to other countries. EC has signed a number of PTAs with the EFTA group and with developing countries under the Generalized System of Preferences (GSP). It is estimated that preferential tariffs are 3 to 4 times lower than tariff charges on imports from socialist countries.[2] On the other hand, one has to admit that even non-preferential tariffs are comparatively low and cannot be regarded in general as major obstacles for imports from non-participants. However, in some commodity groups these charges can be more important in determining the competitive position of outside suppliers. Tariff discrimination against socialist countries is confirmed by the fact, that 75 per cent of external imports

---

[2] E. Synowiec and P. Kitelnicki, *Wplyw rzadow czlonkowskich i Komisji EWG na polityke gospodarcza tego ugrupowania - konsekwencje dla eksportu krajow socjalistycznyh* (Warszawa: Instytut Koniunktur i Cen HZ, 1989).

to the EC are conducted under various PTAs (65 per cent of imports to non-EC European countries).

The use of PTAs to create influence spheres or to consolidate political ties poses a serious threat to international trade because of distortions in the international division of labour. Instead of increasing the volume of trade, imports can rather be reallocated to less efficient partners and global welfare can be reduced.

Quantitative restrictions

In the early 1960s almost all EC imports from socialist countries were subject to quantitative restrictions. In 1967 the Benelux countries waived most of these restrictions on machines and raw materials; France and Italy followed later. In 1970 a list of commodities excluded from quota regulations was specified by the EC (797 tariff positions or 73 per cent of all positions have been liberalized). Other goods are still imported under specified quotas but conditions vary in various countries, with Spain, the FRG, and Italy leading in number of restrictions. *Table 21.3* gives some data on autonomous quotas against imports from Poland. A large proportion of these restrictions (92 per cent) touched upon manufactured goods.

A common opinion is that quantitative restrictions do not constitute a real barrier to East European exports because in most cases these quotas are not filled even by 50 per cent. Taking the case of Poland, for 176 positions the actual import was less than 50 per cent of the limit, and in only 43 positions was the quota filled between 50 and 100 per cent (in leather goods, china and glass, among others). The reason for this is believed to be the generally low quality of exported goods and constraints on the supply side. However, this situation may change in the near future in view of deep systemic market-oriented reforms under way in Poland and Hungary.

The discriminatory effect of autonomous quotas for socialist countries should not be over-emphasized because the EC applies quantitative restrictions against other countries, like Japan or Canada. Further liberalization can be achieved through establishing formal agreements between socialist countries and the EC.

More important than autonomous restrictions for CMEA exports are sectoral agreements between the EC Commission and particular socialist countries. These agreements are types of so-called voluntary export restraints (VERs) and orderly marketing arrangements (OMAs). Since 1978, a steel agreement regulates volume of steel products imports to the EC from the CMEA countries (except the Soviet Union). A similar agreement for textiles has been signed with Poland, Hungary, and Bulgaria in 1979, with Czechoslovakia in 1986 and Romania in 1987. A classical VER-type agreement concerning footwear products exists between Poland and the United Kingdom and Ireland. A number of other VERs and OMAs of lesser significance have been in force for many years, for agricultural products for example. Such sectoral agreements, paradoxically, may carry some advantages for exporting countries. They secure a certain level of foreign sales and sometimes allow the exporter to avoid additional fiscal and customs charges.

Table 21.3

**Autonomous quotas imposed by the EC
on imports from Poland, 1980-1988**

Country	1980	1983	1986	1988
Benelux	27	27	21	21
Denmark	7	6	5	5
Ireland	1	1	-	-
FRG	37	39	40	40
Greece	31	31	15	15
France	20	18	17	17
Italy	38	39	39	39
United Kingdom	15	13	12	12
Portugal	-	-	15	15
Spain	-	-	52	52
Total	176	174	216	216

Source: *Official Journal*, various issues.

Price control measures

Price control measures are applied in the EC to agricultural imports and in exceptional cases to other products. Differential levies are used to equate import price with domestic price for a given product, the latter normally being higher due to EC's protectionist agricultural policy. Differential levies are regarded as much more efficient tools of protection than customs duties, and at the same time their discriminatory power is much higher. If quantitative restrictions affect 7 per cent of total Polish exports to the EC, differential taxation is applied to more than 9 per cent of total exports (although this amounts to 50 per cent of agricultural exports). It should be mentioned that in the past the share of agricultural exports in total CMEA exports to the Common Market was much higher but gradually diminished as result of the severely protectionist Common Agricultural Policy of the EC.

Among price control measures countervailing duties are considered as highly protectionist instruments because of the lack of objective and precise criteria to determine dumping prices. The EC normally refers to some "ideal" markets without specifying the "most efficient producer" to be taken as reference. Such procedures leave the question of estimating the dumping margin to the discretion of the EC officials, and allow for discriminatory treatment of socialist countries. *Table 21.4* presents data on antidumping procedures undertaken by the EEC against exporters from socialist countries. The increased number of anti-dumping procedures against socialist countries in the 1980s may be only partly explained by the imprecise manner of "fair" price estimations by the EC. It is almost certain that since CMEA countries are suppliers of similar products to the West, they frequently compete through price reductions which may lead sometimes to dumping charges.

Table 21.4

Anti-dumping procedures against socialist countries

Country	1970-1979	1980-1983	Total
Bulgaria	5	1	6
Czechoslovakia	12	16	28
GDR	10	14	24
Hungary	8	8	16
Poland	12	8	20
Romania	12	10	22
Soviet Union	9	10	19
Total socialist countries	68	67	135
Other countries	116	102	218
Total	184	169	353

Source: A. Munko and W. Rybowski, "Rozszerzanie sie EWG a dskryminacja Krajow socjalistycznych na tym rynku", *Handel Zagraniczny*, 8 (1987).

Special entry procedures

Sanitary requirements and technical norms are most commonly used by the EC to secure a high technical level and quality of imported goods. If these measures are applied on a non-discriminatory basis (i.e., they are compulsory for imports from all countries), there is little to complain about, except for insisting on having these restrictions widely published to inform all actual and potential exporters. It is worth noting that individual governments are still free to establish national technical and sanitary norms which may be higher than the standard norms recommended by the EC Commission (e.g., French norms for metal products.)

Export Policy

The power of the EC Commission is of much lesser importance as far as exports are concerned. A sigificant degree of supranational intervention is observed only in agricultural exports, where exporters are subsidized up to the level of the internal EC price. More important, however, for export expansion are financial and credit support measures which are still under the control of particular governments. The measures can be classified into two main groups: export credit guarantees and preferential credit conditions for exports.

Every EC country has a government agency for export credits insurance. Government guarantees are granted in cases where export is financed on credit conditions, provided that the importing country satisfies specific economic and political requirements. Economic creditworthiness is measured by various indicators reflecting the level of external debt, balance of payments position, and the overall economic situation. The assessment of political standing depends obviously on subjective judgements of particular governments and reflects priorities in foreign policy. Government guarantees for exports credits became an important tool of foreign policy in the 1980s when the global debt crisis developed and numerous countries got into liquidity problems. Poland's example demonstrates that this tool can be effectively used to freeze the inflow of hard currency funds to the indebted country and can serve as a convenient form of political pressure. Overnight suspension of foreign credits in 1982 caused a tremendous supply-side shock in the Polish economy which was abruptly cut off from Western supplies of raw materials, consumer goods, and machines. Hard currency imports dropped by more than 50 per cent within one year, leading to a deep recession and reduction of output. It must be stressed that credit sanctions were imposed on Poland largely for political reasons. The suspension of guarantees for export credits to Poland by Western governments led to a significant drop in the volume of Polish foreign trade in the 1980s; the pre-crisis level of Polish exports to the West was reestablished only in 1987, although, as of 1989, the import level is still 20 per cent below that of 1979.

Credit sanctions against Poland were not extended to other socialist countries, although in general the financial policy of Western governments towards the East became much more cautious after the debt crisis in 1982. Western countries adopted a policy of careful discrimination, obviously trying to influence the internal situation in Poland. The recent acceleration of democratic processes and the "round-table" debate in Poland are sometimes interpreted as the desired outcome of the West's firm stand on new credits, conditional on political concessions by the Polish government. However, this view is too simplistic. The most important factor that contributed to the political opening in Poland seemed to be the very unfortunate, conservative, and erratic economic policy followed by the Polish government between 1982 and 1988. It was the failure to reactivate the economy and to implement a strong market mechanism that eroded political resistance against democratic reforms. The change of leadership in the Soviet Union also played a very important role in this process. The same line of reasoning may also be valid in explaining the recent acceleration of democratic processes in Hungary in the late 1980s.

Another tool of government intervention largely used for political reasons is official financial assistance. "Soft" credits or grants are extended mostly to developing countries, and are only exceptionally offered to carefully selected socialist countries. Only Romania and Yugoslavia have benefited in the past from concessional financing for development programmes, although the volume of this assistance was negligible as compared with total inflow of funds from other sources.

21.4 Trade control measures applied by other West European countries

As in the case of the EC, non-tariff barriers continue to be the main instrument of government controls of East-West economic relations by other West European countries. Quantitative import restrictions are widely used together with price control measures in EFTA countries. For example, Polish exports of vegetables, frozen fruits, and beef and pork are restricted under quotas in Switzerland (the most severely protected market), Sweden, Finland, Norway, and Austria. Import licenses for Polish meat is required in Sweden and for steel products in Finland. Polish footwear is exported under a VER agreement to Austria, and the same kind of restriction bears on exports of horse-meat to France, cement to Sweden, and steel products to Finland. In sum, the value of Polish exports under quota to EFTA contries reached $ 100 million in 1986 (2.5 per cent of total exports).

Differential taxation applied by the EFTA group is less arduous due to the much lower proportion of agricultural products in Polish exports. Also, anti-dumping procedures have seldom been used against Polish exports; (only twice in 1986, for example, against plywood exports to Finland and Sweden), and involved less than 1 per cent of total exports to EFTA market.[3] In general, trade with EFTA countries has to be regarded as much more liberalized than trade with the EC.

21.5 The role of the Japanese government

The volume of trade between the CMEA countries and Japan has traditionally been of much lesser importance for both sides than trade between CMEA and EC, but the dynamics of Japanese trade was much higher. In 1955 trade with Japan was less than 2 per cent of that with the EC, but by 1986 it has grown to 11 per cent. As can be seen from *Table 21.2*, after a long period of steep increases, CMEA-Japanese trade came to a practical halt at the end of the 1970s, and has since decreased to less than 2.5 per cent of total Japanese merchandise exchange.

As in the case of other market economies, the role of tariffs in regulating Japanese imports declined significantly and has been gradually replaced by non-tariff barriers which, unlike tariffs, offer much larger possibilities for discrimination among trading partners, and therefore are more convenient to achieve non-economic objectives. Indeed, non-tariff restrictive measures are applied in Japan with a far higher incidence to products originating in socialist countries than in other country groups. *Table 21.5* shows the share of imports subject to NTBs in Japan and the EC.

Treatment of particular socialist countries is much more differentiated in Japan than in the EC. For example, up to 78 per cent of Polish exports are subject to quotas in Japan, as compared with 6.3 per cent of Hungarian ex-

---

[3] E. Kawecka-Wyrzjowska and J. Wieczorek, *Przeszkody pozataryfowe w dostepie polskich towarow do rynkow rozwinietych krakow kapitalistycznych w swietle baden ankietowch* (Warszawa: Instytit Koniunktur i Cen HZ, 1989).

ports and only 0.9 per cent of Bulgarian exports. Corresponding figures for the EC are 39.3 per cent, 44.2 per cent, and 36.8 per cent.

Table 21.5

**Role of non-tariff barriers facing imports
to the EC and Japan from main country groups, 1976**

Importing markets	Exporters	Total value of imports	Quotas and licensing	DIC[a]	Other NTBs	NTB index[b]
		($ millions)	(%)	(%)	(%)	(total)
EC	developed	78,918	8.1	10.8	12.0	0.28
	LDCs	77,298	9.3	4.6	20.6	0.28
	CPEs	11,613	27.3	14.8	18.5	0.41
Japan	developed	25,796	23.5	2.1	36.9	0.15
	LDCs	35,811	1.6	1.2	13.2	0.12
	CPEs	1,361	17.9	-	8.7	0.14

a) DIC - direct import controls including minimum prices, VERs, and variable and differential levies.

b) NTB index is the so-called "frequency index" showing the share of tariff lines in a particular product group which are covered by NTBs, in a total number of tariff lines within the product group.

Source: A. Olechowski and A. Yeats, "The Incidence of Non-Tariff Barriers on Socialist Countries' Exports", *Economia Internazionale*, XXXV, no. 2 (1982).

Japan's biggest trading partner among CMEA countries is the Soviet Union which accounts for about 60 per cent of its trade with socialist countries, excluding China. Soviet-Japanese relations are, however, heavily distorted by deep political divergences, concerning mostly the problem of the Northern Territories. The Japanese government makes any further extension of bilateral cooperation and financial assistance conditional on a softening of the Soviet position in the disputed area. For this reason a number of specific restrictions still hamper Japanese-Soviet economic relations in the field of direct foreign investment and capital cooperation, for example.

21.6 The "Paris Club"

The "Paris Club" is an informal intergovernmental organization of Western countries to coordinate official credit policy towards indebted countries. Three CMEA countries ran into balance of payments difficulties at the beginning of the 1980s (Poland, Romania, and Hungary), and the question of restructuring or rescheduling of their external publicly guaranteed debt was discussed in the Club. Poland's case was undoubtedly the most severe one. If the decision to suspend government guarantees in 1982 was obviously motivated by political considerations, there is less evidence to support the view that the Club's policy towards Poland after 1982 was highly discriminatory.

True, Poland was treated extremely severely in negotations with the Club and other equally indebted countries were getting distintly more favourable rescheduling conditions. Hungary and Romania were offered at least some assistance from the Paris Club (as well as from the IMF and the World Bank). A much more cooperative approach has been taken by the Club in the case of Brazil, Mexico, Argentina, Nigeria, and other debtors where sophisticated financial schemes have often been designed and applied in order to alleviate the debt service problem. Poland, in turn, was regarded as a debtor of lowest standing, even though her economic position has not been worse than that of many other countries.

But recent developments indicate that some changes in the Club's policy may be forthcoming. Small amounts of credits for specific investment projects in Poland are already receiving government backing in Austia, Italy, and France. In January 1989 the Japanese government decided to reestablish export credit guarantees by MITI to 18 of the most heavily indebted countries, including Poland and Yugoslavia, but only for carefully selected projects, evaluated on a case-by-case basis. It is more and more clear, that the wait-and-see strategy adopted by the Paris Club does not respond to current needs and undermines the chances for overcoming the global debt crisis.

21.7 The problem of multilateral export controls (COCOM)

Responding to pressure from the United States, Western countries agreed to establish a multilateral system of export controls to socialist countries. The Coordinating Committee for Multilateral Export Controls (COCOM) was created in 1949 as an executive body of the intergovernmental Consultative Committee, which was responsible for the coordination of trade policy vis-à-vis socialist countries. The primary objective of COCOM was to extend controls over exports of products with significant military applications. In the 1970s this objective was reformulated to maintain the strategic advantage of the West in high technology goods. However, the definition of strategic goods has been always very flexible and vague, allowing for the imposition of restrictions and embargoes on numerous manufactured products with little or no military application. This refers in particular to the so-called "dual-use" items. Suffice it to say that the COCOM list includes products of general use like valves, anti-friction bearings, or synthetic rubber. The list of restricted products is revised periodically; since 1985 one-third of the industrial goods list is revised every year.

The number of items on the industrial list fluctuated with the political climate. The list was reduced from 285 items in 1952 to 118 in 1958, oscillated around 150 items in the 1960s and 1970s, coming down to 130 in 1980. Political tensions in the 1980s raised the number of restricted items to 154 in 1986.[4]

Restricted products can sometimes be exported to the East after passing the rather cumbersome licensing procedure. Export permits were granted usually to more than 90 per cent of applications which may suggest both that the controls have some degree of flexibility and that the COCOM system has become over-stretched and redundant.

One should note also that different Western countries approach COCOM procedure and policy somewhat differently. The United States is undoubtedly the most outspoken advocate of strict and widespread controls whereas the West European and Japanese governments have traditionally taken a more moderate position.

COCOM restrictions have been strongly criticized by socialist countries. It has been stressed that embargoes often affect products used for purely civilian purposes, and that the whole idea of strategic controls remains at odds with the principle of mutually beneficial trade and cooperation between East and West. It can also be argued that if COCOM might indeed have had a negative impact on the technological level of the industrial sector in socialist countries, it has neither undermined their military power nor altered the world military balance.

---

[4] A. Rudka, *Systems wielostronnej kontroli eksportu COCOM* (Warszawa: Polskie Towarzystwo Ekonoczne, 1988).

21.8 Conclusions

First, East-West economic relations have fluctuated according to political cycles, reflecting the interaction between the conflicting objectives of political confrontation and economic cooperation.

Second, generally speaking, socialist countries are to a larger extent subject to more discriminatory measures on the part of the West than other groups of countries. The reasons for less favourable treatment are more politically oriented in case of the United States and Japan than in case of West European countries.

Third, tariffs and non-tariff barriers, however, do not at present constitute a major impediment to mutual trade with Western Europe, although in the future the role of protectionist measures is expected to grow, especially in trade with the EC. Financial and credit restrictions and the activity of COCOM are more important than tariffs and NTBs.

Finally, Western governments can do a number of things to improve and enhance East-West economic relations without having to yield on strategic and political principles. In the immediate future they can lift credit sanctions, restoring regular guarantees for exports credits to the East and creating a more favourable climate for capital investments in selected socialist countries and selected sectors. They should also start the process of reducing strategic exports controls. Western goverments can significantly contribute to solving the problem of foreign debt in socialist countries by taking a more constructive and cooperative stand in the Paris Club and encouraging market-oriented reforms and institutional changes. The growing exchange of information and ideas should be accompanied by the removal of obstacles to travel between East and West in order to give more support to the deep democratic transformation of East European countries. While attempting to materialize the concept of the single market, Western governments should not miss the emerging chance for creating a "common house" in Europe.

COMMENTS ON PART IV

Karel Dyba[1]

The first point that needs to be made is that East-West economic relations have never been free from political and national security considerations. And these have frequently prevailed over economic considerations. This was especially so in the late 1940s and early 1950s when East-West trade was abruptly reduced to insignificant levels because of the Cold War. From the mid-1950s until the late 1970s, however, East-West trade expanded quite rapidly (albeit with some political vagaries). This expansion was, of course, from a very low base and was far less impressive than the general expansion in intra-West trade. Because of this relatively low volume, Western governments have had little interest in East-West trade and economic cooperation.

Despite the presence of political factors, it is nevertheless fair to say that, over time, the underlying economic factors have conditioned East-West economic relations. It can be seen, for example, that West European governments have become more and more reluctant to use export licensing, trade embargoes, asset freezing, credit denials, and the like as economic weapons. This has, of course, caused occasional friction between the United States and its European allies; especially at times when U.S.-Soviet relations have been bad.

The different attitudes to East-West trade and economic relations between the United States and the West Europeans are clearly related to differences in economic interests as well as to broader historical, cultural, and even political differences. This comes out clearly in the chapters by Gehart on Austria and Jahnke on the FRG. The Austrian and FRG governments have long stuck to the *Wandel durch Handel* principle, believing that security goals are better served by maintaining and increasing trade and economic ties with Eastern Europe. This principle seems to be supported by the available analytical evidence in the relevant literature; for example, by Adler-Karlsson who examines the grave consequences of the Cold War for East-West economic relations and, more recently, by Holzman who criticizes U.S. East-West trade

---

[1]   Institute for Forecasting, Czechoslovak Academy of Sciences, Prague, Czechoslovakia.

policy and elaborates some more constructive alternative policies.[2] In his analysis of COCOM restrictions, Schiavone provides an even more critical view on the use of economic weapons to achieve security goals.[3] These authors show that economic sanctions are costly to implement and are rarely effective in achieving their security goals. They also suggest alternative East-West economic policies which ask for mutual concessions and shared benefits. (This is the view taken by Rosati in this volume which I tend to support.)

In addition to the economic weaponry related to political and security goals there are more "normal" obstacles to East-West economic cooperation. Rosati, for example, surveys the Western tariff and non-tariff barriers to East-West trade. Although a case can be made for their removal, the issue of effective reciprocity by the Eastern partners has also to be dealt with.

There can be no doubt that the structural problems inherent in trading with unreformed non-market economies constitute a major trade barrier. Structural deficiencies also make these economies uncompetitive, especially in manufactured goods. This point is made in the chapters by Gehart, Jahnke, Schneider, and Nomura. Western countries can help remove this general barrier by offering certain concessions to reforming East European countries.

The East's inability to compete in the West can only be turned around by deep systemic reforms in Eastern Europe's economies which will hopefully make them market-based and market-responsive and, in fact, functionally compatible with any market economies in general. However, Western governments can have a positive impact on the progress of economic reform in Eastern Europe. For example, the removal of Western trade barriers should not wait until the process of reform is complete, and rather it should be a constructive part of this process. Such action by Western governments would help to overcome post-war economic and political divisions and contribute to a sustainable and healthy stability in Europe.

Generally, Western governments (and the EC) have pursued a kind of selective approach in their East-West economic relations, and we should not expect this to change much in the near future. Differences in the economic,

---

[2] G. Adler-Karlsson, *Western Economic Warfare, 1947-1967* (Stockholm: Almquist-Wicksell, 1968); F. D. Holzman, *Foreign Trade Under Central Planning* (Cambridge, MA: Harvard University Press, 1974).

[3] G. Schiavone, "Export Controls: The General Framework" (paper presented at a colloquim on The Political and Legal Framework of Trade Relations between the European Community and Eastern Europe, University of Ghent, Belgium, December 17-18, 1987).

social, and political situations among East European countries should not be underestimated, and Western governments will no doubt tailor their East-West trade policies according to the kinds of responses and concessions they are offered by individual East European governments. This selectivity is evident in Schneider's description of the different agreements reached between the EC, on the one hand, and Czechoslovakia and Hungary, on the other. These agreements differ depending on the mandate, skill, arguments, etc. of the negotiators of the respective East European countries which are, in turn, related to broader differences in the economic, social, and political situations in those countries.

Finally, speaking about selective approaches applied by Western governments towards East-West trade, and referring to Nomura's chapter, I would very much hope to see more Japanese economic presence in the small economies of Eastern Europe. Such a presence would certainly be appropriate given the global importance of the Japanese economy and the responsibility in global affairs which goes with it.

John R. McIntyre[4]

The chapters which address the role of Western European and Japanese governments in East-West economic relations have a number of commonalities from which can be derived one common overarching question: what are the long-term conditions or preconditions which will facilitate or hinder an extension of economic relations in the medium and long term between Western Europe and Japan and the East?

First, trade ought to be based on commercial terms and the benefits should not be one-sided but rather balanced. It is not a matter of economic symmetry in trade flows but rather the broad principles of "free and fair trade" as embodied in the GATT regime and the economic concept of comparative cost advantage that is at issue here. Jahnke's chapter in particular stresses this point in explicit and implicit terms. The question is then one of identifying with some precision - both in macroeconomic terms and in marketing terms - what are the comparative advantages of the Eastern economies in the global economy. A corollary to this question is what internal economic strategy is best suited to produce comparative advantages for the Eastern economies and what the role of government ought to be in the implementation of such a

[4] Associate Professor of International Business, Georgia Institute of Technology, Atlanta, Georgia, U.S.A.

development strategy once it is selected. The age-old debate of import substitution versus export-led growth comes to mind and it takes on a particularly complex colouration in the context of reforming heretofore centrally planned economies where international trade was viewed as a balancing act rather than one of responding to external market needs.

Second, all the authors agree that the intensification of economic relations with the West is predicated on the ongoing process of modernization and reform in the East European economies themselves. It is this process of internal reform and its interfacing with international competitiveness that is problematic. The pace of reform, the type of economic priorities to focus on, the speed of implementation, etc., all raise unanswered questions regarding international competitiveness and integration in the world economy, generally, and with the economies of Western Europe and Japan, more specifically. Some authors have expressed doubts which I share as to how far and how serious internal Soviet economic reforms are meant to be, as made evident by the postponement of general market pricing reforms to the late 1990s.

A related point is that an intensification of trade and economic relations with the West can in no way be considered a panacea for failing internal reforms. Though the two are clearly connected, one cannot be a substitute for the other.

Third, the ability of Eastern economies to integrate currencies and their exchange value in the global monetary and currency system is a *sine qua non* to sucessful, viable, lasting East-West interactions based on the principles of free and fair trade, as generally understood. This is clearly one of the most salient obstacles to the intensification of economic relations. The convertibility of Eastern currencies can be viewed as the tangible proof of the success of internal economic reforms and the eventual hallmark of successful global competition. None of the authors offered tangible suggestions on a Western governmental approach which could assist the Eastern economies in moving along this path. The recent Mitterand proposal to create a European bank to assist Eastern economies does begin, in embryo form, to address this very central concern.

Fourth, a point particularly well made by Gehart and Jahnke and implicit in the others, is that insufficient diversification in the structure of Eastern exports will be a serious impediment to the development of mutually beneficial trade. The current trade situation is characterized by a serious asymmetry in the composition of trade flows between East and West and vice versa. Corrective measures need to be envisaged. A strategy of trade development by Eastern

313

economies is needed. The example of the newly industrializing countries of Asia comes to mind as a possible heuristic model.

Fifth, with the exception of the Schneider and Haus pieces, the historical context of the "failures of the past" are not fully taken into account. Schneider provides a very useful explanation of the changes in Eastern and Soviet attitudes towards the European Community, moving from hostility at first to limited contacts and eventually to normalization. The history of trade relations provides an essential framework and, very possibly, some real constraints to the intensification of trade relations between East and West and to experimenting with particular types of strategies.

Sixth, the linkage to fundamental political and geostrategic realities must be placed in sharper focus. The Japanese approach to trade with the Eastern and Soviet economies has been essentially predicated on Japan's fundamental alignment with the United States on matters of East-West relations when compared and contrasted with the policies of West Germany and Austria, for example. The chapters all implicitly acknowledge strategic constraints but fail to recognize that trade is often viewed as a tool in East-West relations. Haus does, however, acknowledge the fundamental lessons of the negotiations between Eastern European countries and Western economies, in the context of the GATT, and provides much support for the pessimistic outlook of a "realist" (realpolitik) analysis of East-West trade. Her conclusions support Henry Nau's telling point that GATT membership for the Soviet Union is a possibility but that it is too premature, given the obstacles and preconditions that should be surmounted first.

The chapters failed to consider the influence of U.S. East-West policy as a critical determinant of West European and Japanese policies and their willingness to assume credit, commercial, and joint venture risks. While U.S. policy as a central determinant was eclipsed by the events of the closing days of 1989, the structure of international relations will soon recapture center stage in determining outcomes and the euphoria may prove short lived.

Finally, the impact of Europe 1992 was insufficiently analyzed. Not only is it essential to understand the interaction between the momentum of the Single Market Act and economic and political reforms in the East, but the reverse causation needs to be further analyzed. Additionally, the Single Market Act does portend major changes in Western strategic trade controls and export licensing policies. These were insufficiently explored. Ultimately, Europe 1992 as a process may well have been the coda to the Yalta regime of the post-war period, signalling the beginning of a new order, both political and economic.

PART V - PROSPECTS

Chapter 22

GLOBAL ADJUSTMENT PROBLEMS OF THE 1990s: THE EFFECTS ON EAST-WEST TRADE POLICIES

Allen J. Lenz[1]

A series of very large trade deficits have rapidly transformed the United States from the world's largest creditor nation to the world's largest debtor. While these large deficits and the complementary surpluses of some trading partners may continue for some time, global imbalances of recent magnitudes are unsustainable distortions in global capital flows and trading patterns. Both political and economic forces will dictate a narrowing of these imbalances. But doing so while maintaining good global economic growth rates will be a slow and difficult process, with many opportunities for things to go awry along the way. Intense competition for world markets for manufactured goods will risk rising protectionism that could lead to severe global and national economic disruptions.

The first part of this chapter briefly describes the evolution of U.S. deficits and the dominance of manufactured goods trade in the growth of the deficits and in the adjustments to come. The second part examines the potential impact of the coming adjustment process on global trading patterns and notes some problems that may arise. In conclusion, the chapter speculates on how the difficult global adjustment process could affect East-West trade.

---

[1] Director for Trade and Economics, Chemical Manufacturers Association, Washington, D.C., U.S.A.

22.1 Generating unsustainable imbalances

U.S. trade performance

The United States in recent years has recorded very large current account deficits, reflecting large net capital inflows from abroad. Until 1983, the U.S. current account fluctuated in a normal range of relatively small surpluses and deficits. Deficits then began to grow rapidly (*Figure 22.1*). The current account deficit was $ 107 billion in 1984; $ 141 billion in 1986, and $ 154 billion in 1987.

The 1987 current account deficit, equivalent to foreign borrowing of about $ 640 for every person in the United States, may represent a low point in U.S. performance. The 1988 deficit improved modestly to around $ 135 billion, about $ 540 per person.

The recent large current account deficits also represent borrowing from abroad in amounts that are quite large relative to the size of the U.S. economy. The last current account surplus in 1981 was equivalent to only 0.2 per cent of gross national product (GNP) (*Figure 22.2*). Deficits then grew rapidly to the 3 per cent range, peaking at 3.4 per cent of GNP in 1987, with the current account deficit in 1988 shrinking to about 2.8 or 2.9 per cent of GNP.

In essence, this means that from 1984 through 1988 the United States consumed 2.8-3.4 per cent per year more goods and services than it actually produced, with net imports and net borrowing from abroad making up the difference.

As a result of international borrowing, the United States international investor position (IIP) has dramatically changed from that of the world's largest creditor nation to the world's largest debtor nation. (*Figure 22.3*).

The rapid deterioration in the current account balance moved the United States from a creditor position of $ 141 billion in 1981 to a debtor position of $ 368 billion at the end of 1987; about $ 500 billion at end-1988.

It took seventy years to build to the 1981 peak U.S. creditor position, but only seven years to move to the large 1988 debtor position, a swing of about $ 640 billion. In an orderly adjustment of U.S. deficits and complementary trading partner surpluses, however, U.S. current account deficits would narrow only gradually in the 1990s and continued growth of the U.S. international debtor position over the next several years should be expected.

The current U.S. debtor position does not, in itself, pose large, immediate risks. The end-1988 debtor position was quite small relative to GNP, about 10.2 per cent of GNP. Future trends in capital and trade flows are uncertain. Analysts believe, however, that by the end of 1990 the U.S. debtor position could be in the $ 700-$ 800 billion range and that it could reach $ 1 trillion in the early 1990s, an amount perhaps equivalent to 15-20 per cent of GNP. This compares with, for example, a Brazilian ratio of external bank debt to GNP of about 40 per cent of GNP and a Mexican position of about 80 per cent. Other factors, including the fact that the United States has the unique advantage of borrowing in its own currency, also mitigate the problems of its debtor status. However, the rapid change in the U.S. IIP and the long-term implications of continued large current account deficits and continued debt build-up relative to GNP are matters for serious concern and the continuing debt build-up may become an important political issue in the United States.

A dissection of the U.S. current account

The U.S. current account deficits must ultimately narrow because no nation, not even the United States, borrowing in its own currency can indefinitely borrow in amounts that are large relative to its GNP. Indeed, the process of narrowing U.S. current account deficits apparently began in 1988.

The U.S. current account has five major components: merchandise trade, business services, international investment income, other goods and services, and unilateral transfers. The 1981-1987 deterioration of U.S. current account balances was dominated by worsening merchandise trade performance. Of the $ 161 billion slippage from a 1981 surplus to a 1987 deficit of $ 154 billion (BOP basis), $ 132 billion was in merchandise trade and the bulk of the remainder stemmed from debt servicing changes generated by the merchandise trade deficits and accruing debt. Nevertheless, because the United States is rapidly becoming a more service-oriented economy, it is sometimes contended that the large U.S. merchandise trade deficits can be offset by increasing surpluses in business services trade.

However, an examination of the data reveals that business services trade is neither a large component of the current account nor one in which the United States is likely to achieve major gains. Rather, improved U.S. current account performance must come from the merchandise trade sector. Indeed, careful examination shows that deficits have occurred primarily in manufactures trade and improvements will also have to come from that account.[2]

---

[2] For a more detailed disaggregation of recent U.S. manufactures trade performance, see U.S. Department of Commerce, *U.S. Trade Performance in 1987* (Washington, D.C.: U.S. Department of Commerce, International Trade Administration, June, 1988).

U.S. merchandise trade has been in deficit since 1976. Deficits remained relatively modest through 1982, but rapid enlargement began in 1983 (*Figure 22.4*). The merchandise trade deficit reached $ 122 billion in 1984, $ 134 billion in 1985, $ 156 billion in 1986, and peaked at $ 170 billion in 1987 (c.i.f. basis). The 1988 deficit narrowed by $ 33 billion, to $ 137 billion.

Explosive deficit growth in the 1983-1987 period was mostly the result of very strong import growth, concurrent with export declines in 1982 and 1983 and subsequent slow export growth through 1987. Total merchandise imports increased rapidly and by 1987 were 55 per cent above the 1981 level, with a further increase of over 8 per cent in 1988 to about $ 460 billion.

Total merchandise exports in 1987 finally pushed 5.9 per cent above the 1981 level. 1988 exports increased almost 27 per cent above 1987 levels, to reach a new high of $ 322 billion. However, despite the slowing of import growth and the strong export increase, 1988 imports remained just over 1.4 times the level of exports.

A broad categorization of merchandise trade into four principal product groups shows the dominant role of manufactures. Manufactured goods accounted for four-fifths of 1988 U.S. merchandise trade; 79 per cent of exports, 81.5 per cent of imports: only slightly different from the 1987 composition shown in *Figure 22.5*.

The other three main components were much smaller. Mineral fuels (mostly oil) accounted for 10 per cent of imports. Fuels, including coal, were less than 3 per cent of exports. Agricultural products were 12 per cent of 1988 exports, 5 per cent of imports. "Other" is a group of miscellaneous items, including paper pulp, wood, hides and skins. It was only 6 per cent of 1988 exports, 4 per cent of imports.

Manufactures trade not only dwarfs the other components but the massive deterioration in the manufactures balance far outweighs other changes. U.S. manufactures trade fell into deficit in 1982 (*Figure 22.6*). The deficits expanded rapidly thereafter, through 1987, reflecting lagging exports and an explosion of imports. Exports peaked in 1981, than declined in 1982 and again in 1983 before beginning a gradual recovery in 1984.

Manufactures imports, however, increased every year with particularly dramatic gains beginning in 1984. By 1987 manufactures exports were 16 per cent above the 1981 level but imports were 116 per cent higher.

In 1987 manufactures exports were $ 200 billion, but imports, at $ 338 billion, were 1.7 times as large. By 1988 manufactures exports had to grow 1.7 times as fast as imports simply to keep the manufactures deficit from expanding further.

In 1988 manufactures exports grew 27.6 per cent to $ 255 billion; imports only 10.9 per cent to $ 374.4 billion. But manufactures imports remained 47 per cent greater than exports and the manufactures trade balance improved only $ 19 billion to a $ 119 billion deficit.

Manufactures trade has dominated merchandise trade and current account performance. The 1987 deficit of $ 138 billion far outweighed the $ 39 billion mineral fuels deficit (*Figure 22.7*). The modest $ 6.5 billion agricultural trade surplus was relatively insignificant. The manufactures trade deficit was equivalent to 70 percent of the total $ 171 billion deficit. Balances improved only modestly in 1988.

Perhaps most revealing, however, are the changes in balances of individual merchandise trade components over the 1981-1987 period of massive deterioration. U.S. merchandise trade performance may have hit bottom in 1987. Although agricultural trade improved in 1987, yielding a surplus of $ 6.5 billion (*Figure 22.8*), the surplus was $ 18.5 billion less than in 1981. Agricultural trade provided the United States significant surpluses in earlier years. The peak surplus was $ 25 billion in 1981 but surpluses shrank through 1986, before beginning a modest recovery.

The mineral fuels deficit, on the other hand, worsened in 1987 but was still dramatically improved over earlier years. The deficit narrowed from $ 74 billion in 1981 to $ 39 billion in 1987, a $ 35 billion improvement. As a result of declining oil import prices, the 1988 mineral fuels deficit further modestly improved to $ 36 billion.

Other goods trade, a small account, was essentially unchanged in 1987 from its 1981 balance. From 1981 to 1987 exports ranged from $ 11 billion to $ 15 billion and imports from $ 11 billion to $ 17 billion. Balances ranged from a deficit of $ 7 billion to a surplus of $ 900 million. A surplus of $ 1 billion occurred in 1988.

In the six years 1981-1987 the manufactures trade balance worsened by $ 153 billion, significantly more than the $ 136 billion slippage in the whole of the merchandise trade account. The account then improved by $ 19 billion in 1988.

Looking ahead to what can be expected in the next few years, "other" goods will likely continue to be a minor factor in U.S. trade balances. The mineral fuels (oil) account is less predictable. Other things equal, each $ 1 per barrel decline in the oil price saves the United States about $ 2 billion in its oil import bill. But further major improvements in the mineral fuels account seem unlikely. While oil prices were down in 1988, import volumes were up. The result was modest contraction of the oil deficit to about $ 37 billion. Looking to the longer term, however, oil import volumes will likely continue to increase and, although oil prices will likely fluctuate and could decline in the medium term, they may increase in the longer term. There is, therefore, a good chance that the oil import bill may begin to grow significantly again. Indeed, even if oil import prices remain at 1988 levels, the oil deficit will increase as oil import volumes continue to increase.

Although there was a significant $ 8 billion gain in the agricultural balance in 1988, the prospects for a sustained return to the still larger agricultural surpluses of some earlier years are dim. Despite favorable short-term supply-demand changes, the fact remains that because global food supplies are expanding more rapidly than demand, global food surpluses will likely continue, keeping prices low, competition for markets tough, and agricultural surpluses near current levels.

Manufactures trade dominance

As noted above, the deterioration of manufactures trade was the dominant factor in the growth of large U.S. merchandise trade and current account deficits. It must be similarly dominant in any major improvements to come. There is no other likely source of major gains in U.S. trade.

The dominance of manufactures in U.S. trade is not unique. World trade has become very much an exchange of manufactured goods and the manufactures portion has been rising. In 1970, about 70 per cent of world non-energy exports was manufactures. By 1980 the portion had risen to 79 per cent and in 1984 it was 83 per cent. Trade among developed countries is even more heavily concentrated in manufactures. In 1984, over 83 per cent of industrial country non-energy exports and 79.5 per cent of non-energy imports were manufactures.[3] The manufactures portion of non-energy trade is likely to continue to expand as global demand for manufactures continues to increase more rapidly than demand for food and raw materials.

---

[3] U.S. Department of Commerce, *U.S. Trade Performance in 1985 and Outlook* (Washington, D.C.: U.S. Department of Commerce, International Trade Administration, October, 1986), p. 13.

The U.S. role in world manufactures trade is large and changes in U.S. manufactures trade volumes and balances can impact strongly on world trading patterns. In 1986, the United States held a 12.2 per cent share of world exports of manufactured goods to all world destinations including the United States. U.S. manufactures imports, however, were about one-fourth of non-U.S. manufactures exports to the world. The U.S. manufactures deficit alone equalled about 10 per cent of manufactures exports by other countries.

Given the magnitude of U.S. trade, sizeable expansions in U.S. exports and/or shrinkages in the U.S. manufactures imports could bring major disruptions in world trade patterns and create particularly significant problems for countries dependent on exports to the United States.

The future of U.S. manufacturing

The very large U.S. manufacturing deficits of recent years have raised concerns in the United States about the survival of its manufacturing industries. The U.S. manufacturing base has been seen by some as withering away and there have been calls for an "industrial policy" that would preserve U.S. manufacturing. A 1985 *Business Week* cover story raised the possibility that the United States might become "a nation of hollow corporations"; one essentially devoid of manufacturing operations, with corporations performing design, marketing and research functions, but with most manufacturing performed abroad.[4] Among many other problems, such a demise of manufacturing would raise serious national security concerns. But a demise of manufacturing would also generate huge trade deficits that could not be overcome by export income from other sources.

As noted earlier, no nation can borrow indefinitely at rates that rapidly raise its debt relative to its GNP. Thus, because of the dominant role of manufactures in U.S. trade, the United States cannot continue to run very large manufactures trade deficits for very long. There is no source of large export surpluses in other accounts to offset large manufactures deficits. The fact is that the United States cannot run large manufactures deficits and pay its way

---

[4] "The Hollow Corporation", *Business Week*, March 3, 1986, p. 57.

in the world economy. Indeed, over the longer term, the United States must run manufactures trade surpluses to balance its external accounts.[5]

In effect, the workings of the international economic system ensure that the United States will not become "a nation of hollow corporations" and that it will retain a large manufacturing base, ultimately returning to a situation where U.S. manufacturing output is roughly equal to or greater than total U.S. consumption of manufactures. Changes in exchange rates, economic growth rates, inflation rates and other international economic forces will act to preclude huge continuing U.S. current account deficits and, hence to ensure maintenance of a large U.S. manufacturing base.

Most other industrial nations are in a generally similar position. Over the longer term most will have to maintain rough balance in their manufactured goods trade. Few will be able to maintain either huge continuing deficits or surpluses far beyond what is required to pay for imports of primary products and other goods and services.

It can, therefore, be unequivocally stated that the United States will not deindustrialise and that it will not become a nation of hollow corporations. In fact, to balance its external accounts, the United States will have to run substantial manufactures trade surpluses. This fact has significant implications for global trading patterns; particularly, it implies a difficult global adjustment over the next several years.

Size of the required turnaround

The impact of narrowing U.S. trade and current account deficits on global trade patterns may be underrated because the size of the changes required relative to global world manufactures trade markets is not generally recognized. To restore balance to the U.S. current account, manufactures trade performance must improve more than the $ 153 billion decline in performance experienced over the 1981-1987 period. Indeed, to return to balance by 1992, even if oil import deficits do not enlarge, manufactures trade performance would have to improve by about $ 200 billion over 1987 levels, moving from a 1987 deficit of $ 138 billion to a 1992 surplus of about $ 60 billion

---

[5] For an examination of the problems the United States will encounter in expanding its manufactures exports, see Allen Lenz, "Slimming the U.S. Trade and Current Account Deficits", *AMEX Bank Review Special Papers*, no. 16 (London: American Express Bank, October, 1988).

(*Figure 22.9*). The manufactures trade surplus would be required to meet payments on the enlarging U.S. international debt.

Achieving this improvement would require manufactures exports to increase at rates about 15 per cent greater than imports for the five consecutive years 1988 through 1992. Manufactures trade exports actually did grow at about 16 per cent faster than imports in 1988, yielding an improvement of $ 19 billion. Repeating this performance for four additional consecutive years, however, will be very difficult. Indeed, if U.S. imports remained constant and world exports of manufactured goods to non-U.S. destinations grew over the 1988-1992 period at the same rate as they grew over the 1981-1986 period, achieving a $ 200 billion dollar improvement would require capturing about four-fifths of the $ 250 billion growth that would occur. If U.S. imports continued to increase (as they did in 1988), a still larger portion of total growth would have to be captured to yield a $ 200 billion improvement in the U.S. manufactures trade balance.

Moreover, if world exports of manufactures to non-U.S. destinations increased at the 1981-1986 rate, the required increase of U.S. manufactures exports would raise its share of world exports to non-U.S. destinations to almost 29 per cent, nearly twice the 1986 level of 15.5 per cent and much larger than the Japanese 11.7 per cent and German 17.9 per cent 1986 shares. Clearly, such an increase would be extremely difficult to accomplish in a world where manufacturing competition is intensifying as production capabilities are expanding rapidly around the globe. Foreign competitors are unlikely to readily cede large chunks of hard-won market share either in foreign countries or in the United States, probably heralding a period of competition for international markets more intense than ever before experienced.

22.2 Narrowing global imbalances: central problem of the 1990s

The huge U.S. trade deficits have produced complementary large surpluses for some trading partners and temporarily distorted global trading patterns. Narrowing these unsustainable imbalances will likely be a central problem of the world economy and a process stretching well i the 1990s.

Unsustainable U.S. borrowing

The very large U.S. current account deficits of recent years and the external borrowing they represent cannot and will not continue indefinitely. When the net inflow of investment into the United States begins to shrink, trade flows

323

must also alter, narrowing the U.S. trade and current account deficits. Two generalized scenarios summarize different ways in which the U.S. narrowing may occur. First, the U.S. government budget deficits decrease over the next few years, perhaps accompanied by increases in U.S. saving. This gradually reduces U.S. capital import needs and eventually returns the United States to a net capital exporter position. Alternatively, the excess of U.S. investment spending and the government deficit over U.S. saving continues to generate capital inflow needs. But in a changing international environment, international investors begin to perceive U.S. investment opportunities as relatively less attractive than other foreign alternatives. Inter alia, this raises the price of U.S. borrowing and ultimately shrinks it, perhaps rapidly.

The first scenario would allow a "soft landing"; a reduction of global trade imbalances with minimal global economic disruption. Progressively shrinking U.S. deficits would force difficult adjustments in the manufacturing industries of trading partners but the adjustments would be relatively gradual and more manageable. Surplus countries would have to take steps to stimulate domestic consumption to create demand that would replace export demand as surpluses diminish. Exporting industries would have to reorient to that new demand probably for different products.

Getting imbalances down to sustainable levels by this kind of process would probably require five or more years. But even this scenario is not without hazards. As the trade deficit slowly declines, U.S. manufacturing would gradually increase its share of U.S. and foreign markets and progress on reducing the deficits would be evident. Nevertheless, with deficits declining only slowly, the U.S. external debt would continue to enlarge and any softening in the U.S. economy could bring renewed pressures in the United States for protectionist measures.

The second scenario risks a hard, much more dangerous and disruptive landing for the United States and the global economy. Large U.S. borrowing - and current account deficits - continue until foreign investors change their preferences. Should those preferences change abruptly, a rapid, forced closure of U.S. borrowing abroad and the current account deficits could have many serious global repercussions. U.S. interest and inflation rates could rise rapidly, and a sharp U.S. recession could quickly cut U.S. imports. Suddenly deprived of their key U.S. export market, some countries that have not reoriented more to domestic demand and remain dependent on large manufactures trade surpluses for employment and economic growth would likely experience major economic problems and, perhaps, domestic political unrest. A serious global recession and high interest rates could threaten the abilities of less developed countries to continue servicing their debts. In turn, this could pose major problems for some industrialized country lender banks.

Narrowing imbalances: a mutual problem

Narrowing the unsustainably large global current account imbalances of recent years while maintaining good world economic growth rates and not aggravating Third World debt problems promises to be difficult. Indeed, it will likely be the central problem of the world economy in the 1990s. The difficult transition to be made is probably underrated because the magnitude of the changes that will be forced on some economies is not widely appreciated.

There are five major imbalance countries. Large U.S. current account deficits are complemented by surpluses in Japan, the Federal Republic of Germany, Taiwan, and South Korea. Narrowing these global imbalances is not just a U.S. problem. It is a problem as well for U.S. trading partners, particularly those countries with large current account surpluses. Indeed, because of their greater dependence on international trade, some surplus countries probably have even more at stake than does the United States.

When U.S. trade deficits were widening, it was U.S. manufacturing industries that were often forced into cutbacks. In the period ahead, however, it will often be industries in other countries which will bear the brunt of unpleasant adjustments. This may provide a motivation for surplus countries to delay the inevitable and to characterize the imbalances as a U.S. problem; one the U.S. must solve by modifying its behaviour by trimming its budget deficits, improving the quality of its output, and becoming more cost-competitive, for example.

The United States certainly needs to take these kinds of corrective actions but they cannot spare the surplus countries the difficult adjustments involved in shrinking their surpluses. Unsustainable global imbalances do not stem just from U.S. behaviour. Rather, surplus country behaviour contributed to the imbalances and is a complementary problem. Surplus country saving rates have been too high; consumption and investment have lagged. An orderly narrowing of global imbalances will require surplus countries to reduce their saving and expand their consumption; the opposite of the prescription the United States must follow. The surplus countries may criticize the United States for its failure to move promptly to reduce its budget and trade deficits but in private they must surely welcome the slow U.S. progress and, for the most part, they are moving no more rapidly to make their own adjustments.

The surplus countries are aware of the significant impact the required narrowing of U.S. trade deficits will have on their economies and the difficulty of their positions. Just as the U.S. delays the difficult budget decisions involved in getting total U.S. consumption down to match total U.S. production, it is quite natural that the surplus countries should want to delay the painful adjustments they will have to make.

While there is motivation for all parties to delay difficult steps, the long-term interests of the United States and its trading partners lie in shrinking the imbalances in an orderly and gradual but prompt process that would stretch over the next several years. The United States must reduce its dependence on imported capital, while the surplus countries must shrink their manufactures export surpluses. Other things equal, this will have a depressing affect on their employment and economic growth.

Complementarity of U.S. deficits and trading partner surpluses

When U.S. current account performance deteriorated over the 1981-1987 period, offsetting improvements necessarily occurred in the accounts of other countries. Similarly, when U.S. current account balances improve, there must be complementary, offsetting declines in the balances of others.

There are five major current account imbalance countries in recent international trade performance: one very large deficit country, the United States; and the four large surplus countries being Japan, Germany, Taiwan, and South Korea. The whole of the global economy has been impacted by the huge swings in capital and trade flows since 1981, but these five countries have probably been most directly affected.

From 1981 to 1987, the U.S. current account balance declined by $ 161 billion (*Figure 22.10*). During the same period the current accounts of the four surplus countries improved by $ 163 billion. Over the years of increasing deficits, the United States was a "locomotive" for economic growth abroad. But shrinking U.S. deficits will in years ahead mean a "drag" on the economies of trading partners whose surpluses must then decline to accommodate improving U.S. balances.

By 1987 global imbalances had grown very large. The 1987 U.S. deficit of $ 154 billion was complemented by surpluses of Japan, Germany, Taiwan and South Korea totalling $ 160 billion (*Figure 22.11*).

Current account imbalances relative to GNP had also become large. The 1987 U.S. deficit was 3.4 per cent of GNP (*Figure 22.12*); Japan's surplus, 3.6 per cent of GNP; Germany's, 4.0 per cent. Taiwan's surplus was equivalent to a huge 19 per cent of GNP, indicating that country's total consumption was only slightly more than four-fifths of its production with the balance in net exports. The effect was net lending abroad equivalent to about one-fifth of Taiwan's GNP. South Korea's current account surplus was also very large relative to GNP (9.0 per cent), reflecting very high export growth. However, the 1987 surplus was only South Korea's second significant current account surplus. Deficits over a number of prior years have accumulated a very large Korean external debt that is being rapidly reduced by the recent surpluses.

The current account balances cited above are "global" balances of the respective countries; that is, their balances with the world. Reducing U.S. imbalances, of course, must be viewed in a global perspective in which U.S. bilateral trade and current account balances are only one part of the picture. While reducing the U.S. global deficit will inevitably involve a narrowing of its deficits with Japan, the FRG, Taiwan, and South Korea, the thrust of U.S. deficit reduction efforts should not be on its bilateral imbalances, but on adjustments that will narrow the global imbalances of the United States and the surplus countries. For example, while the United States runs large merchandise trade deficits with Canada, the Canadians had a substantial current account deficit in 1987 on their trade with the world. Thus, U.S. and global imbalance problems would not likely be resolved by efforts to eliminate the U.S. trade deficit with Canada. Rather, a country's global imbalances - not its bilateral imbalances - are the measure of its need to adjust in an integrated world economy.

The coming adjustment process will alter world trading patterns in many ways. Nevertheless, it will likely affect the five major imbalance countries more than others. In an orderly reduction of U.S. deficits, the surpluses and foreign lending of Japan, Germany, Taiwan, and South Korea must shrink substantially. If the U.S. deficit is to shrink, there is no apparent alternative to a major reduction of their surpluses and their foreign lending. Their surpluses and lending must decline as U.S. deficits narrow because there is no other country or group of countries sufficiently creditworthy to borrow enough to allow them to continue the large surpluses that have been absorbed and made possible by U.S. deficits.

Throughout much of the 1980s, growth of the U.S. trade deficits caused significant substitution of foreign manufacturing production for U.S. manufacturing production. The result was widespread restructuring of U.S. industry; a painful process. Now, however, the coming adjustment process promises an expansion of U.S. manufacturing that may impose painful cutbacks on the manufacturing industries of some trading partners. To avoid or postpone the pain of restructuring, each surplus country will struggle to retain its surpluses. But the major portion of their surpluses must ultimately disappear if U.S. trade deficits are to narrow significantly.

Changing the underlying fundamentals

"Better coordination of economic policies" is a frequently cited cure for narrowing the existing global imbalances. Most often this is interpreted as a call for faster growth abroad. Faster growth abroad is desirable but is unlikely to be the major factor in narrowing imbalances. What is required are more difficult to achieve, and perhaps more wrenching changes in fundamentals; changes in saving and consumption rates relative to total production in the imbalance countries. Put in simple microeconomic terms, to narrow the existing imbalances, the United States must consume less and save more, *relative to* its total production. The surplus countries must do the opposite; consume more and save less, *relative to* their total production. These changes, concurrent with good global economic growth rates, could provide the optimum adjustment scenario.

Translated into effects on trade, the United States must either export more, import less, or some combination of these two changes. Conversely, the surplus countries must import more, export less, or some combination of the two. The optimum combination would be one in which the imbalances are narrowed predominantly by increased U.S. exports and increased imports by the surplus countries.

How a smooth transition could occur

In theory, the required transition could be accomplished in a situation of continuing global economic growth, without traumatic adjustment-related disruptions to existing industries. In theory, the imbalances could be eliminated without cuts in U.S. imports that would hit exporting industries in partner countries. U.S. imports could stabilize in volume terms or even continue to grow modestly, albeit slower than the U.S. economy, with exports growing much more rapidly than the economy and providing a major stimulus to U.S. production. At the same time, surplus country exports could stabilize, or even

328

continue to grow modestly but at slower rates than their economies. Increased domestic demand in the surplus economies would maintain domestic production and power a rapid growth of their imports (*Figure 22.13*). In this scenario current account imbalances would narrow, as would the wide differences in saving and consumption patterns between the United States and the surplus countries.

In essence, this scenario requires the surplus countries to switch from export-led growth to domestic demand-led growth; that is, they must consume and invest domestically a higher portion of total production that is itself enlarging primarily to satisfy growing domestic demand. Moreover, an increasing portion of their total consumption and investment goods must be satisfied by imports.

In the United States, the deficit country, total consumption would gradually decline relative to an increasing production. Exports would grow rapidly, becoming a larger portion of expanding production, while a decreasing portion of total consumption and investment would be supplied by imports.

Making this transition would be a delicate process but in time the existing imbalances would be eliminated. U.S. export-oriented industries (presumably the country's most efficient industries) would increase their output and capacity. There would not be undue disruption to surplus countries' export-oriented industries, presumably their most efficient industries, because they would not have to cut their exports. For example, in this scenario, strong import increases by Japan could narrow its surpluses without a further major strengthening of the yen, and without a major decline in exports of automobiles and other manufactures to the United States.

There are, however, at least two fundamental difficulties with this scenario: first, the ability of individual countries to quickly and smoothly change their saving versus consumption ratios; second, the ability of the world economy, particularly the surplus countries, to absorb additional manufacturing output.

U.S. and surplus country adjustment problems

Fundamental changes in the saving and consumption ratios and export and import propensities of the five imbalance countries would impact negatively on many different interest groups within each nation. As a result, such changes are likely to come hard and slowly. For example, continued, or even increased, U.S. economic growth does not necessarily rule out the need for fundamental tax and other changes to alter the saving-investment imbalance. There is no assurance that the United States can "grow" its way out of the situation where total national consumption exceeds total national production.

Instead, there is an ever-present tendency for perceived social and other needs and resulting government spending to stay ahead of increasing government revenues. And there is little reason to expect voluntary changes in personal saving and consumption habits that would bring U.S. rates closer to those of other countries. Without major pressures for change, total U.S. consumption (expenditures by government, consumers, and investors) could well continue to grow rapidly enough to stay ahead of total production.

U.S. personal consumption habits and expectations may be difficult to change. A London banker once characterized the United States as "the most efficient consumption society the world has ever known". She allowed that she used her business trips to New York as occasions to shop because "they make everything so easy for you".

It's true. Nowhere else in the world is there the intense pressure to consume and nowhere else is it made so easy. TV, radio, newspaper and magazine advertising incessantly bombard potential consumers. Most Americans can receive numerous TV channels 24 hours a day, almost all heavily laden with advertising. In Britain there are 4 channels. The two BBC channels carry no advertisements and transmit only 18 hours per day. The two commercial channels normally transmit less than 24 hours per day. A Sunday *Washington Post* - mostly advertisements exhorting every conceivable form of consumption - typically weighs in at around 5 lbs, several times the bulk of a week of the London *Times*. Americans are deluged by dozens of junk mail solicitations, pressing credit cards and offers of loans on them for any purpose from home remodeling to vacations.

Credit cards facilitate shopping and the stores are ever ready to help deliver customers of their money. Shopping malls in the United States are open 7 days a week, often 12 hours a day Monday through Saturday and 6 or more hours on Sunday. In the FRG, and much of Europe, stores close at noon on Saturday and do not reopen until Monday. Japan remains on a five and a half day work week, with an average of only six holidays per year versus 11 in the United States, holding down Japan's leisure expenditures.

In the U.S. bumper stickers boast "born to shop" and the average American spends 5.7 hours a week shopping versus 2.8 hours in housecleaning. In the last 20 years shopping malls have become "efficient temples of consumption". Twenty years ago, "few envisioned how television's siren song would unleash cravings to be satisfied with the flick of a magnetically coded plastic card, or how shopping malls would proliferate in response".[6]

The U.S. social security system is also believed to be an important factor in lifetime consumption patterns. Though it was originally intended to supplement rather than replace personal saving, many have come to think of it as the principal income required for retirement and old age, reducing the perceived need for pre-retirement saving.

In short, the U.S. economy is keyed to developing demand and consumption like no other. So long as the economy remains strong and incentive systems unchanged, current patterns of consumption and saving will probably not change dramatically without some new causal factor. To accomplish even marginal changes in personal saving and consumption habits will likely require significant changes in the motivations to save versus the ever-present urgings to spend.

One might think the task in surplus countries - raising consumption relative to production and thus raising living standards - would be much easier. It might be, but more likely changes that would increase consumption and raise the living standards of surplus countries will be resisted because change is invariably seen by some interest groups as undesirable. For example, an important step in changing Japan to a more consumption-oriented society will require reducing the Japanese work week from the current 5.5 days per week to create more time in which to spend. But industries will resist, fearing the effect on international competitiveness. Increasing Japanese consumption to higher levels will also require changing an archaic distribution system and displacing many merchants who operate small, inefficient stores and do not want to give up their livelihoods. And more spending on housing - a logical expansion of Japan's consumption and living standards - will require freeing up land from agricultural uses and displacing small, inefficient farmers who cling tenaciously to a traditional way of life.

Other factors may also change national saving rates and facilitate the adjustment process. In a prize-winning essay, William Emmott notes that Japan's ratio of saving to disposable income has fallen steadily from 23 per cent in 1975 to a low of 16 per cent in 1985 as Japan's pensions and social security schemes have become more generous, eroding the need to save. Emmott also sees the new post-war generation as less prone to save, implying

---

[6] Ellen Graham, "The Pleasure Dome", *Wall Street Journal*, May 13, 1988.

a further continuing fall in the saving rate. Over the longer term he posits that the aging of Japan's population may significantly further reduce the saving rate. Old people typically spend more than they save and, other things equal, the older a population, the lower will be its saving ratio. This demographic factor, however, would not begin to have significant affect until 1995.[7]

Thus, things may be moving in the right direction but probably not rapidly enough to satisfy U.S. and international investor concerns. It seems unlikely that U.S. policies and investor attitudes will sustain continuing very large U.S. borrowing while awaiting a gradual and uncertain evolution of saving and consumption patterns in Japan and elsewhere that would be based on rising affluence and aging populations. Instead, more certain and faster policy solutions will likely be sought. But fundamental changes in U.S. and foreign lifestyles and saving and consumption patterns will probably require major changes in tax and fiscal and other laws and policies that will be controversial and will take time to achieve.

A global glut of manufactures?

The second and, perhaps, even more important obstacle to a trouble-free adjustment is that the manufacturing sectors of the surplus countries may have grown too large in supplying enlarging U.S. deficits. Now, as U.S. manufacturing expands to satisfy a larger portion of U.S. demand, the effects on world trade and some individual economies will be important. The $ 200 billion improvement in the U.S. manufactures trade balance that would be required to balance the U.S. current account by 1992 is large relative to total world manufactures trade and would cause major alterations in world trade flows. A significant reduction of the manufacturing sectors in some surplus countries may be necessary.

On the other hand, an expansion of capacity in the United States seems necessary. In fact, there has been a significant "hollowing" of U.S. manufacturing; a decline of total U.S. manufactures production relative to U.S. consumption. In 1987, U.S. manufacturing output was equivalent to only about 86 per cent of U.S. manufactures consumption, with net imports making up the difference. Now, however, to bring U.S. accounts back into balance, U.S. manufacturing output will have to rise to more than 100 per cent of con-

---

[7] William Emmot, "The Limits to Japanese Power", AMEX Bank Review Special Papers, no. 16 (London: American Express Bank, October, 1988), p. 15.

sumption, perhaps to 103 per cent in 1992, were balance to be achieved that year (*Figure 22.14*). The result would be a significant addition to world manufacturing capacity and global supplies of manufactured goods.

What countries will absorb the U.S. net manufactures exports required to balance U.S. accounts? Will the surplus countries rapidly increase their imports to allow U.S. deficits to decrease? If not, who will take the net exports of Japan, Germany, Taiwan and South Korea that are now absorbed by the United States? As noted earlier, there is no other country or group of countries sufficiently creditworthy to borrow in amounts that would allow current account deficits equivalent to recent very large U.S. deficits. But without such complementary deficits, the large surpluses must also disappear.

Can the surplus countries themselves adjust in a way that will allow them to maintain manufacturing output at current levels, either importing more to close the surplus, or diverting to domestic use manufacturing output currently being exported? Closing the gap via increased imports by the surplus countries would allow their consumers wider choices in an increased consumption of goods and services. Diverting production of their own manufactured goods to domestic consumption would allow increased consumption, but narrow their choices to domestically produced manufactures.

Either alternative would require large increases in domestic demand. For economies like Taiwan, whose manufacturing sector is grossly oversized relative to domestic needs, there would seem little chance of sustaining domestic manufacturing output at existing levels by diverting export surpluses to domestic uses.

Some important conclusions flow from this assessment of the adjustment process to come: a growing global oversupply of manufactures and a resulting intensifying global competition seem in prospect; a reduction of the manufacturing sector and a need to switch more employment and production to service-oriented industries will probably be necessary in some surplus countries.

22.3 Effects of global adjustments on East-West trade policies

The outlook for a smooth adjustment

Given the difficulties in accomplishing fundamental changes in imbalance countries in a timely fashion, the relatively painless, smooth adjustment of global imbalances described earlier is probably unlikely. Consumption in surplus countries seems unlikely to expand rapidly enough relative to production that would continue to grow but would be increasingly oriented to domestic demand and less dependent on export growth. In the United States a complementary early, smooth decline of consumption relative to increasing production, accompanied by rapid export expansion and slowed import growth, seems similarly difficult and unlikely.

A better bet is that if the U.S. current account deficit is to narrow significantly, the adjustments will ultimately be driven by market forces that may produce more painful changes. The U.S. adjustment will likely be manifested in a combination of strong export growth, but also significant import cuts, at least in volume terms, if not in nominal terms. The surplus countries will likely experience significant import growth but will probably also sustain export cuts. These movements will likely be forced by, or accompanied by, significant further dollar depreciation.

If so, the result may be a disruptive global industrial restructuring. In the United States, manufactures imports may decline, at least relative to U.S. production and probably in real volume terms. U.S. manufacturing output may grow, partly to satisfy expanding exports, but mostly to substitute U.S.-based production for foreign imports.

In surplus countries, exports may decline, putting a drag on their domestic economies that would reduce total output unless the exporting industries successfully increase domestic demand and reorient toward products used to satisfy increased domestic consumption. For example, without large increases in Japanese imports that would narrow Japan's surplus and obviate further large yen appreciation, a major portion of the large segment of the Japanese automobile industry now devoted to supplying the U.S. market will probably have to relocate to the United States. This will leave idle capacity in Japan and add additional excess capacity in the United States. With little room for expansion of auto sales in Japan, a successful transition would require excess Japanese domestic auto production capacity to be switched to new products that would satisfy increased Japanese consumption.[8]

For surplus countries whose manufacturing sectors are very much oversized relative to potential domestic consumption - Taiwan, Japan, and South Korea - the disappearance of large export surpluses may mandate

---

[8] The outlook for Japanese automobile exports to the United States is examined in some detail in Lenz, "Slimming the U.S. Trade and Current Account Deficits".

reducing the manufacturing sector, even if domestic demand is successfully stimulated.

For the most part, actions by the surplus countries to increase their domestic demand and consumption relative to production have been inadequate. They recognize that declines in their exports to the United States will cause them major adjustment and structural change problems. This is why they fear and resist further declines in the dollar. On more than one occasion since the 1985 beginning of the dollar decline, German and Japanese officials have complained that the dollar had fallen far enough because it was "beginning to hurt exports." But without any expansion of their imports, this is precisely what must happen if the imbalances are to narrow. Unfortunately, the surplus countries may procrastinate in taking difficult adjustment actions in the same way the United States avoids taking difficult budget-cutting measures. If so, a major slimming of the U.S. current account deficit will ultimately require significant further depreciations of the dollar to levels that surplus country exporters cannot adjust to exchange rates they "cannot live with." The result could be sharp, disruptive changes in global financial flows and trading patterns.

Continued structural change must occur in every economy to implement technological and other changes. However, the wide swings in international trade and capital flows that occurred in the 1980s have imposed difficult and, perhaps, wasteful changes on affected industries. Barring a major global recession, the worst of aggravated structural changes may be over for U.S.-based manufacturing. Earlier, much of U.S. manufacturing scaled down in adjusting to tough foreign competition. But now, in an orderly transition to balanced accounts, U.S. manufacturing employment and output would be stimulated, both by export expansion and by the substitution of U.S. production for foreign production in satisfying domestic demand. U.S. manufacturing, investment, output and employment would increase. U.S. consumers, however, would expect slower growth in their consumption relative to GNP. In an "export less" narrowing of imbalances, surplus country trading partners will be forced to stimulate domestic demand to substitute for declining export demand and will probably have to reduce some export-oriented industries, switching their output to expanded domestic needs in other product lines. In some industries the effects could be wrenching, leading to intensified protectionist pressures in the affected countries.

The more slowly the imbalances narrow, the less painful and disruptive it will be for both the United States and the surplus countries. Unfortunately, however, the slower the narrowing of the imbalances, the larger the U.S. debt accumulation, the greater the potential for U.S. protectionist actions, and the larger U.S. manufactures trade surpluses must ultimately be to balance U.S. accounts. Moreover, without immediate pressure, as would be provided by further dollar depreciation, the natural tendency may be to continue deferring painful changes.

Potential impact on East-West trade policies

During the 1990s there will be continuing movement by the centrally planned economies (CPEs) - the Soviet Union, Eastern Europe, and the People's Republic of China - toward integration into the world economy. Entry of those not yet members into world organisations such as the GATT and IMF poses one set of problems. More difficult problems, however, stem from the increasing participation of these countries in world trade at a time when over-supplies of many goods and trade tensions may be rising.

The intense competition among nations for world manufactures markets that will likely be the result of narrowing global trade imbalances to sustainable levels may have significant implications for East-West trade and Western government policies. Continuing expansion of supplies will likely produce a global glut of manufactures and intense competition for manufactures markets. In turn, attempts to gain a market advantage will speed the pace of techno-logical advance, style changes, and quality improvements. The intense com-petition will hold down prices, probably enlarge the export credits available, press suppliers to search for new markets, and hence provide some advantages to Eastern importers. But at the same time the intense competition will make exporting more difficult. It will disadvantage those suppliers who have quality problems or do not react quickly to style changes and technology advances. It will also handicap those who do not have the ability to move rapidly in responding to other market needs.

On balance, the 1990s may be a particularly difficult time to expand manu-factures exports. There is, however, little prospect that competition will lessen in the foreseeable future and CPEs will necessarily expand their market entry efforts.

Increased CPE participation in world trade will likely disrupt and alter global trade patterns, but in a different way than have the very large U.S. deficits and complementary surpluses of some U.S. trading partners. The CPEs engage in trade not to generate jobs, employ unused resources, or to enlarge their saving. They export simply to be able to import; to be able to buy the goods and services they need to build up their economies. They will not accrue large surpluses that would aggravate global imbalance problems. They pose no such threat, not only because their manufacturing and marketing abilities are inadequate to allow them to do so, but because it is clearly in their interest to use whatever added income they achieve from export increases to buy more imports.

Neither will they be able to accrue large deficits that would allow the surplus countries to defer their adjustment and continue their surpluses as U.S. deficits decline. Thus, increased CPE trade is unlikely, in macroeconomic terms, either to aggravate the global imbalance problem or to aid markedly in its solution. Nevertheless, increased CPE participation in world trade will probably cause some problems in microeconomic terms. To increase their imports, CPEs must increase their exports. Most of the increase will necessarily be in manufactures, primarily in labor-intensive products - including textiles, apparel, electronics, and other items - where trade problems already exist.

To the extent that intense competition for world manufactures markets generates new protectionist pressures, barriers may be raised that will apply to all countries. But non-market economies may be particularly vulnerable to anti-dumping and countervailing duty actions.

22.4 Summary

A deterioration of the manufactures trade account was the dominant factor in growth of huge current account deficits and the U.S. international debtor position. Improved U.S. current account performance must also come from the manufacture trade account. There is no other source of significant improvement.

A balanced current account by 1992 would require a $ 200 billion improvement in U.S. manufactures trade performance, moving from a 1987 deficit of $ 138 billion to a 1992 surplus of about $ 60 billion.

The recent large global current account imbalances cannot be sustained indefinitely because no nation - not even the United States, borrowing in its own currency - can indefinitely continue to accrue large amounts of external debt relative to its GNP.

Narrowing the global imbalances - U.S. deficits and the complementary surpluses of Japan, Germany, Taiwan and South Korea - without serious repercussions for the world economy requires gradually changing the consumption and saving patterns of the United States and the major surplus countries, while maintaining good world economic growth rates.

Gradually changing these consumption and saving patterns will be difficult, both for the United States and the surplus countries, probably requiring major changes in fiscal, tax, monetary and other policies. Such changes will be difficult and controversial and are unlikely to be accomplished quickly.

The difficult adjustment process will likely produce a global glut of manufactures and intense competition for world manufactures markets. The intense competition and struggle for world markets raises the risks of increasing protectionism.

The 1990s will likely be a particularly difficult period for centrally planned economies to increase their exports of manufactures to the West. Moreover, CPEs may be particularly vulnerable to increases in protectionism that may be triggered by the increasingly competitive struggle for world markets.

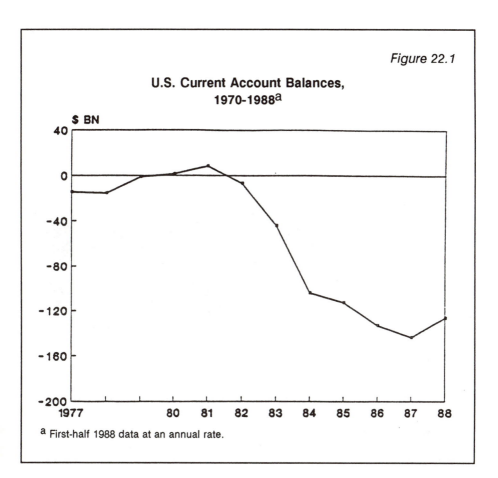

Figure 22.1

U.S. Current Account Balances,
1970-1988[a]

$ BN

a First-half 1988 data at an annual rate.

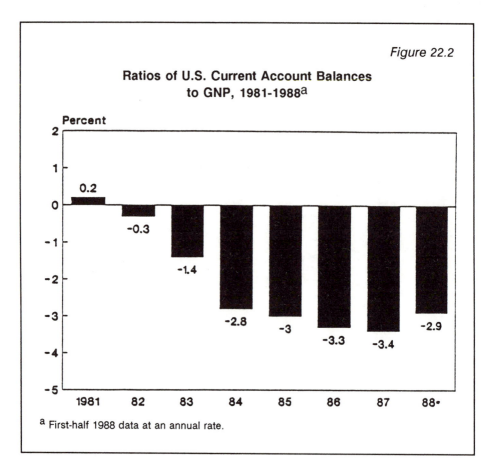

Figure 22.2

Ratios of U.S. Current Account Balances to GNP, 1981-1988[a]

a First-half 1988 data at an annual rate.

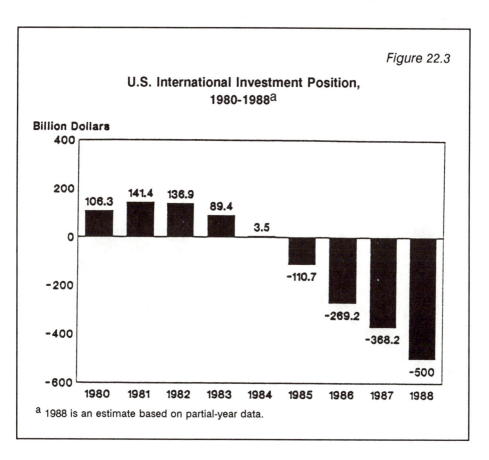

Figure 22.3

**U.S. International Investment Position,
1980-1988[a]**

Billion Dollars

- 1980: 106.3
- 1981: 141.4
- 1982: 136.9
- 1983: 89.4
- 1984: 3.5
- 1985: -110.7
- 1986: -269.2
- 1987: -368.2
- 1988: -500

[a] 1988 is an estimate based on partial-year data.

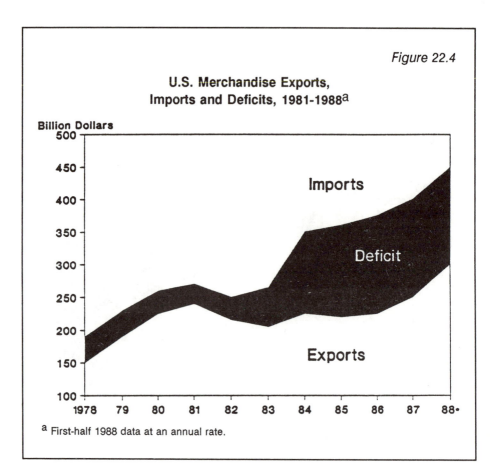

Figure 22.4

**U.S. Merchandise Exports,
Imports and Deficits, 1981-1988[a]**

Billion Dollars

Imports

Deficit

Exports

[a] First-half 1988 data at an annual rate.

342

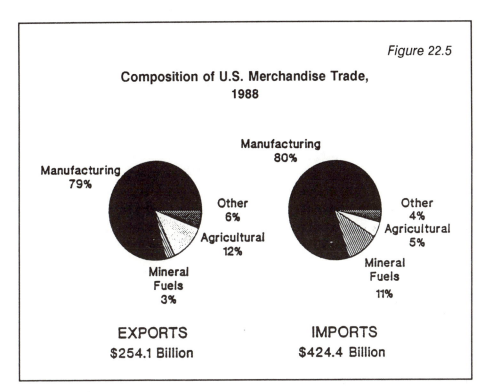

Figure 22.5

**Composition of U.S. Merchandise Trade,
1988**

Manufacturing
79%

Manufacturing
80%

Other
6%

Other
4%

Agricultural
12%

Agricultural
5%

Mineral
Fuels
3%

Mineral
Fuels
11%

EXPORTS
$254.1 Billion

IMPORTS
$424.4 Billion

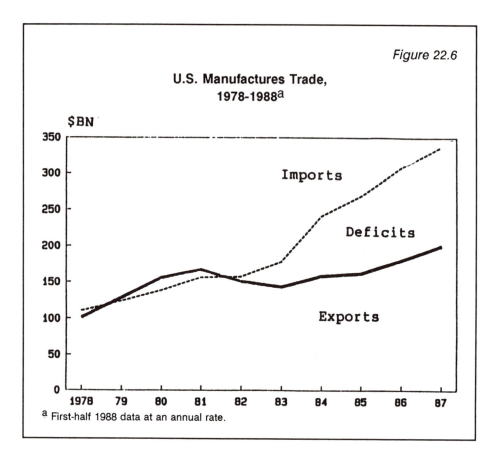

Figure 22.6

U.S. Manufactures Trade,
1978-1988[a]

$BN

Imports

Deficits

Exports

1978 79 80 81 82 83 84 85 86 87

a First-half 1988 data at an annual rate.

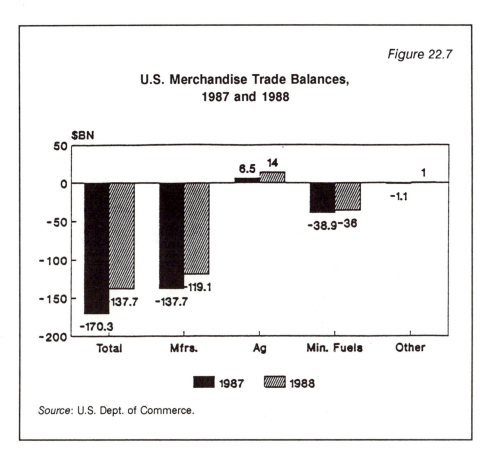

Figure 22.7

**U.S. Merchandise Trade Balances,
1987 and 1988**

$BN

Source: U.S. Dept. of Commerce.

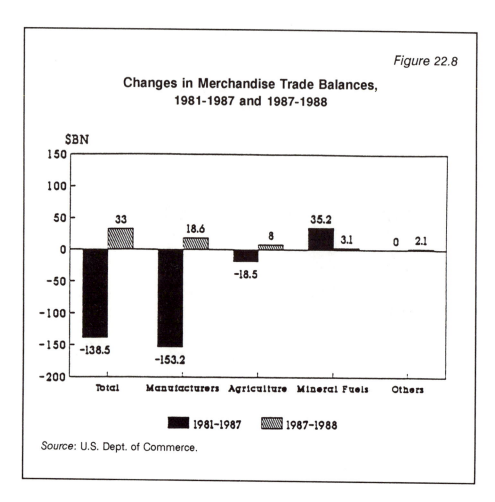

Figure 22.8

**Changes in Merchandise Trade Balances,
1981-1987 and 1987-1988**

Source: U.S. Dept. of Commerce.

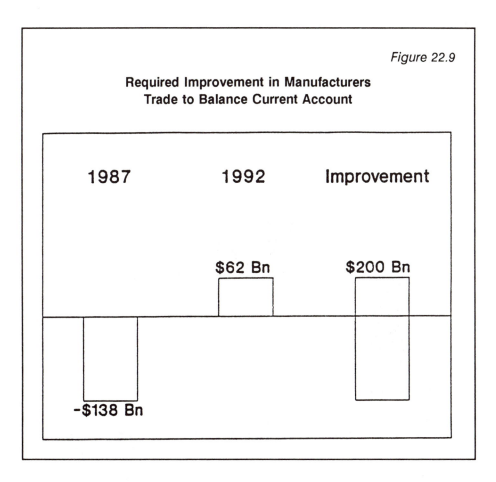

Figure 22.9

**Required Improvement in Manufacturers
Trade to Balance Current Account**

1987   1992   Improvement

$62 Bn $200 Bn

-$138 Bn

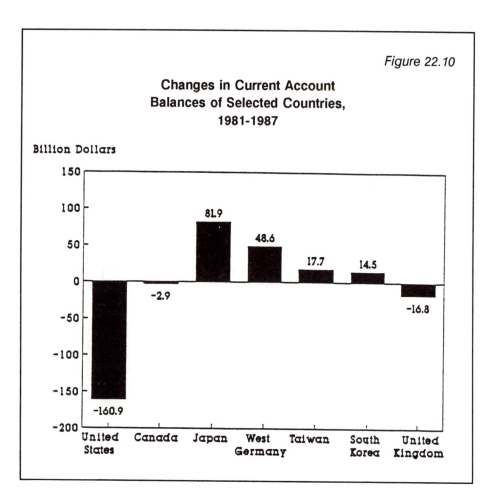

Figure 22.10

Changes in Current Account
Balances of Selected Countries,
1981-1987

Billion Dollars

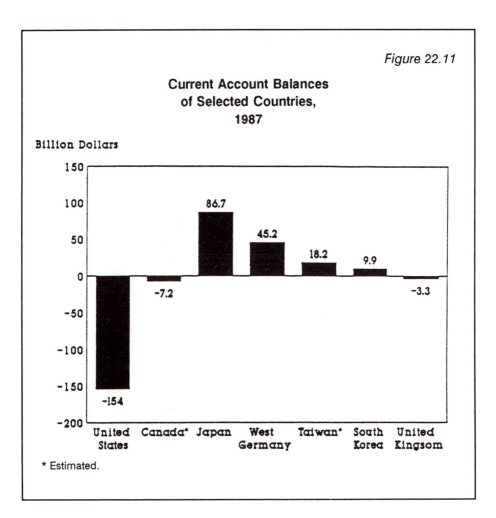

Figure 22.11

**Current Account Balances
of Selected Countries,
1987**

Billion Dollars

* Estimated.

349

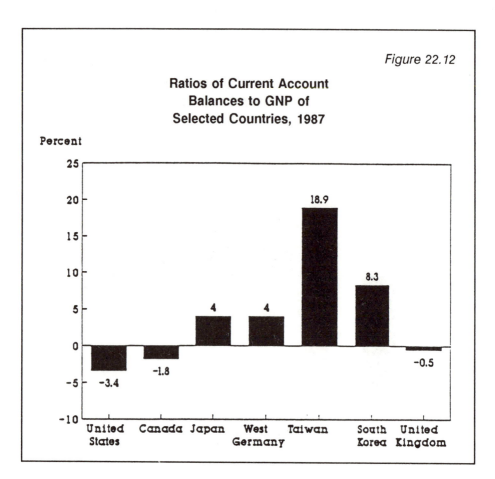

Figure 22.12

Ratios of Current Account
Balances to GNP of
Selected Countries, 1987

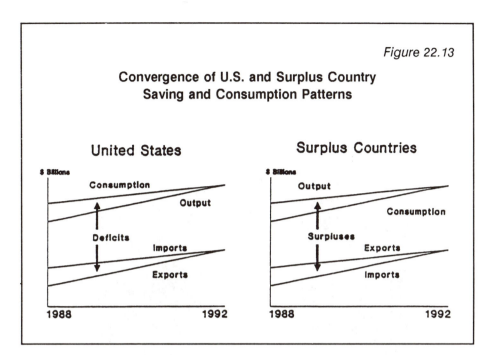

Figure 22.13

**Convergence of U.S. and Surplus Country
Saving and Consumption Patterns**

351

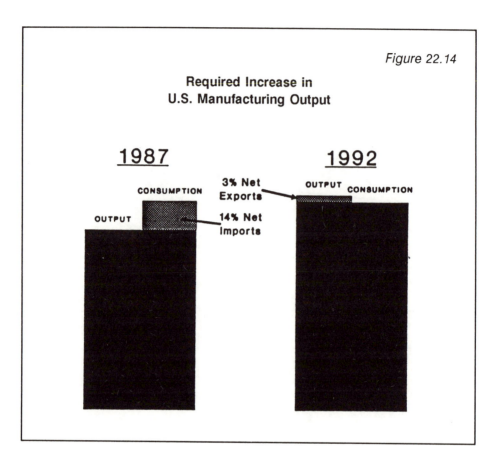

Figure 22.14

Required Increase in
U.S. Manufacturing Output

1987

CONSUMPTION

OUTPUT

3% Net
Exports

14% Net
Imports

1992

OUTPUT   CONSUMPTION

Chapter 23

EAST-WEST ECONOMIC INTERDEPENDENCE AND THE RISE OF FOREIGN TRADE CONSTITUENCIES

John P. Hardt[1]

23.1 Normalization: a movement toward a liberal government role in East-West economic relations

Politics has dominated East-West commerce in the past and government intervention has been mainly restrictive. That seems less likely to be true in the future. A clarification of the future interrelationship of politics and economics in East-West commercial behaviour is essential in order to improve the accuracy of Western forecasts of East-West commerce and for assessing the government role in this area.

In Western Europe, except for intra-German relations, politics has been less of a factor in foreign commerce. Although Western political authorities generally involve themselves in trade issues on grounds of security, sovereignty, and the maintenance of the pluralistic market system, their interventions either to facilitate or to restrict trade are not, as a rule, central to the commercial relationship. This has not been the case with the United States where arms, regional issues, and human rights have been the centre-piece of U.S.-Soviet relations or with Japan where security concerns and the Northern Territory issue have overshadowed commercial considerations. As the political environment between the United States and the Soviet Union appears to be qualitatively changing, the prospects of normalization or facilitation of commerce by the respective governments seem more likely than in the past.

The key to development of U.S.-Soviet economic relations is a general improvement of the political environment. Were we to enter into a period of substantial, predictable improvement in all areas of our relations - arms control, regional issues, and human rights - then the preconditions for economic interdependence would be set. The past experience of Nixon-Brezhnev detente suggests that economic normalization is not likely to precede successful nego-

[1] Associate Director for Research Coordination, Congressional Research Services, Washington, D.C., U.S.A.

tiation of a process of arms control, regional accommodations, and human rights improvements.

An *arms reduction regimen* was initiated with the INF agreement and the "deep intrus...r" for verification and inspection. The changes in military doctrine and new tradeoffs between "guns, growth, and butter" appear likely to precede more Soviet unilateral withdrawals and force reductions through negotiations. An apparent change in both military doctrine and international policy has affected their perceived need for military forces. The reasonable sufficiency doctrine with its defensive orientation requires less and different forces to perform needed missions; "new thinking" in foreign policy calls for a shift away from military to political-economic centered foreign policy. These changes in doctrine and policy make existing and planned weapons systems redundant.

The success of perestroika requires a shift in the resource allocation priorities from "guns" to "growth" and "butter". What now appears to be in conflict is the political security of Gorbachev's regime based on the success of perestroika and traditional views of military security needs. In the short run to 1991 - the next CPSU Congress and the beginning of the new Five Year Plan period - it is necessary to make a substantial start on modernizing the Soviet "rust belt" (their obsolete plant and equipment) and installing equipment and processes using less energy, materials, and manpower to produce goods that are up to world market standards. Similar types of plant and equipment for civilian modernization would be required for military augmentation ("tractors" versus "tanks"). Likewise more investment is needed for increased output of consumer goods, to bring more quality food to the market, increase supplies of medical equipment, and raise the quality of housing. The resource allocation claims are more likely to provide results in the short run than systemic changes involving the use of market forces through decentralization, price reform, and the changing economic roles of the central bureaucracy and party. The longer term goals of perestroika and interdependence for the year 2000 are more ambitious in restructuring, reform, renewal and political reform and interdependence. However, Gorbachev's regime must survive the test of performance in the short run to effectively deal with the more revolutionary changes of the long term. In the short run the "guns, growth, and butter" tradeoff is crucial.

Soviet *new thinking in international affairs* calls for a more pragmatic, less military centered foreign policy, ergo fewer forward deployed offensive and intervention forces and less military aid and sales. Withdrawal from Afghanistan, possible agreements in South Africa and Southeast Asia, an

354

apparent resolution of the Iran-Iraq war, and new initiatives in the Middle East are all examples of the new thinking in foreign policy. The new thinking implications for foreign policy reform laid out by Foreign Minister Shevardnadze in July 1988 indicated that the traditional military-driven foreign policy was often too costly and counterproductive. A model for regional settlements has been suggested with the United States and Soviet Union as Great Power guarantors of crises resolutions.

U.S. policy has established a special relationship between *human rights* and economic normalization. The Soviet Union's perceived domestic discrimination (the nationality question) and restrictions on emigration are issues of particular interest to the United States. Tolerance of Jewish national or ethnic cultures and an acceptable emigration policy for Soviet Jewry and Armenians are specific areas of U.S. interest. To the extent that restrictive nationality policies have limited the human resources available for Gorbachev's ambitious programs, he may have greater interest in equality of opportunity. Elimination of the self-induced "brain-drain" caused by restrictive nationality and ethnic opportunities, such as the prohibition of the teaching of Hebrew on the grounds that it is a religious language and discrimination in educational and employment opportunities, may liberate more productive reserves for what is called the "human factor" in perestroika.

Release of refuseniks, clarification and narrowing of "security" as a basis for emigration denial, and expansion of individual rights to include practices consistent with cultural and religious traditions, as highlighted in the General Secretary's December 7, 1988 United Nations speech, might increase Soviet productive reserves for energizing the human factor in Gorbachev's reform program. This might entail risk, from the Soviet perspective, of increased emigration of talented people, at least initially. Such steps, however, would likely generate positive responses within the CSCE process, especially from the United States. Based on the U.S. policy of relating commercial benefits to human rights, substantial progress by the Soviet Union in these areas tend to make issues such as tariffs, credits, and a CSCE meeting in Moscow more negotiable. Furthermore, such change would provide a basis for a more congenial summitry process. The United States' conditional acceptance of a Soviet proposal to have a Moscow meeting of the CSCE in 1991 was concrete evidence of American and Western acceptance of a favourable process of human rights improvement.

23.2 Competitiveness and commercial normalization

Toward a liberal East-West commercial regimen[2]

In a favourable process of arms negotiations, regional issue resolutions, and human rights improved commercial relations may be more normal in U.S.-Soviet and East-West commerce. In this context consideration of a waiver of the Jackson-Vanik and Byrd amendments to the Trade bill of 1974, and repeal of the Stevenson amendment to the Export-Import Bank bill of 1975 are on the current agenda in the United States. With a change in the political environment, the conditions of a liberal market regime became more relevant and shared mutual interests in commerce may come into play. These common interests in an open global trading system have been the basis of discussions between Eastern and Western economists for some time preceding perestroika and the upgrading of foreign commerce in U.S. policy.

The emphasis on national economic objectives has shifted from quantitative growth, which characterized the economic strategies of the past, to growth with efficiency. The Stalinist policy of extensive growth has given way to the qualitative, intensive growth strategy in Eastern centrally planned economies. The Western economies are, likewise, increasingly concerned with the changing quality of economic performance and less preoccupied with quantitative growth rates.

Comparative advantage and trade normalization

Global interdependence in economic development has been adopted in lieu of the concept of independence or two markets which characterized the policies of the past in both East and West. Eastern economic isolation and self-sufficiency have ceased being ends in themselves. Western denial of Eastern commercial relations on both economic health and military enhancement grounds has been abandoned as a basis of a unified Western policy.

---

[2] This section draws in part on John P. Hardt, "Commentary on Professor Bogomolov's Position", in Zbigniew M. Fallenbuchl and Carl H. McMillan, eds., *Partners in East-West Economic Relations: The Determinants of Choice* (Toronto: Pergamon Press, 1980), pp. 18-27; and A. Kunitsyn, "Socialism: The Choice of Global Economic Strategies", *IMEMO Journal* no. 9, 1, (1989).

Stability, predictability, and responsibility in the world market

Global interdependence has been buttressed by a sense of shared East-West responsibility for stability and economic growth in the international market, in lieu of a general focus on the national and domestic concerns of the past. Eastern and Western economies have been responsive to the need to follow policies conducive to international and inter-regional price stability and economic growth in the world economies. Conversely, the negative impacts of inflation and recession have been recognized as common problems in both East and West. Indeed, budget deficits and inflation are specific common concerns. Western and Eastern industrial economies, especially since the oil price rise of the early 1970s and fall in the 1980s, have become increasingly aware of the interrelations in the global economy and the advantages of stability and reasonable predictability in the world market.

Attention in the East and West has been focused on the economically developing world and some recognition of the task of establishing joint responsibility for a liberal global economic environment. This new perception contrasts with past policies emphasizing national economic independence. While this emphasis on Third and Fourth World economic problems extends to the environment in global warming to the oceans as well as land, the development of policies for the utilization of fish, mineral, and energy resources of the sea has provided opportunities as well as problems in East-West economic policy.

Development of a commercial constituency

Once a threshold is reached in the economic sectors where the critical outcomes for importer and exporter in their domestic economies are substantially influenced by commercial relations, a constituency is likely to develop. For example, U.S. grain exports were considered to be primarily a political issue until the point was reached in the early 1980s where the U.S. farm community determined that the level of Soviet grain imports had a critical impact on the price and profit in the grain growing regions, then the grain trade became an economic rather than a political issue. Indeed, grain was effectively removed from the use of "foreign policy criteria" for controlling exports; the grain trade became embargo-proof with the 1983 Long-Term Grain Agreement.

In 1989 there could be an expansion in commercial relations in food processing, health, environment and housing equipment areas. Joint ventures are being discussed in these non-strategic areas and when substantial, long-term contracts are signed they may lead to the development of constituencies. The increased market share of consumer and agricultural equipment may develop a comercial constituency in the United States comparable to the grain trade. Plants in Peoria, Illinois may relate their employment and production to the Soviet market. Likewise joint ventures in production in the Soviet Union for third country markets, as well as the United States market, can be advantageous to the Western partner.

Just as grain has a constituency in Kansas and Iowa, pipe has a constituency in Dusseldorf. If two-way commerce in non-strategic, profitable commerce expands, there will be indigenous supporters in each Western country supporting trade. This commercial constituency will influence their elected representatives and incline their governments toward commercial normalization policies.

23.3 The implications of perestroika for Soviet foreign economic policy

Perestroika may in the first instance require comprehensive reform of the domestic political economy. Each aspect of perestroika in turn has a relationship to the global developed market which generates the opportunity or necessity of openness for successful domestic transformation.

Technological restructuring uses the second industrial revolution as the framework and the world level of quality goods salable in the convertible currency market as the measure of qualitative improvement in domestic output. The world level of efficiency in inputs - energy, materials, labour inputs per unit of output - is the explicit measuring rod for modernization of the production process. To more effectively and quickly reach the world market level of manufactured goods is crucial to effective modernization and commercial expansion. The historical record indicates that there is no method of domestic modernization as effective as interdependence and openness to the world market. Economic reform involves the use of domestic market forces and international world markets for increasing incentives and introducing competition. World pricing and competition are very useful supplements and stimuli to internal reforms.

Especially difficult in expanding commerce is to develop niches in the global market for manufactured goods. Joint ventures with Western partners provide quality control, management, and other transferred elements of technology and know-how. But a critical benefit is access from the Western partner to the marketing and supply of the global, convertible goods markets. Joint ventures are the currently chosen instrument for this form of interdependence.

In order to be successful in attracting enough joint ventures and exports, it would seem necessary to make working in the Soviet economy attractive for Western partners through special zones; preferences in terms of freedom from tariffs and taxes; special arrangements to assure supply of high quality inputs and quality control of exports, etc. The result could be more exports in value-added materials, such as refined petroleum products and petrochemicals, pulp and processed wood, energy intensive processed metals, and also manufactured goods. Objectively, judging by the success of Asia's developing economies, foreign trade should be assigned first priority in the economy, even higher than defence. With first priority justified by burgeoning hard currency earnings and effective technology transfer, an influential foreign commerce constituency should rise in the Soviet Union. Indeed, in the short run, if foreign economic relations contribute a critical margin to putting quality food on the Soviet table, improved quality of care in the medical system, a better controlled environment and improved housing, the political-economic benefit could be crucial to the success of perestroika. If improvements in the efficiency of the energy chain from well to pump can substantially increase hard currency earnings, the foreign economic sector may claim considerable credit and prestige. Even with small but critical foreign commercial sectors the domestic constituency for interdependence may increase in importance. As foreign trade and investment activities from the West become more important the reciprocal importance of commerce to the success of perestroika and expanding market shares would lead to the development of important constituencies or interest groups affecting the governing bodies both in East and West.

Chapter 24

EAST-WEST ECONOMIC RELATIONS IN THE 1990s: THE DEMANDS ON POLITICS

Wolfgang Heinrichs[1]

24.1 The political climate

In outlining the prospects for East-West economic relations in the 1990s it is necessary to begin with an appraisal of the general political climate. This is important because the new emerging forms of economic cooperation are more complicated than traditional forms of simple commodity exchange and require a far more favourable political and security climate. Their expansion demands a higher degree of trust, mutual accountability in behaviour, and stability in political relations.

While the first half of the 1980s was characterized by conflict and confrontation in the political sphere, and thus inhibited the development of East-West economic relations, more propitious conditions have emerged in the second half of the 1980s. This allowed the emergence of more diverse forms of economic cooperation, such as joint ventures, that were in line with the technological challenges and the growing world-wide economic interdependence. As we enter the 1990s, the policies pursued by governments are faced with great challenges in shaping the general political conditions.

The establishment of official relations in 1988 between the CMEA and the EC and the establishment of diplomatic relations between individual CMEA countries and the EC will lead to an improvement in the general political conditions for economic cooperation between the two big economic organizations and among individual CMEA countries. Even the CSCE process, notably the results reached in Vienna in 1989, testified to the long-term interests in East and West to unfold economic cooperation. The more favourable political climate has not been reflected in a more constructive atmosphere during the EC meetings. The majority of member countries are interested in greater EC activities aimed at an increase in efficiency. Of course, it is possible to refer to additional tendencies and factors, documenting that the general political condi-

---

[1] Director, Central Institute of Economics, Academy of Sciences of the GDR, Berlin, GDR.

tions have invariably improved for East-West economic cooperation and that there is a real chance now of putting them on a stable foundation for a longer period. As a result, the United States and its allies were forced to lift considerable parts of embargoes and sanctions imposed on such fields as grain, credits, large-diameter gas pipes, etc. Obviously these measures that stemmed from the time of political confrontation had come into conflict with certain political and economic interests in Western circles, especially in Western Europe and Japan.

Given the progress reached in favour of the general political conditions it has to be frankly stated that, apart from several neutral countries (such as Austria, Finland, and Sweden), the foreign economic policies pursued by various Western states and groups toward CMEA countries are not yet constructive enough and continue to show illusory aspects.

In this context, however, reference has again to be made to the technology blockade and, specifically, to the continuation of traditional and the introduction of new, yet more subtle, varieties of discrimination. A politically motivated trading policy of differentiation vis-à-vis the CMEA countries, tariff and non-tariff protectionist restrictions by Western industrial countries or the EC, which generally put CMEA countries at a gross disadvantage, are doubtless part of a set of negative factors that affect the general political conditions of East-West economic cooperation. In all probability these factors will continue to be operative in the 1990s, with even heightened intensity. Even at the end of the 1980s it is not possible, notwithstanding all the advances made, to speak of a state of normalcy in the political climate of East-West economic relations. If this abnormality should continue in the 1990s, the new forms of cooperation (such as specialization, delivery of equipment and factories, and joint ventures) would be jeopardized.

24.2 Economic tendencies of the West and their influence on East-West economic relations

Economic development in industrial countries was contradictory in the second half of the 1980s. Since 1980-82 there has, however, been moderate economic growth among OECD countries. But the dynamism of the capitalist world economy had been on the decline. In contrast to 1973-1979 in which average annual industrial production of OECD countries rose by 2.3 per cent and exports (in comparable prices) rose by 5.2 per cent, growth in these areas between 1979 and 1987 was 1.7 per cent and 3.5 per cent, respectively.

Important structural changes in the steel, coal mining, shipbuilding, textile, and construction industries continue. The processes of adaptation have proved complicated and are related to the sudden emergence of social and trade policy tensions. Meanwhile, modern high technology production has accelerated, entailing a radical transformation of the material and technical foundations in macroeconomic dimensions. The governments of developed industrial countries, regardless of declarations to the contrary, are exerting a great influence on this development. Out of the state expenditures on research and development in the middle of the 1980s the United States allocated 22 per cent, Japan 34 per cent, the FRG 24 per cent, France 25 per cent and Great Britain 32 per cent to electronics and communication engineering alone. Within EC-operated research and development programs the high technologies are promoted in an effort to overtake Japan and the United States. This explains the increasing toughness and the new dimension of competition which is virtually spilling over into new technological struggles for the top positions by accepting the devaluation of important productive capabilities. Despite this growth, unemployment is still high in OECD countries and has a restrictive influence on the expansion of private consumption. Competition and pro- tectionism on Western markets have also grown together with the budget and trade deficits perpetuated under U.S. influence. Chronic imbalances in the foreign trade of leading Western industrial countries operate as additional catalysts in the severity of competition, involving fusions and mergers of new dimensions in the same way as bankruptcies with all the social ramifications. Unstable tendencies prevail in finance. Uncertainties have increased in the face of substantive currency fluctuations occurring at shorter intervals. The debt of developing countries reached a record height of $ 1.3 trillion by the end of 1988. What Western governments and international banks are actually capable of doing, as soon as they decided to resort to suitable means, was shown by their "crisis management", when they warded off the onset of an expected general crisis in the Western world economy which would also have affected East-West economic relations.

Apart from these structural tendencies in the world economy it is necessary, from the point of view of future East-West economic relations, to mention the declining consumption of important energy importers in the West; energy products being the major exports of the Soviet Union and other CMEA countries. A 1988 report by the EC Commission concerning the development of energy consumption until 1995 urged that: the consumption of energy should be cut back by 20 per cent from 1987 levels; the consumption of crude oil should be reduced further and oil imports be frozen down on a level corresponding to about one-third of the total energy consumption of 1995; the share of crude oil (19 per cent of EC energy consumption) should be maintained at current levels; the share of solid fuels in consumption should be raised in connection with the higher competitiveness of solid fuels extracted in EC countries; and, finally, the share of hydrocarbons in the generation of electrical energy should be reduced below 15 per cent.

This trend has been intensified by the drastic decline of raw material prices since 1981 and oil prices since the first half of 1986. Since then it has been impossible to offset the downward movement of prices.[2] The so-called threshold countries with their exports into developed industrial markets could also gain favourable positions because they, among other reasons, enjoy trading privileges vis-à-vis the CMEA countries. Apart from the fact that South Korea, Taiwan, Hong Kong, and Singapore are already exporters of high technology, their present export structure corresponds largely to the import structure of OECD countries.[3]

Thus, East-West trade was stagnant in the second half of the 1980s due to the general political climate, certain global economic tendencies in the West, and a number of factors related to the economic efficiency of CMEA countries and the mechanisms underlying their cooperation. It is not possible to say whether and in what way the tendencies observed on Western markets in the 1980s will continue, and whether the East-West economic relations of the 1990s will be positively or negatively influenced by them. Rather, it is justifiable to determine somewhat more precisely the possible effects of an underlying structure of interests and to assess the future East-West economic relations from there.

Despite the comparatively low share of East-West trade in the total trade of the developed capitalist industrial countries (about 3 per cent), the relatively stable interests in the continuation and expansion of East-West economic relations, notably in Western Europe, cannot be ignored. These relations have proved to be stable, and did not suffer any appreciable damage in the early 1980s despite the massive deterioration of the East-West political environment. About 85 per cent of the entire trade of the European CMEA countries with the

---

[2] Annual Report 1988: Zur Wirtschaftslage imperialistischer Länder, IPW-Berichte 8.88, pp. 23 and 33.

[3] Tendenzen des Außenhandels mit Ländern Ost- und Südostasiens, AW 18.88, pp. 8 and 26.

West is done with West European countries. In addition, East-West trade is very important for several West European industries. By the middle of the 1980s one out of eight metal-working machines or machine tools exported by Western Europe was delivered to the CMEA countries, even one out of six from the FRG. In the same period 42 per cent of all exports of such machines from Austria and 35 per cent from Finland were supplied to the CMEA region. The different interest structure underlying East-West economic relations is, among other things, the outcome of the different shares taken by the three western world economic structures in East-West trade.

Table 24.1

**Share of OECD countries' trade
with CMEA countries**
(per cent)

	1980	1985	1986
EC	61.7	62.5	63.6
United States	5.6	6.5	4.9
Japan	6.7	7.2	9.6

Source: W. Nicolai, "Entwicklungstendenzen der Wirtschaftsbeziehungen europäischer RGW-Länder mit kapitalistischen Industrieländern", in *Jahrbuch Politische Ökonomie des Zentralinstituts für Wirtschaftswissenschaften der DDR* (in process).

While the FRG in 1986 reached a turnover in trade with European CMEA countries of $ 389 per capita, France had $ 124, United Kingdom $ 68, Finland $ 1,257, Austria $ 568.5, Japan $ 46, and the United States only $ 16.[4] Obviously, the West Europeans have the greatest interest in stability and an expansion of East-West economic relations. The unfolding of these interests in conjunction with supporting governmental measures and initiatives are a sine qua non of the development of East-West economic relations in the 1990s.

---

[4] W. Nicolai, "Entwicklungstendenzen der Wirtschaftsbeziehungen europäischer RGW-Länder mit kapitalistischen Industrieländern" in *Jahrbuch Politische Ökonomie des Zentralinstituts für Wirtschaftswissenschaften der DDR* (in process).

24.3 The role of reforms in CMEA countries and their influence on future East-West economic relations

In international discussions the continuity and expansion of inter-systemic economic cooperation has often been made exclusively dependent upon the progress of economic and political reform in CMEA countries. Sometimes the progress of reforms is exclusively judged by market economy criteria. Indeed, reforms are of vital significance for the economic and social development of the socialist countries and the global community as a whole. At the same time they turn out to be *one* essential factor of influence on inter-systemic relations. However understandable Western interests in these reforms may be, it would be inaccurate to reduce the interest to this one factor in determining a realistic perspective of East-West relations. As past experience shows, progress reached in inter-systemic economic relations has never been the result of changes occurring only on one side of those involved. This is more valid as simplified views are harboured as a point of departure in studying the influence of these reform processes on East-West economic relations, and since hopes are pinned on the variety into which these reform processes are presently developing, which often result in attempts to pursue an official government policy of differentiation vis-à-vis the individual CMEA national economies. As in any social process of development, short, medium, and long-term interests permeate each other in the development of socialist economies, and they portray their specific forms of manifestation. And apart from the fact that there are phenomena of stagnation, elements of continuity have always combined with those of renewal.

To explain reform processes primarily as the outcome of defective developments of past decades, does not show any claim to ambitious thinking, and still less in those cases that conceive the past development exclusively as a deformation of aims, ideals, and the forces of movement of socialism. However, this very approach would put forward the justified question after the socio-strategic motives of the current reform processes in the East.

All socialist countries, irrespective of the scientific-technical, economic, and social level achieved by them at the beginning of the 1970s, are still faced with the task of effectively utilizing the new technologies and production processes that have emerged for the durable safeguarding of social achievements and their dependable strengthening. Without powerful impulses from modern science, highly productive technologies and their economic utilization it would be less and less possible to attain real economic and social progress. Socialist ownership and production relations per se do not provide sufficient social guarantees, nor is it possible for the advantages of the system to assert themselves if they lack the support of efficient potentials of modern material and technical productive forces and if they cannot be effectively used for the implementation of definite social aims. Thus the primary socio-political objective of the reform processes is to combine scientific-technical progress with economic and social progress, not for a section of society at the expense of other sections, but for all according to the yardstick of social justice.

Since an acceleration of the dynamics of modern production development has to be reckoned with until the turn of the century, the process of reform in all socialist countries will not come to an end in the next few years. Rather, it will continue without interruption. It is quite imaginable, however, that periods of profound and radical change will be followed by periods in which existing and well-tried structures will undergo rather slower, evolutionary change. Moreover, the process of change will not proceed synchronously in all socialist countries. Here a great number of factors are essential which are rooted in the specifics of the countries concerned, such as the social and economic policies so far pursued by them. Thus the generality of the permanent character of reform processes in socialist countries is not synonymous with the generality of the time and the periods at which or in which concrete reform projects are implemented. And the time and periods of reforms in one socialist country do still less determine those in a different country.

Despite the great variety that characterizes the reform process in different socialist countries, there are a number of definite general traits and features underlying it. They include:

1) Provision of economic units with more rights and a higher self-responsibility in the interest of an effective use of resources, judged by economic criteria and a greater consideration of the function of recognition, implementation, and information of domestic and external markets.

2) Increasingly manifest tendencies in the organization of social production and labour (i.e. in the process of socialization) to complete the economic cycle of units (firms and enterprises) both directly by scientific-technical means and/or to integrate it more effectively with the economic cycles of these economic units via various forms of cooperation and research and development.

3) Formation of central state functions of economic management, their statehood including planning, in line with the new socialization tendencies on a

national and international scale and as a result of the growing self-responsibility of economic units. This includes changes in the relationship between direct and normative planning, the transition to normatives valid for several years, towards which flexibly reacting units can orient themselves due to a change of market conditions and requirements by showing a higher degree of self-responsibility, without losing sight of social objectives. This shall run parallel to a radical reduction in plan indicators from top to bottom.

4) Efforts to expand the social component of economic activities and to intensify the necessary strategic work in the scientific-technical, economic, and social fields by the central state level of management which will gain in weight to the extent that self-responsibility is actually exercised by the economic units. And

5) differentiated utilization of different forms of ownership (nationally owned, cooperative, personal, and non-socialist forms) preferably for the improvement of the supply of goods and services.

One of the remarkable features of the reform processes in Eastern Europe is the common recognition that modern productive forces have to be more completely utilized by increasing the international division of labour. This ultimately depends on better control over the integration of internal and external factors of growth. Foreign economic relations no longer form an independent block within the economic mechanism, they are no longer confined to the macro-level, but increasingly involve economic units and their interests at the micro-level. This process is sometimes described as the "opening" of socialist economies to the world economy. Ideally, the process includes: the adaptation of domestic prices to the world market price system via wholesale prices; the development of an effective financing and credit system; the formation of economically substantiated exchange rates; and the introduction of a convertible national currency coupled with the abolition of foreign exchange controls and the development of capital movement for the economic units.

In this way objective economic criteria are created for the economic units which, within the framework of centralized state decisions and in discharge of their self-responsibility, allow them the selection of exclusively internal variants or only those under the influence of external variants. However, these elements of an ideal opening of a socialist national economy remain academic and exist only in abstractions. The actual opening will proceed only step by step. No doubt, it is justifiable to assume that the CMEA countries will first open themselves toward each other step-by-step within the framework of their own community of integration. This will proceed in stages in the direction of the United Market of the CMEA for which the internal economic prerequisites would have to be created from scratch.

Certainly, there is no one-sided and short cut connection between the opening of the socialist economies within their own community of integration and definite steps toward more intensive participation in the world economic division of labour. And it is equally certain that for the sake of stability and security the opening of the socialist economies vis-à-vis the Western economic system is and will be a function of their international competitiveness. This emanates, explicably, from the uncertainties of capitalist commodity and finance markets that will undoubtedly continue into the 1990s, and from the persistence of protectionist measures. Serious prognoses on the role of reform processes in CMEA countries, including the opening of their economies, in the interest of future East-West cooperation should not be entirely based on statements of intent, theoretical models, etc., but should also consider the proceeding changes in terms of international competitiveness and the balanced nature of internal economic processes. However, this empirical material is not yet available. Even more, in those socialist economies in which "more radical reforms" (also in the field of foreign economic relations) are intended or are being put into practice, neither international competitiveness has changed appreciably nor has a new quality emerged in the functioning of domestic economic mechanisms.

A survey of FRG enterprises regarding their cooperation with GDR partners produced results in sharp contrast to the internationally usual subdivision into more or less reform-minded or reform-aspiring CMEA countries. Based on an inquiry of 2,350 enterprises with a return rate of 25 per cent, it was concluded that the facts "stand in clear contradiction to the widely propagated assessment that the GDR would maintain only minimal cooperation relations with the West compared with the other CMEA countries".[5] Obviously there are substantive differences between the claims and realities of reform which should at any rate be taken into account when forecasts are made.

The interesting question regarding the impact of the Eastern reforms on East-West economic relations concerns the role of the state. In view of the great variety of envisaged or already operative regulations, which increased dramatically in the late 1980s, the state will remain involved. To fully under-

---

[5] DIW Wochenbericht 46.88: Die DDR als Kooperationspartner, p. 616.

stand this involvement it is necessary to try to distinguish between the role of the state as set out in the new regulations and its role in practice. In several countries it became necessary to increase centralization and thus the role of the state shortly after the implementation of regulations in order to avert the danger of a deep polarization of social life. Despite the variety of detailed regulations concerning the growing openness of different CMEA economies, three things can be said about the future role of the state in foreign economic relations in these countries.

First, in all CMEA economies foreign trade, by its nature, is a state monopoly which, however, in its instruments of implementation and its technical contents has changed substantially in the past decades. Everywhere the methods of managing foreign trade have increasingly come to the fore together with strict approval procedures by the state. Nowhere, not even in those countries with a high degree of "autonomy" in foreign economic relations, has it been possible to adduce any proof of a perceptible increase in efficiency within foreign economic relations or in the interests of the national economy.

Second, the state is compelled in this or that way to assume its responsibility for foreign economic equilibrium and, in aligning the exchange rates for the regional currency, to steer the export and import interests of economic units into the optimal direction in connection with a much higher self-responsibility, especially for the self-generation of funds.

Finally, the state remains responsible for the constant formation and organization of the general economic conditions. It is held responsible for the operation of economic units according to economic criteria and with an orientation toward the requirements of markets up to their merger within their own community of integration. Thus, in the future any politically and economically harmful effects will be prevented from the national economy or from the social system underlying it.

24.4 Conclusions

The perspectives of East-West economic cooperation are, in the long term, embedded in general political conditions, the more since a stable and longer term conformity of interests in the economic and ecological fields will react on the formation of favourable political conditions. Here governments will be required much more than in former times to put forth adequate political strategies. The requirements of world-wide interdependence have to be recognized in the same way as the longer term coexistence of two opposing social systems. They have to be formed in a way capable of policymaking and, ultimately, be put into reality on the basis of a balancing of interests. Within this fabric of interests, East-West economic relations play a relatively independent role and this is the reason why the policies pursued by the states involved should be measured by the contribution made by them in expanding and deepening East-West economic relations in their own regions by overcoming existing impediments. Stable East-West economic relations in the 1990s will require reciprocal recognition of the ability of learning and reform in the policies of the states and communities involved in the social and economic systems of each side. Such a philosophy underlying government policies will prove to be up-to-date in the 1990s because, apart from the traditional forms of commodity exchange between East and West, completely new areas of scientific-technical cooperation will emerge, such as environmental protection, energetics, transport, statistics, and standardization. New forms of cooperation will be opened up and included, such as information exchange, mediation of know-how in the sphere of hardware, software, and data organization, consulting, training services, further education, etc. The cooperation and trade agreements already concluded or in the process of being concluded on the basis of the establishment of diplomatic relations between CMEA countries and the EC have justified the assumption that Europe will turn into a specifically dynamic continent with both traditional and new forms of economic East-West relations developing there in the 1990s.

Chapter 25

NEW THINKING AND THE ROLE OF GOVERNMENTS IN THE WORLD ECONOMY

Oleg Bogomolov[1]

The development of international economic relations has been significantly shaped by the policy of governments. Acute debates between proponents of free trade and protectionism dating back to the past century burst out from time to time today. These conflicting approaches to foreign trade express the true interests of industrial and agricultural groups in the countries concerned. They, of course, affect world trade and can be illustrated by numerous examples.

The foreign economic policy of governments in the late 1980s undoubtedly consists of a greater number of various components, and its role cannot be assessed unambiguously or simply; the more so that nowadays the relationship between economic and political (military-strategic) interests in foreign policy is manifested more explicitly and clearly than in the past.

The Marxist thesis of the primacy of the economic over the political may hold true in the long run but preserving security quite clearly dominates now over economic interests. Under current conditions the settlement of military and political problems precedes trade and economic relations but offers no guarantees about their normalization, let only their expansion. The recent agreements on disarmament and regional conflicts have opened the way for better East-West business cooperation but the West seems to be in no hurry to reform the terms of trade exchanges with the Soviet Union and some other socialist countries, to stop discriminating against these countries in international commerce, or to accept them as equal partners in world economic exchanges. How can this be explained? Why does economic integration lag behind and why does the desire for greater commercial advantage not pave the way for political detente as some people expected?

In the political sphere there has been a growing conviction that any East-West military conflict could result in total annihilation and that it is in everybody's interest to stabilize and control the East-West situation. No such

---

[1] Director, Institute for the Socialist World Economic System, Academy of Sciences of the USSR, Moscow, USSR.

clear convergence of interests is apparent in the economic sphere. Moreover, it has become more obvious that some Western countries wish to use the growing East-West technology gap not for economic but political advantage.

The Soviet Union and East European countries have lost or are losing their former specialization in world economic exchanges, and have yet to acquire new ones consistent with their capabilities and the requirements of the scientific and technological revolution. The West does not need Russian bread but the Soviet Union needs nearly one-quarter of its required bread from the West. The Soviet Union's raw material resources have also devalued considerable, especially since the West overcame the energy crisis. Gold has lost its "currency of currencies" status and become a mere commodity, though a specific one. The Soviet manufacturing industry remains uncompetitive on world markets. In those areas where the Soviet Union and East European countries can offer final products or good-quality prefabricated products, their export capacities are relatively small.

In short, the East is obviously far more interested in East-West economic cooperation than the West. The problem is compounded by the dramatic changes taking place in the East and the attendant commercial risks and uncertainties for Western investors. Western countries appreciate the potential material and intellectual resources in the Soviet Union and Eastern Europe and the vast markets there. However, these countries have to travel the long and difficult road of perestroika to realize the tremendous trade opportunities. Western governments have not yet decided on how and to what extent they should provide economic assistance to perestroika, and how to handle the Soviet Union's involvement in the world economy. This might explain why economic arguments have acquired their appropriate weight in these policies.

25.1 The new thinking

The Stalinist model of economic development advocated substantial isolation from the world economy because, being of a random nature, it could not be subject to planning; moreover, isolation avoided the threat of dependence on hostile capitalist economies. The new thinking in the Soviet Union rejects such long-standing dogma. It rests on the concept of global and regional interdependence, the necessity of taking this into consideration in foreign policy, and on the pursuit of self-sufficiency only in the most critical areas. This thinking means a greater openness of Soviet society and the economy to the outside world, more active involvement in the global division of labour, and full integration into the world economic system in other ways. The new thinking assumes that the specific interests and expectations of participants in international economic relations will be taken into account.

These conceptual changes in socialist countries' foreign policies are being followed by more practical steps. The Soviet Union, for example, has declared its desire to participate in multilateral discussions of global economic problems and matters of regulating the world economy in various international forums. It has also proposed the principle of ensuring the economic security of individual states which means, amongst other things, the abandonment of policies that are explicitly designed to harm the economic interests of other states. This, of course, requires ideological differences to be set aside or at least de-emphasized to the point where peaceful coexistence and competition are possible within the framework of a pluralistic, interrelated world community. This "deideologization" means respecting any nation's free choice of political system.

Problems that previously faced only individual countries have become global in nature. Such problems include the dangers of thermonuclear war and ecological catastrophe, the inefficient use of natural resources, disease, and starvation. The solution of these global problems should be one of the main objectives of the policies of all governments. However, the solution of global problems requires a global approach involving broad international economic, scientific, and technological cooperation that overcomes narrow, nationalistic interests and the struggle to eliminate competitors.

Such a global approach can begin with regional integration and then inter-regional cooperation. The positive effects of this are proven by the experience of the CMEA and the EC. Formal relations have been established between the two organizations and individual CMEA countries have signed agreements with the EC. This does not mean that CMEA countries deny the advantages of integrational cooperation within the CMEA but they do recognize the limitations, and faced with organizational and structural constraints to an expansion of their mutual trade, they have begun to look outside the CMEA region to obtain a better use of opportunities and advantages of the combination of both regional and global cooperation.

Being fully aware of the importance of further progress of the Helsinki process, and the necessity of intensifying all-European cooperation, the Soviet Union and other East European countries support the idea of a "common European home" and strive to make such a concept meaningful. They have suggested specific measures in the military-political sphere and in the economic, ecological, and cultural spheres. The goal is to gradually shape an appropriate infrastructure which would help to overcome the division of Europe and to build a common European home from the Atlantic to the Urals. It should be noted that all-European cooperation does not, by any means, rule out interaction with other countries and regions. Indeed, the Soviet Union is seeking to enhance its economic and political significance in the vast Asian-Pacific region where the gravity centre of the world economy is gradually shifting. The Soviet Union has proposed a programme for the development of broad, mutually beneficial cooperation to meet the interests of all of the countries of the region. Measures are being undertaken to involve the resource-rich Soviet Far East in trade, production, and scientific and technological cooperation with China, Japan, the Asian NICs, and the United States.

Considering the growing significance of international organizations in the development and regulation of world economic relations, the Soviet Union is seeking more active participation in them; not only the United Nations and its special and regional institutions but other international organizations as well. For example, the Soviet Union has declared its readiness to join the GATT and interact with other international economic organizations and financial institutions to facilitate their constructive activities in all directions, including East-West cooperation. Unfortunately, Western countries continue to resist Soviet participation in global economic processes and international economic organizations.[2] It is believed that Soviet participation would be detrimental to U.S. interests and, more specifically, would weaken the economic and political ties between the United States and its allies.

The domestic policies of the Soviet Union and other countries of Eastern Europe should be analyzed in terms of global problems and East-West relations. Until recently the goal was to minimize economic contact with the world economy. Perestroika is gradually removing the numerous internal obstacles that hampered the interaction of the domestic and world markets.

In the Soviet Union a radical reform of foreign economic activity is taking place. 22,000 state and cooperative enterprises have obtained the right of direct (or through economically responsible intermediaries) access to the world market. Their economic interest in the efficiency of foreign economic operations has been increased, and a system of self-financing was introduced along with exchanges of foreign currencies on the basis of auctions.

---

[2] See Leah Haus, in this volume, for a further discussion of this issue.

The creation of joint enterprises with foreign capital in the Soviet Union has been allowed; as of early 1988 they numbered more than 260. The joint venture legislation was liberalized several times, and now corresponds to international norms. Moreover, the possibilities for the participation of Soviet enterprises in joint entrepreneurship abroad were extended by establishing, amongst other things, joint shareholding and other companies. The next step is to create free economic zones in the East and West of the country with special incentives for both Soviet and foreign businesses. It is intended to introduce a Soviet convertible currency in these zones which may later be extended to other areas of the Soviet Union.

It is recognized that multinational corporations (MNCs) are the main motor of international trade, and Western governments encourage their development and protect their interests in every possible way. However, socialist governments have yet to decisively define their approach to such corporations. The elaboration of a new political approach to MNCs could provide a strong boost to East-West economic relations.

All this points to the fact that greater economic openness of the Soviet Union's economy means greater involvement in the world economy. The main Soviet players in this relationship will be direct producers of goods. The central and regional governments in the Soviet Union will continue their guiding and coordinating functions, providing the necessary organizational, legal, and other preconditions for the independent foreign economic activity of enterprises.

25.2 International cooperation versus confrontation

The internationalization of economic affairs and global interdependence have created contradictions and problems of their own which can only be solved by coordinating the policies of the states of the world.

The coordination of economic policies by governments is a new phenomenon in international life. This has not yet taken global proportions: East and West initiated such coordination separately. The idea of a new international economic order has not yet given birth to institutions capable of controlling international economic processes on a global basis.

Western forums for coordination are the annual meetings of the Group of Seven, meetings of Western finance ministers and the heads of central banks, the Tripartite Commission, regional organizations like the EC, and other international organizations such as the GATT, IMF, IBRD, IEC, and closed-type Western organizations as the OECD, NATO and COCOM. Such forums enable the West to coordinate its efforts to stabilize and promote economic processes, to jointly define domestic and international economic policies, and to smooth contradictions between different countries (which have been especially acute in the late 1980s in the monetary and commercial spheres).

East-West economic relations play an important part of this coordination activity (especially in COCOM, of course) which points to their great political and economic significance in a broader collective Western economic strategy vis-à-vis the East. This collective Western strategy involved restricting East-West economic relations within the framework of "Atlantic solidarity" and the policy of confrontation and deterrence. However, as a result of perestroika in the Soviet Union there is somewhat less consensus in the West on East-West economic policy. While Western Europe, especially the FRG and a number of neutral countries, becomes more interested in expanding and intensifying economic relations with the East, the United States and (under its influence) Japan want additional evidence of the efficiency of perestroika and the new political thinking; they want guarantees of the persistence and irreversibility of the economic reforms.

An appreciation of the significance of global problems and the necessity of finding solutions is a beginning but is not sufficient. The formation of international mechanisms to ensure the effective coordination of efforts should be on the international agenda. In this respect, the Soviet Union supports the activity of the United Nations, and supports the creation of new UN agencies (for cooperation in space, for example) that would help to unite and coordinate efforts to resolve global problems, including emerging ones.

The Soviet approach to trade and economic relations contemplates the universalization of the UNCTAD mandate in respect of its greater involvement not only into the general problem of trade and development but into East-West cooperation as well. The same approach is applicable to the GATT which has frequently been described as a "club of the rich". It would be useful to allow all countries to join the GATT as equal members. This includes the Soviet Union and other socialist countries, especially now that economic reforms make their foreign economic systems more compatible with those of other GATT members.

The Soviet Union has expressed its interest in participating in the Uruguay round of trade negotiations, especially in the discussions of regulating exchanges in technology and services. The idea of meetings of the leaders of the major powers of the world, including the Soviet Union and China, on the problems of development of the world economy also falls within the scope of this policy. The participation of some socialist countries in the OECD could be useful as well since without consideration of economic processes in the socialist world one cannot properly comprehend the present state and future of the global economy.

The policy of the leading Western countries towards Soviet involvement in international economic organizations needs revision. It is time to lift the barriers to Soviet participation in them. The new political thinking advocated by the Soviet Union requires the non-confrontational, complementary development of the two systems.

The success of perestroika determines not only the future of the Soviet Union but the future of the world because it contributes to the elimination of East-West confrontation and thus ensures peace on our planet. It seeks to include the Soviet economy into the world economy in a way that will make the global structural and technological perestroika more rational and successful. The sooner the official policy of the West takes into account the political and economic benefits stemming from Soviet perestroika, the greater are its chances for success and thus the chances of all mankind for survival.

In the late 1980s and early 1990s there is some discussion of a type of Marshall Plan in support of perestroika in the Soviet Union and in some other socialist countries. This idea appears to be rather utopian because nobody is ready for free financial aid, even if it were forthcoming, and additional Western credits could overburden the troubled Eastern economies rather than help them. However, other forms of assistance are possible.

To begin, the West could abandon certain restrictions to East-West economic interaction, including export controls and barriers to MFN status. Western investment in joint ventures in the Soviet Union and Eastern Europe in the special economic zones would also be of great assistance. Another promising form of assistance would be to help train Soviet and East European managers. The scientific potential of the Soviet Union and a number of East European countries might be engaged in international scientific and technological programmes such as Eureka. Opportunities should be found for an expansion of Western exports of consumer goods in return for some kinds of final products, foodstuffs, or raw materials. Finally, the most effective assistance that the West could provide to countries such as Poland and Hungary would be facilitating the present terms of their hard currency debt repayments.

There is no doubt that the governments of the leading countries of the world will have great influence on the future on East-West economic relations and the solution of global problems. We can only hope that this influence will be guided by the spirit of new political thinking.

COMMENTS ON PART V

Norbert Kloten[1]

Allen Lenz's paper is a genuine contribution to "The Impact of Governments on East-West Economic Relations" in the sense that it is focusing on a special set of, doubtless important, problems of the world economy: the unsustainability of balance of payments disequilibria, the prospects and the need for global adjustments, reflecting different scenarios of more or less appropriate politics. What we learn is under intellectual auspices stimulating, under political ones rather depressing. Lenz concludes his chapter by telling us that the "global glut of manufactures", and the intensified competition between the large exporting nations, will increase the risks of protectionism at the probable expense of CMEA countries which are trying to build a position in the world markets.

Given the general topic of the Workshop and this volume, I cannot deal extensively with Lenz's chapter but its valuable insights deserve a comment. I share the foreseen necessity of global adjustment processes. The magnitudes discussed reflect a sober judgement. Nevertheless, the gloomy prospects are too negative. The findings are determined by the type of analysis, the almost exclusive arguing in terms of economic aggregates and of internal and external absorption as substitutes. A microeconomic approach, in addition to the macroeconomic, would have provided us with more confidence in the virtues of new patterns of imports and exports on a world wide level; determined by dynamic market forces, offering chances, not only risks.

The FRG has lost quite a substantial part of its market share in the United States but was able to compensate for that loss in Europe and elsewhere. Accordingly, I do not think that the unavoidable adjustments contain for themselves major problems for the CMEA countries.

I now want to discuss some conceptual aspects of this project on the role and impact of governments on East-West economic relations. Let me start with a concern. Although I think that it is an important and inevitable task to illu-

---

[1] President, Landeszentralbank, Baden-Württemberg, FRG.

380

minate the specific contribution of governments to developments in the past, these issues should not be the centre of attention. If there is a common leitmotif in all of the chapters, it is the fascinating process of economic restructuring which is now under way throughout Eastern Europe and the Soviet Union. Thus, the analysis of the present and the future role of governments deserves our main interest. The most important questions are thus:

1) What was the impact of governments in the past and what is it at present?
2) What is the most likely impact governments will exercise in the future under the auspices of reform policies in the East initiated in the last few years? In this respect the most important issues are the realization of the single market in Europe by the end of 1992 and the more cooperative attitude even in the United States towards the CMEA countries, especially the Soviet Union.
3) The questions of positive analysis have to be supplemented by normative analysis: what should be the impact of governments on East-West economic relations in the future?

Looking back at past economic cooperation between the East and West, the assessment is inevitably characterized by a dominance of political constraints. From the perspective of socialist countries, the COCOM lists as well as quantitive restrictions imposed by OECD countries on CMEA exports to the West have been serious obstacles to a better integration of socialist economies into the world economy. There is no doubt that economic restraints determined by specific political targets (e.g. security and avoidance of unacceptable dependencies) have had detrimental effects on economic performance and that these restrictions should be strictly limited to items of vital military interest, hoping that the available information about modern Western technology will not be absorbed directly or indirectly by the military. But politics are only a part of the story.

I should stress another aspect. The unsatisfactory developments in the past are most of all due to the incompatibilites of the divergent economic systems. The division of labour between the East and West is determined by very peculiar conditions which due to system-immanent reasons cannot lead to an efficient international allocation of resources according to comparative advantage, as it should be. In the period of state monopoly in foreign trade, imports and exports of CMEA countries were an integral part of the central planning process. Exports very often had the main function to provide foreign currencies and, in order to avoid payments in foreign exchange, governments tried to find barter transactions for imports.

At the microeconomic level, the direct impact of OECD governments has traditionally been very limited as most allocative decisions are left to the market. Governments support East-West economic exchange in a more general way; by entering into bilateral cooperation agreements, for example. The Federal Republic of Germany, for instance, has now seven "mixed commissions" with socialist governments. From the perspective of economic theory, the provision of fora for contacts between Western firms and official institutions and enterprises from the East can be regarded as a public good, which justifies governmental interference. The same applies to bilateral agreements between OECD and CMEA states which define the rights of Western firms investing in socialist countries, especially the right to transfer their profits in convertible currencies. But beyond these catalytic functions, the logic of a market economy sets very strict limits to the role of the state.

On the whole, an explanation of the sluggishness in East-West commercial relations in the past should not only and not mainly refer to the restraints imposed by the West but most of all to the obstacles which derive from the incompatibilities arising out of divergent economic systems and structures, which have been the main reason for suboptimal outcomes, especially in the 1970s. Even in the period of detente, the expectations of an intensified division of labour and increasing capital flows into the East did not materialize. Under conditions of rapid technological change and of strong competition by newly industrializing countries, the inflexibility of centrally planned economies resulted in an increasing loss of international competitiveness of their enterprises.

This rather bleak assessment of the past and the present leads to the central question of whether the future will offer better prospects for the division of labour between East and West as well as for the allocation of Western capital in the East. In the last few years, the urgency of an economic restructuring going to the roots has been felt by almost all socialist governments. Considerable reforms have already been initiated. In Hungary, the Soviet Union and in Poland the monopoly of the state in foreign trade was abandoned and the autonomy of exporting enterprises was strengthened. But it is very difficult to figure out how far all this will go and if there are not more drastic reforms necessary to change the mechanisms of economic allocation and control before socialist economies will really become competitive in international markets. There seems to be a difficult dilemma for socialist governments. They realize that restructuring is the only way to modernize the production potential of their countries and they are at the same time aware of the fact that it is not easy to control the dynamics of such processes, which will probably influence the entire social and political realms. Will it be possible to stop perestroika somewhere arbitrarily? I think these challenging questions deserve our attention.

You will have realized that I did not emphasize the role required of Western governments. In the future of East-West economic relations they play a leading role only in a special, but very important sense. It is their task to keep their markets open, to use the COCOM lists in a liberal way, and to reduce the remaining quantitative restrictions for CMEA imports, especially in agreements between the EC and CMEA countries. The recent agreement between the EC and Hungary is a positive example. The European internal market scheduled for the end of 1992 must not and should not become a fortress with additional restrictions for imports from third countries. What is asked for, is to prepare for as much cooperation as can be offered under the given circumstances.

Jozef M. van Brabant[2]

The following comments are based on several of my interventions at the workshop in Athens. The general topic is new organizations and the participation of centrally planned economies (CPEs) in established regimes.

With the new receptivity by CPEs, including China and the Soviet Union, to seek more active participation in international economic relations, including in the existing international economic organizations, the question arises whether these countries can be accommodated therein on a full and equal basis. This is not an easy matter to come to grips with as very often, when placed in a diplomatic, ideological, or political context, the technical issues are confounded. Yet, because international economic organizations are by definition exposed to political pressures, the issues involved in assessing the potential for the CPEs in such organs need to be researched from several dimensions.

Regardless of the priority one wishes to accord to technical matters, one of the dimensions to be analyzed carefully comprises the requirements and

[2] Staff member, International Economic and Social Affairs, United Nations Secretariat, New York, U.S.A.

possibilities of the CPEs in organized international economic relations from a purely technical angle. I feel these topics need to be explored prior to hammering out any kind of political and diplomatic position on the issue. At the very least, it is helpful, even if only for heuristic purposes, to distinguish clearly among the various factors, technical and otherwise, that may complicate more comprehensive participation. Such an inquiry could even benefit CPEs that are already within the organs but that have found it rather difficult to benefit fully from the underlying economic regime for technical reasons.

It would certainly be impractical to answer the question of whether the CPEs belong in international economic organizations in a vacuum, by a simple yes or no. Likewise, it would be injudicious to insist upon the removal of the obstacles to the CPEs being admitted to international economic organizations or to grant accession simply because one or more CPE is now inclined as a matter of policy focus to deepen their involvement in the global economy. The many technical matters involved in ensuring equal access to the international economic regimes in place could usefully be explored comprehensively prior to diplomatic or political negotiations. The objective would be to formulate alternative, technically sound, proposals to be negotiated at the political and diplomatic command levels.

Perhaps the most important factors to be taken into account can be discussed under two headings. First, the international economic organizations in place were created essentially for developed market economies. Some of their fundamental features are ill-suited for countries with different economic and organizational models, including many developing but also the planned economies. Moreover, it is important to recall that the regimes in place have been infringed upon even by developed market economies, and that these regimes were meant in essence to come to grips with conditions prevailing in the aftermath of World War II. The objectives envisaged and the ways in which these goals can be reached could, therefore, usefully be adapted to the requirements of the 1990s and beyond.

Seen against this backdrop, one might be inclined to contemplate in earnest the possibility of replacing the existing institutions. Newly conceived entities would in principle be in a position from the start to better accommodate countries whose economic conditions, systemic or otherwise, diverge from the context of the mainstream developed market economy. Rhetoric and posturing aside, the creation of such organs can be seriously entertained only if there is ample ground to believe that the international community would be prepared to adopt a set of principles for such regimes that differ in minor and major ways from those that in principle shore up the existing regimes. Such consensus could be hammered out only after protracted negotiations even during the extraordinary circumstances of wartime pressures and within the commanding Anglo-American wartime alliance.

Drawing a lesson from the evolution of international economic relations over the past two decades or so, there would appear to be little if any chance of reaching at present a broad consensus among key actors in the global economy on the basic framework of cooperation, the principles buttressing alternative regimes, and the conditions for the functioning of new global institutions. As a result, accommodation for countries and economic models that fit incompletely into the existing regimes and their underlying multilateral economic institutions will have to be sought from within, rather than from outside, the various organs in place.

Second, it is necessary to recognize that by its very nature an economic reform amounts to a complex process that evolves over a protracted period of time. This has been validated even in CPEs that have been enacting modifications in institutions, policies, and policy instruments for years. Furthermore, there is every indication that the reformed CPE, once the process will be completed, is unlikely to exhibit all of the key features of a developed market economy.

Seen against this backdrop, it is not very constructive for Western policy makers or observers to advise the CPEs to complete first their envisaged reforms and only then to commence accession deliberations. Neither is it helpful for representatives from regime participants to suggest that the current agenda for policy deliberations, as for instance in the GATT context, does not permit the examination of questions specific to such CPEs as China, which requested accession in 1986, and the Soviet Union, which is likely to do likewise very early in the 1990s. Certainly, the requirements of the ongoing Uruguay Round of multilateral trade negotiations are straining the commercial and diplomatic resources available for negotiations among key Contracting Parties. That round itself, which started in late 1986, is likely to continue into the mid or even late 1990s, even though officially it should be concluded in 1990 or 1991. Finally, it is not very constructive on the part of the CPE policymakers or their spokespersons simply to request accession to the international economic organizations without offering suggestions or clarifications on how their countries could actually participate more fully and on an equal basis in the regimes in place.

An honest attempt to usher the CPEs more fully into the existing international regimes will therefore need a transition phase. Insiders would be assured that some measures will be taken by new applicants and countries who previously could not fully adhere to the agreed discipline to harmonize their systems with those of the regimes in place and the major actors therein. At the same time, such transitory accession would enable the CPEs to access some of the benefits of the regime. In this way, the international community could avoid, deliberately or by neglect, undermining support for the ongoing reform process in CPEs. It would also provide some assurance that the reforms stay on the course of harmonizing the economic features of CPEs that now inhibit fuller participation in the international economy. Because this is largely uncharted territory, a successful conclusion of the deliberations will by necessity depend on creative, imaginative proposals being formulated by all parties involved; that is, the CPEs themselves, the international organizations, as well as the insiders.

These propositions may be illustrated with respect to the GATT and the Fund. Regarding the GATT, the key features of the international trading regime in place are nondiscrimination, reciprocity, safeguards, and transparency as habitually interpreted under the General Agreement. Of these, only reciprocity poses technically complex demands that have not so far been resolved for CPEs because Contracting Parties have tended to foster adherence to their rules and regulations, and CPEs have hence been brought under the discipline of the General Agreement on the basis of simple substitutes for - in some cases, rather naively forged equivalences to - tariff concessions.

Reciprocity arrangements between market economies and a traditional CPE should instead have been based on commitments, as slated in the relevant socioeconomic development plan, to equivalent increases in imports from Contracting Parties. Whether such targets could be set annually or only within the context of the medium-term plan would have been a simple technical matter to be resolved pragmatically. But it would clearly have been necessary to estimate the increased export capacity of the newly acceding CPE attributable to tariff concessions on the part of the market economies and thus to set an equivalent value of incremental imports from the Contracting Parties that the applicant would have to provide for from within its habitual economic decision-making procedures.

With the genuinely reforming CPE, however, reciprocity should eventually be based on principles that simulate or approximate as closely as possible the basics of the General Agreement. With the move toward market-type decision making in the CPEs, these could entail the following: 1) economic decentralization, 2) commercial decision making by economic agents, 3) making key government preferences on resource allocation and income redistribution explicit in the form of *ad valorem* taxes and subsidies (or other fiscal measures, but they would be of a lesser interest within the context of the General Agreement), and 4) linking domestic with foreign prices, possibly only on an intermittent basis.

I feel that these elements provide sufficient food for thought to commit the CPE that wishes to accede to the discipline of the General Agreement to a reform schedule on the basis of which the Contracting Parties can extend conditional concessions and eventually full Contracting Party status. The commitment need not be so rigid that it would overly constrain the economic sovereignty of the applicant. But it certainly would have to narrow somewhat the extent to which national priorities can be implemented without heeding international obligations.

Technical matters in evaluating accession to the Fund and the Bank are much less involved than they would appear to be in the case of the GATT. Perhaps the most pivotal technical issue, especially in ushering the Soviet Union into the international monetary regime in place, would be currency convertibility. There is simply no practical way in which a country such as the Soviet Union could attain currency convertibility, in the sense delineated in Article VIII of the Fund's Articles of Agreement, in the short to medium run. Yet, it would be unseemly for such a country to be granted accession under the "transitory" arrangements of Article XIV of the Fund's Articles of Agreement.

Instead, it would seem much more realistic to hold the would-be applicant to a firm commitment as concerns movement toward and steady progress with the implementation of currency convertibility. That is, it would be useful to make the transitional provisions to which Article XIV is tacitly welded as explicit as political circumstances and diplomatic protocol permit. Since neither the Fund nor insiders or outsiders of that monetary regime have given much thought to how best to render Article XIV compatible with Article VIII and yet make the institution as universal as possible, there is ample room in this case too for constructive deliberation and professional imagination. In the first instance, such technical suggestions might be tendered by the would-be applicant. Also the organizations themselves could usefully evaluate feasible alternatives to the orthodox model and check it out with "key insiders" to ensure that technical possibilities are not rejected out of hand because of simple political considerations.

In other words, bringing CPEs fully or at all under the discipline of the international monetary regime in place and thus letting them participate in the construction of feasible alternatives to the present arrangements calls for some deviation from the habitual accession arrangements for market economies. Under some circumstances, this might legitimately be perceived as being tantamount to discrimination and infringement upon the economic sovereignty of the applicant. These are certainly real concerns that need to be mitigated through proper diplomatic negotiating procedures. Key would be the desire of the would-be applicant to submit itself to the discipline of the international regime according to criteria that it might find most constructive. To translate these attitudes into a feasible negotiating strategy, it is desirable that the candidate undergirds a position that is more nuanced than unconditional and immediate accession, both of which, in my view, are simply nonstarters.

Henry R. Nau[3]

In 1947-1948, significant differences between the United States and the Soviet Union over how to organize domestic political societies in central Europe led to the Cold War. The United States favoured decentralized competitive forms of political and economic organization; the Soviet Union favoured centralized, command economies and political institutions. These political differences made it impossible for Eastern and Western European states, including East and West Germany, to develop substantial economic relations. The Soviet Union viewed suspiciously the motivations of the Marshall Plan and monetary reforms in the western zone of Germany, and Czechoslovakia and Poland declined to participate in Marshall Plan programs. Eventually, domestic political and economic differences in central Europe led to foreign policy and security alignments (NATO and the Warsaw Pact) that divided East and West.

It is useful to recall this historical sequence because the basic conditions underlying the Cold War may be changing today in central Europe and the Soviet Union. A process of political change is underway in Poland, Hungary, and the Soviet Union that could result in more decentralized and competitive political institutions in these countries. Accompanying and perhaps motivating

---

[3] Professor of Political Science and Associate Dean, Elliott School of International Affairs, The George Washington University, Washington, D.C., U.S.A.

this change, especially in the Soviet Union, is a process of internal economic reform designed to revitalize stagnant economies. If these changes succeed, Eastern and Western countries may become more open to one another, both economically and politically, and the foreign policy and military alliances of the cold war period, which grew out of earlier political and economic differences, may soften.

The potential changes are profound. Equally so, they are complicated. It is essential, therefore, that the countries involved think clearly about their choices and avoid excessive swings of euphoria and despair, concluding neither that change is inevitable (and irreversible), nor that change is threatening. Governments in the West incline toward the first conclusion, assuming that democratic political and competitive economic traditions are deep-seated in many of the Eastern European countries and required by modern technological developments (e.g., the information revolution) in the Soviet Union; communist governments in the East incline toward the second conclusion, worrying that domestic political change may get out of control and that internal economic reforms may upset a stable and secure, albeit unproductive, way of economic life in the past.

Three separate, but interrelated, processes are at work in central Europe today: political glasnost, economic perestroika, and foreign policy detente. The United States and the Soviet Union give different priorities to these various processes. Historically, the United States has had a principal stake in the foreign policy orientation of East European countries, pursuing a policy of differentiation to encourage European "deviation" from Soviet foreign policies. The United States has also sought to protect basic human rights in East European societies. Only peripherally has the United States had a stake in economic relations or reform in Eastern Europe. For years, Romania exemplified U.S. policy, earning favours from the United States for its foreign policy independence of the Soviet Union while remaining one of the least progressive East European countries in terms of basic political and economic reforms. Today, the United States gives greater emphasis to domestic political reforms in Eastern Europe, but it still has little at stake, in terms of potential trade, in economic reforms.

The Soviet Union has an opposite set of priorities. Its key objective is the economic revitalization of the Soviet economy and the related enhancement of East European productivity and growth. Mikhail Gorbachev has also recognized that such economic restructuring is not possible without some political reforms. But it is fair to say that he values political change primarily for its economic benefits. While he may eventually accept multi-party socialism and genuine democratization of political institutions in East Europe, he probably will not accept an early or premature foreign policy realignment of East European countries with the West (e.g., membership of some East European countries in the EC). In this sense, the top priority of the United States, and also that of some of its allies, namely, a loosening of Moscow's grip on East Europe and East Germany, may conflict with Soviet priorities.

Of course, it might be argued that Gorbachev's top priority is a foreign policy one, to induce a weakening of the U.S. position in Western Europe and to draw West European countries into assisting economic and technological change in the East. From this perspective, Gorbachev would welcome vast and immediate Western European economic assisitance to the East, even if such assistance risked a blurring of foreign policy alignments; as long as the U.S. role in Western Europe were diminished. But this perspective assumes a self-confidence on the part of the Soviet Union in dealing with powerful West European states, particularly West Germany, that does not seem to be con- sistent with the deteriorating economic and political conditions in Eastern countries. It is more likely, therefore, that Gorbachev's diplomacy toward the West is a covering and supplementary strategy to aid economic revitalization in the East, not an offensive and priority strategy to divide the West.

In contrast to the Soviet Union and the United States, as well as some of their East European neighbours, Poland and Hungary have still another set of priorities. They undoubtedly give greater weight to domestic political change than to either economic reform or foreign policy realignments. They recognize that basic economic change in their countries is not possible without more legitimate governments. But politicial changes in these countries may work against basic economic reforms. Effective economic forms will require more work and sacrifice, at least in the medium term, from the very groups--workers, farmers, small businessmen, etc.--that stand to gain most from political change. These groups, therefore, may use their newly won political power to resist significant economic reforms. Substantial Western assistance may be useful to these groups to solidify and, hopefully, make irreversible domestic political changes (as in the case of Polish requests for Western aid following the constitutional reforms of Spring 1989), but such assistance may also weaken incentives to work harder by providing immediate opportunities to consume and may threaten political reforms by raising the spectre of Western intervention in delicate domestic political processes.

Given these complicated interactions of political, economic, and foreign policy processes and priorities in central Europe, how should the United States and its allies respond to the hopeful prospects of ending the post-war division of Europe? I would suggest three principles to guide U.S. and Western policies so as to avoid both euphoria and despair:

First, concentrate on assisting genuine economic reforms in Poland, Hungary, and potentially, other East European countries to restructure domestic incentives to work, invest, and compete in these economies, avoiding superficial assistance in the form of credits and consumer goods that may only postpone economic reforms and involve Western countries too visibly in delicate domestic political events going on in Eastern Europe.

Second, recognize that economic reforms, such as laws for owning, registering, and insuring property, competitive institutions for allocating capital (e.g., equity markets), and training programmes to facilitate the redeployment of labour and upgrading of management and entrepreneurial skills, are not only important to restructure incentives to work and invest, but also provide economic supports to advance and defend individual political rights and, thus, secure political reforms in these countries from within these countries, rather than through massive credit and import programmes from the West.

Third, give priority to security (e.g., arms control) and political issues in East-West negotiations, intensifying the dialogue within the alliances and between them about the foreign policy arrangements that might emerge in central Europe if political and economic changes proceed to the point that domestic differences between East and West Europe no longer constrain the development of substantial economic, political, and human contact.

The most immediate economic need in Poland and Hungary, it might be argued, is not capital. Domestic savings are high in both countries, as they are in the Soviet Union. But these savings stagnate in low interest bearing accounts of nationalized banks (or, as often, in mattresses) and are allocated to investment in state enterprises by centralized ministries that pursue political and bureaucratic objectives as much as, or more so than, economic ones. Equity and bond markets would offer competitive alternatives for these savings and, simultaneously, encourage some privitization of state firms, at least the potentially competitive ones; price and tax reforms would encourage private investment and, potentially, more profitable public investment; legal reforms would secure these investments against arbitrary confiscation; and vocational and management training programs would ease the redeployment of labour both within the industrial sector and between agriculture, industry, and services. None of these reforms require massive Western financial assistance, and large imports of consumer goods from the West might actually divert savings from productive investment and future consumption to immediate consumption, adding to domestic and international debt without increasing future supply.

The most important external assistance in these early stages of domestic economic reform might be improved access to Western markets for products of East European countries, rather than consumer exports from Western countries to Eastern markets. Although Poland and Hungary are not likely to improve their competitiveness so rapidly that they will expand exports immediately, reducing tariff and, most importantly, quantitative restrictions on Eastern exports to Western markets, particularly in sectors such as textiles, food products, etc., where Eastern European countries are potentially competitive (and where Western restrictions are often most severe), would put into place another long-term market incentive that would enhance the more efficient allocation of domestic savings and investment in Eastern Europe. It would also encourage foreign investment (e.g., joint ventures) and technology assistance in appropriate sectors, none of which is significantly restricted by East-West export controls (except, perhaps, in the area of sophisticated, computerized factory equipment and machinery where controls are likely to be relaxed for light industries such as textiles before they are for sectors such as telecommunications).

Opening Western markets for East European products will be more difficult for Western countries than supplying credits and consumer goods to the East, given the growing competition and protectionism in world markets. But, to that extent, it will also be a good test of how serious the West is about political and economic reform in Eastern Europe.

For political changes in Eastern Europe and the Soviet Union have the best chance of succeeding if they proceed at their own pace and are not forced by excessive Western aid and enthusiasm. To become irreversible, political reforms have to involve some legal protection for the private rights of citizens, such as the ownership of property, and some pluralist reform of public institutions and political processes to allow citizens to vote for appropriate government officials and legislation (or else legal reforms could be simply rescinded arbitrarily). Such reforms are extraordinarily delicate in any society. The West would do well to respect the right of East European and Soviet societies to decide these issues for themselves. Western countries might assist, when asked, in areas of legal and constitutional reforms from their own experience

392

or through training assistance for workers, managers, and government regulators. But none of these programs need to be so large as to identify foreign interests with a delicate political process that, to be recognized as legitimate, must be indigenous.

Being circumspect about Western involvement in delicate political reforms in Eastern Europe is also a good way to reassure the Soviet Union that the West is not challenging Soviet security and foreign policy interests in central Europe. The West is not indifferent to the outcome of political reform in Eastern Europe; it seeks wider respect for human and political rights. But, in a nuclear world, it also seeks continued peace and stability in this crucible of post-war superpower rivalries. The United States, therefore, can buy time for political reforms in the East to proceed at their own pace by concentrating on security negotiations with the Soviet Union and intensifying its political dialogue with the allies. If arms reductions succeed in significantly lowering levels of conventional and nuclear arms in Europe, the crux of future security in the region will rest on political arrangements. What will these arrangements be, especially as they affect Germany? This is, foremost, a subject that the United States should discuss with its allies, although this discussion can be sufficiently open that the Soviet Union will be able to conduct a similar dialogue with its allies, enabling the two sides to find their way gradually in a non-threatening environment toward mutually satisfactory accommodations.

The foreign policy and security outcomes of changes currently taking place in central Europe depend, ultimately, on the nature of the domestic political and economic societies that emerge in Eastern Europe and the Soviet Union. Security threats derive not from international power rivalries alone or even primarily, but from different domestic political societies and purposes. While peace and prosperity can accommodate a wide variety of domestic political and economic systems, they cannot accommodate, as we learned in 1947-1948, unlimited differences in domestic political values and institutions between Eastern and Western societies.

ANNEX

Philipp Rieger[1]

Introductory remarks to the 12th Workshop, "The Impact of Governments on East-West Economic Relations", *April 1989, Athens, Georgia, U.S.A.*

May I welcome all of you on behalf of the International Steering Committee to our 12th Workshop which is remarkable in many ways. For the first time it is being held outside of Europe and thus breaks from its traditional terms of reference to East-West *European* economic interaction. Joint ventures are fashionable these days and we are fortunate that our hosts at the Center for East-West Trade Policy of The University of Georgia enabled us to leap the Atlantic and come to Athens.

Since the "new thinking" in the Soviet Union started to permeate and revolutionize East European policies and institutions and in turn to have an impact on Western attitudes, there is no lack now of conferences, seminars, and workshops on all aspects of East-West relations. Sometimes, I feel, they are on the way to becoming a new industry.

Allow me, therefore, in all modesty, to point out the rather unique and pioneering character of our workshop series which started 14 years ago as one of the first fruits of the Helsinki Accord of 1975. It was quite natural that in our research programmes the emphasis was put on the European aspects of East-West economic relations, in view of the fact that up to now East-West trade is predominantly a European regional affair, about 80 per cent of that trade alone being conducted with the European OECD countries and more than 40 per cent with the FRG, Finland, and Austria.

But from the start, in matters of organization and concepts, there was always a strong American connection. Without the active encouragement and support of the Ford Foundation, the first series of workshops could not have taken place. And the International Steering Committee could draw on the wide experience and guidance of Fritz Machlup and John Hardt from the very beginning.

The success and survival of our workshop activities during all the ups and downs of superpower relations, often viewed with suspicion on both sides of the ideological divide, was not least due to the circumstance that some of the

---

[1] Consultant, Creditanstalt-Bankverein, Vienna, Austria.

fathers of today's new thinking, like Bogomolov, Bognar, Kohlmey, Land, and Pajestka, were active members of the Steering Committee.

In the course of our periodical meetings we were able to evolve a habit and tradition of dispassionate scientific dialogue and mutual understanding and tolerance. This specific workshop culture enabled us to weather critical situations.

Today, in the climate of spreading glasnost, perestroika, detente, and hopeful disarmament initiatives it seems difficult to recall the precarious situation at our 8th Workshop in Moscow in September 1983, just after the tragic Korean airplane disaster over the sea of Okhotsk, when cold war passions ran high. Lawrence Klein and a number of other invited participants were unable to join us; only the Austrian airlines maintained their flights to Moscow. At that time the idea of holding a workshop in the United States would have appeared totally utopian.

In this field of study we were always aware of the dominant political dimension. It seemed therefore a good idea to devote a whole session to "The Impact of Governments on East-West Economic Relations".

Economic relations will to a large extent evolve within the framework of overall superpower relations and be influenced by the progress of disarmament and detente.

Much will depend on the policy stance of the new Bush administration which is conducting a lengthy review of U.S. foreign policy options; on how the United States will respond to the challenges of the Soviet Union's new foreign policy and to the incipient transformation of some CMEA countries into pluralistic and democratic societies.

West Europeans are occasionally suspected by American observers of being afflicted by "Gorby Fever". This, in my view, is a misleading interpretation. Obviously, our views are partly shaped by differing interests, geographical proximity, and perhaps by a longer and more intimate acquaintance with East European affairs. This does not blind us to the precarious state of the reform process, which has not yet become irreversible. But we are afraid that too much caution, too much foot-dragging might let us miss a unique historic chance. West Europeans generally tend to agree with Sakharov's view that the "West need not fear perestroika's success, but its failure".

The obstacles to further detente, genuine disarmament, and the success of perestroika are still formidable. They include the "military-industrial complex", articulate ideologues in the West, and the huge central planning bureaucracies in the East, all of which have a vital interest in the maintenance of the status quo. But things are on the move and there are grounds for optimism.

In conclusion, allow me to convey to you as an Austrian, a citizen of a neutral central European country bordering on the Iron Curtain, some of the political and psychological atmosphere created by recent developments. On the Hungarian side to all intents and purposes the curtain has already been lifted, only the iron hardware remains to be dismantled.

Without indulging in euphoric moods, the successful conclusion of the Conference on Security and Cooperation will prove of far-reaching significance. In Jean Kirkpatrick's view, the Human Rights Convention embodied in the Vienna Final Document is of far greater weight than even the INF Agreement and START plan taken together. Mr. Gorbachov's announcement that 500,000 men stationed in Hungary, Poland, Czechoslovakia, and the GDR would be unilaterally withdrawn, the new round of negotiations started last month in Vienna between NATO and Warsaw Pact countries on conventional disarmament, the obvious demise of the Brezhnev Doctrine, all add to our sense of relief. We watch with fascination the revolutionary changes taking place in the intellectual and cultural life of the Soviet Union, Hungary, and Poland and would like to share Mr. Shevardnaze's vision, that the Vienna Final Document might help to speed the further "corrosion of the Iron Curtain" and contribute towards ending the division of Europe.

LIST OF PARTICIPANTS

in the 12th international
Workshop on East-West European Economic Interaction
Athens, Georgia, U.S.A., 1-5 April 1989

Christopher Allen - University of Georgia, Athens, Georgia, U.S.A.

Yuri Andreev - Institute for World Economy and International Relations, Moscow, USSR

Wladimir Andreff - University of Social Sciences, Grenoble, France

Tamás Bácskai - Karl Marx University, Budapest, Hungary

Harold Berman - Emory University, Atlanta, Georgia, USA

Gary Bertsch - Center for East-West Trade Policy, University of Georgia, Athens, Georgia, U.S.A.

Oleg Bogomolov - Institute for the Socialist World Economic System, Academy of Sciences of the USSR, Moscow, USSR

Daniel Bond - Export-Import Bank of the United States, Washington, D.C., U.S.A.

Jozef van Brabant - United Nations, New York, U.S.A.

Irène Commeau-Rufin - French Institute of International Relations, Paris, France

Karel Dyba - Institute for Forecasting, Czech Academy of Sciences, Prague, Czechoslovakia

Sue Eckert - Committee on Foreign Affairs, U.S. House of Representatives, Washington, D.C., U.S.A.

Steven Elliott-Gower - Center for East-West Trade Policy, University of Georgia, Athens, Georgia, U.S.A.

Gerhard Fink	- Vienna Institute for Comparative Economic Studies, Vienna, Austria
Friedrich Gehart	- Österreichisches Credit-Institut AG, Vienna, Austria
Carol Rae Hansen	- Foreign Policy Institute, School of Advanced International Studies, Johns Hopkins University, Washington, D.C., U.S.A.
John P. Hardt	- Congressional Research Services, The Library of Congress, Washington, D.C., U.S.A.
Leah Haus	- New York University, New York City, New York, U.S.A.
Wolfgang Heinrichs	- Central Institute of Economics, Academy of Sciences of the GDR, East Berlin, GDR
Martin Hillenbrand	- Center for East-West Trade Policy, University of Georgia, Athens, Georgia, U.S.A.
Jerry Hough	- Duke University, Durham, North Carolina, U.S.A.
Joachim Jahnke	- Federal Ministry of Economics, Bonn, FRG
Richard Kaufman	- Joint Economic Committee of the Congress, Washington, D.C., U.S.A.
Norbert Kloten	- Landeszentralbank Baden-Württemberg, FRG
Váltr Komárek	- Institute for Forecasting, Czech Academy of Sciences, Prague, Czechoslovakia
Alexei Kunitsyn	- Institute of U.S.A. and Canada Studies, Academy of Sciences of the USSR, Moscow, USSR
Laszlo Lang*	- Hungarian Institute for International Affairs, Budapest, Hungary

* Author, but unable to attend the workshop

Allen Lenz	- Chemical Manufacturers Association, Washington, D.C., U.S.A.
Friedrich Levcik	- Vienna Institute for Comparative Economic Studies, Vienna, Austria
Aleksander Lukaszewicz*	- Warsaw University, Warsaw, Poland
Paul Marer	- Indiana University, Bloomington, Indiana, U.S.A.
John McIntyre	- Georgia Institute of Technology, Atlanta, Georgia, U.S.A.
Henry Nau	- George Washington University, Washington, D.C., U.S.A.
Issei Nomura	- Japanese Embassy, Washington, D.C., U.S.A.
Urszula Plowiec	- Foreign Trade Research Institute, Warsaw, Poland
Philipp Rieger	- Creditanstalt-Bankverein, Vienna, Austria
Dariusz Rosati	- Foreign Trade Research Institute, Warsaw, Poland
Andrzej Rudka	- Foreign Trade Research Institute, Warsaw, Poland
Christopher Saunders	- Science Policy Research Unit, University of Sussex, Brighton, Sussex, U.K.
Klaus Schneider	- Commission of the European Community, Brussels, Belgium
Norman Scott	- Economic Commission for Europe, United Nations, Geneva, Switzerland
Nikolai Shmelev	- Institute of U.S.A. and Canada Studies, Academy of Sciences of the USSR, Moscow, USSR

* Author, but unable to attend the workshop

Peter Sydow — Academy of Sciences of the GDR, East Berlin, GDR

Jean Tesche — Emory University, Atlanta, Georgia, U.S.A.

Dragomir Vojnić — Institute of Economics, Zagreb, Yugoslavia

INDEX

Denmark 188, 190
Derix, H.H. 30n
Dole, Senator Robert 59
Donke, Martin 285n

East Germany 10, 23, 36–7, 41, 96, 296
  debt 133–4
  foreign trade 30–3, 39, 43–4, 180–2
  national interests 175–84
  negotiations with the EC 229, 237–8, 250
  reforms 46
East-West trade
  barriers to 197–8
  controls by USA 96–101
  global adjustments 333–8
  'Paris Club' 307, 309
  role of the EC 206–7
  Soviet reforms and 33–43
  trade control measures 297–305
  US policy on 65–72, 90–3
  see also CMEA; COCOM; Eastern
    Europe; individual countries
Eastern Europe
  and the Cold War 120, 124, 388
  balance of trade 128–35
  dollar trade values and shares 124–6
  economic systems 153–5, 388–9, 393
  exports to Soviet Union 142–3
  exports to Western Europe 126–7, 392–3
  foreign trade reforms 25–43
  import substitution 122–3
  investment allocation 122
  joint ventures with the West 43-6
  leadership of 210–11
  membership of GATT 85, 99, 117, 228,
    230, 279–93, 336, 386–8
  MFT 212–17
  ownership and property rights 217–19
  USA policy towards 95–6, 103–4, 388
  see also CMEA; East-West trade;
    individual countries
EFTA
  cooperation with EC 225–6
  trade control measures 304–5
Eisenhower, President 98
Emmott, William 331, 332n
European Community (EC) 52, 58, 79,
    135, 153, 154
  Common Agricultural Policy (CAP)
    229, 230, 302
  cooperation with EFTA 225–6
  and East European membership of
    GATT 284–93
  negotiations with Soviet Union 236–7,
    250

'Ostpolitik' 238–41
  relations with China 229
  relationship with CMEA 107, 151,
    245–6, 250, 361–2, 371, 375, 383
  relationship with Hungary 167–8,
    219-20, 222, 228, 230, 234-5,
    250, 383
  relationship with Poland 171, 250,
    301, 304
  trade control measures 297–304
  trade with CMEA 107, 227–42, 296–304
European Economic Community (EEC) 24
Evstigneev, R. 25n
Export Administration Act (USA) 56–7,
    68, 77, 100
Export Control Act (1962) 99–100
Export Enhancement Program (EEP) 93

Feld, Werner 287n
Finland 35, 36–7, 40, 67, 108, 124, 190,
    365
Foreign Trade Bank 87
France 190
  cost of labour 188
  R.& D. 363
  trade with Eastern Europe 287, 365
  trade with the Soviet Union 35, 36–7,
    40, 67
Franklin, Daniel 74n, 84n, 85n
Funigiello, Phillip 49n

Gardner, Richard 289n
General Agreement on Tariffs and Trade
    (GATT) 96, 224, 229, 231, 274, 385
  Bulgaria and 236, 279–80
  Eastern European countries
    membership 85, 99, 117, 228,
    230, 279–93, 336, 386–8
  Hungary and 85, 163, 228, 230,
    235, 279–85, 289–92
  Poland and 85, 98, 228, 230, 279,
    289–90, 292
  Soviet membership 8, 9, 60, 84, 92,
    111, 336, 376, 378, 385
Germany, Federal Republic of (FRG)
    10, 21, 40, 67, 108, 120, 188, 238,
    296, 326–7, 333, 337–8
  economic policy 249–50
  environmental protection agreements
    251–2
  foreign policy 247–9
  R. & D. 363
  trade with CMEA 247, 365, 378, 382
Gerschenkron, Alexander 286n